For Sir Ranulph

In admiration,

WAR, WINE AND VALOUR

Five Years Fighting the Nazis

by

Douglas M. Baker

Douglas M Baker.

First Published 2005

Printed and bound in England

ISBN 1-901754-00-6

Published

by

Dr. Douglas Baker
"Little Elephant"
High Road
Essendon
Hertfordshire
England.

This work is dedicated to my brother Desmond who
served on His Majesty's battleships and to the
comrades who fought beside me in East
Africa, at Tobruk, Alamein and in Italy.

Author who volunteered to join the
Natal Mounted Rifles in 1939
when sixteen.

Author's Note

Born in North Finchley, I emigrated with my English parents to Natal, South Africa and fought with the Natal Mounted Rifles in World War II, volunteering in 1939 at age sixteen. My regiment faced Axis forces progressively on five fronts – in Kenya, Central Abysinnia, the Western Desert in Egypt and Cyrenaica and Italy. With almost six years of active service and convalescence I came to understand the psychology of men at bay through first-hand experience and the dynamics of acute and sustained terror.

War evoked in me both curiosity and discovery, leading to the mastery of Medicine and Surgery at Sheffield University where the hidden effects of shrapnel and other missiles could be investigated further like those which had penetrated my own body.

In my long standing friendship with Barbara Cartland we sometimes talked of the impact that the World Wars had on society. Barbara, herself, had lost two brothers and her father killed in them. It was Barbara who encouraged me to publish this, my own story which she had seen in my war diaries.

Brute beauty and valour and act, oh, air, pride, plume, here
Buckle! AND the fire that breaks from thee then, a billion
Times told lovelier, more dangerous, O my chevalier!

—Gerard Manley Hopkins

Acknowledgements

The author acknowledges the following for their support in the publication of this book: Arthur Blair; Don Bodine; Ted Capstick; Eric Gregg; David Harvey; Joe Hayes; Marcus Hayward; Alexander Heaton; Raffaele Iandolo; Fred Knights; Mick Lysejko; Dudley Morning; John Paine; Richard Painter; Sue Platt; Jeremy Richardson; Cecil Ritson; Terry Smedley; Brenda Storar; Robert Storar; Lorraine Stringfellow; Mark Weight; Ian Wilson; Margaret Wood; Paul Wright; Imperial War Museum.

CONTENTS

killed: Ammo A.F.V. knocked out: Eddy Sayer platoon runner captured searching for an officer: N.M.R. company withdraws: My friend Terry Smedley shot down and carried out: Under day long bombardment a mile out in no-man's land: Direct hit on our emplacement: Buddy in trouble: Guns and mortars rain down incessantly: Withdrawal at sunset: Post mortem comments: Fighting Mac Lachlan on our right flank.

Entertaining Ito P.O.W's to tea: Fate of the Cauldron and Bir Hachiem: Huge allied tank losses: Gazala, the opportunity lost: Casualty list for June 7th: Exit Free French from Hachiem: N.M.R. 'C' Company called to relieve Guards at Elweit el Tamar box: Cartoon of 8th Army 'in the bag': Ferocious fighting in boxes behind Gazala Line: More boxes overrun: N.M.R. clings on at Elweit el Tamar and captures German prisoners: German prisoners beg for food and water: General retreat to Alamein along the whole front.

Panzers attempt to rout 8th Army: Mess-ups at the passes down the escarpment: Panzers close in and shell escape routes: Valiant reargard sacrificed: Struggle to get to Tobruk: Struggle to get admittance: Appalling state of Tobruk's outer defences: The attack on Tobruk: Stukas neutralise minefields: Artillery creeping barrage in South east: Indian lines penetrated: Port taken: Klopper orders surrender: Most troops not even engaged: Rommel's triumph: We escape towards Alamein: Whisky & beer galore.

Preventing the retreat from becoming a rout: Lili Marlene once more: Alexandria naval base evacuated: Germans occupy Mersa Matruh: Allied confusion and poor leadership: Alamein holds: Nightly fighting patrols: Routine air sentry waiting for Stukas: Comrade killed and wounded on fighting patrol: Zulu war cries and bayonet charges: Laying barbed wire to keep Rommel out: Desert sores and 'sand fly fever': McLachlan wins M.M.: First Battle of Alamein: Rommel defeated at Alam Halfa: McLachlan wounded at Alamein.

around Ismalia on bikes: Silver Nitrate and granulations: I search out my rescuing stretcher bearer: 7000 men in a tub: Hopes and wishes and frustrations on home leave.

Trouble in Durban: Larking about on leave: Re-boarding and recovery: Springbok Legion, a red herring?: Lovely girls and re-embarcation: Ille de France with new hopes and aspirations: Spit and polish outrages: Egypt again: Corp life at Katatba: Big fight, bring your lunch: Victory to the defeated: Desert rats and human mice: Misbehaviours on parades: Group insolence: Troops show their disgust for staged parades.

Interminable training courses for armour: Parallel events in Europe: Secret German report on internal affairs: A night with Geraldo: Another with the Merry Widow: Desert dreams that are portentious: 10,000 soldiers at a rugby match: Groping for renewed faith: Sailing in Alexandria's war torn harbour: S.M. Aga Khan the wise: Bully's proscribed list: Shell-shock friends.

Enter the 'Hunks': Pupils at Alex. Tank school: Ice colds in Alex.: Buller sustains fractures: Little Brown Jug don't I love thee: High tension and sweet poetry: Poor relation, bright connection: An anorexic hero: Drill inside a Sherman turret: Sherman as a death-trap: Staggering displays of sea species in the middle of the Eastern desert: Defects in training: Hullos and goodbyes to Egypt.

Nonsense routine at Altamura: A new patriotism: Threats of incineration: Incineration incorporated: Tommy Cookers and Ronsen lighters: Aga meets U.S. General Mark Clark: Three tanks destroyed in first engagement: Paddy Gill killed: Racing through Rome: Piercing the line at Civita Castellana: Ritson eye witness account: German eye witness.

Bravery in open country: Alexander points to Florence: Two more tanks lost: Howard Butcher, N.M.R. hero killed: Horror at

Bagnoregis: Mass tank attack by S.S.B.: Sitting under the Sobbing Sisters: Why no mountian troops?: Becomes impossible for tanks: Desert Rats and desert mice: Neurosis and battle fatigue: General Patton's assault on soldiers: Sterzel in trouble again.

Advance in the mist: Terrible consequences: German company surrenders: Tank plunges off a bridge: Tall stories home about naughty Germans: Holes punched through our armour plating: Biological demands on army parties: The matter of group rape: Severe casualties on both sides at Orvieto: More premonitions: Pot roast chickens, not humans: Howard Foss killed, notable sportsman: Last of the Mohicans scalped: Hidden self-propelled guns: Tragedy everywhere: Happy John survives a brew-up.

South east of Siena and moreTigers: Wrecking the village of San Felice: The Shadow of Death: A suicide mission: Discord in my tank crew: The aroma of fear: Trapped on a Sherman turret top: Seeing through closed eyelids: Near death inside a Sherman turret: Horrifying conditions in a C.C.S.: Hoddy appears amidst the carnage: Light in the darkness: Trailing bandages on the plane to Naples

Hospital plane to Naples: Piercing wound in chest: Right lung collapsed: Admitted 92nd British General: Naples bombed during night: Two bullet wounds found in right leg: New wonder drug PENICILLIN being given me: Nazi planes bombed Naples again: Pain and bad dreams: South African visitors: 800 c.c. taken from right lung: Flirting with Maria: More surgery: Comforting terminals like Ellis: Zulu fables and history: Hoddy visits: Surgery to extract more shrapnel.

Bad news from N.M.R. at front: 'A' Company severely mauled: Strong determination to go back to regiment: Doc Eddy sends me to convalescent camp: Rome and Juliette: Convalescence on the Volturno: Shell shocked, Stezel visits..

Photographs in page order

Photographs continued...

Maps in page order

Maps continued...

Foreword

Douglas Baker is a remarkable man and has written a remarkable book. He rescued a wounded comrade at Gazala while under intense cross fire. In the carnage at Alamein a shell took away most of his right shoulder blade. He retrained on Sherman tanks. Near Florence an 88mm shell burst on his tank perforating his right lung and almost severing this left arm. He absconded from hospital and fought once more at the front. Although just one man's experience of the war it is a gift to the historian with its engrossing accounts and accurate detail. It is also a fascinating insight into day to day events and personal feelings during this difficult time. He is undecorated and receives no military pension from the British Government.

– William Roach MBE

CHAPTER I

1937 was my last year at school. They were happy days. I was fourteen and had not anticipated interruption of my studies, least of all by the approaching war or by the specific event that forced me out of my pre-matriculation grade. It had become usual for my brother Desmond, two years younger, and I to go away for the month of July to some farm in the Natal midlands. July was the mid-year winter school holidays and, to relieve pressure on my mother, who was the family breadwinner we picked a farm that offered some sort of novelty, even excitement for that month. This year it was Arnold's Hill, an extensive dairy and maize estate with wattle plantations, a tennis court, lively owners and English-speaking. We had been there two years running, the food was good, my mother approved and there would be other kids there our own age.

The farm, on the railway line to the town of Richmond was run by Oliver Arnold who had taken over when his father had died prematurely a decade earlier. The vacation was going well. I was winning our own tennis tournament, and had got two old motor chassis, stripped down to their rims and bare necessities racing each other on a mile of farm road with a steep descent down Arnold's Hill, and had constructed a log cabin deep in the woods out of the plentiful wattles of derelict plantations.

Half way into the month there was a phone call from home. Desmond and I were to return home immediately. Mrs. Arnold, Oliver's mother had delivered the message to me red-eyed. Oliver was glum driving us to Arnold's Hill station but said nothing. As I shook hands with Oliver in a short goodbye, I felt a cold shudder pass between us. It was the last time I saw him. Five years later he was taken prisoner of war at Tobruk and spent three more years in German captivity.

1

My elder sister Kathleen met us at Durban Station. Again silence and then mama had her two boys back and I detected tears there too. She sent Desmond off to the kitchen to get some fruit. He loved fruit so much that the Zulu servants called him 'Inyoni', the toppie-bird that used to peck at the great yellow-orange paw-paws that grew wild on trees in Durban. My mother never balked at the truth and she came out with it immediately. She was dying. Metastases from an unsuccessful breast operation had seeded her abdomen according to a laboratory finding and she had no more than six months. She had no regrets except that she was leaving her two boys at a time when they needed her most.

·I climbed into my tree house in the old avocado pear tree. My mother had pointed out that there would be no funds to pay for further schooling and I would have to fend for myself or go and live with my Uncle Ken whom both of us boys detested and he knew it. My mother had said that her main concern was that I should complete matriculation. There were still a few days of the July holidays to review options. I needed to make some firm decisions about my immediate future and after all was said and done it seemed I should stay at Durban High at least until the end of the year and then leave and take a job. I would be 15 on the 31st of December and more likely to get a better position then. My thoughts turned to ways and means. First of all I would drop the organised games at school which consumed two of my late afternoons every week and the two afternoons involved in cadet training. This would leave me time to help my mother in her last days. She had given me a good schooling and this was a chance to repay her. Our livelihood was a small private hotel she had started high on Durban's Berea, very select with seven Zulu servants and very hard going for her. 'Marine View' it was called with a breathless view of the ocean, harbour and race course.

Durban High School was a good school. Families fed their sons into it and generally it turned out sturdy products, and why not. Rugby football was compulsory and so was cricket. My mother called the two sports 'raw beef and Yorkshire pudding'. Cadet parades were compulsory, traipsing around the sports field in uniform with Boer War carbines was supposed to train you for another Zulu rebellion while you were in early adolescence. There were good teachers and bad ones.

CHARLIE EVANS

Charlie Evans was history master and I couldn't wait for his lessons. Cock-eyed Wilson was a bad teacher, confusing you because you didn't know which one to look at. He insisted you spelt Shakespeare without an 'e' on the end. I mention Charlie Evans because he made every piece of history a story that gripped you and much of it was prophetic. In the loss of Empire, the rape of Abyssinia, one-man-one-vote and his stalking horse, the Polish Corridor, he was telling the classes of adolescents again and again "Watch out lads, a war is coming and you're just the right age." He didn't actually say it but he was against war and talked of the Polish Corridor as the place where a war was bound to start given a treaty as crass as that of Versailles. Charlie loved long words, which could roll off his tongue and impress his classes, historic names like Johan van olden Barneveld. A boy in class was Johannes Von Wermeskerken and calling his name on the register Charlie would shake the last three syllables lovingly off the end of his tongue.

Three years later most of the class was in uniform fighting for Britain who had gone to war with Hitler over the Polish Corridor on Sept. 3rd, 1939. Six of us in the class were in the same local regiment the Natal Mounted Rifles* also a relic of the Boer War.

In my form also was the young Cowley whose elder brother Joe was later shot through the neck in a bayonet charge we made in the battle of Alamein, and lived to tell the story. He was a very shy, nice looking boy who bit his nails and had an appalling handwriting that rivalled my own. He joined the airforce and had half his face shot away. After the war he had difficulty being recognised by anyone. Joe used to share his letters with me and kept me in touch with Cowley Junior.

A very tall companion at D.H.S. was the Norwegian boy Rosholt in our class. We used to meet occasionally in our hotel basement after school and review our armies of tin soldiers. His father was of a wealthy family of merchants at the Point (harbour) in Durban and well off. Their scion had an excellent collection, whereas most of my tin soldiers were limbless or decapitated by my younger brother's

---

*See Appendix One.

3

pellet gun. As I recall the young Rosholt joined the air force and was killed in W.W.II.; he was, being Norwegian, very fair indeed and would have had an awful time in the tropical sun in Abyssinia if he had joined my regiment, because it was for Kenya that the first South African volunteers of the coming war headed and it was on the equator. In any case we decided to cremate all our toy soldiers and made lead fishing sinkers out of them before mobilisation.

Then there was another guy in the class who joined the N.M.R. Bruce Lockyer, diminutive and blonde, always impeccably turned out in the school uniform, did not compete too well in the school's 'beef and Yorkshire pudding' but kept the form entertained with his accounts of 'cher chez la femme'. He let it out that he lived on the beach front in a large block of apartments and that here he had as a neighbour an older lady friend who would entertain him after he got home from school once or twice a week when cadet training did not interfere. There were lewd and exciting accounts of his antics reinforced by his gestures. It kept him popular at school where it had left the class horny for the rest of the day, and I've no doubt his stories changed when we hit Cairo, Alexandria and Rome. When sports day came, Bruce was always surrounded by girls. Whether they were sisters, fans or his various 'femmes', he never elucidated. In Italy driving Shermans in 'B' Squadron he was noteworthy for having been crushed and otherwise injured, a nice guy, brave and articulate.

JOE HOFFENBERG

Joe Hoffenberg was a quiet, diffident Jewish boy who marched in with at least forty others after the Christians had dealt with their prayers at D.H.S's morning assembly. He was more concerned with events developing in Nazi Germany than any. In 'C' Company of the N.M.R. he volunteered for all the dangerous jobs and died grotesquely before the battle of Alamein on a fighting patrol.

GOLDWATER

With succinct cruelty schoolboys called the teacher Mr. Goldwater, 'Pissy' and there was some palpable evidence for this, in that when he got excited he let forth jets of saliva in his enthusiasm. Those pupils sitting in the front rows of the class would hold up their exercise books as mock shields that were to protect them from Pissy's outpourings. But he was an excellent teacher of English and Latin. He pronounced his Latin v's softly saying that was how the Romans did it, but it was rumoured that Mr. Goldwater had once pronounced 'vasto' and other v's so hard that the resulting salivating bombardment was too intense for his pupils and this was why his v's were soft. He liked to stand right in front of your desk so that he could kick you under it if you exceeded the bounds of propriety with him. This meant with the kick your eyes were level and close to another part of his anatomy that had expressed goldwater excessively. This chronic dribble well-ironed into his trousers gave emphasis to his sobriquet. Not usually a spiteful man he couldn't help taunting us every time Ariovistus was read out in Caesar's Gallic Wars with comments like "And I hope the Germans get hold of you Baker and lay you waste you silly fool" with a gentle kick at me under the desk or at anyone else that read Ariovistus or 'vasto…I lay waste' with a hard Vee. His hopes and wishes albeit playful were to be granted.

RAITH HOWES

Raith Howes was another D.H.S. pupil in Charlie Evans' class. He and his brother Duncan would sometimes join us on Durban beach where my brother Desmond, the Howes brothers and I would spend the day surfing the waves and dodging the giant dumpers. Those days in surf and sun were to repeat themselves when Raith, cut off with others in the fall of Tobruk, struggled to escape prisoner-of-war camp by swimming and wading through the seas and channels skirting Tobruk and Bardia.

AUBREY HAMPSON

Aubrey Hampson came from a large, well-known family on the coast south of Durban. He was mischievous and produced all sorts of gizmos in class, which he demonstrated without getting caught out. We both hated cadets and ran foul of the pupil quartermaster, an effeminate boy who we used to call 'Sweetie'. When we joined the N.M.R. regiment together we were both soon in hot water with Sergeant Major John Herbert, Sweetie's elder brother. Aubrey was to have a penchant for escorting enemy P.O.W's and keeping them in order in the Western Desert three years later. In the lunch hour when together we ate our sandwiches in nearby Berea Park, Aubrey smoked two or three cigarettes. I never smoked, but in exchange for his lunch apple or banana I would disperse his smoke with my free hand. The cigarettes were called Myrtle Grove and out of their packets of cardboard and silver paper, in chemistry lessons I fashioned miniature boats, which I floated on water in the lab's bench sinks. If there were chemical stinks on the go, he would light up a fag and sometimes my boats too. But Aubrey was caught out one day when he lit up a 'myrtle grove' while Aunty Armstrong (the chemistry master) was in the fusion cupboard and Jimmy Black, the headmaster, poked his head in the laboratory's back door and caught Aubrey at it. In those days thrashings at school, six of the best on the backside with Mr. Black's deft cane, were not unusual or illegal. The hard part was that the canings were done on the stage in the Assembly Hall in full view of a thousand pupils. Afterwards, I commiserated with Aubrey. He rubbed his backside ruefully and all he said was "Fuck him!"

HAROLD LAKE & GEOFFREY FRANK

One of the most gifted school companions I ever had from the Durban High School and in the N.M.R. was Geoffrey Frank. G.F. died of wounds after the Battle of Gazala, June 7th 1942. From the same class at Durban Prep there emerged the class humorist; a very brilliant and talented boy called Harold Lake. The best description I can give of his appearance was his similarity to Billy Bunter of St. Jim's of Magnet Comics fame. Harold spent 99% of his time in class sketching teachers but also drawing the latest models of motor cars. He was superb in both. But he also had a predilection for theatre. He had played Sir Toby Belch in a scene from *Twelfth Night* staged in the Durban Pavilion. Harold and I met up again at Durban High School and we acted out one of the Sandy Powell sketches "Sandy and the Burglar" in one of my concerts held in the basement of our hotel Marine View in 1937. He became a famous S.A. actor playing at the Criterion theatre and also, as I recall it, singing in opera. I lost track of him when he retired. I used to liken him to Bottom the Weaver because he wanted to poach all the roles in any play being presented. He liked nothing better than to sit and giggle at the weird ways of the schoolteachers and in the breaks to mimic them mercilessly. Harold Lake, as I recall it became involved in ENSA presenting programs for troops in W.W.II. I must say that from an academic point of view there were only two bright stars in the class: Colin Spence and Geoffrey Frank. Each month the results of the tests were read out in front of the school during morning assembly and unfailingly, the first two names read the highest two, were these. I don't know what Colin did in the war. I did meet up with him at University but I felt no rapport with him as I had done with Geoff.

DENNIS THE CHILD

And then at D.H.S. there was Dennis Baker. Through a set of extraordinary circumstances I became more closely associated with a family of old friends whose surname was also Baker and Percy Baker, the father had been a friend of my father Sydney Baker. The two of them had served in the Honourable Artillery Corps in W.W.I. Percy had an only son called Dennis who was born on the same day as myself, the 31st December 1922. Whereas I had been delivered on the stroke of midnight, Dennis had been born earlier at noon. Dennis Baker lived in Puntan's Hill near King's House, N.E. of Durban.

Dennis didn't do very well at school, but he was a very good golf player. One could call him a child protégé, whereas I was very rough-cut, independent and more experienced, even at that age. Dennis was very mollycoddled by his adoring parents. He was naive in just about everything except golf. I would meet him on a bicycle for a jaunt in the Umgeni Valley, which lay northwards of Durban. It was here that we watched Hindu ceremonies at their temples down in the riverbed. The firewalking events there mesmerised us. Watching simple Hindu market gardeners and their families walk barefooted across blazing hot coals staggered me. Whereas Dennis was overawed by the religious implications of these Hindus in semi-trance states, I was more impressed by the insults their actions projected at Newtonian physics. How was it possible for the flesh to remain unseared? How could faith place their consciousness in a position of immunity to fire? On the way back from the Umgeni we would always take the jungle road through Burman Drive stopping for tea at the Elephant Tree where we would have a brew-up and chat.

My own social life was confined to events at my family's hotel where I increasingly shared responsibility for its running. Dennis' social life was expressed through a group in Puntan's Hill called the Odd Fellows. The name meant to include anybody who felt unable to fit to the normal requirements of social life. I myself was ambivalent and capable of joining in with whomever Dennis Baker chose to be associated and to be able to return to my own surroundings (unfettered) by Dennis' involvements. When I stayed for weekends at Puntan's Hill I became more associated with Dennis' elder sister, Vera Baker, a charming English blonde who eventually married a British ex-serviceman. She was bridesmaid at my sister Margaret's wedding and I was best man at hers. I was amazed at the way Dennis Baker's parents cared for him when staying over. Percy Baker, Dennis's father, who worked at Shell Company on the Esplanade, would see us to bed, tucking us into the double bed the couple had once occupied and making sure no draft would threaten our sleep.

I remember the first night I slept there. Dennis put the light out and we lay in the dark silence for a few minutes and then he dug a finger into my ribs and we larked about wrestling for a while. The old bed bumped and thumped a bit and it ended with both of us dumped in the hollow of it, Dennis' right hand still around my neck where, in the frolic he tried to strangle me and with his arm across my chest. We stayed like that a few minutes recovering and it seemed he didn't want to disentangle. I said to him "Explore if you want to" he did. A few minutes passed and I found he had fallen asleep. I disengaged him gently, got out of bed and tiptoed to the door into his sister's room and turned the handle gently. It was locked.

On the last day of 1938 we shared a birthday party. The cake had 16 candles for each of us. With one gasp I blew all mine out. Ominously, I thought, Dennis left two burning.

When war was imminent the Bakers were very alarmed about Dennis' future. He was already a cadet in the R.N.V.R.*. I didn't fancy the navy and his parents wanted Dennis to join the same regiment as me. Percy Baker discussed the matter with some agitation.

*Royal Naval Voluntary Reserves.

Crossing the River at Gidu

The author carrying a Bren gun is probably 6th from the left. Note the stretcher-bearers on the opposite bank.

Of course I wanted everyone around me to join my regiment, but in the end Percy settled for the Royal Navy. That decision was one he blamed himself for, for the rest of his days. Dennis joined the battleship Barham. In November/December 1941 the Allies lost ten battleships between them. Dennis' ship was one.

The night we crossed the swollen river at Gidu two years later, I had a strange dream of Dennis Baker. We were both coming through the forest at Burman Drive, Durban and I had gone ahead along the banks of the Umgeni River again. Then I heard strange sounds coming from behind me. There, struggling across the waters of the river, which had become flooded, was a huge elephant. It was the Elephant Tree torn out by the raging waters and Dennis caught amongst its branches was in great distress calling for me as the tree trunk rolled over in the torrent. I awoke distressed. Over the approaching months the dream repeated itself. *[see plate of crossing the river at Gidu]*

My mother chose to live out her last span of life in her own way and I helped as I could. First of all there was the pain and I learnt to give her the prescribed bromides and not to chide her when she asked for twice the dose. In my own way I was sympathetic to euthanasia and couldn't bear to see her suffer. Almost coinciding with the bad news delivered to Arnold's Hill, a beautiful blue Persian stray cat walked into the house and selecting my mother, attached herself. Mother's favourite hobby was keeping canaries and in her last days she would sit amongst them in their shaded aviary comforted by their songs, rowdy bathing and voluptuous mating. Our pet Alsatian got in on the act too and they all shared a corner of the garden.

When I got home from school I would sit with her and have my afternoon tea and buttered toast and do my homework chatting with her. She had, when I was younger, encouraged me to paint in watercolour and I would try to do English flowers for her, like primrose, impatiens and wild roses.

My father in the Honourable Artillery Corps during W.W.I. had worked on the first tanks in a munitions factory. My Mother was a music teacher and they were married in 1917. Emigrating to South Africa the couple, encouraged by my Uncle Ken, settled in

Durban where I was conceived but my mother decided that I should be born in England. Back in South Africa mother bought a series of private hotels and ran them to keep the family alive. My restless father left home and settled in Umhlali on the north coast about 30 miles from Durban where he opened the Umhlali garage and continued his career as an engineer dealing with Huletts enormous sugar lorries. He died suddenly in 1931 of a heart condition. Only a few weeks before his death he had insured himself for a large sum of money and there was a post-mortem. He had not left a will and my brother and I became wards of the Supreme Court. The upshot of her own impending death was that my mother had little option but to make her brother, my Uncle Ken, our guardian, and to our horror!

My elder sister Kathleen hearing that I was looking for a job knew someone well placed in the printing industry. He approached John Dickinson & Co. who were suppliers to the printing trade and after an interview I succeeded in starting with Dickinson's on January 3rd 1938, and mother died 5 weeks later.

CHAPTER II

In January 1938, as a boy of fifteen, I joined the staff of John Dickinson & Co. (Africa) Ltd. in Durban. My boss was Clem Woods, captain of the infantry, he was partially blinded by gas at the Front in W.W.I. A nice man. Very compassionate and interested in the welfare of his Zulu staff and the Indian community both of whom were suffering from the problems of apartheid, he was also a member of the Oxford Group which I found unpleasant because he was determined to offload his sins with the least provocation. At that age, I was hardly receptive to detailed stories of his intimacies. The white staff was a youngish group held in thrall by the antics of Hitler in the Sudetenland and Poland. War was anticipated at any moment. I was friendly with all of them but particularly with Archie McLachlan, a youth four years older than myself, who had been raised strictly by his Scots mother. He was very green about certain things and so was I for that matter, at age fifteen. I took all my office problems to him for advice and he leant on me for some matters pertaining to social activities. We became firm friends and he became senior salesman and I was allocated the bazaars to sell Dickinson's stationery. We met each morning for anchovy toast and tea in Greenacre's and would discuss everything under the sun except business and then go off and see clients. As it was clear he was going to become a country traveller for Dickinsons and need to drive a car, I taught him how to drive. He was very grateful for my concern. He joined the Royal Durban Light Infantry, and became a hero in Libya the time I was there. He was seen as one of the three fighting macs who had displayed great courage under fire.

At the last moment before departing for base camp Mr. Woods had me in to tell me the company need not pay me on active service because I had only too recently started work. However, because of this consideration and that consideration, he would pay me two pounds and fifty shillings a month while I was away at the war. I was not to know it, but the experience I had already had with Dickinson's would prove invaluable to me all my life. Invoicing, indenting, importing and exporting, paper and book sizes, printing stationery were all to play their part in the post-war years.

More than anything I had made some good friends at my employment, who stood by me till the end of their days.

John Dickinson & Co. (Africa) Ltd., was an overseas branch of the English Company with its headquarters in Old Bailey, London. The English complex had numerous factories in London and the English countryside, which manufactured paper, cardboard and stationery for global sale. The African division was run by two shareholders, a father and son, surnamed Timberlake. The father was a very friendly man hiding a deep grief which was that his son and heir W.H. Timberlake was dying of a wasting, incurable disease and would not be able to retain his direction of Dickinson's in Africa much longer. Old man Timberlake had gone out of his way to act as pater familias to his employees and especially since the beginning of the war. As we left South Africa on active service we kept in touch with him by letter and cards. I was flattered when he replied and wrote to me in Egypt, but when his son died, he faded out of the company and I lost touch even before the war ended.

Alex Giraudeau was the go-getter in the Durban branch, and the ailing Woods relied on him increasingly. Giraudeau took an interest in me since the day I started work in the New Year of 1938. He was a huge, very healthy man, who played league rugby and persuaded me to join his club named "Tech. College." Nothing was too much trouble for him and, always in search of a father I consulted him on all kinds of matters. He was very inspiring and coming from a large family also gregarious, placing his energies where there was weakness and occasionally clipping a wing where there was a budding Icarus. As his name implied he was of French stock, actually Huegenot. He would come into and leave work at all hours, was a merciless slave driver when there was work to be done. He was manager under Woods but no job was too tough or too dirty for him and would drive off up country for a week selling Croxley stationery and printers' requisites to 50 different towns and villages. Alex Giraudeau joined the South African Air Force (S.A.A.F.) when war came and whether in uniform or out of it still threw himself into preparing Dickinson's for a long war siege cut-off from the parent company in England as well as undergoing training on seaplanes for patrolling Atlantic waters.

Alex's favourite was Archie McLachlan, four years my senior, a young Scotsman who was the only person able to outpace him at work. Very slowly Archie and I earned respect for each other. After all he was from that other school, Glenwood High, whereas I was from Durban High School. He was into soccer and I into rugger. Archie went out of his way to teach me the trade and I did my best keeping track of the company's stocks, a thankless, tedious and unrewarding job.

Alex Giraudeau was the Durban branch's first casualty of war. Seven men were on active service out of a male staff of ten. I was up north in East Africa fighting the Italians. Despite being in the thick of things, Giraudeau's demise was still a great shock to me and remained so, for his death was never confirmed to my knowledge. He had been the acme of dedication for me as assistant manager of Dickinson's, and almost a father to whom I had turned to for advice and encouragement. About the same time Dickinson's sustained another dreadful blow. The head offices in Old Bailey were totally destroyed. Everything was consumed by the London Blitz, offices, files, records, and even the office safes.

Alex Giraudeau had a younger brother Gus who was a quartermaster in N.M.R.'s 'C' Company stores. I remember him in British Somaliland and then he disappeared. Rumour had it that Gus had gone back to South Africa on home leave and it was then that I heard that Alex was reported missing. A flight of Sunderland flying boats had gone out on patrol from somewhere off the coast of Central Africa. Funny things were happening at the time with German raiders operating in the South Atlantic. One of these had been the Graf Spee, the German pocket battleship. I wondered whether Alex's plane might not have been brought down by one of these raiders operating in the Atlantic.

At that time, another member of Dickinson's staff was Jack Smith, a few months older than myself. He joined the Naval Reserves part-time. In late 1939, he was called up for duty, surprisingly, and disappeared for weeks on end. It was a worrying time for the South African Navy because the Germans had a pirate ship off Durban sinking merchantmen of any nationality. Several ships of the South African Navy were destroyed but Jack Smith survived.

Jack Smith's long absences at sea were later explained when the activities of the German raiders Graf Spee and Atlantis were revealed. ATLANTIS, launched in December 1939, converted from a freighter into an 8,000 ton armed cruiser with six, six-inch guns camouflaged and a special room capable of holding 90 magnetic mines, the ship also carried fake flags of the British, the Dutch and the Norwegians. The records claim twenty-two sinkings by Atlantis amounting to almost 150,000 tons mainly in the South Atlantic and as far as Cape Town, near Jack Smith's naval base in Simonstown and Durban, which is in the Indian Ocean.

Jack had been involved in many grim experiences, rescues and agonising searches for mines and for the ruthless raiders of the South African coast. He had of course been silent about shipping movements during the war, but through him, after hostilities ended, I heard that Atlantis had been sunk by the British cruiser Devonshire. The Nazi pocket battleship Graf Spee had also been one of the culprits involved in predatory actions off the coast of Southern Africa.

Graf Spee's war cruise lasted 77 days taking her at one time eastwards into the Indian Ocean where nine British merchant ships were sunk off Lourenco Marques and Durban totalling 50,000 tons. A year later the N.M.R. embarked at Durban for the East African Campaign against the Italians, escaping the German raiders.

Forced to leave school because of my mother's death I had retained my strong desire to matriculate even though working full time at John Dickinson & Co. Enrolling at the Natal Technical College I went from work at five o'clock each day to evening classes completing the usual studies for matric in Math's, English and Commerce. A fourth subject eluded me, perhaps a Freudian matter deriving from primary schooling. It was Afrikaans, the Boer War heritage that the English

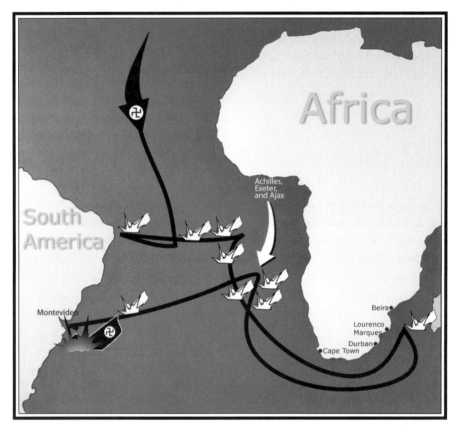

Route of the Graf Spee

Route taken in South Africa by the pocket battleship Graf Spee which sank 50,000 tons of shipping off Portuguese East Africa and Natal in September / October 1939 before returning to the South Atlantic meeting her demise at the hands of the three British Cruisers Achilles, Exeter and Ajax. Some months later our own troop ships bearing us north to Kenya and Abysinnia were to ply the same waters as Graf Spee had off Durban and Portuguese East Africa.

community had to endure as part of the Act of Union of 1910 which brought resolution of Anglo-Boer difficulties. The new South Africa had a tiny white population of less than 2 million and only 37 per cent of it was of English origin. The rest of it was of Dutch descent, mainly the embittered remnants of the two Boer Republics, which had invaded Natal to start the Anglo-Boer Wars of 1899-03. This of course was only the political background to the undeniable fact that this country, still an integral part of the British Empire was sitting on the largest deposits of diamonds and gold in the whole world. The second and ultimately more decisive factor in this equation was the existence of a black population that was many, many times more populous than the white community and which had practically no political representation for its tremendous problems mainly accentuated by its collective poverty.

Racial inequality was part of the everyday life. You just grew up in it. Most of the white English-speaking community had no option but to accept the situation as they were in the voting minority and held on to their British links with the Empire with a determination which bordered on jingoism. The Afrikaner element made some attempt to unite with their English-speaking brothers but its hard republican core consolidated itself wherever possible at the expense of the white English moderates and the black native population could go suck eggs.

Political opportunism was continually employed by both sides. On the side of the Anglos there was the English monarchy and its ongoing events such as Durbars, coronations, and life events of its royals e.g: births, deaths, abdications and visits.

On the side of Afrikaans, public emphasis was placed on historic and centennial anniversaries like the Battle of Blood River where a handful of Boers defeated the might of the Zulu nation and the centennial celebration of the Great Trek in which the Dutch element in 1838, rather than submit to British rule's anti-slavery laws, fled into the hinterland to escape it [to **trek** away from it].

In South Africa, these various tensions had come to a head on both sides when in 1938 the Trekker Centennial celebration bubbled up in the South African cauldron and in 1939 the threat of a British war with Germany rattled the sabres of the English white community of which I was one.

1938/39 was the critical period in which Britain and France had to weigh up Nazi Germany's intentions. Revolutions require both drive and direction. I was then considering a university degree reading history and English literature, and had privately poured over the events in France after 1789. The extraordinary success of the revolution there seemed to hinge firstly on the impetus of an emerging middle class out of the liberated peasantry. Despite its drive utter chaos had existed until the young Napoleon had provided direction through his expertise, generally leading on to imperialism via a 'New Order'.

Germany's national socialism had provided impetus for a successful revolution, but had to await for Hitler to give it direction. Hitler's New Order was old wine in new bottles. It was the slick presentation of Nazism, which fascinated the youth of the pre-war days both in Germany and in the British Empire's bored capitalistic youth. The daily press presented the events of each day so dramatically that you, the reader, was also drawn towards Hitler's direction without any threat of disloyalty to the Allied cause. It was the newness of it all. None of us had witnessed the tactics of confrontation that Hitler was concocting and despite its evil and bullying, it thrilled and most of us, covertly at least, succumbed. It was effective war mongering. The Nazis called it propaganda. A war situation offered alternatives and we welcomed them. We did not volunteer despondently but with all the hubris of the patriotic young.

My mother's youngest brother Kenneth Browne became the state appointed guardian of my younger brother Desmond and I. We both detested him for what he was – a brash ignoramus hardened by having to live out a life in which he chose to make all his own decisions and then lived by them, though in most instances they were the worst imaginable. He had opted to leave home without an education at the very early age of thirteen. In search of work he had drifted into the Thames dockside and stowed away on ships or accepted menial tasks until he was sufficiently adult and developed to undertake physical labour that paid reasonably.

He had lost what money he made in foolish enterprises and only began to acquire wealth and property when, on his travels he had met a Dutch girl who had her head screwed on and saved money she had earned and invested it, purchasing a hotel on the Natal South Coast which he had helped to manage. His experiences had hardened him to such an extent that he conducted his life never, ever trusting anyone, proudly stating "I don't borrow from anyone; I don't lend to anyone and I never stand as bank guarantor for anyone."

Ken Browne was huge in frame and a nasty merciless man with it whom I once as a boy saw beat up a black vagrant mercilessly who happened to stray on to his land. That there were fine points in his life I would agree, but they rarely showed themselves.

He once knelt down and sucked the poison of a puff adder out of my brother Desmond's foot when he was bitten while we were both staying at his hotel. His strength was immense and he frightened people with it. I found his ignorance more frightening when he was put in charge of my affairs.

During the war he joined some volunteer group that did part-time service. To his credit he had some patriotic vein in him that gave him a uniform to wear.

Early in 1945 my Uncle Ken suffered a serious heart attack. I sat at his bedside and noticed his alarm as he questioned me about death. He died unexpectedly three days later.

Uncle Ken had purchased a house on the esplanade in Durban and with it an 022-class sailboat to take trips on Durban Bay with his wife my Aunt Margaret. Two blocks from him on the esplanade was an old red brick colonial building which housed the local Y.M.C.A. With tall ceilings, concrete floors and capacious windows it was an ideal structure for the sixty odd youths that lodged there. My uncle made the acquaintance of its General Secretary, John Hunt who had his own red brick establishment next door. The Y.M.C.A. was to become my home of convenience for the turbulent years of 1938 to 1940. It was handy to the town centre, to John Dickinson's & Co., where I worked and to Natal Technical College where I attended night classes for the Matric which I had promised my dying mother I would complete.

Cleverly my uncle had secured a place in a dormitory for three at the Y.M. for me with a broad veranda on the top floor overlooking the

The author's brother Desmond, a boy in the British Navy at the outbreak of war.

busy yacht club (housing my uncle's boat) and the even busier new harbour T-jetty, and an eyesore railway line that ran the length of the esplanade serving the harbour. Right next door to the Y.M. on its right side, were the spacious lawns of one of Durban's poshest hotels, The Marine. On the esplanade abutting a subway isDick King's statue, a local hero who reminded Afrikaners that Anglo-Boer disharmony was much older than the Boer War and in Durban, dated back another fifty years or so to an encirclement of the British in the old Fort at what is currently Kingsmead, the site of Test Match cricket. Dick King was the British hero who rode horseback 600 miles cross-country down to Grahamstown to get a British squadron to come up by ship to relieve besieged Durban. In the Y.M. we didn't know too much about the current fragile new King George VI and our loyalties centred more around Dick King and his horse in 1939. At that time the national anthem of the land was "God save the King" but as its words suggested it was under threat of being replaced by an Afrikaans reciprocate which nobody had successfully been able to translate into English. It was no wonder that the nation was willy-nilly taking sides again as war clouds threatened in Europe, which had been the origin of both Boer and Briton. I was reminded of the disturbing words in Kubla Khan that I had just learnt at school…

> "And midst this tumult
> Kubla heard from far
> Ancestral voices prophesying war."

Life at the Y.M. brought a complete change. Suddenly I was cut off, as a boy of fifteen from my school chums, who were replaced by my colleagues at work where I was virtually a dog's body as the new office boy.

Associates at the Y.M. were, in the first few months distant. I had very little money and was expected by my uncle (and legal guardian) to pay board and lodging myself from my tiny wages. With night classes my schedule was tight and stressful. Even confirmation classes at St. Paul's Cathedral locally, ate up my time and even soured my attitude to Christian dictates. All this changed when my room mates found other accommodation and two bronzed lifesavers from the south coast took their place.

Winston Churchill and Field Marshall Smuts, his wartime confidant, who led South Africa into the war to assist Britian and was C-in-C of the South African military forces

Eric Gregg and Tommy Haylock were anything but beach boys. Eric worked for the Durban City Council and Tommy was apprenticed to a sign writer. Living 25 miles south of Durban they felt the grind of commuting by train to Durban from Warner Beach each day too demanding. They were able to stay at the Y.M. five days mid-week and go back to their Warnadoone Life Saving Club weekends.

Eric, lanky, fair-haired and always very sunburnt was two years older than I and we got on well together as companions, room mates and as students of Tech. College where we met for evening classes. We had both lost our fathers in the early thirties, his knocked out by the Great Depression and edged into alcoholism, mine through a massive single heart attack. Our communal lifestyle brought home the fact that we were now poor! It was a revelation to me but an old acquaintance to Eric whose two elder sisters had taken jobs in Durban to help the family out. Eric sharpened me up as to where expenses could be reduced and I gave help with his studies.

Tommy was extrovert, always busy with outlandish hours on sign writing jobs. Tall, swarthy and very practical, he looked like a Roman eaglet with his very aquiline features. Eric kept Tommy's feet on the ground and both cared for me in many ways. Unfortunately they both smoked and I didn't think it went well with their life-saving disciplines.

Politics began to permeate almost everything. The media just poured out the war mongering incessantly. The national republicanism of South Africa was increasingly identified with German, Nazi attitudes and various institutions began to reflect this. General Smuts had an awful time keeping the state in one piece with his United Party. 1938 was election year and political meetings became hot stuff for youths fed on media hype. Inevitably, with war approaching, the English-speaking section of the nation became suspicious of Afrikaner intent and Jan Smuts in Parliament had to hold political rallies to keep his United Party alive. Secretly, I admired the old general but adopted jingoism as being more loyal to my own British connection. At one political rally held by Smuts in Durban's City Hall, I was in a crowd of youths, provocatively English, which surrounded his limousine baying jingo slogans. Smuts was unmoved at the taunts as he sat in the brightly-lit interior of the car. I couldn't have been more than two feet from him and I shouted, "We don't want you! Go back to the Platteland!"*

His steely blue eyes looked deeply into mine as the vehicle took off. Within 18 months, against frightful odds Smuts took South Africa into World War II to stand by the side of his old enemy, Great Britain.

With Britain at war with Germany, the extremists in the republican movement in South Africa became emboldened. Those M.P's who had voted against war in the parliament in Cape Town were investigated by the English press and found to have German connections in their ancestry. Stellenbosch University was a hotbed of Nazi sympathisers and everywhere there were resurrected old Boer War sympathies. The concept of a fifth column hostile to pro-war elements, soldiers and military establishments became more evident. There emerged with sabres rattling the 'Ossewa Brandwag' intent on sabotaging Smut's pro-Empire stand and South Africa's military participation. This only stirred up patriotic groups and everywhere men were rushing to old established regiments to join up. Eric, Brian Massey and Tommy Haylock were no less enthused than myself. We turned to look for a hero figure and discovered we didn't even know what the new king looked like. Tommy discovered a fairly recent portrait of George VI and set his artistic talents to reproducing it. Meanwhile, in the Y.M. we had stirred up enough war fervour to insist all residents there should make themselves clear as to what side they were on. The division was hardly clear cut but certainly the pro-war backers were in the majority.

Colin MacArthur headed a young group of my own age and ilk and we decided to have an unveiling of Tommy's royal portrait at the esplanade end of the top floor of the Y.M. right outside our dormitory. My brother-in-law who was managing the French Bottle store just down the road, supplied us with 2 demijohns of Cape Jeripigo sweet wine and we had one helluvan unveiling. The General Secretary had me in to register his disapproval. Eric came into his office with me for the ticking off and told him to grow up. Quinn, the doorman secretly approved and tried to pacify the outraged Y.M. resident republican nationalists. After the unveiling the revelry began to get unruly, the

---

*The Afrikaner outback territory that was once the Boer Republic.

demijohns were emptied and we all decamped on to the esplanade around Dick King's statue. Several of us gave speeches with avowals of undying loyalty, a good number of us were able to muster a notable rendering of 'God save the King' and only a few of the bravest actually mounted Dick King's horse and cheered the big knobs on the verandas of the overlooking hotels, who had come out to see what was going on.

One weekend when Eric Gregg had taken me back to Warner Beach on the South Coast for a weekend I met Brian Massey, a big, muscular, lifesaver friend of his who was very blonde and susceptible to sunburn. It was the year the war broke out and later he, Eric and I joined the N.M.R. at the same time. Eric's sister Margery Gregg worked for the Natal Mercury Newspaper, a publisher, big boned, attractive with bronzed skin and suited neatly; she reviewed books and novels mainly, almost weekly and passed them on to Eric. Too poor to buy expensive topical and contemporary works I seized on them and developed a bookworm enthusiasm for reading, which broadened my outlook at a time when Hitlerism was in total occupation of the media.

Margery met and married Brian's brother. Brian was constantly active with cher chez les femme and so handsomely presentable that his efforts were frequently crowned with success but Eric, equally poor, found him too tight with his money to be a good companion at all times.

Watching the girls flocking around him on the beaches, you had the feeling that Brian would be hit with a polycratian fate somewhere in his successful young life.

At the Battle of Dadaba in southern Abysinnia two years later, a bullet shattered his right shoulder and he was invalided back to South Africa via Berbera. But fate dealt him a final and mortal blow, when a few years after the war he was stricken with cancer against which he had no defence.

I had not wept for the virgins he de-flowered but with his death I first began to sense the remorselessness of karma.

"Golden lads and girls all must
As chimney sweepers, come to dust."

The early 1940's was a dreadful time for young Britishers wherever they were. The motherland was embroiled in a fast developing European debacle and the young men of the Commonwealth itching to get involved were signing up with regiments everywhere. Australia, New Zealand, Canada and South Africa were all re-establishing old regiments out of the tatters of W.W.I and even the Boer War. Restlessness was everywhere. We all clung on to our civilian jobs and waited for mobilisation orders, which would take our regiments into training. In this disordered state Eric Gregg had left the Y.M.C.A. and gone back to his family in Warner Beach, 20 miles down the South Coast. He had invited me, equally restless, down to stay with him, weekends and anytime I was free.

On a sunny day staying with Eric down at the Warner Beach, I was with a group of guys seated near the lifesaver stand. They, with me, had all joined the N.M.R. and shared my impatience for mobilisation. Henry Rule, nice guy but a bit of a lout had joined the regiment with Eric and Brian Massey. All three were lifesavers and had earlier put on a pretty good demonstration of life-saving techniques on the beach followed by a sturdy march past. We, the spectators, had settled down again on to our beach towels in the hot sun idly watching the passing parade. There was the usual conglomerate of bathers between the safety pylons placed by the lifeguards. Beyond them there were surfers taking the surf's slides which brought them right up to the beach.

Some 200 yards beyond the furthest of the surfers, was an aquaplane mounted by Dennis Nourse and with him, in the water was Fred Hooper, another lifesaver who had just joined the S.A.A.F. Watched from the lifesaver's platform, all seemed peaceful.

Suddenly there was a commotion and people stood up looking out to beyond the swimmers, some thinking it was another demonstration of rescue. But there were gasps of horror and I saw a wave engulf Fred Hooper and break reddened. He had been taken by a shark. Desperately, Dennis Nourse grasped at Fred with one arm and held the other arm up to signal for help. Brian Massey hooked the lifeline around himself and Eric and Tommy Haylock followed him as he dashed into the water to the rescue. I joined the crowd gasping at

Fred Hooper's injury as he was brought out of the water haemorrhaging massively from the shark's bite in his right thigh.

Alas, the event did not end happily. Rushed to hospital immediately. Fred died that night from loss of blood and from shock. As a child I had often swum in the lovely, warm lagoon at Warner Beach and surfed with a board at first and later without a board through just hunching the shoulders. Too often the carnage of that day would be repeated on the battlefields over the next five years in the North African desert and the Italian Apennines with Nazis in the role of predators.

For his valour Dennis Nourse, who became a teacher at Durban High was awarded the George Medal.

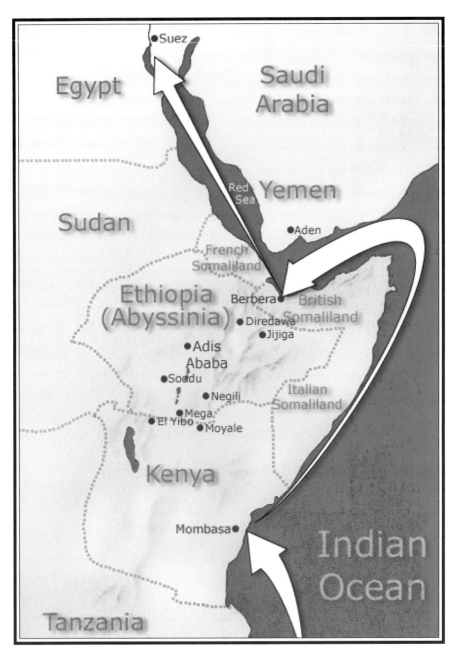

Troopships laden with soldiers and equipment left Durban for Mombasa, Kenya in 1940/41. They were to spearhead attacks that drove the Italians to surrender in southern and central Abysinnia in 1941.

CHAPTER III

In mid-May 1940, my orders for full time service with the N.M.R. came through virtually as a Mobilisation Order! The word 'mobilisation' bore special significance to every young man wishing with all his heart to say "Goodbye to all that!" 'That' was civilian life, families that crowded your ambitions, employers who offered dull prospects, the 'African Mirror' with its stereo weekly news strip at the local bioscope, tiresome parades half-uniformed and without weapons, confirmation classes at St. Paul's Cathedral and so on. Three or four of us at the Y.M.C.A. received the same orders and it was a signal for some sort of special celebration. Departure date was a month away but I began saying goodbye to almost everyone, beginning with the Zulu staff at work who did a little war dance for me. Two years later I was to give that war cry in earnest when we charged the Italians at Alamein.

Mobilisation orders happened to synchronise with the issue of true army style great coats, which flattered and suggested serious military involvement, and seventeen was an impressionable age. I took the great coat to Dickinson's & Co. and donned it to say goodbye to the staff Zulus. It was all quite ridiculous with autumn temperatures still high, but sounded the note of the day. The typists in the front office thought I looked cute and queued up for kisses, but I sighted the boss Clem Woods arriving and parking his car. So I discreetly crept out and returned the coat to its wrappings and sat at my desk again. The head typist Vivienne Thornton went out and bought a cake for the office's morning tea and Captain Woods hearing the news began to remember Delville Wood and other W.W.I. episodes.

With mobilisation came military training, which I found to be a very sketchy affair in which you now endeavoured to deal with another new set of relationships. There were the roots of what you had come from, the links with the civilian company you still worked for and the various military hierarchies emerging in the training camps you were shunted around to. Military training was elementary enough in weapons you knew were either obsolete or generally ineffectual compared to those which had overwhelmed Norway, Holland, Belgium, France, Poland etc., etc., and the list was long. Then there were the imponderables like Russia, Japan and the U.S.A. who might be on either side. The base camps were poorly equipped, crowded and in the mid-winter unheated. Dangerous illnesses emerged like epidemics of meningitis. You just had to adjust. If you did not drink, and at seventeen I was hardly likely to, you had to learn to or you had no friends. You learnt how much beer you could swallow before you were sick. At least your new tent mates tended to you when you overshot the mark. The food was endurable, but you learnt to banish all your fads and fancies. The squad drill was demanding and sharpened your wits. You learnt to swallow hard when confronted with fatigues and unpleasant duties like serving at table in the officers' mess, digging latrines and respecting orders given by permanent force soldiers who couldn't even speak your language. You learnt to recognise rank and when to salute it and when not to. You were used and abused by those scrambling for promotion, to accept the nonsense of prayers and Christian platitudes when you knew you would soon be killing and maiming. But I swallowed it all and if you didn't think too hard, you enjoyed it. Your clothes were provided free, the accommodation was clean, and you ate communally and made a lot of friends. Some had cars and took you into town. Leave for the unmarried was generous. You just grew into it if you were young enough and looked forward to a good scrap on some frontier. Most importantly you were a volunteer ready to serve by attestation for King and Empire. Beyond all this there were only thought's wildernesses which would confront you soon enough in some of the appalling places and situations that would develop and in which you grew and grew while you at least served a noble cause.

We were just a bunch of schoolboys, farmers and clerks when we joined up and somehow training had to change us. (see Appendix Two.)

RAY LEE

Ray Lee was my age, just sixteen when we joined the regiment together at its base in Durban our hometown. We came from totally different backgrounds. He was an apprenticed boilermaker and I was a sales clerk at a paper company. I had soldiered my way through to matriculation; Ray was silent about his schooling. His refinement was in his slender physical form and chiselled features, more a soccer player, whereas I was top heavy and more the rugby type. He grew a better moustache, and mine at that age had required pencilling to get me through recruitment. He was fair with blue eyes and Bohemian in civvy-wear. In childhood I was blonde, but in adolescence my prolific head and body hair became dark.

Only my skin remained fair and sensitive. It too had to be soldiered through controlled sun tanning to a walnut brown, so that it could brave the Libyan sun.

Ray was madly in love, and her family and his all turned up to see him off with the huge crowd at Durban station. I was already orphaned, and what pals I had were either mobilised with me or in our sister regiment, the Royal Durban Light Infantry including my workmates. Ray's teeth were good and creamy, having escaped the ravages of his cigarette habit. We treated each other with some reserve. He had his friends in regimental headquarters, but mine were spread out in the rifle companies. Ray was always on the defensive, hiding things like family, schooling, sport and hobbies. My accent was very English and suffered from the elocution lessons imposed on me to overcome a childhood lisp. Our sufferings however, were sometimes shared when we met on kitchen fatigue or over too much beer in the mess. It was when sharing drinks that I discovered Ray had a temper and it sprang into action if anyone probed his clandestine circumstances too pointedly. There was another matter. His girlfriend had two brothers in the same regiment and one of them was a dark horse whose background I happened, purely by chance, to know about. Ray was also totally without any enthusiasm for warfare, and you had the feeling he had been caught up in the wave of war fever that was awash everytime Hitler invaded a new country. In the army he paid little attention to the numerous obligatory courses that were part of our training and ended up as an ammunition carrier in my Bren gun crew.

It was on one of the protracted route marches at Gilgil, Kenya that Ray and I clashed. The rule was a ten-minute break in every hour of marching. It gave the smokers a chance to light up and the foot-sore time to get a boot off to examine a blister or adjust a plaster. Ray was characteristically, doing all three at once. I thought he smoked too much anyway. Somehow or the other, Ray, hot and sweaty and sitting on the grassy bank, had placed his lighted cigarette on a flat stone while he rolled his putties back on. I, still booted, trod on his cigarette; he jumped to his fee in rage screaming epithets and tore into me. Stepping back from his assault I went down the bank falling flat on my back. Fortunately, the cluster of other blokes pulled him off me or I would have been kicked to death. We were made to shake hands, and the incident was over. Paradoxically, Ray and I became even closer friends and shared many of the terrible events that lay ahead – Stuka attacks, high fever, fighting patrols and bombardment.

DEREK STREET

Derek Street was one of the first friends I made in the army. He was heavily built, but light on his feet and you had to see him on the rugby field to appreciate why he played for the regiment's first fifteen. Derek was half-French on his mother's side. He was a 'L'Allegro' type, always seeking the comedy in our martial circumstances. He detested authority in the regiment and shared my aversion for arsecreepers. In civilian life he had a good job in wool industry marketing – a better job than most of the creatures he waited on in the officers' mess fatigue and he occasionally told them so.

Despite the genteel family background, Derek was sloppy. None of his uniforms seemed to fit. His slight gynacomastia and developing pot seemed to heighten his insouciance. Bad news, and there was a lot of it about for francophiles in W.W.II., beetled his brows but never depressed him for long. After France's fall, he turned to me, eight years his junior, for direction. Watching a newsreel of a barrage balloon breaking its moorings over London and floating around out of control made me utter his name 'Derek', and he laughed nodding his head in agreement. He was brave under fire, even if some of it was friendly.

In his work, meeting with wool farmers he had developed a frightful appetite for alcohol, and after the war it became a problem, but I never saw him drunk or belligerent. He had fellow imbibers and he loved a good story and risqué jokes. I knew him when he was heart-sore for France's plight. I was too, but still indignant at the course Vichy took. I had to be careful about French honour in his presence. Derek laughed in suppressed giggles, often with tears in his eyes and loved the resentful terms that I used to describe some of our worst officers and the fuck-ups they made.

He had rugby injuries which, with appropriate self-applied pressures would show bruises and contusions that were helpful in getting him excused duty, and even into hospital. After Alemain, hearing I was badly wounded, he turned up as a patient at the 92nd British hospital in Kassasin and even secured a bed near me, with rugby injuries of course. I met the girl he married after the war, a wise and kind person who knew how to handle Derek's drink problems and other idiosyncrasies.

JIMMY REEN

Jimmy Reen had been the baby of his family and with many aunts to fuss him, being spoilt was a chronic feature of his character. Only about 25 years old he was wise enough to grasp the fact that he would have to make changes in himself if he was to survive in the army at all. He was usually pleasant but sometimes had a sulky expression which, with flaccid features, reminded you of a bulldog in deep depression. Jim had signed up with the N.M.R. because he had fallen, like all of us, for the absurd war propaganda of the day. His elder brother Jock had been another who had spoilt Jimmy fussing over his childhood complaints and mishaps. Jock worried about others but Jimmy only worried about himself. Concerned about how Jimmy would manage Jock followed him into the N.M.R.

In short Jimmy was a hypochondriac and he to-and-froed with the regiment's medical unit, often with Jock's instancing. He was never going to make a good soldier but you still accepted him because he had two outstanding gifts which could be milked. He was an excellent cook/scrounger very much like the olden days when certain types were good hunter/gatherers. Secondly, he sang beautifully, an attractive baritone with songs that stirred.

Jimmy's elder brother was Jock, a dour Scot in name as well as in his gloomy nature. He was nanny to his younger brother and had joined the regiment probably on the advice of his Auntie Vi, to see that Jimmy wore warm socks with his clammy cold feet. Jock was skinny, sallow and always appeared dehydrated with creases around his mouth and sunken, jaundiced eyes. In the early days of army training, Jimmy a good cook, would volunteer for kitchen fatigue in the officers' mess, bringing back sirloin steaks, frying them in butter and chips. No wonder Jock was jaundiced. Allowed one weekend out of the camp a month, the Reen brothers would book in at the local hotel where their aunts would join them and the family smoothed away their hurts. On at least one occasion the brothers brought Aunties M and Vi (I called them M & V*) back to camp to introduce them around. It was then the four of them, four aunties did not look dissimilar... dour, gloomy, grim Cassandras, sour, morose, worried and forbidding beneath their jocular handshakes.

Desert life, when it came, did not suit Jimmy and he would not have survived the dust storms, scorpions and bully beef without Jock as his infrastructure. I used to hum the old army tune "Good Morning Sergeant Major..." in the background when the two brothers appeared together. The words fitted Jock, who later became a sergeant, and his brother, perfectly, but in cockney:

> "Now what's the matter with you Freaks? Homesick?
> Cor stone a crow sergeant,
> I don't half miss my missus -
> Holes in me stockings -
> No perishin hot water bottle,
> I ain't half fed up..."

Sept/Oct 1940

My own disgust at the demise of France clashed with the forlorn hopes of Derek Street who was now promising that the French fleet would side with Britain and the Free French and show this soon in its ports at Dakar in Northwest Africa and at Oran in Algeria. It came as a shock to both of us when news filtered through in September (of

---

*Army ration of tins of meat and vegetables.

The Author in fatigue suit (1940) training for active service 'anywhere in Africa', so proclaimed in the Oath of Allegiance he swore.

1940) that a British attack on Dakar had been called off because the French battleship Richelieu had, with her 15-inch guns, sided with Vichy France and engaged the British warships some of which were hit. Notably, the British battleship Barham had been plastered by Dakar's shore batteries at 16,000 feet and, the next day was damaged again by a near miss from Richelieu's 15-inch guns. Derek was heartbroken. My own concern was also aroused because my childhood buddy Dennis Baker was on the Barham and my dream life had been disturbed a few weeks earlier by his presence. To make matters worse, I knew that my brother, younger by two years, a boy in the British navy had been posted to a battleship, the HMS. Revenge or Valiant. We were already in East Africa when we heard that the Barham accompanied by other British warships had left Gibraltar and safely crossed the torpedo infested waters of the Mediterranean to reach and reinforce the navy in Alexandria. Dennis and I were both approaching disaster lying only a year or more away. The N.M.R. had a fine military band of pipers and buglers, which officiated handsomely at the beginning of the war but tended to bolster only the regimental elitism as the going got harder. But I was stirred by the bugle call for officers' mess. Reveille and 'lights out' calls of course were early casualties. They were sometimes mixed up in the minds of rookies and in those suffering from hangovers. In the early days of training we had an ageing volunteer in our barrack-room. A veteran of World War I he had rejoined the regiment in 1940 and was as keen as mustard to go through the ranks and enter the Officers Training Corps (O.T.C). He was always up first in the morning and before the last notes of reveille sounded he was in the communal bathroom taking a cold shower. On one occasion a group of boozers had come in and were getting into bed just as the last sounds of 'lights out' died away. They were rowdy and awakened the veteran with their noise. Confused, "World War I" (as we had nicknamed him) rose suddenly and flew into the shower room to take his early morning cold ablution nine hours before time!

When the days became warmer, it was a bungalow joke to carry drunken buddies while asleep, in their beds outside the barrack room where they could puke their hearts out with impunity. The practice halted abruptly when the drunkards, exiled outside, got up in the middle of the night, staggered semi-somnambulantly over to the nearest windows to relieve themselves, pissing into the bungalow over the sleeping inhabitants and causing uproar. Life in Barracks was like cabbage in the army diet. I hated it at first and then grew to enjoy it. After 'lights out' the barrack room sometimes became a forum partly for serious debate about our current company affairs, but more often it encouraged personal reminiscences, especially if they were humourous and frankly critical. Insights of character would emerge and gossip too especially if the bungalow had inmates who were functioning in the medical unit, the quartermaster's stores, at headquarters or in the orderly room. Of course there were problems.

In October, our training in South Africa ended and the N.M.R. sailed in the Llangibby Castle for Mombassa, Kenya's seaport. It was an easy trip followed by a monotonous train journey from Mombassa to Gilgil in Kenya, which lies 100 miles north of Kenya's capital Nairobi.

Campaigning in North-Eastern Africa and its horn was vastly interesting to any romantic young man. It was romantic in the sense of fever trees, volcanic lakes, flamingos and salt pans, trails that once may have been trodden by the Queen of Sheba travelling north to meet Solomon, the heat that produced the fascinating varieties of mirage which made distant trucks suddenly take off and end up in the sky and palm tree fronds become images of distant marching men. The purpose of the East African event was to clear the Italians out of East Africa once and for all. They had been part of Mussolini's dream of a Roman Empire settled around the entire Mediterranean shores. This would have to include Egypt, the Sudan, without which Egypt's security could not be guaranteed and the ancient Christian land of the Coptics, Abysinnia ruled over by Emperor Hailie Selassi, Lion of Juda, King of Kings. The Italians had come across the frontier into Kenya. The British aim was to attack the underbelly of Abyssinia and to kick the Italians out. As South Africans it was our job to boot them out of Kenya first and then to invade Abyssinia and Italian Somaliland.

Training was required for the special kind of warfare that would be necessary to achieve these objectives. This really meant, for me, as part of the air defence of the regiment, the Natal Mounted Rifles, learning the silhouette of the Italian and German planes. At this stage generally the planes were all radial engines, which means the pistons were arranged round a single crankshaft. We had also to learn how to combat hidden enemies like malaria and the inhumane heat. Kenya straddles the equator right down to a bar in Nahuru, which is said to mark exactly the equator. You are in Southern Africa on one side of the bar and Northern Africa on the other side of the bar. More specifically, my role in the first platoon of the regiment was to ensure that the headquarters were not strafed or bombed by a chance enemy patrol. In practice, this meant going out into the bush and establishing three main anti-aircraft positions, which would command as much of the horizon as possible. As it happened the East African venture only produced a minimum of air assaults because of the incredible problems the Italians had to face if they were going to change from the defensive to the offensive. In practice, it also meant reading and writing for most of the day with your ears alert for aircraft and a steak lunch fried in butter over a fire of thornybush sticks and trying to dose off in leisure time with only the help of the same thornybush's shade in a ferocious sticky heat.

The training took place in a town called Gilgil. The town was a series of mud-built banda, with corrugated iron roofing offering only comfort from the wind and the rain. There was a military airport at Gilgil from which South Africans of the local airforce offered flights to reservations and wild areas where game teemed.

The day I had accepted such an excursion coincided with a mock attack on the Gilgil camp, which was to be dive-bombed by British bi-planes, a flight of Hawker Harts. My own ride included first of all participating in the bombing attack which literally meant dive-bombing from two or three thousand feet to twenty feet above the camp so close that I could wave at some of my comrades in the bandas in which we were housed. I had just managed to capture the ride because I happened to be there at the right moment. With no helmet, my hair very long at that stage beat into my eyes. In a two-seater plane, no helmet on, everything wildly exciting and diverting, I later found that the young pilot, who was only my own age, had a reputation for self-destruction. After the air raid which lasted twenty minutes or so he flew me on to the saltpans (pans where there was water) in Marsabit National Park. The pilot would dive on concentrations of wild life skimming along the flat catchment area about five feet off the ground. Sometimes the wheels would even touch the ground. You would see giraffe running next to you on the same level, literally just beyond the wings, ostriches, occasionally hippos turning to the side. It was absolutely staggering for me, a wonderful experience I never forgot. It was rumoured later that the pilot had killed himself in an accident.

The other part of the training was endless route marches. By route marches we meant marching from the camp, raw, in long columns of three for an afternoon at quite a quick pace coming back for a foot inspection immediately so that we were really capable of infantry work in bush country. Our target was anticipated to be Italian black troops lead by white officers usually dug-in inside Northern Kenya at first and later in Southern Abysinnia. The main problem of the South African forces was the logistics of supplying such a large army through such a dry desert. And all that entailed. The impedimenta of this army was carried in Ford trucks and I always said, again and again, that I would express wherever possible my admiration for the sheer guts and versatility of these Ford V-8 trucks whose bodies had been put on them in South Africa and which had been then driven up overland to Kenya. They were our transport and our refuge in which each carried about eight to eleven men. Our Bren guns were mounted in them to counter any strafing that might occur from Italian planes. They carried our food and cooking utensils, our blankets and our ammunition. But nothing in them could save us from the terrible bumps, and from being thrown about crossing the lava-strewn flat lands around the saltpans of the Kenyan's deserts.

KENYA IN TRAINING

Training of South African infantry in Kenya continued intensely at Gilgil, about 100 miles northwest of Nairobi, the nation's capital. We were about to enter some of the worst terrain in Africa to drive Mussolini's blackshirts and colonial troops out of Abyssinia and Somaliland. Route marches became de rigeuer. Everyone hated them, but they did sort out the sick, lame and lazy from those who had genuinely volunteered to fight a war. It decided for many, whether they would see things out to the bitter end, despite the insects, the training and tropical temperatures of more than a 140 degrees

Fahrenheit encountered later on the Ethiopian-Kenya frontier. Age counted significantly in this culling and family ties just as much. The older men, usually married, began to pine for their loved ones and the comforts of civilian life. Gulfs began to yawn between the under twenty-five's and the over thirties. Many of the latter had secured promotion to the few non-commissioned ranks, not always because of merit, but rather out of respect and popularity, remembering that this was a recently-mobilised civilian army of volunteers. Many soldiers were crack-shots coming as farmers straight off the veldt with the history of the Boer War and the Great War experiences of their grandfathers tingling their ears. Preparatory and High Schools had compulsorily drilled all South African boys as cadets on their playgrounds and rifle ranges. Respect worked both ways. You might as a youngster respect your older comrades, but not the many wimps who spent most of their time agonising about home leave, their absent wives and fatherless children.

The route marches brought popularity to the Reen brothers. Jock, well into his thirties, earned his stripes repairing his comrades' blistered and bruised feet and of course, the younger brother's ailments. But Jimmy had won respect another way. He could sing; he didn't join the lusty throats of the mess room choruses, but began to lead marching men, tired and footsore into song. Several of his songs were adapted and harkened back to when resentment was in the air. 'The Legion of the Lost' said it all, and even today viewing any desert globally, brings back some of the song's refrains:

> "…Over the desert where the red sun glares
> Staggering blindly along,
> There comes a party of legionnaires
> Singing their daredevil song.
> They sing a song mingled with despair,
> They sing the song of the legionnaire."

We had all felt a bit neglected, Jimmy most of all, and his rich baritone voice stressed our bitterness and sometimes our wrath. The slam of co-ordinated feet on tarmac and even on harsh earth brought out the full measure of the song's words:

40

"The 'legion of the lost' they call us
The legion of the lost are we;
Legionnaires and outcasts
With beau geste and infamy…"

The song always ended in the sine qua non verse of expressed abuse:

"Scum, scum, every tip of the drum
Says scum of the earth, scum of the earth,
Still we come…To fight and die for La Belle France,
The legion of the lost are we…"

France had not long fallen and there was wide sympathy for her plight and not a little for our route-marched own. Though essentially used at this stage of the war as an infantry battalion, our origins were in cavalry countering the raiding commandos of the Boers. Early in the twentieth century, Putties* were at first used widely; ours were khaki felt and rolled on to the calves up to the knee, flattering if you had good legs and acting as leggings convenient on horseback. They were smart and went with short trousers and regimental dress, but were soon replaced when battle dress was introduced to cover and protect the knees with the ankles gaitered.

On Jock, putties were superb; on his brother they were a mess and both knew it. Eighteen months later in the Western Desert just before Alamein; we were all winding a very different puttee around legs torn by the erecting of defensive barbed wire to keep Rommel out of Egypt. Cuts and abrasions from laying minefields turned to desert sores**, which wouldn't heal, and bandaging to keep dust and flies off was the order of the day. You remained at the front and were not hospitalised for desert sores, and you bandaged your own; putties had taught us how too.

I don't know if there is any literature on it, but binding the legs as tightly as you did with putties is the treatment for varicose veins, where venous blood is shunted to deep veins and with daily exercise, it thus widens them.

---

*Putties – a sock-like leg covering; either a long cloth strip for winding, or a wide canvas strip for buckling round the leg.

** Pneumococcal infections contributing to massive puss formation

The author's Uncle Mac in puttees

CHAPTER IV

For a while we were in the regiment's anti-aircraft platoon, stationed in Kenya. This involved a daily walk on to air sentry with Bren guns, tripods and ammunition to high points around the encampment. The position I remember best is where the Reen brothers and I staggered to the fringes of Marsabit forest and set up on a knoll clear of jungle with a good view of the skies. Here Italian aircraft were anticipated from their bases in Ethiopia.

So it was not only the thought of Jimmy's beautiful Kenyan steaks for a late lunch that kept our party alert. There were problems besides peering into the scorching skies for approaching hostile aircraft. The forest was still inhabited by wildlife, latter day hominids, various types of baboons, the females with their young either riding their mothers like jockeys, or hanging on to dried out udders desperately, and males with spectacular blue and red gonads.

Generally, the troops of baboons plundered the forest undergrowth of their fruits, or occupied the rocky outcrops that buttressed our knoll. Confusion and terror would only break out amongst the baboon troops if they were threatened by wild beasts or men in khaki laden with ammunition and Brens traipsing through their preserves. They were usually warned of our approach by their sentry perched on a prominent rock and would then rush helter-skelter, families by tens and dozens, brothers, sisters, husbands and wives for the safety of the rocky krantzes.

Three years earlier I had been at (Durban) High School where my favourite poem was about a baboon sentinel:

> "Upon the summit of the height
> Where only windswept lichens grow
> Bongwi, lit by dawning light
> Watches the plain below…etc."

On this particular day the baboons had been disturbed by a wild animal, probably a snorting, tusked boar, and the sentinel had not done his job. Our arrival was like Greeks bearing presents, most unwelcome. The males hooted in chorus and the mothers shrieked as they gathered up their young. The scattered groups coalesced and made for the krantz, right across our path. The males, with tails erect, bared their long fangs at us prancing on all fours with raised eyebrows forming a phalanx between us and their stampeding families. We had enough firepower to take out the whole tribe, but we froze where we stood.

> Low brows, small eyes, short hands
> That twitch and twitch again.
> The hairy gargoyle of the south
> A man without a brain.

More hoots and "wha-hoos" and then the baboons were gone, and it was a very late lunch that day prepared by hands that trembled. Binoculared, I searched the skies and Jock nursed his brother's aggravated hypochondriasis. We made sure of getting back to camp before darkness fell.

Jock rallied our whole section when he could take time off from Jimmy. Bare feet are always vulnerable in tropical Africa. In Kenya he scraped a jiggerflea's bag of eggs out of my reddened big toe. Kenya straddles the equator and had attracted the jigger-flea which arrived in Angola from South America in 1872.

GEORGE WILTON

George Wilton was another of the 'old guard' who had volunteered to fight the war but, as it turned out, not its elements. George was fastidious in everything and tried to maintain the highest standards in what became steadily worsening conditions – dust, heat, flies and food. When weighing him up you always had to consider that he meant well. He would have done better in the hygiene squad. But at 35, he had won enough respect for his mysophobia to give him the rank of corporal. Watching him perform his ablutions in the common shower room was enough to put us younger nips into fits of laughter. Flies did not show their respect and menaced him during shaving. George kept a special cologne handy (really intended as a decontaminant) to dab wherever and whenever a fly landed on his skin. It was well known that he had terrible thoughts about where he urinated. He really believed that bacteria were able to pass up the piss stream into the sacred member and gave army urinals a careful once over before letting go.

But his main disapproval was for those despicable people who farted near him and according to the item on the army menu (chilli con carne being not infrequent) they were many. That George had detected a smell in confined circumstances, was signalled by his pinching the end of his nose and holding it until long after the offence had faded.

George never liked the four-lettered word 'fart' and considered it indelicate, possibly because of its onomatopoeia. He preferred the word 'browse' and himself always walked over to the barrack room door or the dugout entrance to do so. Confining conditions abound of course, where troops are being moved by train, truck or troop ship. Confined too many to a compartment, I would always make for the luggage racks, eventually becoming inured to their narrowness and to this day can lie on the tightest of beds without having to toss and turn. This acquisition turned out to be useful in my extended convalescence from war injuries, when I could only sleep on my right side.

The long journeys we frequently had to take to get up to the front or to the port of embarkation; the many weeks cooped-up in tents or dugouts, often enduring dust storms confronted us with boredom. Here the oldies helped us, teaching us 'bridge', and to play cribbage, occasionally for money and to share our correspondence – girlfriends, parents and good friends.

Some unfortunates can't bear to lose at games. George was one, and he would flush almost purple if he lost at cribbage, especially if he was losing to a young'n like me.

On this particular day, crowded in the back of a troop truck, crossing the desert in Somaliland, the gods were with me and George was down quite a few rupees. And then I did the unforgivable...I browsed with great glee. It was enough, and George pinching his proboscis with the fingers of his right hand, tipped the crib board over with his left. George was livid; he hammered on the cab roof for the driver to stop and called me out to fight. George's cronies stood up to show they backed him; things looked nasty. And then rescue came.

Derek, who had been quietly crowing as he watched the game, pushed forward and stood between George and me and staring out George's ferocious glare said: "Well George, you'll have to fight me first." The Wilton supporters sank back into their seats. Wilton threw me a demonic look and gathered the cards up, and Jock said: "Let's have a brew-up", and it all blew over.

CORP. CECIL RITSON

Somewhat in the background to the friendly rivalry between Durban High School's Old Boys and Glenwood High School's was Cecil Ritson. Also a rugby player like his pal Dennis Bell but, on the contrary, very unprepossessing open and friendly, Cecil was a tireless worker in the rugby scrum and very responsible as a tank commander and compassionate in the running of fatigues.

Heavily built, he carried a Bren gun and was rock solid in nasty situations. He attracted the milder elements of the platoon who were never going to be after heroics and favoured his good common sense of fair play. He and I shared the friendships of one or two chaps who really should have been invalided out of the army or put into reserves because of battle fatigue, rank cowardice, ducking fighting patrols and other calculated slackness. I liked him for his doggedness, his stability and his valour.

I shared a banda* with Charlie Roper, the kehla** of the platoon, just forty and one of many from the south coast of Natal. Fair-headed, his skin suffered from any prolonged African sun, even from windburn. Very popular, extrovert and full of wise sayings and modern analogies, he had a vocabulary of his own which soon caught on amongst his buddies. He was clever at talking the youngsters into taking on the heavier part of his fatigues. He was very short but sturdily built. I had met his wife Violet who was a tall, delicate brunette. They were very much in love but they were childless.

---

*A very open hut of crude thatching and mud-and-straw walls.

** Zulu for 'Wise old man'.

Cecil Ritson

Charlie was a humourist and his banter would keep up the morale. He was subtle in setting up amusing conflicts between the picturesque figures of the platoon... the singers, the mysophobics, the dietary fanatics and the bridge players. He had a proverb or a comment for every occasion. George Wilton was a natural target and Charlie would dig you in the ribs with his elbow whenever Wilton began to get worked up over something... the flies, delays in the mail, a forthcoming patrol, an over-keen officer, faulty equipment etc., and with encouraging comments like "Good boy George" and "you tell 'em."

In his own realm the comments were on himself, directly and indirectly. If upset he would always threaten to go sick or to get out of the army, immediately citing his age as justification. If Charlie was happy or winning at crib and he usually did, his carping and comment would be appropriate and loud like "If you've got pigeons, I say 'pluck em'".

In the banda, on days off duty, he scrounged and I cooked which meant he would visit friends, especially amongst the company cooks and always come back with something tasty to add to the meal, a tin of pineapple pieces, or pork sausages. He was a heavy smoker and usually it went late into the night. Sometimes it was a bottle of whisky from the sergeants' mess or cypress brandy and he would invite someone to share the supper. You knew when you had amused him; he giggled inwardly and outwardly dropped comments like "Ha-ha…hey Christ!" When things were going badly wrong his ruddy complexion would flush deeply; he would give a chesty smoker's cough and snarl "F∗∗∗ this, I'm getting out." He was an arch flatterer of the young set, especially when he needed help, and a sly fox at influencing platoon affairs through communicating his feelings to the older. He was not an arse-creeper and sought no promotion and always wrote home to Violet punctually. He survived the war, by eventually "getting out" and we later met up under more fortunate circumstances. In his time Charlie had been an excellent soccer player.

Charlie gave me good advice on several occasions and got me back very tight to the banda on the night of my eighteenth birthday, Hogmany 1940/41.

EL YIBO

The battle of El Yibo was the regiment's first real encounter of the war. The minor fortified position was the furthest reached by the Italian groundforces invading Kenya and was only just inside Kenya's borders. It constituted several well-sited strong points on top of a 'Sugar Loaf Hill, which overlooked a long lugga and surrounding bush country. Just below it were water wells and some shady trees where probably the few white soldiers lingered during the day. There were no indications that the Italians were planning a full-scale invasion southwards, certainly not to cross the infernos of desert and lava rock we had traversed to reach El Yibo. (see *map page 50*).

Everyone who participated in the first encounter would have agreed that the main opposition was the massive heat that surrounded El Yibo baking its sugar loaf fort.

The preliminaries to the final assault meant that almost the entire regiment dressed in scanty khaki shorts and shirts had to lay out all day and half a night in temperatures that reached 145°F., a heat that scorched not only your skin, but heated up the lava rocks on which you lay. The area was reputed to be held by 300 banda (black soldiers). The actual target was unclear and was presumed to have been occupied in the first skirmish, which occurred between 10.00 and 15.00 hours. This alone had tired out our forces through heat exhaustion. Then it was found that El Yibo hadn't been attacked at all! The target lay a few further miles on. By now the regiment was exhausted and had run out of the most precious of all commodities at this stage which was …Water.

Our forces, waterless and exhausted, were now, with night approaching vulnerable to counterattack. We had kept back no reserves and the men were strung out over a distance of four miles. Withdrawal to higher ground for the night was inevitable. There had not been a single regimental casualty, but Colonel McMillan now called for reinforcements saying that the enemy had been reinforced.

The regiment spent a sleepless night in discovering that the extreme heat by day of semi-desert is exchanged in the night by freezing conditions. Worse! Water supplies did not get through until next day. The following day was almost as frustrating. The enemy, 150 strong, counterattacked but were driven off after they had reached a point 100 yards distant from battalion headquarters. More 'humming and aharring' around and after this further day of heat exposure the exhausted regiment had to spend a further night on the bare mountain.

On the following morning El Yibo was occupied by the N.M.R. In fact 'the birds had flown' the night before.

Around a campfire that night I heard some survivors of El Heatbo sing:

> "*My old man, says follow the band*
> *And don't dilly-dally on the way!*"

It seemed to me that at the top there had been a lot of dilly-dallying on the way!

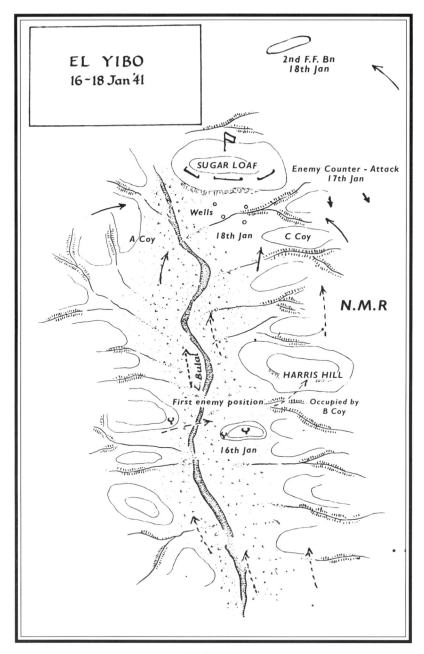

EL YIBO

Also that night, another important omission emerged concerning burial of the dead. Large graves had been dug for the dead, about ten black soldiers. Everyone was in favour of this being done immediately for olfactory reasons. Volunteers were called for to climb 'Sugar Loaf' and bring down the dead from there. It was my first encounter embracing the dead and mutilated. Before this fatigue began we had the opportunity to examine the fort and its circumstances. In one of the machine gun positions was a dead Italian lieutenant still seated at the machine gun in rigor mortis.

He had been firing through the gap in the wall of his redoubt. A bullet through his temple had killed him. It was of course supposed that it was one of our bullets, but through the years I have considered the matter further and believe he had been shot by one of his own soldiers, making the withdrawal of the banda a safer proposition than having to stay and fight it out.

Some of the banda had later spoken to the more communicative of the South African soldiers and they were doubtful about reports they had already had that these South African white men would even think about operating a campaign that meant fighting in a tropical sun like theirs. I thought of Noel Coward's "Mad dogs and Englishmen go out in the Midday Sun."

It ended up that four of us were required to carry our particular corpse down to the flat for burial. It had been a big guy, it was a steep hill and the going was tough. In the hot sun the body had become bloated and as Derek Street and I wrestled with a leg each, sliding and jolting down Sugar Loaf, it let out its gases with realistic farts. Our only compensation was that details might be passed on to George Wilton, which they were.

But George had his glory next morning when he and I were on the mounted Bren gun doing our ack-ack duty. Two Italian bombers came over and we let fly:

Two Italian bombers appeared and began circling over the N.M.R. positions. All ranks took cover immediately. The battalion anti-aircraft platoon opened fire with their Bren-guns and the tracer bullets seemed to be going into one of the planes.

They moved off and a few minutes later the troops could hear bombs being dropped behind them.

Stan Sears added a sad epilogue to proceedings. S.M. John Herbert had approached him the night before, just when the sun was setting and borrowed Stan's towel. There had been a tiny issue of water and Sherbet, huge and dripping with sweat had decided to seize the opportunity to give himself an on-the-spot wash down, but needed a towel and borrowed Stan's. There was not much water and the soap was hardly effective. Stan's towel, when it was all over was unusable. There were many stinks around that day but this was the worst, and Stan had to wait till morning for the next water issue. The total of enemy casualties were:

Killed: 3 Europeans and 20 Banda
Wounded: 1 European and 40/50 Banda

The wounded were petrified because they had been told the South Africans ate their prisoners.

Author's Diary

Friday, 17th January '41 – El Yibo.

This morning at 3a.m. H.Q. ack-ack got the order to move, and we were at the firing line by 11a.m. Just as our convoy came to a halt a British plane was bombing the enemy about 2 miles off. He gave them hell and machine-gunned their positions and a convoy of camels. He killed 3 camels and gave Battalion H.Q. the enemy position. Throughout the day our rifle companies pummelled them with Vickers, mortars and rifle fire. We sustained no casualties and the fort of El Yibo was still in enemy hands. Were sent back half-a-mile to sleep.

Saturday, 18th January '41 – El Yibo.

After arriving back at the line this morning early, bombers soon arrived to bomb El Yibo. We had a good view of the raid. Our three machines unloaded all their bombs on the retreating Italians. No sooner had the raid ceased, than our artillery with direct shelling pummelled the fort with 18lb shells. This was too much for the remaining enemy and they retreated while 'C' Company advanced to occupy El Yibo. There were no casualties on our side, but the enemy lost a white officer and 30 natives. In addition 2 were captured. Left for captured fort at about 5p.m. and arrived about 9.30p.m. after being held up for hours by sand on the road. Like a fool I volunteered to assist burying the dead and didn't finish till 11.30p.m. It was a ghastly experience, which I will never volunteer for again; made me nearly sick with the smell.

Sunday, 19th January '41 – El Yibo.

Arose early as I was No. 2 on our gun and we expected an attack from aircraft. Sure enough, after dawn two Caproni heavy bombers flew over the fort at about 4,000 feet. They re-crossed our path and then bombed a stationary convoy in a pass about half-a-mile away. They dropped all their bombs and then crossed over our position again. This time they were lower (about 1500 feet) and as they passed overhead all of our three guns opened fire. The fire from our gunner (George) Wilton was extremely accurate and it is believed a piece of a bomber was shot away. I managed to get one shot in with a rifle as well. Apart from friendly reconnaissance all quiet for the rest of the day. Had my first bath since Dukana.

After El Yibo.

Friday, 24th January '41 – El Yibo.

Officially it is my day off today. However was caught again for hygiene fatigues, but soon slipped it and wrote 3 letters and read till lunch. Went along to waterhole and had a wonderful bath. Had talk with Derek. We both want to get (transferred) to a Rifle Company. I'm sick of ack-ack and interference with my private opinions. Slept right on the hill (Sugar Loaf) and slept badly. Sleep troubled by peculiar dreams.

Friday, 1st February '41 – Road to Gorai.

Shifted again early this morning, back about half-a-mile to our old gun spot and are very comfortable with plenty of water and some bread. Action taking place at Gorai. Four battalions (ours) are attacking. We (N.M.R.) are in reserve and hating it. Spoke to the padre (Nap Wheeler) about hypocrisy tonight.

EL YIBO & HEATSTROKE*

Personally, I found that I had a propensity for extreme sensitivity to cold after the East African campaign and had to bind a long, broad scarf around my waist when going on night patrol or extended guard duty when temperatures were low in the winter months. The sensitive area to cold was that of the kidneys (above and below the 12th rib).

<u>Sunday, 2nd February '41 – Gorai</u>

Had news today that Gorai fell with 50 prisoners. We had ten casualties. Hobak has also fallen with about 1000 prisoners. I saw some of them today; most appeared very thin and badly clothed. Had a disgraceful fatigue – all morning collecting rubbish.

<u>Thursday, 13th February '41 – Dukana</u>

Italian roads proved much better. They were wider and smoother. After ascending a somewhat steep hill a beautiful scene lay before us, a huge yellow valley sprinkled plentifully with large, dark trees and fringed by mountains. There in the centre stood two mountain peaks with a few miles of forest below. That was our destination. Before long however a storm broke. It was our first experience of rain for three months and was surely a great welcome to a new country. We gloried in the large drops that fell and by the time the shower was over, some had washed one's tins others themselves. Before the sun dipped and we arrived at our camping spot we saw the most brilliant stretches of scenery I have yet viewed; I shall when my colours arrive attempt to copy them. Then we saw a jackal and a peculiar ostrich cum crane bird, and hundreds of 9ft high to 20ft antheaps. Before arriving, I saw a most amazing sunset. There was no food to greet us, but I was too tired to be hungry.

---

* Today we know that heatstroke can cause kidney damage and blood clotting abnormalities where it is associated with overexertion. The classic treatment is to reduce body temperature as soon as possible, preferably cooling in an ice bath. In Africa fighting in deserts did not allow you such luxury treatment. Many soldiers must have suffered kidney damage.

Friday, 14th February '41 – Ganchiaro

We are camped in a valley between two mountain ranges. It is about the best spot since Marsabit. Intense air activity. Mega, about 50 miles away is being bombed all day. Attacking Mega tomorrow. Expect it to be divisional attack.

Saturday, 15th February '41 – Mega

The whole day rumours circulating about our troops contacting enemy in approach to Mega. Nothing definite yet. Lorry with Platoon B.10 chaps overturned, 4 miles up. None seriously injured. Most had bruises and small cuts. Rained in the afternoon and I caught enough in my groundsheet to bath with.

Tuesday, 18th February '41 – Mega

Mega has fallen. The news came through this afternoon. Every person of course was elated. There is no definite version of the scrap, but as far as I know they used artillery on our road. There was a ring of forts 4 miles out of Mega. They say the Irish were so mad about their Major being killed that they shot some Italian prisoners who were screaming "Komaraad". We captured 910 prisoners of these 400 are white. Our casualties I believe were not too heavy. Had a night guard.

Wednesday, February 19th '41 – Mega

Had rather a bad day today. At first we had a 9-mile patrol out to the foot of some neighbouring hills. It was fairly interesting but damn strenuous. In the afternoon I had two teeth out sans injection. What pain! Injuring my back had nothing on this. A guinea fowl was caught and we had it for dinner. Then post arrived. I bagged three.

Thursday, 20th February '41 – Mega

I had trouble with my teeth which bled all night and most of the morning. Had the gaps plugged and now they are fine. Wrote several letters. Was put on to guard Italian prisoners. There are hundreds of them and they appear to be more black than white and ridden with venereal disease.

Saturday, 22nd February '41 – Mega

The convoy left this morning around 6:45am. It was, for a change, very fast as the roads were good. The scenery soon became very green and before arriving at Mega we climbed considerably. Mega has an impressive but weak fort, several small well-built houses, and is in a saucer at the top of a hill. Quite pretty and was well defended. Saw the notorious Bebes, hundreds of captured weapons, ammunition etc. They must have been yellow to give up such a place without a good scrap. Off to take Moyale tomorrow morning. Am happy as blazes.

Sunday, 23rd February '41 – Mega

What a sell! Moyale has fallen!! Not a shot was fired, not a bomb was dropped yet the birds had flown. We left Mega early with the expectation of trouble. The road was rough and dusty but nowhere did we encounter enemy opposition. Planes returned still loaded. A few miles out of Moyale we heard that the scum had evacuated six days earlier. The place though undefended was larger than Mega. I saw British Moyale fort and several other large buildings. Place was filthy and full of flies. It had been bombed though natives were still in occupation. No war material except medical equipment was taken as the Borau had been earlier. I was disappointed but elated at our occupation.

Saturday, 8th March '41 – Marsabit

To start with we went over hell. However, after a few hours of these lava stones in which often nestled pans of water we ploughed our way through sand and mud. Coming into Marsabit in the early afternoon a wind laden with mist swept across the road. We passed a gigantic crater, an airport etc. The roads were ghastly and we barely did our 8 miles an hour. After passing through Marsabit we came on to the 230 mile road to Nanyuki. Here our engineers have made a brilliant job of work and at times we hit up to 55m.p.h.

Sunday, 9th March '41 – Isiolo

After tearing along for 135 miles over lovely S.A. made roads all day, we arrived at Isiolo in the late afternoon. On the way we

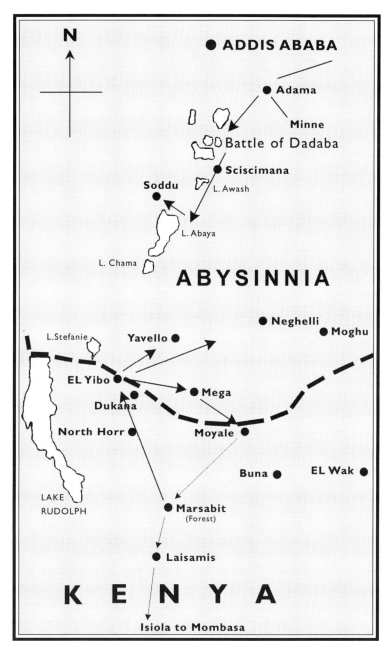

Operations in South and Central Abyssinia

The Italians in Abyssinia were attacked from the south from bases in Kenya early in 1941 and again in April and May '41 by forces landed at Berbera, in British Somaliland.

passed several mountain ranges and peaks. The veldt was covered with small colourful flowers after the rains. Even now we are not certain where we are going or what is going to happen. The rains seem to be closing in. We had one shower this afternoon. It was a treat to taste bread again.

Wednesday, 12th March '41 – Mount Kenya

The convoy took to the road for Nanyuki (50 miles away) about 11:30a.m. The roads were fairly good and the country beautiful and green. We noticed many familiar old scenes, Happy Valley where we were drenched solidly for 3 days. Another embankment that we nearly left through the mud. Rain fell as the journey ended and we are now encamped in tents at the base of snowy Mount Kenya.

Thursday, 13th March '41 – Nanyuki

Prepared to settle down when we heard intense rumours that we were moving tomorrow. Then we were informed that tomorrow we embark at Mombasa for a northerly destination. The camp went mad and became an orgy of drunkards. Our section alone had 12 bottles of brandy. Everywhere lay men paralytic. I held my horses till the evening. When I was just about tight I was put on a fatigue from 10 p.m. till 3 a.m. Mount Kenya snow sparkled under the full moon when I retired.

Saturday, 15th March '41 – Nairobi

For once we were not buggered about in entraining. After a somewhat gruelling march of a mile with full kit to the station we steamed out of Nanyuki at the scheduled time of 9:30 a.m. Then began one of the most beautiful journeys we have yet experienced. It appeared as if spring had kissed every leaf and blade of grass. Mile followed mile of verdant pasture across which full streams bubbled eagerly. I took a bet on for our arrival at Mombasa at 11:21 a.m. tomorrow. At Nairobi we had a splendid welcome by the local blacks. The white people whom we have been defending were non-existing as were sandwiches.

<u>Sunday, 16th March '41 – en route to Mombasa</u>

After a night of horror in which, I got horribly tight, puked, slept for 5 hours, sat awkwardly awake for another 5, and dreamt abominably. 7 a.m. found us already many miles passed up. Tropical undergrowth replaced rolling plains and at 9:45 a.m. Mombasa hoved into sight. We detrained at 10:30 a.m. and I collected my 20 shillings sweep bet. Our ship was already alongside. It is a 7,000 tonner named 'Duniera' and is a proper troop-carrier. We embarked early and sweated like pigs with our kits. We are very cramped with 3,000 on the one ship. Left at 6 p.m. with hardly a civilian to thank us for our protection. Usual natives who fought for the gifts of money.

<u>Tuesday, 25th March '41 – Berbera</u>

Starvation diet in the form of bully beef was our menu for two days. The whole battalion has been working since disembarkation on roads, sewerboring, water laying pipes etc., in fact we are merely a poor white labour Corps. I made an attempt to paint a scene of the town but doubt its success. Our transport is arriving daily.

BERBERA

Even a week confined on the Duniera did not prepare us for the appalling combination of elements in Berbera, British Somaliland, a nasty place set in a tropical climate, and devastated by war and rumours of war.

<u>Saturday, 29th March '41 – Berbera</u>

Have spoken to chaps in (Natal) Carbineers about the action at Jejega. It appears there were several Italians with a white officer and they put up a white flag. The officer came forward to talk with our chaps. Suddenly he rapped out a command and fell flat on his stomach. The Itos opened fire with a machine gun on to our men and killed thirteen before we could stop them. Needless to say the Ito officer was the first killed.

Sunday, 30th March '41 – Berbera

Was on kitchen fatigue for the day. What a dirty, filthy job it is. Managed to get a swim in though. Heard of the Italian machine gun attack on the aerodrome at Jejega. We lost five planes on the ground before they could take off. One eventually got off and brought a Caproni down and a returning Hurricane brought another down.

Friday, 4th April '41 – Jejega

Continuous heavy rain all night left the road rather sticky, but after a few bad patches we got well under way. Most of the local native inhabitants had gathered to grab our discarded petrol tins but were chased away with a length of hose-pipe by a big buck Afrikaner. We crossed into Ethiopia after half-an-hour's run and the road became a perfect highway. After 50 miles the green, grassy plain gave way once more to the inevitable thorny bush. The country however was very pretty and our speed was fast and consistent while a nip in the air made the trip delightful. In no time we were at Jejega, the scene of our reverses I wrote of earlier. The planes were visible in the form of charred frames. The town was small and though mud huts were predominant many European brick houses were visible including the governor's residence. Even as ———————— graveyards were everywhere. The road still behaved well and we mounted the hills around Jejega on the way to Harrar. Then we descended again on a well-built road through a pass. For most of the way down it there was a sheer drop on one side and many bridges and parapets had been built. Rocky koppies covered in greenery lined the route thereafter. We passed through the pass, which the brigade had fought for earlier and came across the first terraces surrounding Harrar. Here were grapevines and every type of fruit grown on most terraces. Harrar hove into sight about 3 p.m. My first impression of the town reminded me of the Casbah in Algiers. This was the native quarter. It was surrounded by a dilapidated ancient wall and appeared to have no regularity or sanitation. In fact it was a veritable jumble of stone and mud huts. There was however the Imperial Palace on the top of the town hill and several other buildings. To its west, outside its walls was the Italian part. Here it was different. Here were flats and cottages, shops and tar roads like a modern European town. Everywhere there were beautiful gardens and trees, hospitals and warehouses could be seen and business seemed to be uninterrupted. Some civilian people though rather dark were quite refined but most were ragged. We camped just outside the town for the night just as it began to pour.

Saturday, 5th April '41 – Harrar

Terrific rains fell all night, but I managed to sleep dry. Shifted into Harrar and I went into the town with Derek for a stroll. We had about a dozen drinks of sweet wine and vermouth. In this bar there was a brawl but I kept out of it. The Italian people were fairly friendly. They seemed confident about ultimate victory yet longed for the fall of Addis Ababa so their relatives could return. Bought some weevill-ridden bread – had a few more drinks – tried to enter Arab quarters no success – enquired after 'senoritas' and hear they are at Diredowa. Got back late at camp. Sorted by Sergeant but didn't give a damn. Some very pretty women in the town.

Sunday, April 20th '41 – Harrar

Was called off guard to move to Harrar but didn't get away till 5 p.m. A storm broke before we left and I was nearly electrocuted when touching a G.S. Then we set out in a heavy downpour for Harrar. We tore through a raging torrent of a drift and nearly went over a forty-foot drop but arrived at Harrar about midnight.

Monday, 21st April '41 – Diredowa

Undertook to help with cooking. After doing a little bartering I obtained some odds & ends of souvenirs. About eleven we pushed on for Diredowa and passed gardens, lakes and descended the most wonderful pass I have yet come across. Diredowa was disappointing. There was much havoc from R.A.F. bombs and many Ito planes were on the drome damaged. The railway was battered somewhat. The country then became bushy and sprinkled with many streams whose bridges were blown up.

Tuesday, 22nd April '41

Cooked breakfast early and continued on our way. We passed El Wash whose magnificent bridge now lay a twisted, mangled wreck, the river was rather swollen and roared down the narrow, rocky gorge. Several lakes with hundreds of wild duck also bumped into view. Then a tragedy followed. We found a still smoking burnt out vehicle with every article of its contents and frame charred. Later we heard that two chaps were filling the car with petrol held a lamp near and three 20-gallon drums of petrol went up. Both were badly burned.

Wednesday, 23rd April '41 – at Adama

At Adama now we are settled for several days, (we expect). Today meaning the 23rd of each month seems to be my most fateful date of each month. This morning I was granted a day's leave into Addis Ababa. I was pleased and we arrived there about eleven after a two-hour journey over 60 miles. The town is larger than P.M.B. but is quite pretty. Commerce seems as lively as possible. The pound was worth 400 lira. Bought souvenirs, had plenty of drinks, a macaroni lunch, and saw Haile's palace and finally returning at 8 p.m.

Wednesday, 30th April '41 – Neghelli

Had a long route march of about 6 miles duration towards Neghelli. Had a pick-up game of cricket in the afternoon. Our side with Joe Cowley as captain won. Derek and Joe played well and I managed to rake up 19 in the first innings and a measly one in the second. It was good fun and exciting.
The score was:

WE 1st innings	61	THEY	38
WE 2nd innings	69	THEY	85

Thursday, 1st May '41 – Minne

Was in the middle of a football match against the M.A.P. when I was called off to pack my kit for a trip. The trip is out to 'A' Company at Guna who have just taken prisoners at Minne. 12 of us were crowded into a G.S. and of course I was in the rear. The journey is about 70 miles and we did 22 miles before we camped for the night. We crossed the El Wasch River and several others. An icy wind blew all night and when rain broke during my beat on picquet. I ended up under the lorry.

Friday, May 2nd, '41 – Guna

I am frankly amazed – I would never have believed it possible that motors could cover such hazardous tracks with ditches feet deep, with swollen (rivers) drifts, with 1:4 gradients with mud up to the axles. We struck trouble soon after striking camp at 5.30a.m. We meandered through a fertile plain covered with a patchwork of crops and began to climb an escarpment of a couple of thousand feet. Patches of mud and slush brought the convoy often to a standstill. During these delays I often got out and wandered into the glades and over the verdant lawns which reminded me of Ovid. Several large native villages were passed as they perched on the summit of colossal natural bastions. On top of the escarpment before entering a rolling plain of succulent grass which was literally a veritable ceiling of the earth we gazed over 50 miles of plain that lay thousands of feet below us. In this plateau were many farms with roaming herds of cattle. Land that would have turned South African farmers' faces as green with envy as the grasses on it.

What a dirty shame that such a land of milk and honey should be dominated by – simple decadents. Many wheat-fields graced the scenery with their husks still green. Before long we descended the plateau into a veritable parkland. Finally we got to Guna fairly late and had a picketless night.

Sunday, 4th May '41 – Guna

Guna is surrounded by a high palisade and wire works which enclose a score or more of mud huts and vegetable gardens. In the morning I picked a handful of shallots and some roses. A Ras was dividing the booty captured from the Itos at Minne amidst much squabbling and a native was then wounded in the thigh by a stray bullet. Minne is 18 miles away and to get to it, it is necessary to descend a cliff many thousands of feet high by mule. Our job was officially to escort the Ito prisoners up this cliff and to stop the patriots firing at them. Was not sorry to return the same day on our journey back.

Monday, 5th May '41 – Siri Village

Rain nearly caused our destruction descending the plateau into the village of Siri, where the population presented us with gifts of 4 sheep and eggs and Kaffir beer. We camped the night and crawled into Adama the following morning where we bought bread and went over the cotton mills before tracking the battalion towards Gimma. Another night in the wilds (of Abyssinia) followed and we found the battalion a few miles past the great and beautiful Lake Zuai and heard that we are about ten miles from the Itos, and that an Ito plane had strafed near their encampment the night before.

Tuesday, 6th May '41 – Dadaba

Settled down for a rest and had one for two days with some good food for a change. Rain fell and was annoying. Vic (Knott) had given us lectures on aircraft (recognition) which was also interesting. Hear that 'B' and 'C' Companies are going into action tomorrow and we are to be left behind (guarding H.Q.) Am I mad!

As the 'C' Company lorries moved out of camp up to the firing line, I jumped in one as I planned. The section was No.2 of No.13 platoon. They were good chaps and saw me right with things I hadn't brought. The convoy stopped just a mile before the river and we jumped out and advanced across the drift, which had been taken earlier by the K.A.R. The water came up to my thighs. In extended order the two companies advanced along the heavy bush country between the road and the river. It was terribly hard going and our section and another soon got lost and eventually we saw our chaps in the distance and at the same time banda, 100 yards ahead. Our (Section) Bren opened up on them – and two Bredas and rifle fire sent us grovelling in the dirt. I became No.2 on the gun and we pumped them for a quarter-of-an-hour. Then I moved out to the flank to help counter the enemy's movement and was there till 4.30. Here I had two narrow escapes when bushes snapped (with bullets) a foot above my head. Then we fixed bayonets and charged. Then down after 50 yards till our mortars stopped firing and in that quarter-hour, the Itos got away. After a 2000-yard trot through the bush, a tank scare and capturing 3 prisoners we congregated on the road, while a Hawker (Hart) and tanks strafed the village 400 yards away and we occupied it just before 8p.m. Got back after a weary march across the river at 10.30p.m. and had a hell of a night with mosquitoes and rain.

Sunday, 11th May '41 – Dadaba

Artillery fired all night and all today. Terrific fusillade is going on, on the ridge. The ration question is hopeless. Food is being cut down more and more. We are on quarter ration for most foods. Rained heavily. Had a shock to hear that Brian Massey was shot through the shoulder but is quite OK and cheerful He has gone back 8 miles to have the bullet out.

Monday, 12th May '41 – Dadaba

Nothing of interest in the morning as I was on the (ack-ack) gun. Volunteers were called to supplement runners in a Rifle Company. 3 of us out of 24 volunteered... Derek, Joe (Cowley) and myself. The attack was on a couple of thousand Itos five miles away. The manoeuvre was to get on to their left flank and rear. Derek and I with 'C' Company and the others with 'A' and 'B'. Marched all night but got lost with Captain Freeman and had a narrow escape as scouts when trying to make contact with our troops. The barrage opened at 5.15a.m. and we attacked with Bren and rifles soon after and drove, without officers, and with bayonet charges galore, the Itos into a rout. I had quite an exciting time. We killed a 180, and the carnage was ghastly. Captured 600 prisoners, 5 tanks, and 2 batteries of artillery and thousands of rounds of ammo, rifles, grenades and food. Our casualties were 3 dead and 15 wounded.

(Gordon) Lacey in a gun accident was wounded in the shoulder. Derek and I escorted 54 prisoners back 8 miles. Felt badly messed-up after doing nearly 35 miles. There were no armoured cars or Vickers. The Itos fought badly except for the natives. Got a primus (stove) and several articles from the dead. Our boys were magnificent. Slept the clock right round.

<u>Thursday, 15th May '41 – Dadaba</u>

We moved only a few miles today and parked for the night near the first Italian river of defence and waited till the bridge was rebuilt and the road hardened. Derek and I roamed the battlefield but found it stripped apart from the dead naked blacks one of which had half his head missing.

It is difficult to give an accurate and balanced account of the Battle of Dadaba. More than half the regiment was involved in it somewhere, somehow. There was hand-to-hand fighting, infantry taking on Italian tanks, an ongoing artillery exchange, terrible carnage in places and vacuums in others. There were rivers to be waded across, heavy mortar equipment to be humped. The overall plan was simple; an attack from the flank in which the whole regiment was strung out in a single line across the battlefield and once the attack started told not to stop till the job was done. Various impediments broke the line and groups of men and even their officers got lost. But the momentum was maintained and bayonet charges in places were frequently necessary. The regimental Colonel had faded out just before the operation, and the acting Colonel, Major Harris did well to pull the thing off.

The ultimate central hero of the engagement climbed on to the enemy tanks in the absence of suitable anti-tank weapons. Captain Chooks Blamey secured the squadron's demise and actual defeat. This incident occurred after an argument with the acting Colonel who had told the hero off for trying to alter the battle plan.

Reaching the Italian artillery emplacements signalled the end. Their gun blasts, at point blank range nearly knocked us off our feet but the shells were going over our heads. By that time the artillery command post was in disarray with both its Italian Major and Colonel fatally wounded.

When I first saw the Italian artillery commanding officer he was still alive lying, not stretched out, rather half-reclining on a hastily prepared table. I thought he was wearing a new red and yellow pullover, which seemed so bizarre against the plain grey-green of his uniform. Then I realised he was in a reflexed position taking tension off his abdominal muscles, for his whole belly had been sliced open

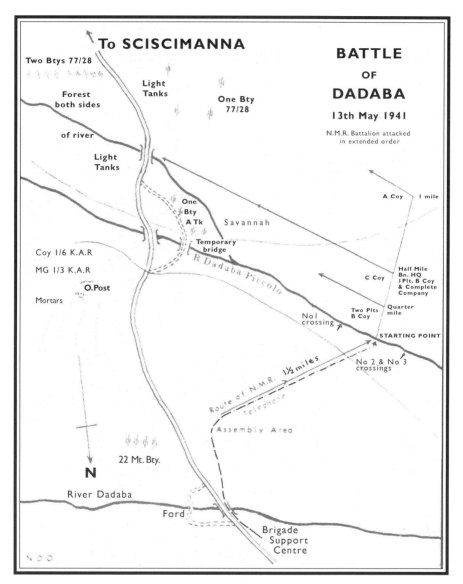

To SCISCIMANNA

Two Btys 77/28

Forest
both sides

of river

Light
Tanks

Light
Tanks

One Bty
77/28

BATTLE

OF

DADABA

13th May 1941

N.M.R. Battalion attacked
in extended order

A Coy   I mile

One
Bty
A Tk   Savannah

Temporary
bridge

Coy 1/6 K.A.R

MG 1/3 K.A.R

O.Post

Mortars

R Dadaba Piccolo

C Coy

Half Mile
Bn. HQ
I Plt. B Coy
& Complete
Company

Two Plts
B Coy

Quarter
mile

No I
crossing

STARTING POINT

No 2 & No 3
crossings

Route of N.M.R.   1½ miles

Telephone

Assembly Area

22 Mt. Bty.

N

River Dadaba

Ford

Brigade
Support
Centre

Battle of Dadaba

The Italians anticipated an advance from the south but the N.M.R. attacked from
the north. Heavily laden with equipment there was an initial haul at night overland
from the ford shown mid centre at the bottom of the map. From the starting point
at crossing No. 2 the N.M.R. was spread out and advanced in a single long line
with its left flank moving along the Dadaba River (Piccolo).

by a Bren-gun burst and his entrails had ballooned out, and the garish yellow patterns were the transverse colon and the red, the haemorrhage in his abdominal wall. He was conscious in his despair and quietly moaning but died shortly.

My own roll was to carry a mortar base-plate several miles into the battle where it was used in the frontal action and then to rejoin a Rifle Company in the bayonet charge from the flank. The element of surprise in the attack was a success; otherwise the enemy's superior numbers and dug-in fire positions could never have been overpowered. The keywords in the success of the mission were BRAINS, INITIATIVE, BAYONETS and VALOUR.

The hero, Captain Blamey later reported:

We were now in the open without a vestige of cover anywhere... We got to a rise (in the ground) shot or captured the machine-gunners, left a couple of fellows to guard them and on we charged. At this point, the fire was murderous, everything seemed to be banging around us. Nevertheless, we went on at the double with Bren-gunners firing from the hip interspersed amongst the line of charging bayonets... I remember seeing during the encounter many acts of valour, but no one individual was more outstanding than another.

N.M.R. casualties: 3 killed and 12 wounded.

Enemy casualties: 41 killed and 21 wounded
796 Prisoners.

Captured enemy weapons:

12 Field guns
8 Anti-tank guns
9 Light tanks
35 x 10-ton lorries
17 Heavy machine-guns
18 Light machine-guns
178 Rifles
200 Cases of ammunition
37 Drums of oil
1 Mobile bakery.

So called Abyssinian patriots, often more of a hindrance in their search for loot. Note the water cart being filled by South African soldiers in the rear across the river.

Looting by the irregulars, the patriots and the you-name-it, evoked a tremendous reaction of contempt from the South Africans. This revulsion was partly responsible for the worries amongst us for the white Italian settlers who were vulnerable everywhere at this time. Nobody wanted to see the country given over to chaos and barbarism. It even became necessary to rearm some of the Italians where their lives were being threatened.

Willie Grobler who later survived a bullet through the head at Alamein recalled with some glee an event to Eric Gregg of a banda warrior who had already filched two rifles for himself then escaping with an opportunity to loot a third. Celebrating his booty of a rifle slung on each shoulder by firing them loudly, he now slung No.3, already loaded, between the two. Unfortunately, it was short-barrelled and discharged through his chin taking the top of his head off.

WINDING UP

Sunday, 18th May, '41 – Sciscimano

Parked with Derek Street, Cecil Ritson and Piet de Beer, on the side of the road and played poker till were given a lift to our platoon 8 miles up. Saw Captain Henfrey laying into the patriots for looting. Have taken snaps of prisoners captured. Reached platoon and shooting on fixed line all night. Has poured with rain.

Monday, 19th May '41 – Sciscimano

Italian prisoners have been pouring in all day. Moved back 3 miles to guard the rear of the Nigerian artillery. On guard again all night. Artillery been firing at Itos in the hills.

Tuesday, 20th May '41 – Sciscimano

The Duke of D'Aosta has surrendered and it seems the show is over. Went hunting in the afternoon with a Nigerian but had no luck. News was bad but Churchill says South African troops are for Egypt.

<u>Wednesday, 21st May '41 – Sciscimano</u>

Back to Battalion H.Q and to guards (bandit country) 4 from the platoon including myself volunteered to drive two Italian tanks for patrolling (and protecting) prisoners and pulling out bogged cars. On guard all night, very little sleep.

EXITING

<u>Thursday, 22nd May '41 – Soddu</u>

Learnt to drive the (Italian) tanks and helped test machine-guns. Still on guard. Wrote several letters. Our two (South African) divisions have now bridged the gap and have joined. Itos have retreated on horseback; the rest have given up. Guards all night (in total blackness). Boar snorting around all night.

<u>Friday, 23rd May '41 – Soddu</u>

Soddu captured by us. Notice of move then cancelled. While on beat at 9.30 p.m. had orders to pack and move for Berbera and I presume from there to Egypt. Got away by the afternoon and because of the crush while travelling with No.2 (anti-tank) platoon. Stopped for a good night's sleep near Sciscimana.

<u>Sunday, 1st June '41 – Berbera</u>

After a harrowing trip from Hargeisa driving, in which we had radiator trouble and nearly sunstroke, we struck the arid, barren wastes of Berbera. A wind sprang up and dust blew all night.

<u>Monday, 2nd June '41 – Berbera</u>

Concluding a short drive down to the docks, such that they are, we boarded an Arab dhow (see overleaf) and made a trip to the Takliwa (ship) for practice. Landed and had a feed – and when the wind dropped we again boarded the filthy, stinking dhows and got to the ship safely. The heat was terrific and I fear the ship is another repetition of the Altmark. At 5p.m. we sailed north for Aden. (See Map page 28)

Embarking by Arab dhow at Berbera

CHAPTER V

The campaign in East Africa and Abyssinia had been what one might call the last of the gentleman's wars. Firstly, you were victorious because you could see what you were firing at and they needed exterminating anyway. As cadets at high school we had inherited the Victorian rifles from the Boer War which were antiquated and ineffectual even in a war where soldiers of the Queen had worn bright red tunics so that the Boers could get them unerringly in their targets and casualties in the field had just managed to out-pace those dying of food poison. Things in Egypt, we thought, would be more or less the same, Omdurman and all that! Lots of heat and fuzzy wuzzies and quick walkovers with weapons always better than the enemy's. This was the confusion of mood as our ship the Takliwa tied up at Suez after a long hot trip up the Red Sea. We just did not know what to expect. First appearances were not encouraging. (See map page 75)

"Takliwa" arrived at Suez early on the morning of the 8th June 1941.

After disembarking the regiment loaded kit and equipment on to a train which was standing on the wharf. We were then taken to a transit camp at Amiriya near Alexandria. Heavy enemy air-raids at that time were being made on the port of Alexandria, where for the first time we saw the barrage of anti-aircraft shells being fired from our shore batteries. In the distance, the thunderous explosions of bombs could be distinctly heard.

Captain Blamey commented:

Normally, I am not a victim of moods or fits of depression, but never have I been more depressed than I was when I landed on Egyptian soil. I was plunged into further despondency on arrival at

Amiriya. I thought it was impossible for any human being to exist, let alone fight a campaign in such a dreadful land. It was no wonder that later on many poor fellows became victims of Caffard, or desert madness. So this was the Western Desert, mile upon mile of red dust, strewn with patches of camel thorn not more than eighteen inches high. The country was flat as far as the eye could see; there were no features or land marks; not a blade of grass or even a thorn tree could be seen, just desert and, except for human beings and camels, seemingly not a living creature existed. The sun beat down relentlessly from a cloudless sky, and shimmering heat waves danced before one's eyes. Whenever a breeze came up everything was enveloped in choking red dust. How aptly this vile country was described as: "Land of bondage, land of hell!"

Almost before we had scratched our patrol tents into the endless sand dunes surrounding Mersa Matruh, Eric Gregg and Aubrey Hampson of "C" Company, were off on a secret assignment. The moment we reached Matruh a push into the desert west of us called 'Battle Axe' had begun and enemy prisoners had to be brought down from the front, which was a hundred miles to the west. The interrogation and consignment of the Italo-German P.O.W.'s had to be under strict control and Eric Gregg's company went up to Sidi Barrani and did the job. Unfortunately though, concentrations of our vehicles attracted Messerschmitts and they strafed our column from one end to the other. Three of our men were wounded. They were the first South African casualties in Egypt.

The enemy prisoners had been brought to "C" Company by British guardsmen. All were desperately thirsty with the Italian soldiers calling out for "Aqua, aqua!"

The German soldiers in the group were youths all under 20 and diminutive. They distanced themselves from the Italians and showed some arrogance. Within 24 hours there were signs that 'Battle Axe' had gone wrong, the front line had oscillated and some of the soft vehicles and supply trucks had panicked and fled the frontier area eastwards making for Mersa Matruh, where we the "new boys", very green at desert warfare were still without tin hats.

Operation Battle Axe did not go well.

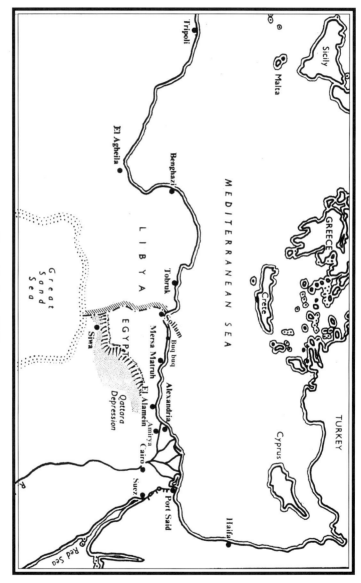

Egypt in June 1941

Front Line – 15th June 1941

In the N.M.R.'s first assignment, 'C' Company with Eric Gregg and Aubrey Hampson travelled up to Sidi Barrani, to take charge of German P.O.W.'s. Operation 'Battle Axe' had just begun at the front line 100 miles to the west of Mersa Matruh, half way to Tobruk.

Unbeknown to the allies, the Germans had landed their new 88mm guns which had great versatility and were used eventually in their Tiger tanks as artillery, and even, some say, in anti-aircraft defence. They completely outclassed the British two-pounder in range and penetrating power. But the Germans, having done our armoured forces great damage, withdrew into their enclave at the top of Halfaya Pass and the panic retreat into Egypt dried up.

Comparative calm ruled the front for the next four months until operation 'Crusader' was set in motion. Rommel's supplies were inhibited by the onset of the Nazi attack on Russia on June 22nd and the war in the desert was sidelined.

Stuck as garrisoning troops in Mersa Matruh, great resourcefulness was required to offset boredom and monotony.

At this stage the Germans had air superiority. Messerschmitts strafed daily, bombers attacked nightly and we never saw any kind of allied air formations.

Comparing dates in my diary correspondence to those of Chief of the Imperial and General Staff, Sir Alan Brooke wrote for June 30th 1941:

> Finally after dinner went to the War Office to meet Dill and Portal* at 9:45pm to discuss organisation of airforce to work with army. Did not get home till midnight. It is an uphill battle to try and get an adequate allotment of airforce for the army!

As I recall it, I don't remember seeing a Spitfire in action over the Western Desert frontline for almost another year.

Saturday 14th June 1941 – Mersa Matruh

Had three more air raids in an hour. Many bombs were dropped, but little damage done.

Sunday 15th June 1941 – Mersa Matruh

Four air-raids last night. One plane brought down. Little damage done.

---

* Field Marshall Sir John Dill and Vicount Portal, Chief of Staff, R.A.F.

<u>Tuesday 17th June 1941 Mersa Matruh</u>

More air raids. Getting a nuisance now as sleep is interrupted. "C" Company was machine gunned by Messerschmitts. Three wounded.

JUNE '41, GERMANY / RUSSIA

On June 22nd 1941 Germany attacked Russia. It came at a time when our part of the South African division had been dumped on the seas of sand surrounding the war redoubt of Mersa Matruh, still at that time rivalling Malta as the worst bombed place on earth. This new development caught us by as much surprise as it had Stalin and even the British high command which still had its anxiety that Britain would be Hitler's next target. We in the Western Desert became even less informed than the British Isles, struggling to dig slit trenches on sand dunes which were whisked by persistent winds into dust storms that penned you into a patrol tent with a companion for hours, even days. My first inclination was to ask which of the antagonists, Germany and Russia would we, the British side, ally ourselves with because Britain at that time was not capable of helping or hindering either. Those of us able to philosophise our remoteness beyond the sand dunes of Mersa, bombed and strafed daily, had to calculate what our actions would be if we were overrun by the Germans as they continued their devastating successes on all fronts. Our attitude was not defeatism but one of assessing how to survive, overwhelmed in the desert. The generally accepted escape route would be to retreat down the Nile valley and rearguard our way back to South Africa. Churchill of course gave the lead in a few days and British troops everywhere began to reorientate their hopes towards 'Uncle Joe' Stalin as a plausible hero. Euphoria developed as the Russians held on. German strength was underrated but in the desert we knew only too well what danger they posed. Here in Egypt, and on all fronts, which they chose to operate, their progressive control of the skies was inexorable.

TWO-POUNDER

Bombed nightly we could be forgiven for the alarm we felt about Nazi air power but soon our attention was drawn to land defences.

2-Pounder in Action

The South African division had arrived equipped with only the Boyes antitank rifle guns. We soon heard horrible things said about the ineffectuality of British armour in action and its weapons.

What we, the infantry, did not know as we prepared to join Auchinleck's 'Crusader' operation scheduled for November 1941, and other operations later, was that we were going into battle with panzers minus a single effective weapon against them. The two-pounder gun on the Crusader tank was hopelessly out-classed. Its range was less than one thousand yards whereas the panzers and their antitank guns had a range of a mile or more (one thousand seven hundred and sixty yards, least we forget!)

Major General Verney of the Seventh Armoured Division recalling the events of that time wrote "Everyone had seen the British shot bouncing off the German tanks, and the enemy knocking out the Crusaders and Light tanks at ranges far beyond the limits of the miserable two-pounder gun that the War Office had been so extremely ill-advised to adopt as the principal armament against German tanks. Even outside the armour there was no anti-tank gun that could worry a German tank except at point-blank range. It is pitiful to contemplate the situation in which the infantry had to be placed deprived of a single weapon with which to protect themselves against what was known long before the war to be Germany's principal arm. Not even an adequate telescopic sight was available. Time and again it happened that we had had more tanks than the enemy, the operation had been brilliantly prepared, full surprise had been achieved, the country favoured tank action and the side with the most tanks, and the troops had fought with much gallantry. Yet we had been driven back on the south flank of the desert because the Army was supplied with tanks and guns of markedly inferior type to those of their opponents.

Talking to N.M.R. infantry survivors I could find no-one who saw a six pounder anti-tank gun until they were wheeled into the line at Alamein just before the big battle, October 23rd '42. In fact, not even the two-pounder was ever part and parcel of the myriad earth works we dug on the front line to survive. This horror in high places didn't really filter through. There never was a credible defence against the 88mm German gun when placed in enemy tanks or dug in and subtly camouflaged against allied tanks. In the hands of the Nazis, to oppose it was like asking a householder to argue with an intruder with a shotgun pointed at him. Sidi Rezegh was an early warning to South African infantry and carried off 3,000 infantrymen into captivity before they had barely got out of their trucks.

Of the many hazards that confronted South African volunteers, enveloped in the battles for North East Africa, the one that frightened me most was malaria. Suddenly, in the Horn of Africa, we were confronted with it. Landing in Berbera, the regiment went on to a daily dose of a quinine-like drug, *mepacrine* as I recall it. It had a grossly bitter taste and made your ears ring. Mosquito nets were also issued and you just had to accept the malarial regimen as a part of your night and day reality.

Some of the guys went down with the disease almost immediately, with its obvious signs and symptoms so dramatically demonstrated by them when eventually you visited them in military hospitals. When malaria patients recovered, they were sent back to the regiment. Ray Lee was one of these. I was staggered by the change in him. He was cheerful enough and pleased to be back with his buddies but had now lost his resilience, especially to heat and cold. The regiment was at present in Egypt and based at Mersa Matruh. As fate would have it, Ray shared a dugout with me there.

At that stage of the desert war in Mersa Matruh it was rare for the fortress not to be attacked by air, at lease once during the night. You could tell when German planes were approaching from their characteristic whine supposed to come from their engine cowlings which were peculiarly streamlined. Close encounters with bombings in Mersa Matruh were so commonplace at night, that you just hugged your pillow, or even sat out on the sand dunes in the pleasant evening air, and watched the nightly displays allowing your tin hat to shield you from falling, or stray shrapnel coming from the overhead ack-ack barrages.

Ray, to my surprise, now found these almost routine air attacks deeply disturbing. Daily conditions, living in the dugouts and unending nightly raids depressed him, so that he seemed to be suffering from what the French in Alexandria called 'Caffard', or desert madness. Sometimes during air attacks he would break down in tears and become hysterical and shiver as if he was repeating a malarial rigor. He was embarrassed at these lapses. I often had to comfort him, or cover him with my own blanket to reduce his shivers. In one attack he confessed that he had 'lost his bottle', by which term picked up from cockney patients in his recent hospitalisation, he meant he had lost his nerve and was fearful that he would be seen as a coward.

Fortunately these situations, acute at the time, would pass as his malarial symptoms went into remission and he became once more the happy, gallant youngster of earlier days. He was not to know that the dismal spectre of defeat forthcoming in the Western desert would take him beyond the limits of his weakened physical and psychological state.

Later, much later on the battle fronts of Italy, I remembered the circulating belief that a malarial like illness had knocked the stuffing out of the Roman legions and brought about the fall of the Roman Empire; and had also forced the people of what is now Italy to build villages in high places out of reach of this terrible scourge.

Plainly and simply the explanation for the continuous defeats of the British Army in the Western Desert was that equipment for Britain's only viable and active ground forces was diverted elsewhere.

Churchill in war cabinets had raged against his defeated commanders and generals. He asked how it was that the Allies could have 750,000 men in the Middle East drawing rations and pay and yet on the fighting front of the desert field only 100,000 men. But he well knew that at various stages lesser actions were on-going in the three Somalilands, Abyssinia, Eritrea, Palestine, Lebanon, Iraq, Malta, Greece, Crete and Persia and after Pearl Harbour, India, Burma, Malaysia and Australia were added to the equation. Russia too was like a vixen gnawing at the vitals of the spartan Churchill asking for help. Until the Americans came to her aid Britain had stood alone and even had to deal with possible Vichy French aggression in far flung places like Madagascar and Dakar (West Africa). There was just not enough equipment to go round from 1940-42.

The defeats were a sensitive political issue for Churchill who was leading a national coalition in government in Britain and had to face parliament. Of course, heads had to roll and generals were always the first to suffer. Through a combination of these political factors and sheer bad luck the replacement of desert commanders became a bewildering imponderable to other ranks. It had begun with the removal of the one-eyed General Gort, through Chief of the General Staff Dill, Ironside, Wavell and ultimately, Ritchie and Cunningham and the predecessor of Alexander and Montgomery, Auchinleck. Gott had been killed in an air crash in Egypt even while Churchill was there. Amongst the Air Marshalls it had been the same story.

To make matters worse equipment reaching the desert was often damaged by long sea journeys or outranked by the Germans. This was most true of guns. Hansard records Oliver Lyttleton's speech to the House of Commons during the debate over the loss of Tobruk. He had told the House that England had had to choose between making a greater number of inferior tanks and guns or a very few of better quality than those of the Germans and had decided on the former. It meant that in the absence of tanks my own regiment in the desert had only anti-tank rifles to defend themselves against panzers. Later in desperation, we were issued with Sticky bombs, the most bizarre kind of weapon since the Molotov Cocktail. It was 'popski'-like in its morphology, a 5" diameter ball of high explosive wrapped in a felt covering of goo. The ball was encased in a thin glass container which stopped the goo from oozing and the whole thing placed in a thin black metal casing with an 18" handle on it for carrying. The aim was to engage tanks at close range (about 25 feet as I recall) by unclipping the outer casings and throwing the gooey mass at the hostile tank's hull. If the bomb stuck to the tank you then had a few seconds to escape death from the exploding bomb by flinging yourself flat or diving into a trench slit. If the bomb missed, or if it came unstuck after hitting its target, it was anybody's guess as to what your chances were. All you had to do then was to evade the tank's machine guns and the fire from the other tanks.

These Sticky bombs were not all that popular and somebody (usually in the tail of a patrol) carried one. Mercifully, as a Bren gunner, I had more than enough to carry on my own. At the battle of Alamein, a good friend of mine, carrying a sticky bomb was struck by shrapnel and he and the platoon officer were killed when the sticky bomb exploded.

At the same time as my own regiment reached Egypt from East Africa (June 1941), the first German 88mm guns were landed at Benghazi. They were dual purpose anti-tank and anti-aircraft weapons, which were to dominate tank warfare in the desert until the Afrika Corp's final surrender in North Africa in Tunisia in 1943. Later, in Italy, by then mechanised, we were to know the horrors of meeting the same guns mounted in the monster Nazi Tiger Tanks. Our beautiful Shermans, with their 75mm's were no match and their shells bounced off the Tiger turrets.

In the desert in 1941 the new cruiser British Crusader tanks, immaculate to look at, were a disappointment. Their tiny two-pounder guns were ineffectual in range and firepower for all the compensatory speed of the tank. Rommel loved them and used them occasionally from which to direct his battles. It was reputed that at one stage a whole squadron of the Afrika Corps had been fitted out with captured Crusaders. German tanks could hit their targets in the desert a mile away and penetrate allied armour-plating whereas the effective range of the British tanks was half that... a demoralising factor for the allies even if you were only watching a tank battle as powerless infantry often did.

ALI BABA

"They say there's a troop ship
That's leaving Port Said
Bound for old Blighty's shore
Heavily laden with time expired men
Bound for the land they adore…"

The old British army song could have applied to Private Eustace Barber. He could have bunked off the boat at Port Said. He was so typical in dress and mannerisms of a permanent force man straight out of the Imperial Army. In fact he had just terminated 5 years in the Palestine Police Service. He never wore badges, decorations or flashes; nor did he seek or expect promotion or advancement and in a regiment like ours, that was refreshing. We inevitably called him Ali Baba. He welcomed the sobriquet because the other alternative would have been 'useless' (Eustace), an uncomplimentary term related to a then currently popular cartoon in the British media. Ali knew all the ropes; how to duck the fatigues; miss roll call, fighting patrols and squad drill. But he never missed a kit issue, cigarette ration or mail from Blighty. Ali knew, somehow, all the red light districts in the delta…the Burka, Sister Street et alias.

He liked attending the Cairo cinemas and avoided paying the price of eating their ice creams which gave you certain gastro-enteritis known in army lingo as 'gypo-guts'. Ali always knew when a film was about to end and sat strategically near the exit so that he could escape the national anthem, which was a panegyric on King Farouk, said to be sympathetic to the Italian forces invading Egypt at the time. Soldiers who stayed and braved this musical eulogy, instead sang the army accompaniment which roughly went:

"King Farouk, King Farouk
You're a bugger and a crook
King Farouk, King Farouk
Hang your bollocks on a hook.
Stand esquire, pull your wire
King Farouk."

There was some justification for this ad lib interpretation of the young king's reputation. After his removal from the throne Farouk's outrageous behaviour, while on it became known and circulated; it was also apparent that his pornographic collection shocked even investigators and media.

Whenever he could, Ali gave a twist to army conversation, its words and phrases being punned, or given slimy innuendo, and the additions were always sexual in some way. His interjections became tedious after a while and some took umbrage; but there was something much more nefarious in his behaviour and it was tactile. If you are a private in a busy army you are always bending to lift something, most often heavy, like ammunition cases, rolls of barbed wire and other impedimenta. At these times, bent over and especially in short trousers, which were de riguer in the desert, you presented prominently the most unattractive part of your anatomy, but by far the most sensitive. This awkward stance of a presenting backside was an open invitation to Ali to take quick action. He would advance on the victim and run his forefinger up the central seam of momentarily tightened trousers and shout "How's that for centre?" Only when you have had it done to you once or twice can you realise just how sensitive that area is, where both sciatic nerves emerge from the spine and spread out down the legs. The victim's reaction both psychologically and anatomically is to straighten up briskly and let loose an enraged catharsis.

At places like Mersa Matruh where there would be a daily epidemic of sandbag filling and lifting to counter air raids, Ali would have a field day. His habit disgusted most and dark hints were impugned, especially by the married soldiers if not by the youngsters who would laugh away their embarrassment.

George Wilton of course was married and no longer young with a 'piss stream' sensitivity. It was one of the gayest moments of my army life when Ali trapped George with his first assault. And it *was* an assault in George's eyes. He read into it every gloomy scenario he could think of and because he was a lance-corporal even suggested to Ali that he had assaulted a senior officer (albeit non-commissioned) and he even looked around for witnesses. I was rolling on the desert sand in laughter and would not have made a reliable witness. George Wilton was not amused.

Being sourly spoken to, Ali made one concession. He stopped calling 'centre!' Instead he would let out a short whistle as his finger traced its way up the central trouser seam. Alas, he disappeared from the ranks, somewhat mysteriously. Perhaps after a leave in Cairo or Alex he made the short trip to Port Said and finally caught a boat to Blighty. When he left, he took away some of the colour from our battalion of volunteers.

> "...*Remember the boys at the front*
> *No beer, no brandy, no c****
> *You'll get no promotion*
> *This side of the ocean*
> *So cheer up my lads, bless'em all.*"

And goodbye Ali.

Cairo was Cairo; just what you expected, the coat of many colours, a sin for every vice, a blessing for every virtue. She adapts herself to war as she adjusts herself to peace and tourism. With it, always a superfluity of everything, cars, restaurants, pensions and poverty, and mixing with it unashamedly, the rich and the very rich. Slums, half-finished new houses, houses with their windows walled to save tax, dilapidations, hovels ground into the dust and indistinguishable from desert sand. Dragomans, shoeshine boys, and boys for other purposes. As the Tommies would repeat:

> "*Streets of sorrow, streets of shame*
> *Streets without a bleeding name...*"

Parks and gardens for the exclusive rich and canals and riverbanks for the poor to shit on. Bargain trams and taxis, their drivers cursing each other and their epithets and phrases half sung out aloud in Arabic mixing with the yelling of newsboys and La Bourse. Vendors of filthy pictures and dirty books, flyswatters and pyramid trinkets, pimps offering every kind of delight made to measure your purse and so on. It was all in the streets. If you were a soldier not too stressed by the war it was good fun as a passing parade if not picturesque and caught up in the midst of it, uniformed men at play from every conceivable country, assembled from the ends of the earth to enjoy it. You could sit on the sidewalks outside a tavern and sip a Marsala from Sicily, a

Hiram Walker's gin from New York or just about anything genuine or ersatz, light a few joss sticks to counter the stench of the Nile or even enjoy a bulimbo beer, iced from Australia.

Of course the deeper and darker side of Cairo was there. Some of it was awful and you participated in it as little as possible and often with regret afterwards. The Egyptian monarchy was having a bad time.

Dreadful traffic jams are a feature of everyday life in the West, but the congestion of traffic, pedestrians, stall holders and their barrows nearly drove the taxi drivers in Cairo round the bend and their driving showed it. Hair's-breadth misses of collision, worn tyres, a shaky steering wheel, jumps and starts in travelling and the strange oscillation in the meter-reading contributed to your nightmare journey, and always the Nile, the Pyramids and Sphinx in the background.

The Nile in the 1940's had an unenviable reputation as a source of many diseases rather than as the sacred repository of Egyptian gods and Pharoanic culture. Amongst soldiers it was said to be the main element in the Egyptian beer of the day, as well as the country's principal sewer and the expert conveyance of the felucca, a sailboat that can still outdistance modern craft. The river then was the carrier of hookworm and its stagnant pools gave the naked children who swam in them schistosomiasis, once called bilharzia, where the worm enters the urethra and bladder of the male bather and he consequently urinates blood. Military authorities in the Western Desert preferred to use wells there instead of having to purify Nile water and transport it.

Both sides were greatly dependent on the 'birs' or wells for water and salted them if they had to leave them behind in a retreat. These were some of the reasons why the rank and file were often desperately short of water for drinking, shaving, body washing and laundering. The 'hubbly-bubbies' and hash-smokers you could see everywhere in the streets at this time, acted as painkillers for the effects of the diseases contracted from the Nile, but they were used also to take the sting out of life. I asked an Arab one day why he smoked hash or drew on his hubbly-bubby. He responded with a voice deep in veneration "Hashish good! Hashish quoisketeer! It bring happiness to the body!" and then dissolved into a paroxysm of coughing, patting his chest at the same time.

SERGEANT MAJOR HERBERT

Sergeant Major John Herbert was spit-and-polish personified. When he walked the creak of his boots and the shine on his Sam Browne gave you the whole story – a lifetime in the army – more than that – six brothers with him had joined the Army for the duration. I had suffered under one of them in Durban High School Cadets, the youngest brother apparently. He was cadet quartermaster and if you had some excuse or temporary disability you were let off cadet parade but had to help in the quartermaster stores. Cadet parades were compulsory and everyone hated them. Young Herbert (actually 3 years older than I) was very effeminate and we called him 'Sweetie'. If you played your cards right and used a bit of flattery you could laze about, polish rifles with two-by-four or even crib your homework from other more saintly defaulters in the QM store. Sweet Sherbet had obviously been spoiled by his elder brothers, something wicked.

But in the N.M.R., Sergeant Major Herbert was not an easy touch. He hadn't too much in the belfry but his bats flew out each in many directions and could be obnoxious to those caught unawares with some petty infringement of the daily order of things. He was massively overweight and in hot weather testy and revengeful, not good augurs for serving actively in the hottest places on earth viz. Abyssinia, Egypt and Libya, which was his destiny. He was courted in his very important post, but his harshness was superficial and intended to hide weaknesses in judgement and appearance. John Herbert was pigeon-chested all the way down and when he broadened and threw back his shoulders every time he challenged somebody's behaviour, dress or deportment, his pot belly rose to fill his midriff, and it was difficult to hold down a giggle. John's appetite was voluminous. Occasionally on his rounds he would be invited to step in by a group of chaps and share their lunch. After one such visit our ration box, at a single sitting was nigh emptied.

Jimmy Reen almost wept at the depredations made on Auntie Vi's anchovy paste from home, and Stan Sears was inveighed into opening a vacuum-sealed cake being kept to celebrate his wife's birthday.

Stan was one of John Herbert's favourites. He had a few whom he called on regularly being sure of semi-divine respect and who still believed in his brand of British Army code of conduct and duties. Inevitably they climbed rapidly in promotion and sometimes they were admirable choices. However, as battle conditions began their onset his own sponsored promotions, clandestine or out in the open, didn't seem to work out and those based on valour and leadership reasserted themselves. In his peregrinations through the regimental lines or positions John kept his ears open and noted what N.C.O's were well thought of even amongst other ranks. Stan Sears was well thought of by rank and file, gave wise counsel and set a good example by way of calmness during a flap and stability when there was monotony and tedium. He soon became a sergeant at a time when doubt about the performance of indifferent sergeants was openly expressed. My clash with S.M. Herbert was unplanned and not vindictive even if not entirely innocent.

Throughout the war Churchill in victory or defeat, was continuously admired by Middle East forces. The Australian soldiers lost some respect for Britain's war leader after the military catastrophe in Greece as had the Australian people after the loss of Singapore and Hong Kong but otherwise support for him was strong, being later only eclipsed by Joseph Stalin because of the latter's victorious and valiant Red Army.

Until America came into the war, in the ranks we did not feel the Allies had much going for them except Churchill and his Bomber Command. His words instilled everyone with confidence though everywhere victory was elusive. In particular there stood out in my mind his words in August 1940:

"Even if Nazi legions stood triumphant on the Black Sea, or indeed the Caspian, even if Hitler were at the gates of India, it would profit him nothing, if at the same time the entire economic and scientific apparatus of German war power lay shattered and pulverised at home…because British bombers would continue to strike at German military industries and communications."

Churchill had reiterated again and again with his mighty tautology that bombing Germany at its very heart and on an ever-increasing scale would continue to the end of the war because it was the most certain road to victory. He meant it; we believed him and he persisted with it and BBC Radio made sure that the troops, spread globally, knew about it. It was the great morale booster at the end of the hot weary days in the desert as it had been in the drenching monsoon-like forests of Ethiopia. Those who, because of their duties could not hear the latest BBC news craved it from news bearers who had. In the Western Desert bearing the 9 o'clock news to eager ears was euphemistically called "bringing back the bacon." Myself, only just out of high school, I preferred, when the news was exciting, the opening lines from "How they brought the good news from Aix to Ghent" especially as ours was traditionally a cavalry regiment and should have been then if the tanks and armoured cars had not been retained in Britain against the threat of Nazi invasion.

What all ranks in the desert did not know at that time and indeed at any time, was that British bombing of Europe was ineffectual and would not be significant for a very long time. The cause was not just bad weather alone. Bombing of Germany was then almost confined to night raids because England had insufficient fighter planes to protect her bombers over long distances.

But the BBC was a morale booster to news-thirsty soldiers in the desert for all its defects. It was amidst this scenario of news fetching that my row with Sergeant Major Herbert hatched. As the sun went down men would gather around the very few competent radios to hear the BBC news. Most especially it was the bombing of Germany that lifted the spirits… how many planes in the attacks? What tonnage was dropped and the briefings, the testimony of the pilots who were eye witnesses. Those hearing the news would return to their section post haste to give the guys the facts.

Herbert chose these precious moments to be at his most obnoxious. At the radio set anxious ears listened for every detail so that accurate information could be passed on. It was then that the Sergeant Major would bellow at any miscreant listener who dared to light up a ciggy with "Put that light out!" It might be repeated again and again as latecomers would arrive or, if the news was exciting and anxious soldiers forgettingly lit-up.

It really was an aggravating intrusion no matter how justified. Ears straining to hear were suddenly bludgeoned into these monstrous intrusions and there were under-the-breath mutterings.

On one of such occasions, as a news-bearer, I had just got back to the platoon area hotfoot with 'bacon' and blurted it out. Coming to the end of it I commented "And that pot-gutted old bitch Herbert spoilt everything with his shouting." Sympathetic voices were adding their note when out of the gloom the S.M. himself emerged.

Herbert must already have had something of a rough handling because he was steaming with rage. He had heard my loud, irritated comments and taken massive offence at them believing I had addressed them directly at him. There was a hullabaloo in which he had got little sympathy from the rank and file and the next morning I was placed under arrest. The charge was swearing at a Warrant Officer.

Wednesday, 10th September '41, Nr Mersa

Left on battalion manoeuvres about 9am. Went thru Matruh and formed up, along the Sidi Barrani Road and turned off into the desert. Did a good deal of desert manoeuvring and drill. The (army) lorries crossing the desert reminded me of cavalry charges in the film 'Balaclava'. On kitchen fatigue in the evening.

Thursday, 11th September '41, Nr. Matruh

Continued on the (manoeuvre) triangle in the desert. Mortars and Vickers practised during the day and our Ack-Ack fired tracers in the evening. I fired our (Bren) gun and the shooting all round was good. Listened to the (BBC) news and on giving my opinion of the S.M. (Herbert) to someone else was heard by the R.S.M himself. There was naturally a terrific row but he has let me off. Afterwards I intended apologising for the personal remarks but he was out of sight and I couldn't have found him in the dark.

Captain Bello Theunissen M.C.

CHAPTER VI

What we loved about our company commander, the ageing Bello Theunissen was that he did not make us, the men of the regiment, feel the generation gap or sense it himself. In our early days of training he unashamedly crawled on the ground and using the lie of the land and a little personal camouflage, demonstrated the basics of scoutmanship. He was no Baden Powell, but he too quickly won, firstly the interest of his young soldiers, then their cooperation and finally the loyalty that comes with camaraderie. Bello was a thorough extrovert with loud, bullying speech for men in groups and a soft spoken, coaxing dialogue for individual men of the ranks in trouble. He made no bones about what he (and anybody with him) would do to the enemy, and when the time came, in actual combat, led his men accordingly. When I heard he was going to try me I rejoiced inwardly. His history was impressive and strode in company with the ribbons he wore from service in W.W.I. Bello would often stop to have a cheery word when we were on air sentry near his headquarters, always enquiring about our needs, what was our field of fire and such things as what happened to the Bren's barrel when you put on the special circular drum which could fire a hundred rounds through it non-stop.

Bello was always attempting the unethical to get results which gave my unethical action some hope at my trial. At El Yibo, during action on the eve of our assault on the stony positions (sangers) occupied by Italian officers and black troops, Bello had approached the enemy alone in the dead of night. Barefooted he had crawled up to the sangars on Sugarloaf to ascertain if they were occupied. They were not and on his return journey to our lines he had injured a bare foot. The following morning a Captain Leary had questioned why he limped. Bello told him his story and also that he had scratched his initials "H.B.T' on a rock near the sangars. El Yibo was attacked later that day occupied and the initials were discovered. So concerned was Theunissen for 'my boys' he had reconnoitred the positions, unofficially in advance of the action.

Sometimes in the early days of the war in Abysinnia, the average age of soldiers in his platoon was less than 21 years (I was then just 18). Of the youngsters under his command he reported at the time:

"They compared with seasoned soldiers in the cool, efficient manner in which they carried out their duties. Not a single man showed fear though we expected to have many casualties."

At 11a.m. on Sept. 13, I was put on trial before Capt. Bello Theunissen. Herbert, still at full steam, maintained I had sworn at him. A conduct report was read out.

I was marched into a court that was tiny occupying an E.P.I.P. tent but everything indicated the paraphernalia of an Imperial Army court-marshall as if S.M. Herbert had set it up. In front of me seated was Captain Theunissen whose blue eyes immediately fixed on mine and when I looked back at him I could tell he remembered me from some patrol, air guard or other operation. A subaltern ran the proceedings and another was presumably there for my defence. The charge was read out in that I had sworn at the S.M. and that he had been there personally. He was then called and asked to say what happened. His evidence was short and simple that Private Baker had been talking loudly to a group of men and when he had walked into the circle of other ranks, Baker had called him a quote "F—ing old sh—."

Things didn't look too good and I felt isolated. When the turn came to give my account of what happened, I spoke out and my words were meant to be tinged with some indignation. I explained that the news every night was important to us and it had become my routine chore to get it from the Company radio and to bring it back as verbatim as possible. Everyone thought the S.M's interruptions were 'infra dig' and distracting in the midst of the news bulletin. At the end of my report I had told the gathering that "that pot-gutted old bitch Jack Herbert had interrupted the news with his shouts or there would have been more for me to tell them."

The E.P.I.P. army standard equipment tent in the Middle East could be linked together to form large hospital wards. Picture shows Tommies digging shell slits.

The atmosphere in the court immediately became more relaxed. Bello's eyes began to twinkle; the S.M's face reddened and he had to clear a dry mouth. My defence subaltern shrugged his shoulders as if to say the whole matter was trivial or to show where his sympathy lay. The court was then adjourned for half-an-hour and the officers went off to tea. I was seated at the back of the tent until their return. Recommencing the proceedings Bello appeared to be examining various records, presumably mine and then I was called to attention before him. He addressed me in his gruff voice and the twinkle was gone. Herbert stood poker-like at attention with his jaw jutting in profile only a yard away.

Captain Theunissen said: "No.1068 Private Baker you have admitted referring to S.M. Herbert as a 'pot-gutted old bitch'" and as he spoke the words very emphatically and measuredly, his gaze roamed very slowly up and down the figure of S.M pausing at the part of his anatomy that had been accused. Herbert stared straight ahead and flushed uncomfortably. He knew what was implied. Bello went on saying, "Now Baker I note from your number you are a volunteer. It takes guts for anyone to volunteer, to leave his homeland to fight in a war overseas like you have. But there are two kinds of guts." The twinkle was back in Bello's eyes. "There is physical guts and anyone can bring that out." Herbert's eyes began to turn towards the respected Captain as he developed his theme. He was quite sure that his own protruding guts weren't to come under attack once more. Bello continued, "And there is moral guts." There was a long pause as he ran his fingers through the reports on the table in front of him. "Moral guts is a hard thing to bring out," and he glanced again at Jack Herbert's offending belly. "You Baker have moral guts because you spoke out for what you thought was the truth, but I don't want to hear about this case again. Have you anything to say?" And I did what my council had advised me pre-trial. I apologised for being so rude. Herbert was mollified and Theunissen said, again gruffly "Case dismissed" and gave me another penetrating stare.

The feeling in the ranks was that Bello had stuck by his 'boys' and against British permanent army standards. Only then did it come out that there had been a similar piece of nonsense when Herbert had wanted to charge my friend Dennis McCullugh (later Captain McCullugh) with 'dumb insolence' straight out of his army manual.

Parcels from home reminded the infantryman of the autonomy he had surrendered to king and country. There was no real substitute for them. Each item in the parcel bore a remnant of a long since parted emotional tag. Why had this or that been sent? What sacrifice or struggle had there been to obtain it? Did it have a special meaning or tug at a memory string or act like a memento? Often the enclosures in a parcel were anachronistic or downright silly and wasteful and some soldiers, for this and other reasons opened their parcels alone. Sometimes items were included at special request, especially sugar, Nescafe and condensed milk, all of which would have to be pooled with whatever was your immediate army unit – section, troop or squad. The most enthusiastic parcel senders were wives and parents. I had no parents, was single and had only sisters and girl friends all of whom were hard working and parcels were a rarity for me.

Inevitably there were included foolish and unnecessary items like woollen gloves and socks in midsummer. Pure sentiment might cause them to be retained. It was during long periods of monotony that such items would be stock taken or at least reviewed. The amount of kit an infantryman could carry was strictly limited…tiny chess sets, postcards of home, obscure friends and distant relatives, novels unread and unattractive (usually Penguin editions), comfort boxes with needles and cotton, elastic and tiny scissors, balaclavas and scarves in excess and reminders of W.W.I., powder, a variety of toothpaste, mouth washes, liver salts.

For those bored to tears and torn with the loneliness that dugout life could present, the display of these sensitive reminders of the world out of reach were insidiously resorted to. They were, for many, especially to those most susceptible to battle stress, an incipient therapy. Little knick-knacks, mementoes, reminders of once thriving domestic and emotional processes, were balm to the heartsick and lovelorn, to the shell-shocked and emotionally exhausted. Thenceforth I was to note it was a therapy to which the rich and the poor, subjected to intense grief or trauma, turned. They had to become magpies collecting and reviewing small items out of their environment to divert attention from their miseries. I was never a magpie, but after the war I met hundreds who were and the idiosyncrasy saved many from neurosis and in the desert a lonely infantryman under the whip would find an excuse to sit quietly re-packing his backpack and reviewing items from home.

BERNARD NOTCUTT

I first met Lieutenant Notcutt when he had been posted as information officer to the N.M.R. in – 1941. He had come out of the blue, to give the various assembled platoons in situ, an update on the war… a new experience for most of us. We had relied on the BBC 9 o'clock news for that sort of thing taking much of its news service as pure propaganda and tongue in cheek nonsense. Notcutt's one pip on his shoulder (sub- lieutenant), freshly scrubbed appearance and straight out-of-the-stores uniform did not project an encouraging image for an army that had not won a single major battle in its two-year record. He even wore a red and khaki spine protector against the sun, when everyone in his audience was copper-tanned to the waist.

Notcutt thought that psychologists were too timid, lacked direct experience, and because of their academic and intellectual dispositions, shied from emotional contact with real people. He certainly knew about these weaknesses because he himself was timidity and introversion incarnate. His survey of the background features of the war was informative but dull. At question time I had monopolised his attention. He seemed grateful that someone from the ranks was interested in his lecture series and was happy to exchange ideas oft times distant from the war. I told him about strange dreams I had had that were vividly real, sometimes of dead comrades and asked whether he believed in the survival of consciousness after death, a hot military question amongst soldiers in dangerous times.

Bernard became as friendly as any officer and private might… which was not that much. But there was something about his demeanour that worried me. He would occasionally become distant during conversation, always lucid, but as if distracted by some inner tension. Bernard always looked as if the Egyptian sun and its noonday brilliance were affecting him even when he was in the shelter of Smuggler's Cove, talking to us.

I once told him the cave we were in reminded me of the cave scene in Plato's Republic and that I had mystical experiences in which I felt that I too had broken away from being chained to the cave wall of material existence. He was startled and led me on to see how much I knew of that subject. I said that for me, the pathway up to sunlight out of the cave would open at death, and I would learn then the secret of the soul.

Bernard replied: 'I am a psychologist and don't accept the existence of the soul.' Impudently I quoted the psychologist Frome back at him:

"Psyche means soul – psychology should be the study of the soul, but the soul is never mentioned."

Notcutt was a gentle, humble person and a good friend. After Smuggler's Cove we didn't meet again until the war was over, and it was at the University of Natal.

Bernard's quietly, determined voice at lectures was a contrast to the eternal bullshit and shoptalk floating about in the regiment. He earned the sobriquet of 'Sober' partly because he spoke sense amongst a group of inebriates in the Officers' Mess, but also because some likened him to a St. Bernard dog in the Swiss Alps which brought alcoholic spirit to distressed and lost travellers in the winter snows and who could be more distressed and lost than we in the dust storms of Smugglers' Cove?

Invited to play rugby in the competing company teams, you put your name forward with some trepidation. In pre-war civilian days I had played for one of the lesser fifteens under the name Natal Technical College and had been sponsored by John Dickinson & Co.'s assistant manager Giraudeau.

Competing teams then had been roughly comparable in anatomical size and age but the N.M.R. Company teams contained all sizes and ages. You never knew who (or what) you were pitted against. The regimental personnel were mainly farmers; most were heavily built, older than me and frequently bald and toothless. Playing hooker in the front row of the first match I was reminded of these unpleasant factors when I lifted my right leg to do the necessary in about the fourth scrum. To my astonishment an immense hairy hand crossed the front

Two Springbok rugby players, Ebbo Bastard and Pat Lyster.

rank divide and clamped itself on my right thigh anchoring my leg to the ground. I was shocked when I discovered that the same action was not accidental but repeated throughout the match making my own performance ineffectual. But when I eventually traced the culprit amidst the rough and tumble of arms and legs I was horrified to discover it was a giant-sized gargoyle, toothless with scalp closely shaved who, under pressure uttered curses in German, a volunteer from South West Africa, formerly mandated to South Africa after the Great War. Timidly and with respect at half-time, I pointed out the error he was making. He looked at me incredulously, snorted and turned away with a "Fok you." I asked the captain to change my position and I then played number eight. In the next match I broke a rib cartilage on my sternum and that was the end of my rugby career.

Fortunately our regiment had its own Rugby Stalwarts to represent it, ex-Springboks like Pat Lyster and Ebbo Bastard (see above) and lesser lights like my friend Cecil Ritson.

But in the Western Desert there were serious weaknesses in the leadership at all levels of command. Regiments and even armies suffered malaise. Churchill had innumerable army commanders sacked, not only for incompetence, but simply for their inaction. Even within the battalions and companies there was a malaise that had worsened as defeat followed defeat. Officers could not navigate and had to learn how to use a compass on the flat, featureless desert. Others could not read a map or calculate a position with accuracy, and this lead to appalling fuck-ups that enraged the rank and file. It risked life and limb and made friendly fire commonplace. Even Captain Blamey, a hero and ever a friend of the rank and file had to comment:

> "The uninitiated must picture most parts of the Western Desert as a vast expanse of country as bare and featureless as the ocean and absolutely flat as far as the eye can see. It is so. Consequently, there are no landmarks whatsoever to guide one. Thus it is essential to navigate by compass. One of the most important subjects of our training was, therefore, navigation and much time was spent on exercises in this by day and night. This was usually done by setting a course from the map, taking a bearing and mileage from one bir to another, over a distance of anything up to forty miles. It was amazing how accurate we became over long distances, frequently arriving within a few yards of our objective and sometimes directly on it. Over long distances in transport one, of course, checked the mileage from the odometer but, if operating on foot, the number of paces were counted. On some rare occasions we came to the conclusion that the map was inaccurate and were able to prove that the fault was not due to faulty navigation."

Worse still, the malaise was propagated around 'home leave'…the concept that being volunteers, everyone was entitled to a break after 18 months of active service, and, if you were married with children, your entitlement to home leave was undeniable, despite the precarious circumstances of British forces in the Middle East. All that was needed was a good excuse backed by confirmation from the family at home to get 'compassionate leave'. It was pure madness when the regiment was already under strength and struggling with incessant reverses and casualties.

It wasn't long before bleating wives and mothers began to call for their men in Egypt.

Any and every reason was given to get home. Then there was officers' training, which took the best men home and assisted the disaffecting process. It percolated down to the rank and file and created hornets' nests of discontent and resentment. Even the Commander-in-Chief Field Marshall Smuts was drawn into it. Captain Blamey a keenly perceptive man of action had these comments:

"During this period there were many genuine applications for compassionate leave, either on the grounds of domestic troubles, or urgent business reasons. These cases were thoroughly investigated. If one or two men got away with some cock-and-bull story, I hope their consciences troubled them. Apart altogether for the reasons I have just mentioned, we were soon to be advised that General Smuts had resolved to send many married men home. Officers and other ranks with large families were given priority over those with smaller broods. The "Ou Baas" in his wisdom did not want the nation to be denuded of young "livestock", but it appeared to me that if this had been his main purpose it would have been more logical to have reversed the policy and sent the younger and more virile men home first."

This brought about a clash between temporal and spiritual powers within the regiment. Captain Blamey continued:

"On Sunday the 19th an impressive service was attended by all ranks at Battalion Headquarters to commemorate the completion of our first year on active service. The brigade band, which we now seldom heard, was in attendance thus adding to the impressiveness of the occasion. Padre Wheeler gave an excellent sermon and ended by telling us that we had sterner tasks ahead, greater hardships would have to be endured and many sacrifices made. He particularly stressed the point that we had to abandon all thoughts of home leave. The moment the service was over the C.O. ordered everybody to stand fast and then announced that fifteen men, including officers and other ranks, would depart almost immediately on Union leave. This news had just been phoned through from brigade to the battalion orderly room. Later that afternoon another message was received to the effect that an additional thirty-five men would be included to the previous figure.

So much for Nap's sermon! The news caused much amusement and chaffing at the Padre's expense. He chuckled and said: "I should become extremely popular if I gave a similar sermon every Sunday."

The sudden departure during the next few days of fifty men of all ranks seriously affected the establishment of all companies in the battalion and a reshuffle had to be made. Lt. Col. McMillan, who had been suffering ill health ever since the Abyssinian campaign, left for the Union.

Derek and I thought it a huge joke and put in claims for home leave of the most ridiculous nature, very much like wags pestering agony aunts in a lacklustre media.

Stan Sears was almost a father to the whole platoon. In his civilian job he worked in S.A. Railway offices and was used to handling all types. He would make an effort to establish a working relationship with everyone, usually finding common, even private ground for discussion. Letters from home, attitudes to the war, home leave, health …were subjects he would find time to share with you. Youngsters straight out of school, Afrikaners barely able to speak English, cooks, arse-creepers, men in shock, fiances, artful dodgers, platoon commanders, company sergeant majors, all were given his time and consideration. Often as he was used to settle arguments with impartiality Stan was also called upon even as advisor to higher ranks.

After the platoon had had a rough time Stan Sears usually found someone at Battalion Headquarters who would intervene and give the battered section or platoon a posting that was nicely situated or easy going in responsibilities. Stan Sears was now sergeant or about to become so, and maybe this greatly loved and charismatic figure was being smiled on, because we were sent to Mersa Matruh's inner harbour to strengthen its defences against air and amphibious tank attack, and were sited in a rambling estate then almost completely in ruins, on the beach at the water's edge. I was billeted with Stan Harrison, he with a Boyes anti-tank rifle and me with my Bren. Stan Sears being in charge decided that with the old wood stove and huge dining room table still functioning in the bomb wrecked kitchen, we might attempt to cook some decent meals for a change. Having selected suitable battle positions we were then left entirely alone from 4th October to the 17th, 1941. It was absolute heaven. Stan Sears had me elected mess president and a group with Derek Street went scrounging for 'fortuitous' additions to our meagre rations. We collectively maintained a pretty good table and I had hours and hours on the beach to do what I liked.

Sharing a capacious dugout with Stan Harrison was good fun. He was a tall hilarious chap with chirpy remarks and sly banter. Sleeping in the dugout, he would grunt and titter as the bombs came down, sometimes right through the night. You could hear the growl of the Nazi planes coming in, first over the waters of the Mediterranean from Sicily and then a change in the direction of sound as they hit the white shore of the Egyptian coast and turned left along the coastline to Mersa Matruh harbour. But it was the sticks of bombs screaming down that you were really waiting for. They would start their descent perhaps half-a-mile over terra firma and then cross the harbour trying to straddle the tiny ships and barges there. Several times our dugout and the mess room were inches rather than feet from disaster. We both endured the bombings night after night with philosophical fortitude, even sitting on the dugout rampart, dazzled by the closeness of our searchlights and the barking of multiple Bofor guns, occasionally joined by naval gun responses if there was a significantly large warship in port. These German attacks by air were not always at height. Sometimes planes would come in at night so low, that in the dark their outlines could be seen. At height they would drop as many as sixteen bombs in a stick, the scream of each following the next combining with the background aerial barrage flung up by our own guns, and the large developing black plumes of explosions and fires. The whole would become a visual, almost nightly display overhead I would not have missed.

During the day we had the radio on and there were occasionally broadcasts from the Germans of their shellings falling on the perimeter of the Russian capital, Moscow. The Allies had never had, up to this stage of the war, a victory of any consequence, and the overthrow of the Russian army was now anticipated. We were consequently

The Harbour at Mersa Matruh was a forward railway base for supplying the beseiged Tobruk. Small vessels laiden with food and munitions would leave Alexandria and travelling overnight could enter Matruh harbour safely for transhipment to Tobruk in the same way.

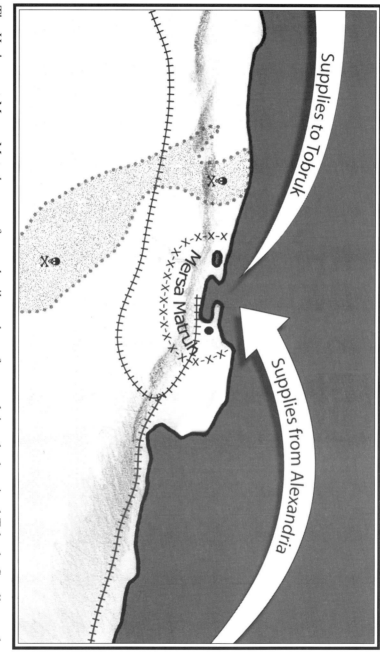

concerned, but not alarmed. Even when the Germans were only 20 miles from Moscow and could see the gleam of the turrets in the Kremlin we all expected Uncle Joe to turn the tables.

Almost exactly a year later both the Russian triumph at Stalingrad and ourselves at Alamein would begin to reverse the German steamrollers.

CANOEING

If anywhere in Egypt there is a place of natural beauty, it is on the coastline at Mersa Matruh where, it is reputed, Cleopatra occasionally visited and would have swum.

The Mediterranean is very beautiful off the Egyptian coast, especially at Mersa Matruh. Its Oxford and Cambridge blues intermingle but still leave room for slashes of mauve and purple where the waters are deeper and where seaweed may be hiding. The rolling white dunes of sand marking the coastline contrast strongly with the glittering greens and radiant blues. The overall freshness of the clear waters always delighted the naked soldiers plunging into their tiny breakers.

When such swimming was available and war conditions allowed the relaxation, you built your day around it. Our fortnight on the harbour shore was one of the few times of real happiness in nearly six years of my war. Only half a decade earlier I had frisked about gaily with friends on the quiet lagoons and in the rough surfs of Natal's beautiful South coast – Uvongo, Umkomaas, Amanzimtoti, Zulu names that brought memories back. Now, living on the small beach, the hot sun could beat down on you and relief would follow every ten minutes, dipping in the emerald greens and lapis lazuli waters of Egypt's finest beach. Inevitably my memory was stirred by the plentiful sheets of corrugated iron protruding from the ruins of houses on the foreshore and soon I was flattening out the corrugations of a selected, un-perforated and long quadrilateral of tin for fashioning a canoe. Stan Harrison helped me to get it to the lapping waters of Mersa's small bay and soon I was paddling, often dipping the canoe too deeply for a red buoy bobbing in the middle of the harbour. It became a daily entry into a forgotten childhood paradise. Rarely, I would swim out alone to the buoy and back…about a thousand yards I calculated. It was to be the last times that I would ever be able to swim such a distance again. Alamein made sure of that.

MATRUH HARBOUR – OCT. 1941

From Mersa Matruh, Alexandria and even Port Said, needed supplies had to be sent overnight to besieged Tobruk.

These were transported in barges and small ships and made the three ports liable to heavy nightly bombing. Mersa Matruh was nearest to axis forces and bore the brunt of these attacks. Tobruk itself, where nightly attacks occurred, had its specially trained Indian stevedores to do the unloading of precious supplies quickly and efficiently in the dark.

BILL STEVENS

Long days in the hot sand of Mersa Matruh were always ended by a dazzling sunset with the characteristic three bands of inter-blending colours, roseate, with pale green and yellow. But this was also time for stand-to. During this quiet watch you let the tautness of muscle and limb loosen, and maybe someone back from Cairo-leave would share a bottle of hooch, cypress brandy most often and tongues would also loosen, stand-to would lapse, and particularly if there was a special occasion, a sing-song would develop. War weary soldiers, most of them still boys would call upon someone who sang to start something up. I still remember three noteworthy songsters Jimmy Reen who had entertained us on route marches in East Africa; Len Clark, a Durbanite who sang there at churches, and for me most loveable of all was Bill Stevens, a tall, gangly amiable youth with a guitar who could bring tears to your eyes when he sang hill-billies or softly yodelled "The Mocking Bird". He was quite the most charismatic heart-throb you could meet under such difficult circumstances. Steve was modest and, at that time had only a small range of songs that he could accompany with his guitar, but if someone else played the instrument his repertoire was usually only halted by the onset of the nightly bombing of Mersa. First of all the hum of planes, not many of them at that stage (mid 1941), then the ack-ack guns putting up a barrage with its shrapnel spitting into the white sands and finally the Bofor guns that

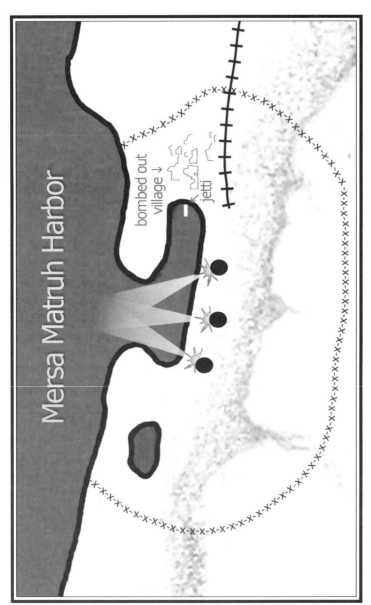

Mersa Matruh Harbor

bombed out
village ↓

jetti

Our platoon's task at the tiny Matruh harbour was to lay down lines of fire for our Bren-guns so as to engage attacking boats coming through the harbour entrance. Crete, recently occupied by enemy paratroopers is only 250 miles to the north.

pom-pommed as the German planes closed in from the beleaguered town's periphery. Any low flying aircraft met with our Bren gun fire. It was never just routine in the defences. Aerial displays, darting searchlights and then finally the bombs, usually straddling the harbour or in sticks almost anywhere were all close enough to keep the adrenaline level high.

But for me always rivalling the fireworks of aerial belligerence there was nature's glory of the inverted celestial bowl of the heavens. To lie out on the sand dunes when all the fuss and bother of the nightly barrage was over, to roll out your blanket and tuck your jerkin in for a pillow under your head, and gaze up into the rich indigo and patinaed heavens was magic.

There was one song Bill Stevens sang that I always associated with nature's mighty firmament, my version being a corruption of it went to the tune of 'Home on the Range' which was a company favourite anyway:

> *"How oft while at night*
> *When the heavens are bright*
> *By the light of the glittering stars*
> *Have I stood here amazed*
> *At the heavenly blaze*
> *And at the glory that's been here of old."*

The song, by association, had a special meaning for me. Sleeping out under the stars beneath the clear skies of almost any desert at night, grips me almost in a rigor with each major brilliance standing out like organ stops. It had taken months for me, used to the whiting out of a city's night sky by its light blaze to get used to this celestial parade of stars in the desert. Out of it had come the sense of immortality – "I have lived before and I will live again whatever the outcome of this war." Immortality is a conviction that has stayed with me ever since and with it I associate immortals like Bill Stevens.

CHAPTER VII

So often events in North African campaigns were decided by factors beyond the control of allied army commanders, so that, for instance, stagnation and boredom could overcome enthusiasm. When opportunities presented for new experience, they were seized upon. The fairly recent aerial Battle of Britain had exposed an alarming shortage of pilots whose replacement had become more desperate than loss of combat planes. The R.A.F. turned to the huge Empire forces for recruitment. What it sought was men with flying experience, a good education and that je ne sais quoi, which was very obvious in 'the few'; a psychological type almost school-boyish that had accepted the appalling stress of fighting the Luftwaffe over Britain, hour by hour, week by week resolutely.

A call came to our brigade for volunteers to train for the R.A.F. who would have to be sifted and vetted for such qualities by a visiting and selecting body. Gordon Lacey and I were chosen from the ack-ack platoon, but there were many others of my friends from the rifle and support companies, in all some 75 from our regiment had applied for transfer to the air force.

Several interviews had to be weathered at brigade and divisional levels. Lacey and I had heard that we would all be tested for lung capacity, and as preparation we practised holding our breaths and doing long runs on the beach. My diary records achieving a breath-holding capacity for a 105 seconds. At the final (divisional) interview, as candidates we sat together awaiting our individual calls. With us sat Edwin Swales, older than me by several years, a Durban boy. We had both attended the same high school. The matter of education came up; you had to be matriculated. I had written successful examinations for most of the subjects, but not all before war broke out. Edwin had not. We discussed what we could tell the board. Edwin said that he was going to claim to be fully matriculated, and they (the examining board) could never check up. I had strong reservations about 'pork pies'* and stuck by the exact truth. These decisions were crucial in the mapping out of both our futures.

Almost all of the 30 selected for the brigade lost their lives over Germany, including Gordon Lacey and Edwin Swales. The latter won the D.F.C., and posthumously, the Victoria Cross. Truth had saved my life.**

At eighteen I had by now just enough driving experience to be collared for a three-day fatigue towing shot-up vehicles from Mersa Matruh to the Delta, even Cairo. My driving partner was Ralph Humphries (see photo page 112) who was the platoon joker and tried perhaps for my sake, to turn every unnerving crisis into an absurdity. It was hard enough for him to keep the towing car on the Cairo road, but my task of keeping the wrecked chassis of the towed truck on course seemed even worse.

Monday, 10th November '41 – Mersa Matruh

At about 8:30a.m. about 55 useless lorries were towed off by 55 good ones and we from the N.M.R. were the drivers. I towed an L.D. (Light Delivery) and then was towed by an L.D. It was hard to get used to towing, but it was hard work concentrating all the time. Did 110 miles and stopped for the night. Went to see R.D.L.I. who were close by and saw Arntzen and Mac (Lachlan). Had plenty of beers and a good talk and then returned at midnight.

Tuesday, 11th November '41 – Alexandria

Left at eight (a.m.) and except for slipping the tow a few times had an uneventful trip. Reached Alex. At twelve and were buggered about between the car park and the transit camp till 5p.m. Took French leave and were given a nightmarish lift by some Aussies. Had dinner at the Minorah Club and thence to Thief of Baghdad. Had several drinks and thence to Sister Street cabarets and smashed about six of them up – more drinks – later dinner. To bed in Victory Hotel at midnight.

---

* Cockney for telling lies.

** See citatioton for V.C. Appendix V.

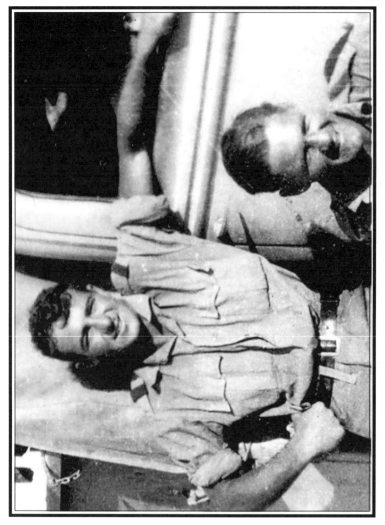

The Author, standing with Ralph Humphries on a task force driving shot-up trucks back from the front for repairs in workshops in the Delta.

<u>Wednesday, 12th November '41 – Alex.</u>

Returned by taxi to car park but were granted leave and went into Alex. again at about 11a.m. I had a haircut, bath and did shopping. Thence to lunch and a drive around the esplanade. Saw 1,000,000 B.C. and had dinner at Minorah. To a dance and then to all the cabarets and home (Victory Hotel) by 1:30a.m.

<u>Thursday, 13th November '41</u>

Left in a slow convoy fairly early and made bad time with the result that we slept about 35 miles from Matruh. Saw terrific air activity and many damaged planes. Push has started we think.

Auchinleck visiting Indian positions. Note the Bren gun mounted for anti-aircraft on its tripod with 100-round circular drain.

AUCHINLECK IN ACTION

The first thing that struck me when we assembled to hear our supremo, Claude Auchinleck was that he had the unruffled confidence of knowing what he was talking about and that he had the backing of those who had appointed him. Indeed, in all the to and fro of travail and triumph that was about to involve all of us during the following year I retained that impression.

Auck was an ageing lion who knew the ropes and would not be easily rattled whatever our joint fate might throw at him. But I was not impressed by his staff that flapped around him and even less by his speech which, as my diary records, told the men from his army assembled to hear him, absolutely nothing.

As I recall it, the old lion was not caught out by the unseasonal weather. The men may have been in brand new winter battle dress, perhaps for the sake of the official cine-cameras, but Auck was in khaki shorts and the hot sun did not disturb him; the rest of us sweltered.

Monday, Nov. 3rd 1941

We went in to represent No.1 Platoon at Auchinleck's speech in Mersa Matruh. Terrific farce of officers' snobbery. Good but uninformative slush. Cameras took scenes of all of us in battle dress, which was disgustingly hot.

My opinion of the coterie of officers surrounding our new Commander-in-Chief (C.I.C) was also immediately voiced by the other representatives of the regiment on return. "Auk was OK but that awful mob around him!…" was the general consensus. In fairness to Auchinleck's uninformative oration, the war diaries of Alanbrooke at the time and later show clearly that the communications Auchinleck had had with the highest authority (Churchill) were very soon to be out of date and superseded by events.

On December 6th Japan attacked Pearl Harbour. Hong Kong and Singapore were under threat; Britain had lost two battleships off Malaya. On December 24 Alanbrooke wrote:

"…Auchinleck struggling along with the forces at his disposal and sending optimistic, personal and private messages to the

P.M. (Churchill) little knowing that his activities must shortly be curtailed owing to transfer of air and sea reinforcements from the Middle East to the Far East."

And then of course there were the more extrovert magpies often with feelings of cowardice who like magpies, chattered and gossiped, nattered and babbled to hide their deep discomforts especially during bombardment and if there was no one to do it with, they gabbled amongst themselves. Harmless enough and better than going into shock. But it was sometimes a cover up for true cowardice and it took on one of the most detestable characteristics of desert mice… which was to highlight all their experiences of the war, even those that were insignificant or with which they were barely involved. If anyone greeted them (they were often popular) with the usual "Hi, how you doing?" out would pour a diatribe like "Yeah, I'm all right now but you should have seen us last week! The sky was black with Stukas. They went for our dugout. Bombs landed all around us." The victim might then say "Did you give them hell?" and the well-rehearsed answer would come, "Boy did we give them hell…etc., etc."

In truth magpie was deep in his trench slit while his mates managed as best they could to fight off the challenge.

Typically, such creatures gravitated to become cooks, hygiene staff, postmen and quartermaster stores. Those that stuck it out on the front line positions avoided patrol and other fighting duties. Tom Patterson, an effective cook, dishing out food near the front line would start running for cover before even putting his ladle down when the hum of approaching aircraft began, friend or foe.

It had become routine to comment in our regiment on approaching aircraft with upward glances and the words "Ullo, ullo, ullo!" also mounting the octave. Subjected to this background, desert mice would run for cover and the bravest in the mess queues would help themselves. If the food was good which was rare, unfounded "ullos" would guarantee more of the feast for the brave.

In the Western Desert, a major offensive against Rommel's front was undertaken on Nov. 18, 1941, by the British 8th Army, commanded by Cunningham under the Command-in-chief of Wavell's successor in the Middle East, General Sir Claude Auchinleck. The offensive was routed. General Neil Methuen Ritchie took Cunningham's place on November 25, still more tanks were brought up, and a fortnight's resumed pressure constrained Rommel to evacuate Cyrenaica and to retreat to Agedabia.

On 19th November '41, The Eight Army launched its offensive against the axis forces in the area around Sollum – Halfaya and Bardia specifically to relieve Tobruk. The presence of a large number of fast moving American Honey tanks now encouraged the allies to believe they could overwhelm German tank forces bearing such large and powerful anti-tank guns that they out-ranged the Allied armour by a thousand yards and penetrated British turrets with ease. The operation was called 'Crusader' and was watched anxiously especially by Commonwealth infantry divisions.

Crusader aborted and British forces ended up after ten days of fighting in almost the same position as when they started. The same old mistakes were made by allied armour. The Seventh Armoured Division split its forces into brigades not each of them strong enough to deal with Rommel's 15th and 21st Panzer Divisions. A whole South African Division of infantry became isolated and unprotected from Panzer attack. The American Honey tanks were practically wiped out through being out-ranged. Rommel, with luck on his side struck right across the desert area between besieged Tobruk and the Egyptian frontier, sent all the allied soft transport vehicles into a panicked retreat, wiped out the 5th South African Infantry Brigade at Sidi Rezegh taking more than 2000 prisoners before most of them had even been able to get out of their transport and then taken refuge in the enclave at Halfaya.

Auchinleck had to take over the leadership of the Eighth Army from General Sir Alan Cunningham, whom he dismissed and forbade very courageously any retreat back into Egypt. The New Zealand Division of Infantry resorted to the bayonet to retain the position on the escarpment at Gambut and the allies crept back into Tobruk after attempting a breakout. Rommel flew back to Germany and both sides sank into an inertia until the Eighth Army began a new offensive in January '42. But some lessons were learnt particularly through the tragic loss of the Fifth Brigade at Sidi Rezegh on Nov. 22nd. The lesson learnt was to give motorised and even static infantry a reasonably secure base to operate from or to defend and this led to the emergence of the Box.

The result of Crusader was that 500 tanks of both sides had fought themselves to a standstill. The New Zealanders had, with bayonets opened a way into the besieged Tobruk. The enemy had retired into Bardia and their redoubt at Sollum/Halfaya.

No one had won as Crusader ended.

SIDI REZEGH

On the afternoon of the 23rd November '41, the Fifth South African Infantry Brigade was crossing the desert south of Sidi Rezegh when its south flank was savagely attacked by Panzer forces. There were many soft vehicles with the South African Brigade which had only just leaguered. Casualties were very heavy indeed. Columns of British armour did their best to divert the Germans to no avail. As a fighting force the brigade had ceased to exist by nightfall. About 3,000 men were lost in the encounter. The impact on South Africa was devastating. With such a tiny population there was hardly a family unaffected by the disaster. Partly as the result of Sidi Rezegh boxes for infantry were employed which became the salient feature later in the Gazala line.

Using hindsight one must say that from the way armoured confrontations turned out in the Western Desert it seems that they all had to become cauldrons of chaos, panic and good or bad luck before an outcome could be decided.

The evolving of these 'circuses' had alarming effects on the anxious infantry quivering in their boxes or troop carriers awaiting their appropriate commitment. This held good from the level of the generals that commanded the infantry all the way down to men in the ranks. There seemed to have been preliminary cauldrons around Msus, at Sidi Rezegh, Gazala and even a rapidly formed one at Tobruk with infantry hardly getting a chance to operate in their true roles. To the outsider the desert antics of British armoured forces seem to have been nothing short of comic opera despite the valour and heartbreaks, achievements and defeats. For the South African infantry this spelt

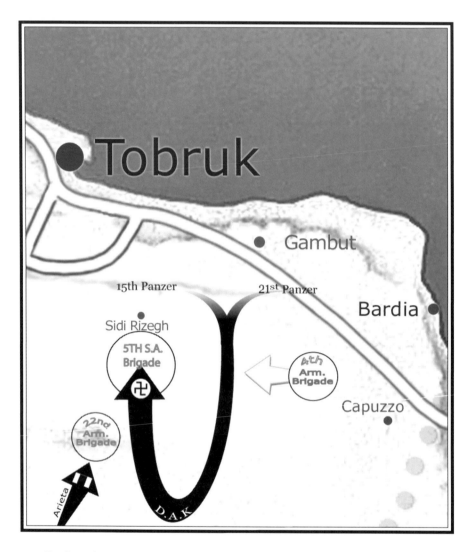

During the operation 'Crusader ' the enemy panzers attacked the South African 5th Infantry Brigade at Sidi Rezegh, unprotected by armour. It was overrun completely.

out a note of desperation, even alarm resulting from the disaster that struck the Fifth Brigade at Rezegh.

It was significant that before operation Crusader, General Brink the Commander of the First South African Division had advised delay in the start of the Crusader operations because his South African division was not yet experienced enough in desert warfare, nor sufficiently armoured. This would have contributed to the debacle at Sidi Rezegh where the 5th Brigade, for instance, was armed only with Boyes anti-tank rifles and Sticky bombs and was annihilated.

THE USE OF BOXES

Boxes were at least focal points that could be placed on a map of the flat, featureless desert wasteland, which was nine-tenths of Libya.

Difficulties
> There was no cover except what you dug.
> The boxes were so far apart, the communications between them were ineffectual especially in battle.
> They were all waterless but often susceptible to flooding.
> They had to have large numbers of men in them to make them workable.
> The occupants had to be kept supplied.
> Without adequate anti-tank guns they were vulnerable to tanks.
> The concept of boxes was intended to avoid disasters like Sidi Rezegh where infantry without protective armour were massacred.
> They could not launch planes (esp. fighters) from within their limited perimeter.

Advantages
> Boxes were points of stability in an otherwise featureless desert.
> They could house artillery, tanks, gasoline, ammo and rations in security.
> From these advanced strongholds armoured patrols could be operated.
> They were places of rest when the battle shifted.

The Twenty Five Pounder

In the first half of the war when action was focused mainly in the Western Desert the 25-pounder was regarded as the "darling" of the infantry and was called upon to act in many capacities apart from its usefulness as an artillery piece. Placed in the centre of the Boxes at Gazala it often held off panzer attacks and stopped infantry being overrun as at Elweit el Tamar.

British strategy in the Western Desert from July 1941 onwards was to relieve Tobruk. Apart from desperate situations like having no suitable anti-tank guns to fight Rommel's panzers with, which meant that the 100,000 British in the desert infantry could not be adequately protected, there was the matter of Malta. The loss of ships evacuating Crete and Greece in April/May 1941 in the Eastern Mediterranean aggravated the struggle to keep Malta supplied, because it was from Malta that bombers decimated the Axis ships supplying armaments to Benghazi and Tripoli.

Auchinleck launched his offensive to relieve Tobruk in between November 17th and December 7th, '41.

We, the N.M.R. were advancing westward towards the Halfaya enclave on Tuesday 25th November when there occurred over the German held Sollum massive explosions as if from persistent shellfire. My assessment was that they were too heavy to be our own 25 pounders and more like 210mm shells typical of Italian naval guns, and yet couldn't be because the Italians and Germans were occupying Sollum themselves. But they could have come from the H.M.S. Barham. The battleship was just off the coast at Sollum on that day and we now know that for sure because it was sunk there at the time, by a German U-boat. What we saw from Buq buq could have been the magazine of 15-inch shells of the Barham, which we also now know exploded together in a mighty detonation four minutes after being torpedoed. This may have affected the combined operations on that day because, unaccountably they were called off later in the day and we, greatly disappointed were returned to Mersa Matruh.

862 crewmen were lost on the Barham. About 400 men survived and they would have had to be taken from the water. Certainly all shipping in the area would have been alerted. The disaster had to be kept secret because the balance of naval power in the Mediterranean was only very finely in Britain's favour. The matter of secrecy was even further emphasised by the fact that less than a month later the two British battleships Valiant and Queen Elizabeth were put out of action by a midget Italian submarine in Alexandria harbour, settling fortunately in the mud on the harbour's floor. They were ultimately salvaged and fully restored, but the British went to extraordinary lengths

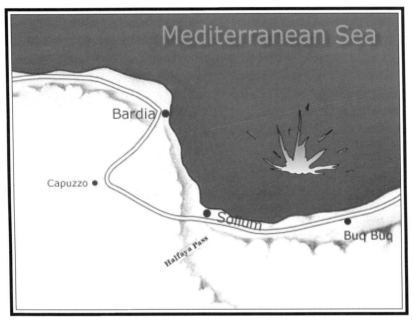

Suggested locations of an explosion in Sollum Bay seen from the Egyptian coast at Buq buq, believed by author to be the torpedoing of the battleship H.M.S. Barham.

to cover up the loss. As it was, even the Italian navy was unaware their midget submarine had scored such successes.

But I myself was personally involved in the tragic destruction of the Barham. (See photo of Bahram exploding, page 124)

Dennis Baker, 'lost at sea' or 'killed in action' was a personal tragedy. The warning dreams of Dennis, the Elephant Tree and the rivers in flood continued until the war was over with Dennis in them fading and the tree becoming undeniably a large tank and myself in trouble on top of it.

The tragic loss of their son was a disaster from which neither of Dennis' parents ever recovered. After the war they offered me a home but they knew I would not be an adequate substitute for Dennis' freshness and naiveté. I too managed to grieve, mainly in dust storms, alone and wrapped in a head towel for hours when I would think morbidly that if I had been born 12 hours earlier we would both have been on the ill-fated Barham or together in the Western Desert, ill-fated twins astrologically.

Coincidence of surname, of date of birth and closeness at the time of his death albeit I on land and he at sea suggested a synchrony of fate that might repeat itself even yet.

1941 NAVAL ACTIVITY

By 1941, Naval emphasis was placed on a strategy for the Mediterranean. Britain was desperately trying to ensure the survival both of Malta and of her extended lines of communication on land in Libya and Egypt. Battleships were at a premium and Britain had both Gibraltar in the West and Alexandria in the East to sustain with naval power. The loss of just one major vessel could upset the fine balance of sea forces operated by Italy in opposition to Britain and her sorely mauled Empire. Italy and Germany had to maintain supplies to North Africa and were soon in trouble doing just this. My brother Desmond was caught up as was Dennis Baker in this tragic power struggle, Dennis being on the Battleship Barham and my brother being temporarily based in Alexandria on a battlecruiser. With my buddy Len Clark I had often gone sailing in Alexandria harbour. It delighted me to wave hello to the British sailors and occasionally to call out for my brother to come up on deck. In December of 1941 my regiment was posted to the Libyan frontier and we had dug in at a place called Buq buq where we waited to make the attack on Halfaya Pass which was held by the Italians. Rumours were always running rife especially about our lines of communication throughout the Mediterranean. The sinking of any major British vessel would set alarm bells ringing. It was touch and go as to whether Malta could survive. At that time, indeed for most of the war, any news about shipping was very hush-hush indeed. In January 1942 rumour had it that we had lost the Battleship HMS Queen Elizabeth and that she had been sunk in Alexandria harbour, not by bombing but through torpedoing. How this could be possible I could not understand because I had personally from our yacht seen the torpedo nets in place around the battleship.

The Sinking of HMS Barham

Matters were even worse than the rumours as it turned out because a second battleship HMS Valiant was also sunk at the same time in Alexandria. Few knew it but Britain's whole strategy was now in disarray. The troops in North Africa, hundreds of thousands of them, could have their supply routes cut off by an Italian sea landing anywhere along the Libyan or Egyptian coastline. What made the whole episode more confusing was reports deliberately published widely in the Egyptian press of parties of diplomats and their families on board the two ships celebrating some event or the other. Dignitaries were photographed at the parties and they were also published in the Egyptian press. The truth was that the two ships had settled into the muddy bottom of Alexandrian harbour but their decks were still above water. Italian midget submarines were able to penetrate the harbour defences and their operators had been able to lay three mines under the hulls of both British battleships. The Italian crew of two were caught trying to escape and were hauled onto the quarterdeck of the Queen Elizabeth. The captain interrogated them himself. The Italians refused to let on where they had placed the limpet mines on the ships' hulls. Half an hour before explosion time in order to save life the Italians reported their action. This attack had been completely successful. In all, over the last two months with Repulse and Prince of Wales off Malaya, Britain had lost 5 battleships and an aircraft carrier and her naval power was near breaking point. The brilliant idea of holding parties on the decks of the sunken ships worked. The Italians had triumphed with a naval victory but the British countered it with photos. The delay enabled the British Naval engineers to repair both ships to restore them to the line.

My brother Desmond had joined the navy at age fourteen. As a "boy" and in the Alexandria episode he would have been seventeen. When his ship whatever it was, reached home waters he would stay with my aged aunt who had fled the bombing of London to Potters Bar. I was surprised from her letters not to hear much news of my brother for he used this facility quite frequently. In 1959 I solved the mystery when talking to my Aunt Lily. It seems that Des had become involved with a girl in the area and that matter had become serious enough for marriage to be considered and then he was called away to a new ship and that was the end of that affair. He was always having other liaisons, as he was a very attractive person both in personality and looks. Years later we shared a small farm in KwaZulu which we called Potter's Bar on my brother's insistence and the author has been associated with Potter's Bar where he has lived ever since.

It was an old tradition born out of the regiment's early days in the Boer War, in cavalry and horse-grooming to call each other 'Horse-stallion' during celebrations and conviviality. It was a recognition call indicating respect for your regimental history, your likeness to the vigour of a stallion (and possibly its private parts) and your capacity to drink as much beer as a stallion could water from its trough. After a communal booze-up, there would be the usual larking about, rowdyism and attempts to call each other into troops and even a semi-balaclava charge might be attempted such as storming the sergeant's mess if the privates' beer had run out. Occasionally the officers would be inebriated enough to join in and give uninvited speeches attempting to restore order. It all became very jolly and unmanageable especially if a few of the regiment's trumpeters appeared and trumpeted something of each of the regiment's calls, from 'Reveille,' and 'Officers' Mess' to 'Lights Out.' Troopers even ran around clattering like horses, with their army boots. Some could not, or did not care to shake off these regimental ghosts of past days and past drunk-ups.

Commonly someone earned for himself the fair entitlement of 'Horse', short for horse-stallion.

Amongst large bodies of soldiers you will always find the sensitives who are liable to fall prey to practical jokes and become targets for coarseness.

Not only that, but somehow they are by nature accident prone to what is current and what hurts. Early in the events occurring in Egypt were the short leaves in Cairo and everyone was still very green in understanding the local population and their attitudes. Being broke but loathe to miss an opportunity for leave I found myself in a pension in Cairo where you slept in dormitories and ate together in a converted lounge-dining room. As I recall, Richard Platt and Joe Cowley were part of the well-knowns in our entourage. One not so close was a very sensitive fellow just up from South Africa. He used to shy like a startled horse at anything unusual and Cairo was the place for the bizarre if anything. This guy, whose real name must remain unrevealed had a George Formby set of gravestone teeth and clattered about like a carthorse to such an extent that he earned the nickname 'Horse.' Friendly enough, he nevertheless remained in the background being very uncertain of anyone in the group until he knew them well enough to strike up a real friendship. The pension accommodation itself was very low in tone and we treated it accordingly. 'Nothing was for nothing' which meant you paid for the day's bed & breakfast in advance and anything extra you had to pay for immediately and on the spot. It was a noisy part of Cairo and cheap. Our first night there went off more or less routinely. Five or six of us, including Horse had got no further than the bar opposite and were pleasantly sloshed except for Horse who had probably found the general consumption rate a bit too high and had surreptitiously to empty some of his drinks into a spittoon.

Then, of course, someone had to mix him a Mickey-Finn that made him clatter even more volubly and when he passed out ensured that he was carried back across the road to the pension. He was flopped into bed and somebody took his boots off.

Next morning breakfast was going smoothly when the dormitory wallah appeared with a face like thunder. He was clutching something rolled up into a ball and took up a position with some authority in front of the cracked old marble Victorian fireplace. Mark Anthony before the Roman mob could not have looked more imperious and out it came in a loud monotone. "Who shit the bed?" There was an incredulous silence in the breakfast room except for the sound of a hoof-like clatter. The wallah straightened his fez and brought up his punchline "It cost 50 piasters to shit the bed." His voice had dropped an octave menacingly. Suddenly there was tittering and we all began to laugh and make gestures rejecting the sight and smell of the rolled-up sheet. Horse gave a pitiful neigh as his teeth chattered. He jumped to his feet, thus attracting attention, rushed across to the bedroom wallah and stuffed an Egyptian One Pound note into the rolled-up sheet and fled the room. We didn't see him again till that evening in the same pub opposite. Nobody said anything, not there or even back at camp. They didn't need to.

DECEMBER 1941

In operation 'Crusader' Tobruk was relieved on 5th December, but our task of dealing with Germans besieged at Halfaya remained. The weather turned nasty and we moved in with the platoon to guard the water point at Buq buq. Rommel had left his troops at Halfaya in a sorry state, ill-equipped to meet the onset of winter.

CHAPTER VIII

Halfaya was a redoubt built into the pass on the escarpment south of Sollum and a remnant of earlier desert actions. The actual pass called Halfaya, was no more than a track up the cliff face. Enemy transport could be observed using it from our positions surrounding the enclave west of Buq buq. Sollum itself was the site of old army barracks and a tortuous macadamised road that wound up the cliff face of the escarpment giving breathtaking views of the Egyptian coastline below.

Sollum was part of the enclave that included Halfaya.

The besieged Bardia was, with Halfaya a refuge and refuelling area for Rommel and his panzers.

HALFAYA

The N.M.R. faced the Germans and Italians at Halfaya by occupying the line next to the sea. The appalling weather was background to tense days of vigilance divided between long hours on guard, sometimes by day but mainly by night and rest periods. It was rare for us to have a whole day free from the khamsin that made life miserable and in which the sun rarely showed itself at the water point we were guarding. In the line itself enemy deserters drifted in starved and disconsolate. Our platoon commander was Ken Clarke who did his best to keep up the spirits of his men. Everyone wanted an end to the winter siege.

On January 2nd, 1942 the Second Division of South African Infantry captured Bardia in a cacophony of bombardments we heard while on guard. Thereafter Ken Clarke acted on orders that the regiment would attack Halfaya a few days later, and made the most of it by telling us all that he expected to be killed leading his platoon, or

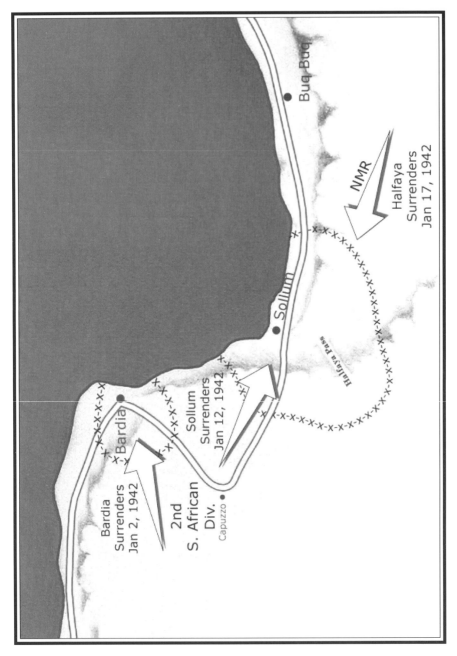

On January 17th 1942, the enclave of German troops at Halfaya surrendered to South African forces.

at the very least lose a leg. His comments were extremely unpopular amongst our married men anxious as always to get home to their wives and children. On the 12th of January, Sollum fell to our forces and the rising tension in anticipation of our own attack on Halfaya Pass scheduled for the next day was deflated by the news that the attack was called off. In fact surrender terms were being negotiated and Halfaya gave in on the 17th. The regiment, exhausted by so many weeks of being under observation beneath the Halfaya escarpment was returned to Mersa Matruh for a rest.

Before the attacks on the Halfaya-Bardia-Sollum enclave Rommel had returned to Germany

The man behind the biggest and most constant binoculars in our anti-aircraft platoon was Private Ernie Oram. He was aircraft crazy from the start and carried around silhouettes of both allied and enemy aircraft of W.W.II. Through him we were taught in advance to recognise attacking planes so that we not only opened fire on them as early as possible, but did not try to shoot down our own planes with friendly fire. It was a comfort to have such an enthusiast give early warning if the sun was suddenly blacked out with tightly packed Stukas or, always coming from the east, a friendly, tightly packed bevy of American Bostons were approaching in silver array with R.A.F. markings.

Private Oram was a popular figure always with a cheery word. In the desert he tanned well and wore snazzy shorts with a good torso. Not much of a gambler he would still come over to play a game of cribbage with Ray Lee at Gazala or even for a sing-song with a couple of beers. He survived the war and is equally popular in peace time Durban.

Aside from the agony of it all, Gazala provided him with a paradise of opportunity to participate in wartime aircraft displays first hand in their naked cruelty and more as a voyeur than as a participator.

When the division reached the Western Desert it had been put into the much-bombed fortress of Mersa Matruh. But there was also a danger that paratroopers would be dropped. Only a few weeks earlier, in late May 1941, German paratroopers had completed the conquest of the island of Crete, only 250 miles across the Mediterranean north of Mersa. We were desperately short of equipment; our platoon alone possessed only three of its complement of six Bren guns. Even simple items like tin hats and sandbags were in short supply. But slowly, over the next year as the regiment moved westward, occupying the front line frequently, it acquired more and more machine guns of every kind, stripped from British and American planes that had crashed, shot down above our lines. There were Italian Breda M.G's and German captured weapons, including machine guns which were too heavy to keep moving from position to position as we advanced and withdrew. The line was always in a state of flux and these M.G's were mounted in our infantry gun pits. The American Brownings firing 1200 rounds a minute were always a delight, excellent in defence, no use on patrols.

We had little firepower to offer against marauding hostile fighters that strafed the shit out of any kind of troop concentrations and army vehicles advancing or retreating. A Bren gun magazine of 28 rounds was hardly a realistic anti-aircraft weapon against Messerschmitts strafing at 400 miles per hour, even when mounted on a sturdy tripod. [See page 113]

To overcome this difficulty, at least in part, I clamped three Bren magazines together, two pointing downwards, and the third placed between the first two pointing upwards. The three were held together with circular one-and-a-half inch rubber bands cut from tyre tubes off shot-up derelict trucks. It meant that this simple device, immediately available, could allow an ack-ack Bren gunner (or anyone) to treble his firing time and thus to engage more than one flypast of a Messerschmitt, and they often hunted in threes.

The device was officially recommended to the Eighth Army and gives an idea as to the vulnerability of advanced infantry in the desert campaign before Alamein. It was better than one silly-arse officer of ours who shouted to his platoon to take cover and in his exhibitionist display shot at the attacking Italian plane with his .45 pistol!

About the same time the army made up our complement of Brens to the correct six!

The infantry ground defence, against tanks at this stage of the war, was still in no less a parlous state, an anti-tank rifle to begin with,

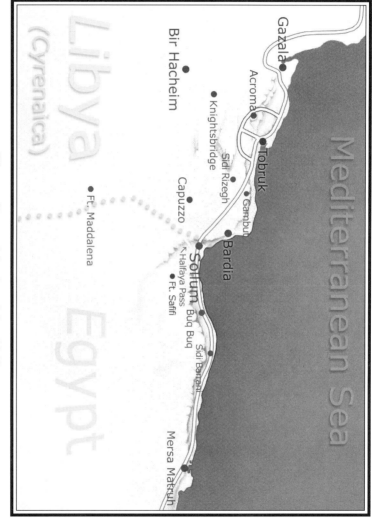

Western Desert March to May 1942

After the surrender of enemy forces in the enclave at Halfaya Pass the N.M.R. moved up to occupy the Boxes in the precincts of Tobruk shown here at Knightsbridge, Acroma, Gazala and Tobruk.

added to by a 'sticky bomb' that promised certain death to the user if he did not employ total precaution and lunatic valour in its application.

In London, by the 25th January '42, the War Office began to have the same misgivings about Auchinleck's staff and their information, which we, in the forces were already having in November '41.

The recapture of Benghazi by Rommel and the Msus gallop that then followed showed, as Alanbrooke noted, that the Auchinleck staff had got the figures of German losses in the desert wrong, overestimating them and consequently was unable to counter Rommel's reoccupation of Benghazi. Alanbrooke's conclusion was that the Auk's greatest weakness was his inability to select appropriate staff to serve him. This was true, but he also had the courage to remove two of his commanders smartly, when they were failing in leadership at critical moments in the desert warfare and to assume their commands himself immediately. This happened when Cunningham made a mess of his role in operation Crusader in December 1941 and Ritchie after the fall of Tobruk in June '42.

In the spring of 1942 Churchill was fighting off political defeat in the House of Commons and needed another victory in the desert.

Auchinleck, who had already given him the relief of Tobruk felt now that he was being prodded into another action before he was ready. For one thing, the advance of the Eighth Army to take up positions and dig in around Tobruk in the form of boxes from Gazala to El Adem was not complete and another, the failure yet to secure control of the air over these regions made a major operation before May 1942 unlikely of success.

My own diaries stressed these tense times.

With the surrender of enemy forces besieged in the enclave around Halfaya and Sollum, we moved forward passing through battlefields that had been torn by shellfire and bombs in the past and would be again. Diary entries cover our advance to take up positions in the Gazala line 20 miles west of Tobruk. On many days it was a matter of playing hide-and-seek with Messerschmitts in a total absence of air cover.

Saturday, 7th February '42 – Nr. Safafi

At barely a moment's notice we were ordered to pack and move up to Tobruk. We had two trucks for the platoon. Over a bumpy road we made Safafi Fort by 3p.m. Thence we descended the escarpment through minefields into the dusty coastal plain and camped for the night several miles from the coastal road. Restless night.

Sunday, 8th February '42 – Halfaya

Left camp at 7a.m. and reached the road without incident. Before Halfaya we struck a colossal traffic jam when a certain body of troops (Polish?) left the front on the way down. At Sollum after seeing the Halfaya Pass which was disappointing, we climbed an amazing (tarmac) pass (above Sollum). Capuzzo and Bardia in afternoon and parked 10 miles past Bardia. Saw battlefields strewn with debris.

Monday, 9th February '42 – Tobruk Perimeter

Made the 60 odd miles to Tobruk (perimeter) in good time. Saw much air activity and the raiding of our dromes. More equipment strewing the Sidi Rizegh area. Skirted Tobruk on the axis (built) road. Saw many crashed planes of both sides. Camped at about 12 noon. Stay indefinite.

Tuesday, 10th February '42 – Tobruk

Rose late after a good night's sleep. Took things easy until after lunch. Was in (patrol) tent reading Tolstoy (War & Peace) when three Messerschmitts strafed the road 100 yards away. All over in 5 secs. Barely had time to get out of tents. Many narrow escapes – 3 killed and 3 lorries of petrol destroyed in terrific blaze. Well prepared for next one now.

Wednesday, 11th February '42 – Tobruk

After yesterday's raid were very alert all day. Terrific aerial activity continually. Enemy planes overhead as well. In the afternoon had a grand view of a dogfight between 4 Messerschmitts 109's and 10 Hurricanes. Saw no crashes but only two enemy passed (over) us again. Dug gun hole and read for the rest of the day.

<u>Thursday, 12th February '42 – ibid</u>

More bombings and air activity. Played cards (during air guards) read and wrote letters home.

<u>Saturday, 14th February '42 – Acroma</u>

Terrific air activity. At one time Messerschmitts north, south, west and east of us. No strafing in our area. Saw 109 brought down in flames by our ack-ack over Tobruk and it crashed about half-a-mile away. Moved to new positions and dug all afternoon. Stukas to the extent of 14 we saw dive and bomb some distance away.

STUKAS (APRIL 1942)

It seemed to me that the long purposeful dive of the Stuka was a determined effort to take the bombs right to the target in the absence of a reliable bomb aimer.

Over Germany, it had been quickly realised by the R.A.F. that, for the most, their bombs were missing the target both at night and during the day and continued in this way some years into the war.

Acroma was a box that no one wanted. The famous box of guardsmen at Knightsbridge was situated in a hollow, one of a million hollows in the Libyan Desert. Acroma was plonked on a ridge or outcropping, also one of a million in the desert. Even after we had slaved at its fortification the Germans didn't want it either, not until the last moment when they had practically overrun the guards in the Knightsbridge box and were hell-bent for Tobruk.

Ray Lee and I hollowed out a 6-foot square hole on the Acroma site and helped Corporal Roger Ellis to complete his dugout too. Roger (I believe he was once in the King's African Rifles) was a stickler for maintaining army code, written or unwritten even in dugout construction. He had chosen his site about 20 feet from our domain. It was in a slight wadi where there was more sand and digging, now in his hands rather than in the hands of others, was easy going. I had thought his positioning unwise but said nothing. Roger ultimately proved to be a very courageous officer under fire and was badly wounded in

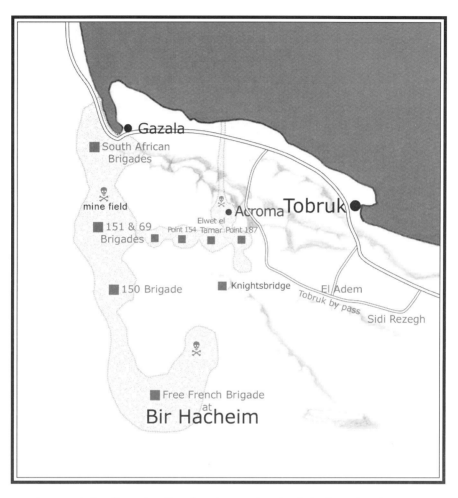

Boxes defending the Gazala Line and Tobruk before the German
onslaught of 26th May 1942.Note the vulnerability of the 150 Brigade
Box and also that of Bir Hacheim.

action, but in these early days his vanity was hard to bear. He was immaculate in wearing even our somewhat gross summer uniform and shorts (with putties of course). He appeared groomed even in sandstorms. His kit received almost as much loving care as did his side-burns and moustache. In carving out his dugout he had shaped one wall into ledges for his kit; boots on one ledge shaving gear on another. His wife's picture was nicely placed where he could feast on its image at all times. Mildred was important to him and he wanted visitors to know it. Still another chosen location was for his letter-writing materials housed in a zip-up with a Croxley linen-faced Cambridge blue pad.

Roger had to confront boredom as we all did, and routine army spit-and-polish was a comfort to him. Those boots were correctly dubboned and yet gave off a glow and the army leather belt knew well the special make of his polish and the shine of its brass buckle. I could always sense when Ray Lee wanted to be alone and would crawl over to visit Corporal Ellis. Occasionally I would arrive when he was about to shave. Instead of being put out he welcomed my intrusion and I soon learnt why. Shaving was the highlight of his day. He deeply admired his own features and would gaze lovingly at them in vastly protracted shaves. The soaping and the actual scrape were daily events in his life that vied only with his devotion to grooming, hair by hair, his dark moustache. I felt totally non-descript in my own appearance on these occasions. But boredom and tedium were so relentless that I sought out his company more and more. We read out letters from home to each other. I occasionally painted in watercolour and offered to do a portrait of Mildred. He accepted with alacrity and my every stroke of the brush drew comments about Mildred, which acted, on him like a catharsis. In turn I also read him my war diaries.

A climax came when there was a cloudburst in the middle of the night. Our own dugout covered by a rough canvas miraculously weathered the storm and Roger's canvas did too. But shouts rang out despairingly. A calamity had occurred. A flash flood rushed down from the Acroma outcrop and of course those who had chosen to dig their dugouts in the bed of any sort of watercourse were washed out with incredible suddenness, some almost drowned. The contents of Roger's dugout were under water including his bedroll. He spent the

Author's father, Sidney Baker, H.A.C. who worked on
the first tanks in 1917/18.

remainder of the harassing night with us, pitched as we were a few feet higher on a knoll, safe as I knew we would be from such hazards. Over the next week or so, Roger had time to reflect on the sweet uses of adversity as he scraped desert mud lovingly from his steel mirror and his wife's photo-frame and restored them to their proper places. He soon went off on an officer's training course and was transferred to another regiment where he gave a good account of himself and the N.M.R. moved into the Gazala line.

Mid-February to mid-May of 1942 were three of the most tedious months spent on what was to be nearly six years of active service. Everyone looked for some kind of diversion, anything that took your attention away from the endless round of guards at night, fatigues by day and dreary food in giant thermos flasks. You read each others' letters, even wrote to each others' girls, commented repeatedly on the same private photographs, exchanged literature, magazines and newspaper, did crosswords, played cribbage, poker and bridge, pined for the beer lorry, shot at any planes that came in range and at many that didn't. It was awful. The two sides built up their forces and it was touch and go as to which would attack first. You even began to join in the most ridiculous activities. In search of exercise you sought out rounded stones and used a shovel as a golf stick to hit them around a small golf course and played each other several rounds of this lunacy. Some carved novelties and nonsense out of derelict wood. Some stared into the blue endlessly and dangerously:

> "Sometimes I sit and think
> And sometimes I just sit."

Many sat and blew small bubbles with their saliva by curling the tongue and blew them at you if you were reading or writing letters.

Any kind of insect diverted you, particularly the dung beetles, which tirelessly rolled their dung ball to some distant hole for burial.

Some seemed to have an attraction or phobia for specific creatures. My own predilection was the snake; Eric Gregg's was the scorpions which on two occasions, in the army and out of it hospitalised him with their stings. Richard Platt's phobia was the desert dog and Joss Deacon's the desert rat that would nest under his bed-rolls.

Life in the desert was uncomfortable and dispiriting. It was very hot during the day and bitterly cold at night. It was also dangerous from the point of view that German raiding parties would make sudden attacks so there was a constant state of alert. We were dug-in to a depth of about five feet, with our tents acting as a shade during the day and a cover at night. Water was strictly rationed – a pint per man per day – and when we suddenly had a storm which lasted about half-an-hour we quickly threw off our shorts and boots and stood in the rain for our first bath for months. We were told that it was the only time it had rained in this area for eighteen years. The desert blossomed, and we saw great areas of small flowers and even ears of wheat – left behind by the Romans who had used this part of Libya as a granary. This vegetation disappeared as rapidly as it arrived.

There were almost incessant attacks on Tobruk from Italian and German aircraft. We were just out of range, but we had a grandstand view of the proceedings.

We were soon on our way again, and little did we realise what was going to happen when we set up a new position near Gazala. We had become part of the Gazala box which was meant to impede the German land advance on Tobruk and to stop any attempt by them to get into Egypt.

And there was time to re-read letters from more distant family members... my cousin Ken Haslewood floating around linked to the N.A.A.F.I. units in the delta, and whom I was to meet up with dramatically six months later. There was also my old Aunt Rose who had put on a uniform and got into an ambulance to drive the wounded and maimed during the blitz of Plymouth and recommended for the George Medal by Winston Churchill. And I still carried in my kit bag a photo of my dad who was in the H.A.C. and helped to build the first tanks in 1917/18 for use on the Western Front. Then there was the signet ring fashioned from my parents' wedding rings for me by my elder sister Kathleen who had inscribed it with the word **'COURAGE.'**

AIR ONSLAUGHT

In hindsight there is no doubt Rommel had already made up his mind to make Tobruk his primary target in his comeback. The Germans had learnt the lesson early on that the skies above their objective is most easily secured if control of its air-space is held in advance.

From March 1942 until he began his offensive on May 26th, that control was ruthlessly sought in the skies above the Gazala-Tobruk axis and its boxes. Extracts from my diaries tell the story of the kind of air activity the boxes were engaged in before the offensive began.

Friday 6th March '42

5 bombs dropped on our box at Acroma. No damage.

Monday 9th March '42

Air activity slight.

Thursday 12th March '42

Another air raid in the afternoon. Two M.E.109's dropped two lots of bombs (on the axis by-pass) a few hundred yards away.

Friday 13th March '42

Enemy planes overhead. Our ack-ack shells burst close to them. M.E. 109's machine-gunned targets close to us. Fired a magazine (one hundred round drum) at them.

Wednesday 18th March '42

Air raid in the morning. Shot at M.E.110 but had a bloody stoppage. Bofors guns cracked him on the fuselage.

Friday 20th March '42

While shaving had a visit from our pal the M.E.110. Fired two Bren magazines at him. Our small arm fire and the Bofors soon dispatched him on his way. Another magazine at an M.E.109 slightly out of range.

Saturday 21st March '42

Very little air activity.

J.U. 87, Stuka dive-bomber used mercilessly against targets in the Western Desert. Note the rear gunner who was seated behind armour-plating.

Monday 23rd March '42

Had some fun from the air in the morning. Two Macchis flew over and I let two mags go at them (from Bren mounted on tripod). Then an M.E.109 followed and I got two more mags off.

Tuesday 24th March '42

There is a plane controversy going on. I think I had as bigger a part in bringing it down as any.

Friday 27th March '42

A report supporting my claim for bringing down an aircraft (Macchi 200 which crashed in our lines) on the 23rd.

Saturday 28th March '42

Perfected new device for increasing firepower of the Bren gun against aircraft.

The interludes between days of air activity were usually caused by dust storms which made low flying hazardous and virtually impossible. On Sundays, the Italians didn't want to fly probably because of the Sabbath.

Tuesday 7th April '42

Fired 4 magazines on two planes just about 5p.m.

Wednesday 8th April '42

Fired off six magazines at two pairs of M.E.109's.

Thursday 9th April '42

Some shooting in the morning at a beautiful target in the form of an M.E.110.

GAZALA STUKAS

It was just after lunch on the 11th April that the air was filled with a distant droning that became louder as the ground also began to vibrate and then literally to shake. Snooky Oram, Ray Lee and I were watching our Brigade headquarters taking a pounding some distance behind

Stukas flying in formation ready to dive-bomb.

the lines. And then the droning amplified and we became aware that our own area was about to be attacked from the air. Automatically Snooks turned his binoculars towards the sun out of which Stukas usually dived as a ploy to blind defenders in their terrifying attacks. Instead of getting a running account of approaching enemy from him with types of plane, number of waves, etc., there was silence as his binoculars trained and retrained on the now horrendous noise. Then the sun was blacked out and Oram made the terse comment "Shit! They're Stukas… and they're in waves…and too many to count."

Everyone on the flats had had no time to site or dig a gun pit and my Bren was on its tripod standing upright amongst the desert scrub without any cover. The loud drone turned into the wail of sirens and then into a protracted scream as the Stukas began their powered dives aimed at the battalion transport dug in a few hundred yards behind where we were, in the foremost positions. The release of their bombs brought an added hellzappopin to the already present cacophony and added more smoke and flame to the fumes carried on the breeze from earlier and more distant attacks. The few Bofors ack-ack guns added their pounding to the chaotic scene. My own machine gun was a thin treble amidst such orchestration.

The Stukas had dropped their bombs and were coming out low over us, not perhaps still in formation but more or less together and certainly not in any kind of ragged fashion. The sight of these monsters heading for us spread out across the desert flats at about 100 feet was too much for Lee who now, shaking all over, had been yanking off the empty magazines from the Bren and slapping on new. His face contorted into a rictus of horror as these barbaric instruments of destruction straightened out of their dives and flapping like take-off ducks came towards us. I knew from experience by now that only when they passed over you, very low and you were then behind them that they were most dangerous from their rear guns. The crunching of the Stuka bombs had already raised Lee's malarial bout of shakes to a severely agitated level. The jaundiced whites of his eyes now showed. He just dropped everything, gave me a sickly smile and the oncoming debauched enemy planes a horrified glance and ran for cover with a "Fuck this!" I was so concentrated on keeping the swines in my sights, one after the other, I hardly noticed I was now alone. One German pilot was so close that as he shot by, almost overhead, I could see the rear gunner. He must have been laughing at my absurd ineffectual stand and waved a hand at me safe as he was behind the Stukas rear armour. Whether he was out of ammo or merely exultant at their success, I will never know. As the waves of Stukas ended, Lee came hobbling across from the dugout with a bucket filled with brackish Gazala water. By then, the Bren gun's barrel had become almost red hot. He disengaged it from the gun, taking it gingerly by its handle and flung it into the water. It shot up a spout of steam and bubbles and I fixed the spare second barrel in place, on the Bren, none too soon, for another final, rather half-hearted wave of Stukas was upon us and Lee bravely stuck that one out.

When it was all over the platoon officer Ken Clarke did his round of the six guns. As I recall only two of them had fired, my own and Cecil Ritson's. Clarke was delighted at my ammo returns and drew them (1800 X .303 small arms) himself from the quartermaster. Later he made Ritson and I lance-corporals. It wasn't much of a promotion but after the war Ken Clarke became a firm friend and Mayor of Durban.

That day Ken Clarke asked me for a special report on the Stuka attacks to support battalion claims as to what was shot down. It was not recorded in my diaries and should have been copied there later. But the report was lost with Tobruk.

AIR ONSLAUGHT continued…
More Diary dates!

<u>Saturday 11th April '42</u>

Had the most exciting afternoon of my life when 10 Stukas and 20 M.E.109's raided us. There was no damage on either side worth mentioning. In the whole raid I fired 14 magazines. Planes as low as (50 to) 500 feet. Bad shooting by the Bofors. Our Bren gun tripod surrounded with machine gun bullet marks but none hurt in the battalion – very close shave. Our tracers bounced off the planes. Saw their tracers whipping past Ray and I.

Seeing our tracers bouncing off the planes meant that the armour plating in the Stukas that protected their rear gunners was effective.

Sunday 12th April '42

Demonstrated my new Bren gun magazine invention to the Brigadier who was delighted and it has gone up to division for interview.

Thursday 23rd April '42

Very dusty day. Slight air activity. Fired four magazines.

In early May the heat became intense and we began to feel the full effects of extended lines of communication. Malta was under constant attack and on the brink of starvation. In the Gazala line the food situation seemed to worsen by the day and with the temperature in the forties centigrade and no adequate cover, water rationing became drastic. Water fatigues, manhandling forty-gallon drums knocked you out for days. Fleas and rats pestered and all the time tension grew and the mystery as to which side would attack first deepened. The Gazala line had been taken over by us from the Poles and the weapon pits always needed deepening, widening and strengthening. There seemed to be no strategy behind our defence system and all was made worse by the Germans retaining air superiority.

The whole Gazala defensive area had been set up believing the enemy would attack the north of the line in strength and would try to outflank in the south with the use of his Panzers and other motorised infantry.

There were many lines of defence for Tobruk.

1. There was the Gazala line stretching from the Gazala inlet on the Mediterranean 50 miles south to Bir Hacheim. This line was reinforced with minefields and was held strongly by infantry brigades.

2. A system of Boxes consolidated the Gazala line.

3. If Rommel attacked from the south there were three lines of Boxes which would prevent his cutting off the Gazala line.

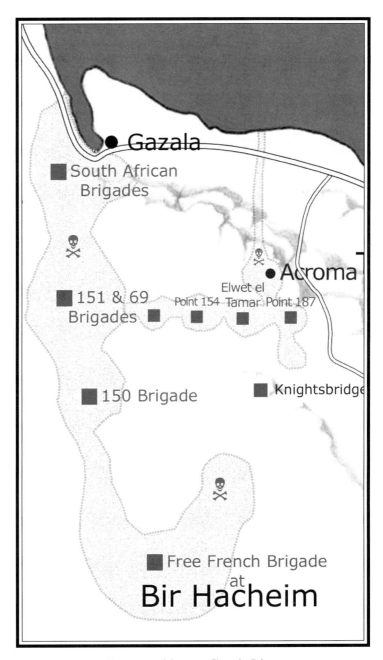

Boxes making up Gazala Line

4. Brigades of allied armour were free to move around behind the Gazala line and in amongst the infantry Boxes.

These factors represented the outer defences of Tobruk. Tobruk itself had its own garrison and fortifications.

It should be remembered that it was not the intention to maintain the fortifications within Tobruk itself. Tobruk could not be held by supplying it from the sea any longer.

AUTHOR BRINGS DOWN A PLANE

On one of the days in mid-March, near Acroma, the day's dust storm had just begun to die down around 5p.m. and we had all come out of our dust-filled dugouts for some fresh air. The author had just removed the dust cover from his Bren gun and fixed the 100-round circular drum to it when the sound of an approaching enemy aircraft was signalled. The sky above us was just clear enough to see it approaching travelling from east to west at about 1,500 feet altitude. Firing from the hip and helped by tracers I was able to bring a steady stream of shots into the macchi by aiming off ahead of it. Even before it disappeared into the west above the dust we could all hear it in trouble, spluttering with misfire, and leaving a trail of black smoke while descending all the time.

The guys around all cheered and were certain the macchi had been brought down. It was later established that it crashed ahead of us in our own lines, the pilot apparently taken prisoner. The platoon officer put in a claim for it, but it was some time before we were credited with it.

Identification of the plane was confirmed when I was able to report having seen the Roman fasciculi on the Italian plane's wings as it flew overhead.

From across the gun pits Cecil Ritson shouted, "Up Durban High School!" and I answered, "Up Glenwood High School!" and we both felt that settled the matter of school rivalry between us.

The Roman Fasciculus was part of the regalia displayed by Mussolini's empire in places like Fort Capuzzo. It was also placed as an insigna on the wings of Italian military aircraft.

CHAPTER IX

The first impression you had of the Gazala line was of its incompleteness if not actual chaos. It was a loose connection of boxes, tracts, minefields and barbed wire strung hastily together to stop Rommel advancing from positions he held in El Agheila, Msus and Benghazi. It was made even more a mysterious site by the ridges and wadis, which furrowed the desert there. Multi-national troops had garrisoned Gazala until the arrival of the First Division of South Africans in April 1942. Minefields were not clearly defined and the Polish previous occupants had not been able to hand over relevant diagrams to us, the new tenants, indicating mine-free areas.

Uncharted mines were everywhere and of every kind, planted indiscriminately. The Polish homeland had been ravaged by the Germans in 1939 and the Poles were revengeful. It was our first encounter with such an attitude amongst Allied soldiers. The Poles had haphazardly planted mines close to their pathways and positions. Even the Germans were a little careless in their own mine laying. Consequently we lost men. Richard Platt, later, at Alamein, told me how he lost his dugout mate there and poured out the whole story.

Defence positions were mainly scratched out of the desert scrub and in places where rock was less likely to interfere with burrowing. New positions were constantly being built but enemy surveillance made it risky and likely to bring down a hail of enemy artillery fire.

The Gazala line ran for 40 miles more or less south from an inlet on the Mediterranean coastline to Bir Hacheim (See page 133).

The Gazala area was intended as the main bulwark defending Tobruk and lay some 30 miles to the west of it. If Rommel struck northeastwards it would be with an attack on this, the most northern sector of the front line guarding the coastal road into Tobruk. It would

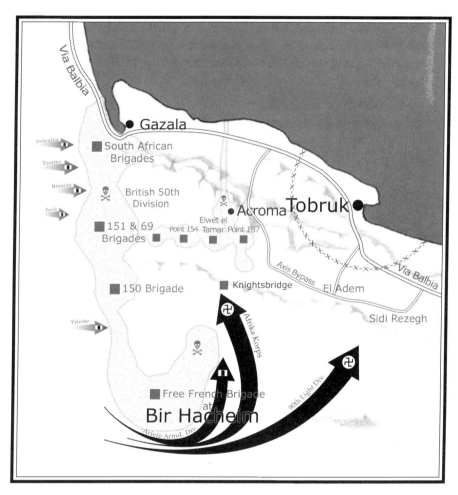

The Gazala Line attacked on 26th May 1942, showing all the boxes at the outer defences of Tobruk, the infantry attacks on the South African brigades in the north at Gazala and the enemy panzers of the Afrika Corps surrounding Bir Hachiem in the south.

also be the site of any major advance of the allies and with these factors in mind the front was kept fighting trim, possibly to the detriment of defending Tobruk itself. The deteriorated situation of the British Fleet in the Mediterranean had put the defence of Malta at risk and the navy had made it clear that it would not be in a position to guarantee supplying yet another siege of Tobruk for very long. There was no doubt in the minds of the infantry holding the Gazala line in strength that, with appropriate armour, the way should be forward and towards the west. At no stage of holding this line was there any suggestion of withdrawal from it, but certain fatal mistakes were made at the highest rank which were to turn the whole Gazala front into a living hell.

The anti-tank defences of the front line where I fought were the totally discredited Boyes anti-tank rifle and Sticky bombs – no match for German weaponry or even Italian. Of course we had tanks, but they were scattered piecemeal over a forty-mile front and roamed around between the boxes in the south and east.

MAY 26TH 1942

On May 26th at 3pm Ray Lee had succeeded in smashing the protruding face of a rock in our weapon pit facing the Italo-Germans at Gazala and having emerged from my afternoon nap, I was filling sand bags to strengthen the parapet when the enemy attacked the Gazala line in force. It had been considered touch-and-go as to whether our own offensive would come before Rommel's. Whichever, would have been welcomed. Everyone in the line was bored to tears and mid-summer in the Libyan desert didn't help. My Bren gun was tripod-mounted for anti-aircraft and we had a Browning off one of our crashed aircraft at the ready with long belts of ammunition for ground defence. Four Italian divisions of infantry were now flung headlong against the northern sector of the Gazala positions and before their infantry became visible there had been a short, sustained Italian artillery barrage which had included 210mm shells from what was said to be naval guns. Shells exploded on and around our positions churning up the desert and splintering rocks with ferocious bangs, and it was apparent they were a part of a generalised attack but tanks in number were notably absent. It meant they would be in use elsewhere, probably in the south.

We were delighted when Support Company on our right began to train their Vickers on mid-distant figures flitting in short rushes towards our entrenchments. Within a few minutes of intensive fire, the Vickers had the Italians in a near panic. They called in distress to each other and stretcher-bearers came out for the wounded. Hours passed and their ground attack petered out. It was then the Stuka attacks followed.

Blamey O.C. of 'C' Company described the Stuka raids graphically:

Usually seven to nine planes came over together to attack. When the Stukas arrived there was no question of inactivity, for every gun and rifle opened up on them, thus giving us the opportunity of hitting back.

Everybody was keyed up and excitement rose to fever pitch, especially when a direct hit was scored on an attacker. Bedlam seemed to be let loose with the rattle of small arms fire and the deep throated bark of the Bofors-guns. The noise was intensified by the scream of the Stukas as they dived down on their targets, to be followed by the crunch, crunch of exploding bombs.

One Stuka collected a direct hit from a Bofors-gun when it was directly over our positions. For one horrible moment I thought it was coming down on top of us but, with a terrific roar, it crashed and burst into flames in the minefield immediately to our front. This was a thrilling sight; there were yells of applause and some wit called out, "Fresh meat for dinner tonight!" It is extraordinary how callous we became. The crew of two were of course burnt with the wreckage. Later they were buried and crosses erected over the graves.

The total score that afternoon in our regimental area was five Stukas shot down and eleven were damaged.

Italian prisoners taken said they had been told the desert ahead of them was clear all the way to Tobruk. They were surprised and anguished to discover our resistance.

My own diary reads:

Tuesday, 26th May '42

Awoke with a shock in the afternoon when Jerry artillery advanced and shelled us. It became an absolute inferno of bursting shells along the whole line. In front, behind and on the flanks they burst at close quarters showering us with shrapnel. Then during this, 107 dive-bombers in eleven waves attacked the line.

Damage and casualties were slight but it was nonetheless beautiful and spectacular. Stood-to all night and this morning (27th May) the enemy infantry had closed to 700 yards and mortars and shelling continued afresh. Intermittent firing of all weapons all day. Under small arms fire towards evening.

On 27 May parties of enemy infantry could be seen approaching the minefields before the South Africa front and were fired on by the defending artillery and machine guns. Two enemy armoured cars were knocked out. Fourteen P.O.W's were taken by 'B' Company that day: all were identified as belonging to No. 8 Company, 2nd Battalion, 361 German Lorried infantry Regiment. Two battalions were estimated to be facing the S.A. front at this stage. Next day enemy forces advanced against the South African positions in some strength, supported by tanks and gained a lodgement in the minefields, but they went no further and suffered casualties from defensive fire. At dawn on 29 May, the Italian Nabratha Division made an attack in some force, which was pinned down and collapsed under heavy fire from the positions held by the C.T.H. and T.S.

After their failure in this attack, 200-250 Italians approached the C.T.H. under cover of a white flag; they were made prisoners-of-war by 1/T.S. and N.M.R. Approximately 20 minutes later, another 100 odd enemy surrendered to C.T.H.

Thursday, 28th May '42

Artillery fire more intense during the day. Practically no appearance of our planes at all. Terrific luftwaffe activity, but order (came) through not to fire at aircraft or to wash in order to save water and ammo. Believe tank battles to south are very successful for our side.

Friday, 29th May '42

Still great artillery activity. German and Ito. aircraft in supreme command of sky over our line. See on average one of ours (planes) a day. Order to fire on planes reinstated. Heavy mortar fire with shrapnel showering all over the place.

<u>Saturday, 30th May '42</u>

Savoia Machetti* bomber direct from Rome carrying big shots brought down half a mile away before our eyes. Ito and Jerry fighters strafing at low height continuously all day. Tickled them up with the Bren. Artillery very alive on both sides.

<u>Sunday, 31st May '42</u>

Front considerably quieter. News of battle behind us still uncertain, but everyone very confident. Sun bloody hot all day and life is unbearable in the early afternoon.

<u>Monday, 1st June '42</u>

Usual shelling and air activity. Stukas by the hundreds going over all day. Still no appearance of our air force.

150 BRIGADE BOX

The 150th Brigade held a Box west of the Knightsbridge Box, between Bir Hacheim and Gazala. It now became the centre of Rommel's attention. His panzers penetrated the minefields on each side of the 150th's box and on June 1st at noon it was completely overrun as part of the battle in the Cauldron which later attracted so much international attention of the media. With this success Rommel was able to take up defensive positions in the cauldron; his supplies began to come in directly from the west through the minefields instead of around Bir Hacheim.

The loss of the 150th Brigade Box was deliberately withheld from us in the north and our attention was drawn to events occurring in the Cauldron and at Bir Hacheim. The Box had been overrun by Rommel in 12 hours with the loss of 3000 men. (see map page 158)

<u>Tuesday, 2nd June '42</u>

Artillery (fire) very close this morning and destroyed the Officers' Mess and the Colonel's car. Both of which brought out little

---

*The aircraft obviously making for Bir Hacheim and the Cauldron carried two Italian colonels, four subaltens and important documents.

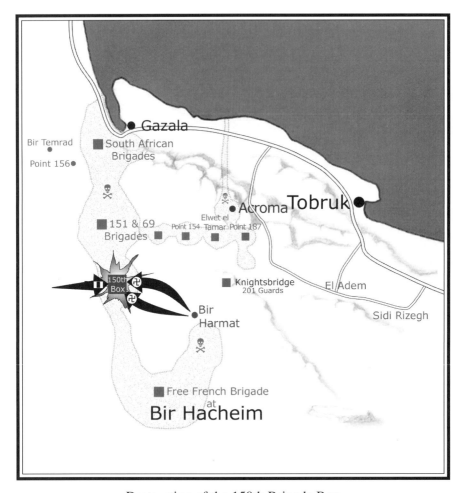

Destruction of the 150th Brigade Box

On 1st June '42 the 150th Brigade box was fiercely attacked by Rommel who penetrated it from two sides. The loss of this box was deliberately withheld from the troops at Gazala in the north.

sympathy. Wind blowing off the desert and the worst sand-dust storm for many months. News of Jerry defeat came through. They lost 260 tanks, etc. Enemy fighter activity in the afternoon.

During these awful days we were disturbed by news filtering through from areas where German tanks and motorised infantry had once struck at Sidi Rezegh* thirty miles **behind** our lines at Gazala. We knew that the whole battle for Tobruk hinged on the boxes at Bir Hacheim to the south and on the guards regiments holding the boxes at Tamar, Acroma and Knightsbridge immediately behind us. Our respect for guardsmen went back beyond W.W.I. to the Boer War and their debacle at Spion Kop, and triumph on Wagon Hill at the seige of Ladysmith where, in this war we had trained.

"The English Guards with their strange and slightly automaton code of behaviour were peculiarly suited to this sort of action. It was something they understood. A position was given you to fortify, and then you got the order to hold it to the last round and the last man. It was simply a matter of progressing to that final point, unless, of course, the enemy got tired first. One simply had to remain there firing through the dust and something or other would come out of the muddle. Whether or not the ground was wisely chosen, whether or not victory or disaster emerged from the struggle, was not the essential point. The essential thing was that the Guards had been given this piece of ground to hold and the reputation of the regiment required that it should not be given up until the regiment was wiped out or got the order to retire." **

The Box at Knightsbridge was the next most important focus of attention after Bir Hacheim. General Ritchie's main problem during the Gazala debacle had been to give infantry protection with tanks to the many boxes now in danger of being overrun or by-passed by the Germans. It meant splitting his armour and in this piecemeal state it was liable to be obliterated by the panzers. Frustrated by the delays at Bir Hacheim Rommel turned on Knightsbridge and its 201 Guards:

---

* Where a whole brigade of South African Infantry less than a year earlier had been destroyed.

** Alan Moorehead "A Year of Battle"

"The 90th Light combined with Italian infantrymen, tanks, artillery and dive-bombers fell upon the box in a series of massed attacks from all sides. An immense battle-cloud rolled across the Capuzzo track and the whole area was enveloped in continuous sandstorms. In the unreal gloom the men fought. The Stukas came back again and again. The enemy artillery got on to the box from several sides at once, and there was hardly a yard in the target area that was not ripped and ravaged with high explosive. In regular waves the German and Italian infantry came right up to the minefields, and there they broke, divided and fell back. It was Waterloo all over again.

"So these odd gawky officers with their prickly moustachios, their little military affectations, their high-pitched voices and their little jokes from the world of Mayfair and Ascot, kept bringing their men up to the enemy, and the men, because they were the picked soldiers of the regular army and native Englishmen and Scots, did exactly as they were told. Knightsbridge did not break because it could not break. It stood through this maelstrom as a rock will stand against the sea."*

Bad News & Dust Storms

Apart from bad news out of your own front line, the dust storm is probably the most devastating demoraliser in desert warfare. Its smell, its attack on the eyes and the very water you drink, its capacity to get you lost and to alienate you from everyone and everything and to reduce armies to entropy has to be experienced. Alan Moorhead, a visiting reporter to the Gazala front commented descriptively on his first encounter with one:

> "Millions of tank and tyre treads had ground the thin crust on top of the sand into a loose powder. When a hot, strong wind blew from the south yesterday morning everyone got ready. At midday the visibility was fifty yards with occasional clear patches. At 14:00 hours it was 20 yards; at 16:00 hours for the most part it was nil."

Illusory shapes could arise from churned-up dust to merge with heat mirages creating phantasmagoria, sometimes beautiful sometimes

---

* Alan Moorehead "A Year of Battle"

ominous. There was nothing anyone could do about it. Usually with such a storm you lay doggo. Having located your favourite spot for such an emergency you covered your head with a towel, newspaper or piece of calico. It was rare to be able to share such occasions with a friend in discussion or a game of cards, or even writing letters because of the intrusive thrusts of dust until it was over.

> "It was not until nearly 21:00 hours, when the sun, coloured pale ice-blue by the sand, was setting, that the storm began to die down. One by one the things around us took shape, and as visibility extended from a hundred to five hundred yards the desert began to take on its normal contours again. The whole landscape looked worn-out and utterly desolate after this hateful day."*

Wednesday, 3rd June '42

Before breakfast stukas overhead. Bofors ack-ack brought down a stuka before our eyes…In the evening more stukas bombed close by and snapped the effect. Artillery shelling more accurate and some casualties.

On June 5th and 6th our armour met Rommel's in the cauldron and the Seventh Armoured Division was scattered for the second time in ten days.

At Gazala we had been told that all was well and we were winning in the Cauldron. The next moment we had to create a diversion in the north to take pressure off Bir Hacheim and convoys trying to get through to Malta. In fact our attack on June 7th was that of only a boy doing a man's job, a composite battalion doing the work of a division.

When you study the map of Gazala/Tobruk region the Gazala Line appears convoluted by the shape of the minefield which extended solidly for 40 miles southward from the sea coast to Bir Hacheim. The decision to lay it was made by General Ritchie and his two lieutenant generals. Strategically it was a splendid idea. The mistake was that it was vulnerable because it was not fully manned. It meant

---

*ibid

that while Rommel was heavily engaged at Bir Hacheim and killing British armour off piecemeal in the Cauldron, German and Italian sappers were clearing a way through the 'solid' minefield halfway along the 40 mile course. This let German reinforcements through and the trap laid for Rommel in the Cauldron was aborted. From that moment the 8th Army was faced with a Dunkirk. Everyone would have to get out quick or be 'put in the bag.'* The infantry dug in securely in the North, were outraged. The battlefield was to become a W.W.I. Mons with thousands of men able and ready to fight moving westward to Benghazi but instead to retreat under orders eastwards.

It soon became apparent that the attack begun on the 26th May and first directed at the northern sector of Gazala was a feint and that the main attack was southwards towards the box at Bir Hacheim. What had always worried the Allied infantry most was the German panzers. Now they and their motorised infantry, had begun their assault on the southern flank of the Gazala line supported by waves of aircraft, mainly stuka dive-bombers.

Included in the hostile forces was the 90th Light Division which always headed Rommel's major attacks. The South African Second Division had lost a whole brigade of infantry, albeit motorised, at Sidi Rezegh in November of the previous year and there was hardly a man in the First South African Division dug in at Gazala that did not have a friend or relative lost at Rezegh to German armour. Divisional H.Q. were aware of this sensitivity and made every effort to keep all ranks informed about events at Bir Hacheim.

The Free French there fought with great valour and for nearly two weeks the B.B.C. nine o'clock news as well as that of nine Battalion H.Q.'s of the First S.A. Division updated the troops. First of all the information was that Rommel's armour was trapped in the British minefields north of Bir Hacheim and south of us; then that British tanks were moving into the resulting cauldron for the kill; then that Rommel had broken out of the cauldron and had turned his attention to the Free French but things were still favourable; then that the outcome at Bir Hacheim was hopeless; then oh, oh! that allied tank

---

*Be made 'P.O.W' ... prisoner of war.

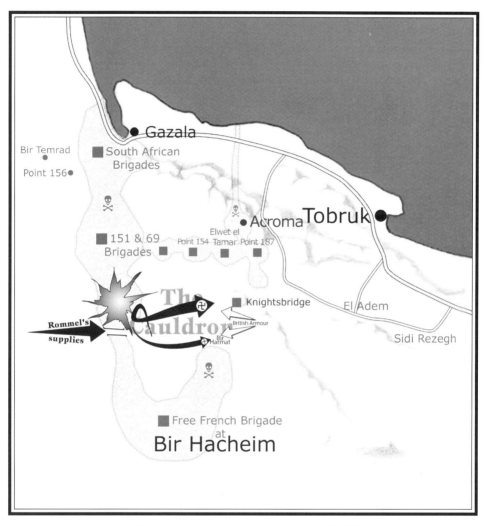

Bir Temrad
South African Brigades
Point 156
Gazala
151 & 69 Brigades
Elwet el
Point 154 Tamar Point 187
Acroma
Tobruk
The Cauldron
Knightsbridge
El Adem
British Armour
Rommel's supplies
Bir Harmat
Sidi Rezegh
Free French Brigade at
Bir Hacheim

British Armour counter attacks in the Cauldron.

The piecemeal attacks of British tanks on the Germans dug-in 88mm guns were ineffectual and Allied armour was practically wiped out.

forces had had a setback, Bir Hacheim had fallen and then the silence which always warned of bad news.

In the Gazala line there were signs everywhere of deep resentment at the prospect of the whole army being bullied into a retreat by circumstances beyond us, some 25 miles away. The percolating news was that bad no one could sleep and simultaneously man guns at the alert day after day. As the evening of the 13th June drew on, resentment turned to ribaldry and faintly across the dugouts and slit trenches I remember someone singing "The Wings of an Angel" to the army doggerel:

> *'I wish I had the balls of an elephant*
> *and the prick of a kangaroo,*
> *I'd fuck all the girls in creation*
> *And I'd send the results to the zoo.'*

Up to this stage the Gazala line had held, and the effectiveness of its boxes had been demonstrated, always providing the British armour remained reasonably intact. General Auchinleck was pleased with his Eighth Army and our First Division in the Gazala northern sector received warm congratulations from its supremo general Dan Pienaar. After this however, the joyride became potholed and bumpy. Eyes now focused on the Free French Box at Bir Hacheim (the Well of Dogs) in the southernmost pole of the Gazala line. Their connection with the Foreign Legion reminded us of Jimmy Reen's song "The Legion of the Lost" which was still sung out of exasperation when the dust and sandstorms blew relentlessly. Remembering the defeatism of France in 1940 and her subsequent actions under the Vichy government I was personally uneasy about anything Francaise especially when it constituted our extreme left wing against the panzer might of Erwin Rommel and his lore of outflanking movements which had caught us with our pants down several times in the past. In the event we suffered in another manner at Gazala. Somehow the battle at Bir Hacheim gained the hype of the media and the R.A.F entered into a remarkable love affair with the Free French at Hacheim. Whilst at Gazala we were being bombed almost hourly by Stukas completely without R.A.F. air support, Hacheim also being bombed mercilessly <u>was</u> supported readily and persistently by the R.A.F.

Meanwhile, at Gazala, we came under merciless shell fire day in and day out. Some of the shelling was from 210mm Italian naval guns.

The ways in which men dealt with incessant bombardment of their dug-in positions were legion. There was no recommended procedure laid down in an army manual. If your mind could still do as it was told, you made yourself smaller, crouching or drawing your knees up to your chest trying to get your face into your own lap. In the end, it didn't matter too much what you did with your body because it was your mind which was suffering. Usually, in despair, it was liable to pick itself clean of all relevances except the malignant process of the bombardment itself like you pick a bunch of grapes until you have only the bared stalk left with its sad little points where the grapes had once held on to their sanity. The grapes were the things you valued in your life; somehow you had stored them in the spare rooms of your militarised mind…loved ones, even those you detested, if they could hold your attention, fragments of poetry, whole tracts of it even Paradise Lost appropriately if you were lucky, not in a flowing stream like Virginia Woolf, or as Milton's fabled, mythical and allusive scenarios. And through the long days, even weeks of shelling you shook them out with every cannonade, again and again, until the mind became slowly or quickly threadbare and all you had left then were its rags and tatters of barrage and bombardment. You retained then, only by the skin of its teeth, the skeletal stalk of cause and effect.

The cause could be isolated by your esoleptic senses driven inwards by a hostile world and now sharpened just to detect the 'be-boom' of the particular gun that had your range closest… and then the whisper and slither of approaching hell as it first licked its way through the ethers and begins to shriek as it closes in on the dust and smokey precincts of your fragile earthwork and inevitably, the unhideable monstrous bang of its trying to marry with and elope with the vestige of your consciousness. Usually it was only for a few hours at a time, but enraged barrages could go on all night, pounding and crashing so that the brittle stem of reason might crumble. It was then finally I might have to repeat my kindergarten times table as a last resort surrounding and defending my cringing sanity with its protecting laager.

There were those who swallowed their dignity and made themselves as small a target as possible by merely sitting on the floor in a corner with their knees bent and grasped around by the arms and with head bowed in their laps, reminding me of the current war song "Knees up Mother Brown."

> *"Knees up Mother Brown,*
> *Knees up Mother Brown,*
> *If you don't get your knees up*
> *You'll get the breeze-up*
> *Knees up Mother Brown."*

DISASTER IN THE CAULDRON

The finale in the Cauldron was June 5th and 6th when Rommel laid a trap for British armour that was totally successful. He had 200 anti-tank guns partly dug-in and camouflaged, mainly 88mm against which no tank could survive for long.

The British armour, most of it, but never enough of it was led on to the trap by the usual ruse of some retreating, easy targets. When the range was right the German anti-tank guns burst into action and immediately the allied atack was halted. The 22nd Armoured Brigades, the same which had failed to protect the 5th Infantry Brigade of South Africans at Sidi Rezegh ran straight into the trap. Dozens of Crusaders and Grants (U.S.A. supplied) brewed up as the 88mm guns got them into their sights. It was the most brilliantly successful ambush of the desert war. It spelt out the doom of fortress Tobruk, the Gazala Line and Allied hopes and wishes to reach Tripoli for another year. Up north in Gazala the South African Infantry Division set out on our ill-starred diversion to relieve pressure on the Cauldron and Bir Hacheim. No one can say to this day how many British troops were lost on that day. The Cauldron which was supposed to destroy Rommell had swallowed all hope of Armoured superiority for the Allies until El Alameim. Rommel after June 7th was able to devote almost his entire attention then to attacking Bir Hacheim.

CHAPTER X

ACTION ON JUNE 7th. '42

With great bravery time and again the Free French beat off attacks on their Box and the world watched breathless. At Gazala however we were not surprised when ordered to create a diversion to relieve the pressures down south. Our rank and file would have preferred a divisional onslaught on enemy positions dug in to our front.

To relieve pressure on the southern sectors of the Gazala line a diversion was ordered against the enemy opposite to three battalions of the First South African Infantry Division in the northern sector. From north to south these three regiments were the Royal Durban Light Infantry (R.D.L.I.), the N.M.R. and the Cape Town Highlanders (C.T.H.). Each battalion was to attack the enemy (four Italian infantry divisions) emplacements facing the Gazala line with a company of about 120 men. The combined attack began two hours before daylight on June 7th. Captain Blamey M.C was in command of the three N.M.R. platoons and their supporting mortars. He had wanted to take his own 'C' Company some of whom knew the ground which contained as its two objectives firstly a wadi called "Outpost Wadi", a few hundred yards in front of the N.M.R. and thereafter Point 156 which was a further 1200 yards due west which was known to be occupied by the enemy in force. At the gap in the wire leading out into no-man's-land in the dark at 3:00am there was a delay because certain supporting elements like signallers were late in assembling. This was a critical factor because the operation was timed to occur just before dawn and to coincide with a plastering of Point 156 with 25-pounder gunfire precisely at 5:00am It had also made the waiting troops anxious to get on with the job and to rush things.

Captain Blamey had asked to have his own complete company under his command but was overruled by the Colonel who had been newly-posted to the regiment and decided that a composite attack be undertaken with a platoon from each of the three rifle companies, an unfortunate decision which added to the resulting confusion.

The operation was a complete failure in front of the N.M.R., with the R.D.L.I on its right flank and the C.T.H on its left. All N.M.R. platoons were under-strength and volunteers were called on to fill the gaps. This was how I came to volunteer for the operation. Merging into the riflemen before the attack I linked up with Jack Gray, from Matatiele in Natal. Jack, always a great sportsman saw it as an impending innings like a game of cricket and offered me a massive slug from a bottle of gin he was carrying with him. I took to the event thereafter with greater enthusiasm. I had never tasted neat gin before and Jack and I decided to stick together. We were soon to be disillusioned and in the course of events became separated.

As dawn began to break, our fears mounted. I had seen no officers since the attack began. We were just behind B9 platoon's advanced position. Away down on our left flank I saw men of the Cape Town Highlanders advancing, the rising sun, behind us, beginning to pick out their tunics and helmets. Then a murderous fire opened up from the front pinning down platoon B9 with anti-tank guns firing against us with open sights. The dawning light made us increasingly sitting targets for these and the Italian machine gunners. Casualties were occurring all along the line and calls for stretcher bearers intermingled with the cries of wounded men. Amongst those who rushed to help with the wounded was Bill Stevens, another volunteer on that terrible morning. Bill's songs took on a haunting note after June 7th.

Until that moment there were no officers apparent.

Amongst my many friends in the attack on that day there was Geoffrey Frank.

Geoffrey Frank was a fresh-faced, very bright school companion of mine in the top form of Durban Preparatory High School. He and his buddy Colin Spence occupied the first two places read out at

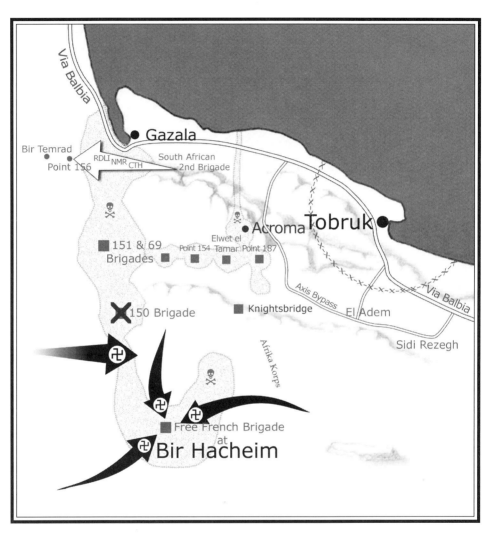

Diversion at Gazala to help Bir Hacheim in south,
7th June 1942

school assembly weekly, by the headmaster who thus emphasised the importance of learning and school reports.

But Geoffrey was becoming even better known for his remarkable talent as a pianist. These two boys later carried their intellectual avant-garde right through all grades at Durban High School as well, a very remarkable achievement. At prep school, they had attracted a group around them, similar to themselves of which I was on the periphery, only because the singing teacher, Miss Dora Jackson had discovered I had a good voice. I was therefore invited with the 'two' and some other pupils for special coaching in singing followed by high tea at Miss Jackson's residence.

When war broke out I found myself in the same regiment as Geoffrey and many others from school. We were in different regimental companies, and I soon discovered that his family had four members spread around the battalion made up of different ranks and of which Geoffrey was the youngest and a private. On active service the battalion's mustering dropped dramatically, through sustaining casualties, and I soon found myself in a rifle platoon, as a Bren gunner under sergeant Ken Frank, one of Geoffrey's elder brothers.

In the regiment I was on nodding terms with Geoffrey and didn't get too close, not because at school he had been an egghead, but for another more embarrassing reason. In the last year of prep school our class had produced an act from Shakespeare's Twelfth Night which was presented for parental viewing in a concert at the Durban Beach Pavilion, and who should be given, in true Shakespearean mode, the two female leads Olivia and Viola but both these pupils who were also the class teacher's favourites. The pair, entering the world of histrionics for the first time, took to it with gusto, gathering their feminine attributes into a presentation that was very realistic, even if not viewed with too much approval by the more macho pupils of the school.

No doubt my presence in the same regiment brought back memories of their 'first night' and a dress rehearsal Geoffrey would now rather not have recalled.

7th JUNE 1942 – A VERY LONG DAY
Written testimony of Private Richard Platt M.M.*

The Free French down South at Bir Hacheim were taking a hammering, so in order to create a diversion it was decided to mount an attack in our sector.

Alan Morehead in his book '*The Desert War*' is critical of the Allied High Command for not having launched a full-scale attack from the Gazala line at that time. The 2nd Brigade was fighting fit and ready to go, but all we engaged in, using Morehead's words, were 'penny packet patrols' which were ineffective and could only result in heavy casualties.

Our platoon B9 was chosen from 'B' Company, and since we had been in dugouts for about two months were keen to get off our bums and get into action. The monotony had been relieved at the end of May when the Italians attacked in strength on the flats to our right, between us and the R.D.L.I. It was an abortive effort dealt with by our Vickers machine guns with their new Mark VIII ammunition. The enemy withdrew in disorder with heavy casualties. Their turn was to come.

On the morning of June 7th we were ordered to rendezvous at 3:30am at a position in front of our lines known as 'Outpost Wadi'.** Most of us knew this area well having previously patrolled there.

I had picked up a German Mauser rifle on one of these patrols. It was in beautiful condition and I used it to fire at low flying enemy aircraft. I loaded the magazine with one ball, one armour piercing and one tracer to indicate where my shots were going.

Our platoon was on the left flank, C.11 on our right with A5 on the flats on our right. We downed a mug of coffee before we left, and little did we know that this was to sustain us for the next sixteen hours.

---

* Later to win the Military Medal for other actions.
** The Polish troops before our occupation had called it 'Cossack Wadi.'

The attack was doomed from the start. The signallers failed to arrive so we advanced without proper communications. In the dark, we overshot our objective without knowing it as the enemy laid low and let us pass. On we blissfully went into 'the Devil's Cauldron.' We came up against a minefield and a few of the enemy on outpost beat it as we fired on them. Then all hell let loose. As it became lighter we discovered that we were up against a heavily defended position. It later transpired that it was an Italian machine gun battalion.

I have never known such concentrated fire from such an assortment of weaponry. Light machine guns, heavy machine guns, anti-tank guns, twenty millimetre Bredas, forty millimetre Bredas, you name it, they let us have the lot. The anti-tank gun was firing tracer shells from the right flank. The shells were whooshing past like an express train, great balls of fire grinding their way into the distance as they ricocheted off the hard ground. The C.T.H. on the ridge to our left were taking a similar pounding, and before long they were withdrawing under heavy shellfire.

Before we set out we were each given a rack of two-inch mortar bombs to carry. These were to serve the two-inch mortar that was operated by Nigel Downes. The mortar was a simple contraption consisting of a base plate, a spirit level, two-inch pipe and a protractor-like gadget to measure the angle of fire. Nigel went into action immediately, and we were only too pleased to keep him well supplied with bombs and thus get rid of our lethal parcels. Why they picked on the biggest man in the platoon to do this job I will never know. He was magnificent. Lying there on the open ground he must have been a prime target, whilst he methodically plonked his bombs into the enemy positions. Our riflemen were finding targets, and Pooch Marais firing the Bren hit the box of ammunition a man was carrying on his back. Man and box vanished in a ball of flame.

Our casualties started to mount. Geoff Frank was hit in the arm; Johnnie Chowles in the head, and Peter Edmonds our corporal in the knee; all three were attended to by a medical orderly by the name of Folkey. He went from man to man cursing as the bullets whizzed around him. It was an absolute miracle he wasn't hit. For his bravery he was awarded the M.M. Jock Gordon Cumming was hit by a shell from the anti-tank gun, and I think Ron Brown died a similar fate.

A Basuto medical orderly was looking after Peter Edmonds and Johnnie Chowles in a shell crater, when a shell from one of our own 25 pounders burst next to them. I remember the black man's tin hat bowling across the desert. It must have been the end of all three of them. I remember thinking some time later, what must have gone through the mind of that black medical orderly. There he was mixed up in the white man's war devotedly serving his white masters.

Geoff Frank was a brilliant pianist. He died of shock the following day in Italian hands. There was simply no way we could move him under such murderous fire. Peter Edmonds was a very popular section leader. He was full of fun. We used to sit outside our dugouts in the Gazala Line at night watching the Italian anti aircraft guns firing tracers at our planes. Peter used to shout "*there go the goofu guns shooting shit balls at the moon.*"

Johnnie Chowles another fun loving youngster had only recently joined us. I think he must have had a premonition of what was to come. He was very silent when we set out from our dugouts early that morning.

It was obvious that we were serving no purpose staying where we were. We had lost contact with our platoon commander and sergeant, having simply left them way behind in the dark. We were being carved up, and the shells from our own artillery meant for the enemy, were falling amongst us. I shouted to the chaps to withdraw section by section, with the other two sections giving covering fire. I recall Brian Keal crawling towards me whilst I was standing, firing my tommy gun over his head. His eyes seemed to be pleading '*keep that bloody gun up!*' Suddenly, the gun bucked in my hands and blood was spurting out of the top of my left thumb. I thought the drum must have exploded. In fact an enemy bullet had hit the drum magazine plumb centre thus preventing it from giving me another navel.

We gradually got ourselves out of trouble and headed for the shelter of Cossack Wadi. On the way I met a very dejected Pooch Marais. He was very down at the loss of his friend Johnnie Chowles whom he knew well in civvy life. I relieved him of the Bren. We were being shelled heavily but under cover of the forward slope of the Wadi were fairly safe. We were short of ammo, and before long an armoured car was on its way. As it entered the Wadi the anti-tank gun on the flats scored a direct hit. In seconds the car was a blazing inferno; the poor driver and his mate didn't stand a chance. Another car followed shortly and was hit in the wheel. The driver, an F.F.B. chap by the name of Naude baled out, but later returned and drove the car in. He was awarded the M.M. for his brave act. I went to fetch some ammo for the Bren when a shell exploded close by. I felt a wrench on my left arm. My bunny jacket sleeve from the cuff to the elbow was in shreds and my arm hadn't been touched. I began to think I was immortal.

I grabbed some ammo for the Bren and went to the edge of the Wadi to try and get a sight of the anti-tank gun that had knocked out our two armoured cars. Bob Bluett our platoon officer shouted across, *"are you trying to win a gong?"*

I replied that I wasn't prepared to sit on my bum facing the wrong way when we had an enemy to our front. We made our peace about a month later when he took me out to dinner at a posh restaurant in Alexandria.

I didn't have to wait long before I saw an Ito strutting nonchalantly across the desert 600 yards away. I put the sight up to 600 yards and gave him a burst. I forgot to aim off, for the dust kicked up behind him and he dived into what appeared to be a gun pit. At that moment an artillery officer came up looking for a target. I gave him the range and within minutes the 25 pounder plastered the gun pit.

We were sporadically shelled for the rest of the day, and at sundown our artillery hammered away at the enemy position prior to our withdrawal to our starting positions. At about 9:30pm we pulled out, and at about midnight were back in our dugouts, worn out and totally demoralised.

Five of the chaps from our platoon we would never see again, whilst five were wounded. It was a fruitless exercise which, if it had been properly planned and supported with armour could have resulted in a major success, thus relieving the Free French at Bir Hacheim.

SAYER ON THE SEVENTH

Poor Eddy Sayer! His doting parents, upper middle class Durbanites, had allowed him to join the war at an early age. He was younger than I was and had, until then, been the youngest in the platoon. Yet he brought with him qualities derived from both parents, wisdom from his father and a freshness and naivete from his mother. He had the elders of the platoon in fits of laughter and they competed for his attention. Eddy's advent in the regiment began a friendship for me that extended many years into our post demobilisation which had been premature, he being released early from war-torn Europe as a prisoner-of-war, and my discharge incapacitated by wounds just before the war's end.

Like me he had volunteered to supplement the fighting patrol of divisional troops going out to create a diversion in front of the Gazala Line, some said to help an allied convoy struggling to reach Malta, others said to draw off Rommel's forces fighting our armour in the cauldron behind the Gazala minefields. In the day-long mayhem of June 7th Eddy had just disappeared along with scores of others apart from the known wounded who could not be carried off the battlefield. Even in the happy times we shared after demob, Eddy had been reticent to discuss his capture. The event had humiliated him, and his P.O.W. experiences added to his gloom. I was accepted into his family, often living with them, because more than anything they said I could make their son happy.

On June 7th 1942 according to Eddy he was given a message to take to the platoon commander on his flank. It was still dark; he had no idea of troop dispositions and soon ran into continuous fire whichever way he turned. As dawn broke he was able to observe Italian troops all around him. He lay doggo until he was discovered by the enemy and made a prisoner unscathed physically but scarred mentally for years to come.

TERRY SMEDLEY

This is my own account of the demise of my friend Terry Smedley. In the retreat on June 7th, and it was a retreat, let's not make any bones about that, Terry Smedley was on my left and, two men separated me from Jack Gray on my right. The machine gun fire from the rear and the left flank was merciless, zipping and streaking, whizzing and ricocheting with arching and windings of tracers. Suddenly Terry wasn't there. I looked back and at the same time heard him shout that he'd been hit. I ran over to him and flung myself down next to him. He had been hit low in the back of the calf, penetrating through to the front and couldn't walk. His Achilles tendon had been severed.

Fortunately Terry had got his webbing and side pack off and I yanked him to his feet. Together we made a larger blob on the featureless flat and must have stuck out because we attracted even heavier fire. At first he grasped me around the waist and used me as a crutch heaving himself with one leg careering like a hobbled giraffe. We fell once or twice. I shed my side pack and that helped. We got going again. Anti-tank shells came from the left, red hot and screaming tearing up the ground and ahead tracers still criss-crossed. I saw someone hit directly. He went down, dying without even a cry. We were both exhausted and breathless and near the end of our tether when we heard our artillery going off and shells began whistling down on to our area. Some started to fall amongst us but the salvos did silence the tracers as the enemy began to get the message. With our last gasp Terry Smedley and I reached the cover of Outpost Wadi. There, Terry's elder brother Jack Smedley anxiously awaited him and grasped him from me.

Having got Terry back to the medics who evacuated him and others wounded, under a Red Cross flagged ambulance, I searched for my own platoon A5 who were taking up a defensive position on the enemy side of the Outpost Wadi. There I found Jack Gray rebuilding very rapidly a stone sangar that had been flattened by shelling, probably some days before. We were still 2½ miles in front of the Gazala line. Our stony residence did not look too cosy to me, but shells began to fall around us and we took occupation of it horizontally and prepared for an enemy counterattack. The sangar rose 18 inches above a flat stone plinth and was comprised of loose, ill-fitting whitish limestone that rattled a little when you brushed against it. But the walls were about 20 inches thick, just enough to keep out shell fragments. None in the hastily prepared line had cover from a direct hit. Jack and I were both exhausted and hoped for some rest before resuming battle with the Italians or falling back to the Gazala line. As it happened we were to spend another 13 hours in the sanger under almost persistent fire and exposed to a merciless sun. Unbeknown to us, a decision had been taken by the officer in command not to withdraw back into the Gazala line from the Wadi until the day's end and darkness had fallen. We had no air or tank support and it was considered too dangerous even to move from our precariously exposed state in daylight. Enemy weapons, especially anti-tank and heavy machine guns had us pinpointed and in no time at all were plastering anything that moved, and they covered the entrances to the Wadi behind us.

Desperately short of ammunition Captain Blamey had signalled for more. The first response was an armoured car loaded down with the desperately needed ammo. As it approached the entrance to the Wadi, it was picked off by the Italian anti-tank guns, brewing up in a thick, black billowing smoke. Two were killed, one was a Durban boy, a member of the Dove family who were the city's funeral directors and had buried my mother just before the war started. A second armoured car heroically repeated the efforts to bring ammo up, and succeeded amidst a hail of shells and machine gun fire.

Shells and mortars kept screaming down on to the area of our flimsy sangars, which were clearly visible to the enemy gunners. And then calamity!… A shell hit the sangar and blew in the wall. All I remember was the shriek of the missile, an ear splitting bang and heavy debris falling on my back.

JACK GRAY

Part of the debris was Jack Gray. In the prolonging silence that always follows such close-call events (I had three of them through the war years) you checked yourself out to see if you were still whole, and then I was aware from groans and expletives and a terrible shuddering that Jack was still alive and so was I. His curses it turned out were not so much for the Italian gunners, as for the fact that the impact had caused him to lose control of his bowels. He was wet through and above the usual sulphurous and cordite fumes of the explosion there was an unholy faecal stench.

Still having to lie flat in the broken sanger we managed to restore the gap in its fragmented wall and then we took stock of ourselves. Neither of us was injured, but Jack was more dazed and shaken than me. He still had some gin left in his liquor flask but we had to help each other drink lest we broke our teeth against the lip of the metal bottle in our rigors. I assisted him off with his trousers, which I spread out decorously to dry in the hot sun for they were only urine stained. But his underpants were badly soiled and I helped cut them off his body with my scout knife. I had had to dump most of my heavy webbing assisting the wounded Smedley, but had fortunately retained in a bren gun pouch a change of underwear amongst some loose 303 cartridges. I gave the underpants to Jack who somehow had cleaned himself up. He received the garment as if it were manna from heaven and soon began to get control of himself. It was then that he began to release throughout the hot long day pent up feelings, which he said had pestered him for some months. His dreams had been warning him of the crisis ahead; as I recall dreams of games like cricket in which he had been frozen stiff at the wicket unable to strike, or even block the oncoming balls; and on sinking ships unable to rescue himself from the rising waters.

While in his shocked state, Jack poured out his miseries which reminded me of my younger brother knocked down by a bicycle while we were at play on a corner near our home in Durban's Florida Road. Unhurt physically, he had remained shocked, dazed and incoherent for several minutes. Jack's shock was not like that which I had seen in others associated with battle fatigue. This was something deeper which I felt was linked to a hidden malaise because he raged on about a growing incapacity to manage the demands of the many sports he had played.

Of course, during those long hours, we talked about 'back home' and our families and did I know any of the Grays at Matatiele. With a snigger I said the only Gray I knew was Oscar Wilde's 'Dorian' (we had a copy circulating somewhere in the squadron). It was always a delicate subject to broach in barrack room talk. He wanted to know what Dorian Gray was about, and we got into surrealism and he raised the matter of a recurrent dream he'd been having but the Italians opened up again with the Besa 40mm.

The sun was stuck overhead and the shimmering heat turned everything into make-believe. Today June 7th 1942 every wiggling mirage was a band of charging troops or an armoured car. The shelling had halted; Jack's damp trousers were steaming on the baking stonework.

"Bastards have gone quiet" Jack said.

"They're having their siesta" I remarked, "usually after lunch between two and four."

"How the hell you know that?" said Jack, turning one of his pockets over to toast dry in the sun.

"In 1934 I went to England with my mama on an Italian boat via Genoa. It was called the Giulio Cesare of course."

Jack came out of his boredom and said: "You must have been there when Musso was strutting around."

"Yes" I answered, "he was threatening everyone with 6 million Italian bayonets."

"That would have scared the shit out of me," Jack retorted.

"As I recall, I nipped a bit, but my mother never turned a hair. When the train from London crossed the frontier back into Italy, and the border guards wanted to search our compartment, she glared at them and ran her fingers across her throat. They just laughed and left us alone."

"That must have been before the Abysinnia war; they hate us now," Jack said as desultory machine gun fire interrupted from mid-distance.

"Oh! They're not like the Germans. Germans are ingrained with arrogance; the Italians have to assume it."

With that I took out my pocket diary and reported the morning's ghastly events.

The bombardment of our three platoons continued off and on during the long, hateful day with the sun beating down on us remorselessly. The glare of the red devil in the sky maintained its malevolent effects on its desert habitat below. June the 7th, midsummer in the Libyan desert and not a single plane, bomber or fighter to give us relief from the enemy gun batteries on the north-west flank pounding our positions.

In the sangar we were spitting stone splinters inhaled from shells bursting on the rocks about us. Cleaned and respectable and now dressed in his trousers, Jack had re-orientated himself and we were lying stretched out close together, head to head. I felt like resuming my anti-shock remedy of shouting the Catholic Credo to shut out the horror of it all. It was comforting to have Jack Gray's comments, even if mainly invectives whenever they came. I began to understand why soldiers became such good comrades as to value each other's loyalty and camaraderie above all else. Jack promised me a bottle of gin if we got through the day alive. I promised him a treat of the biggest meal of rare steaks my favourite restaurant in Cairo could provide for us on our next leave. Sharing the fusillades helped, and when a mortar or even a shell landed very close showering the top stones of the sangar on to our backs I would shout: "You alright?" and thankfully Jack would grunt or give my shoulder an OK squeeze to show that he was whole, still.

It was almost the last bombardment that smashed through the fragile bulwark of the sangar again. Fortunately my rifle lying longways beside me took the main force of the explosion which ripped most of the wood from its butt and even some from the barrel covering. It was then that abrasions of the inner aspect of my right thigh had occurred. Jack cleaned me up this time and wiped away the small haemorrhage. Only much later after being X-rayed hurt in subsequent battles, was I told of small pieces of shrapnel still lodged there (and to this day).

As the sun began to dip we had it confirmed by some poor damned company runner, that withdrawal back to the Gazala line would happen under a protective barrage if necessary, from our own guns at 8:45 pm. Meanwhile vigilance!

As the time for withdrawal drew close our line contracted, officers and N.C.O.'s appeared, binoculars came out of cases, eyes seared by the long days' exposure to the desert sun stared at the horizon searching for any advancing enemy. But while those shadows began to lengthen so did our hopes that we would escape alive, and we dared to look back at what had gone wrong, and it was in anger mainly.

Richard Platt M.M.

As often, our blame was heaped firstly on the officers. In them there was a kind of arrogance that they well knew about and felt bound to endorse, that other ranks need not know the scheme of things which was safe in officers' hands.

The R.A.F. had learnt the lesson of briefing all the crews and all of each crew before raids. As usual in such actions no one in advance had the slightest idea of the lie of the land or the plan of action for June 7th and this was evident throughout the whole of our attacking force apart from its officers. Only the officers knew the score, and once somehow they got detached from their men, a disaster was inevitable. We remembered lying spread out that morning, pinned down in the dawning light, calling to each other: "Where the hell are the officers?" and "We're going to get murdered here... tell us what to do!"

My war diary says that we lay there leaderless for three hours under a withering fire from everything conceivable until an order came from Pat Frank the platoon commander of the most forward group B9 who, assessing the hopeless situation ordered a withdrawal. Even then the orderliness of such a manoeuvre lay mainly in the hands of privates like Richard Platt whose voice we could hear shouting orders. We had to endure another five months of frequently flawed leadership before General Montgomery showed how staff work and comprehension of the orders involved in battle should be passed on to every man participating.

At 8:45pm our 25 pounders started to thump enemy positions in front and we slipped away like Will O the Wisps as our shells dropped a protective screen. We all agreed later, it was the longest day.

My diary entry for June 7th, though fragmentary, reflects what the ranks thought, no matter what the subsequent post mortems concocted:

Sunday, 7th June 1942

Today was the most horrible in my life. Never have I felt so disgusted, sickened, frightened or fatigued or angered. Last night obtained consent to fill vacancy in No.5 section of A5 platoon in the attack on Jerry. Never again will I volunteer for trouble.

Left our lines two hours before sunrise and attacked. Considerable success until main German line struck. Here we were pinned down on open, coverless ground by mortars, machine guns and 40mm Bredas for three hours while casualties mounted rapidly. Withdrew finally when our own artillery shelled us. Dumped all my equipment except rifle to help Terry Smedley who was wounded. Reached a lugger and took up defensive positions and were shelled by artillery and mortars for most of the day. Direct hit on my sangar but I escaped only dazed. Came out unscathed by a miracle. No more words necessary to imprint the horrors of that day upon my mind forever.

The disgust was with the quality of leadership that morning. The fear was that the war had only just begun and, as a volunteer, I had put myself into the hands of such monstrous inexpertise and might have to do so again. I was sickened by the mutilations ongoing for so many hours, that had matched flesh and blood against anti-tank guns operating at almost point blank range and in crossfire. It was also my first experience of total exhaustion.

Anger came in retrospect after a sincere attempt at extracting us had brought friendly artillery fire down upon our own heads when a simple device like smoke bombs could have been ordered to cover withdrawal.

Whilst in the same positions at Gazala, news came through of my colleague at John Dickinsons, Archie McLachlan, now a corporal in 'A' Company of the R.D.L.I. who had been assigned to a listening post in front of the barbed wire of their sector of the front. Archie was carring a tommygun and was accompanied by two privates. The trio had been ordered to advance from the listening post into the enemy line and reconnoiter. They soon spotted three stony sangars ahead of them occupied by German infantry of the 361 Afrika Corps Regiment. Corporal McLachlan ordered an attack and in severe hand to hand fighting the three overcame the German opposition, sangar by sangar. It then became apparent that there was a fourth command post which was besetting the R.D.L.I. men with stick grenades. Archie McLachlan sent one of his men for help and attacked the sangar. Help arrived with a Bren-gunner and the Germans surrendered. The result was 5

Germans killed, three captured along with spandaus, Lugers and ammunition. Archie was awarded the Military Medal immediately.

The Author Wins a Stripe

After shooting down a Machi 200 and being actively engaged in the Gazala stuka attacks, the Author was promoted to Lance Corporal by Lieutenant Ken Clarke who later became Mayor of Durban, the Author's hometown. He returned his stripe when his regiment was merged with another regiment which had an excess number of corporals.

CHAPTER XI

These were difficult days in which you were called upon to perform many varied and sometimes dangerous tasks. Even still they had their rare moments of humour. There were pilots and sometimes just their anatomical parts to be retrieved from the minefields in front of us, forty gallon drums of water to be manhandled, ammunition cases slogged, slit trenches to be deepened, gun pits and patrols to be manned and so on. And then there were the prisoners coming in night and day, sometimes under a white flag, sometimes just jittery, and others in pure panic. Making yourself an Allied prisoner was not an easy task especially for Italians. They might themselves be fired on deliberately in the process by their 'friends' the Germans. Eric Gregg and Aubrey Hampson had this experience bringing in a group of about 50 at a time when the line had been pushed forward some two or three miles as in the nightmare of June 7th.

Aubrey was at Durban High School with me. In the same form, we used to sit at the back of the science laboratory and pot at kids in the forward rows with orange peel and elastic bands and share lunch packs in nearby Berea Park. 'Aunty' Armstrong, the science master recognised that converting to the metric system was not everybody's piece of cake and tolerated semi-drop outs like Hampson and Baker, providing they didn't foul the ink pots with carbide. Everyone in the class read 'Billy Bunter' boys' magazines of the time and "Yarooped" with excessive cries of pain when hit with orange peel. Auntie never suspected the cause.

Like the stone sangar Jack Gray and I had occupied on the 7th, Aubrey's had sustained shattering gunfire and chips of stonework had hit him on the face and scalp and made him bleed. He was a terrible sight with blood still caked to the side of his face. His appearance gave alarm to the prisoners who always feared reprisals.

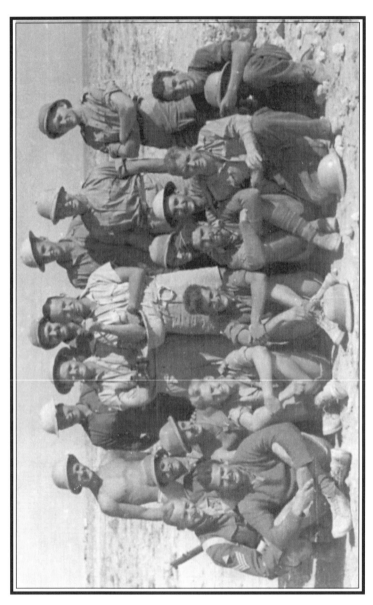

No. 1 Platoon N.M.R., at Gazala, June 1942. From left to right back row standing: Ralph Humphries, Piet de Beer, Lieut. Ken Clarke, Brian Lloyd, Cary Nash, Mousie Bell, Cecil Ritson, Johnny Clark. Middle row seated: Jock Reen, Joe Cowley, Ray Lee, Unknown, Jimmy Shrimpton, Douglas Baker. Front row, Derek Street. Cowboy Drennan, Walter Beangstrom, Roger Ellis, Charlie Roper.

It was just like Eric Gregg and certainly like Aubrey Hampson to come in through the mine gap unheralded and to my dugout for tea. The prisoners of course remained outside while Ray Lee brewed a cuppa on our battered primus for Aubrey and Eric. The Italians preoccupied me and I walked amongst them as they huddled together occupying several dilapidated trench slits. I began to hum again the strains of Giovanezza that I had learnt on my trip to Italy in 1934. Sure enough, the fascist anthem widened their eyes and drew forth mutterings. They didn't know what to make of it, just as the prisoners at the Battle of Dadaba had done a year earlier. Amazed, some thought I was a fifth columnist, even a rescuer. Eric enjoyed the prank and remembers it to this day. It gave me a buzz too and I shared out our precious water with them and a few cigarettes. After the tea they all moved off, the prisoners scattering a little as the enemy restarted shelling the area. I jutted my jaw and gave them a goodbye with a broad Mussolini smile and the fascist salute. Bemused, some waved back.

Aubrey, after hand-over of the prisoners, was evacuated and ended up in a field hospital none the worse.

So frequent had been the disappointing performance of our tank forces in the desert that dips in the morale of the infantry could be correlated with such armoured reverses and this even affected strategy. The evolution of the box system to house infantry in front line conditions had resulted from this awful weakness in armour. Even when our tank numbers greatly exceeded those of the Germans, lack of confidence in the outcome of tank battles was always a demoralising doubt haunting Allied infantry. It was spectacularly true in the Gazala line before the surrender at Tobruk in June 1942. While the B.B.C. Overseas News Service was singing the praises of the Free French's triumph in holding on to Bir Hacheim and describing the hell state of Rommel's forces trapped in the Cauldron of mines and barbed wire, the infantry of the British and South African divisions safe in the Gazala box just a few miles to the north and ready for action had to wait anxiously for the outcome of the inevitable tank battle. Even with the Allied armour in overwhelming superiority in tank numbers, poorly commanded it fell prey to dug-in batteries of German 88mm guns and was annihilated, and the infantry divisions at Gazala were ordered to flee for their lives. It was a similar story in the last days of Tobruk a week later when Rommel's penetrating, superiorly commanded armour smashed its way through the Indian infantry at Tobruk.

A year earlier the widespread weaknesses in command and its incapacity to handle tank warfare had been noted by Lord Alanbrooke, Commander-in-Chief of the home forces in Britain.

It had been made clear to the infantry in the Gazala line that the British had Rommel trapped in what only later was called the Cauldron and that we had a huge tank superiority. Events demonstrated the complete reverse of this. Our tanks failed in the Cauldron and the two infantry divisions in the Gazala line and the string of boxes supporting it were overrun or forced to run for dear life! Historic events showed that though at first Rommel did some damage to the British tanks as they came into action piecemeal from a weak position, he failed to break through to the coast behind Gazala. In a single day one-third of Rommel's tank force was lost; and, after another unsuccessful effort to reach the coast, he decided, on May 29th, to take up a defensive position. The new German position, aptly known as the Cauldron, seemed indeed to be perilously exposed; and throughout the first days of June the British attacked it continually by air and from the ground, imagining that Rommel's armour was caught at last. The British tanks, however, persisted in making direct assaults in small groups against the Cauldron and were beaten off with very heavy losses each time; and Rommel meanwhile, secured his rear and his line of supply by overwhelming several isolated British positions to the south. Whereas in May 1942 the British had had 700 tanks, with 200 more in reserve, against Rommel's 525, by June 10 their present armoured strength was reduced, through their wasteful tactics against the Cauldron, to 170, and most of the reserve was exhausted. Suddenly then, on June 11, Rommel struck eastward, to catch most of the remaining British armour in the converging fire of two panzer divisions. By nightfall on June 13 the British had barely 70 tanks left, and Rommel, with some 150 still fit for action, was master of the battlefield. The British on June 14 began a precipitate retreat from the Gazala line toward the Egyptian frontier.

Rommel had said to a British brigadier whom he had captured in the desert winter campaign: "I don't care how many tanks you British have so long as you keep splitting them up the way you do. I shall just continue to destroy them piecemeal."

There was a post-mortem to the tragic events of June 7th at Gazala. Later, enquiries revealed that only officers had been at the order group where the Colonel's instructions had been given. In the action which followed, the officers became detached from their men and the company, a composite one with platoons drawn from three different companies became a headless leviathan pinned down for three hours on an almost featureless terrain, ahead of the objectives it had been intended to reach and officer-less.

It would also seem that something went radically wrong with the overall planning of what was really a simple manoeuvre. The ultimate objective was Point 156 but although it was almost reached and we were being raked by its fire, our own company H.Q., a thousand yards behind us was under attack and too preoccupied with it to be able to re-establish contact with its advanced platoons.

There is no better description of the firing from Point 156 which we were sustaining than that of the officer conducting the operation:

"It was just getting light, when suddenly all hell seemed to be let loose as the enemy began firing from Point 156 with anti-tank guns, mortars and machine-guns. The anti-tank shells screeched like wild cats as red-hot balls of fire came towards us, sometimes ricochetting off stones, or bursting overhead. The tracer bullets from their machine-guns looked like jets of fire streaking along above the ground, and each bullet seemed to be coming straight at one. Another frightening weapon was something which made a noise like the rumble of an old-fashioned tram car setting off a double explosion when the shell burst. Nobody knew what it was. My headquarters were only a few yards from the crest of the eastern slope of the ridge which ran down to the Wadi. Consequently, most of the shells and bullets passed over us. We had found stone sangars which gave us a certain amount of protection from mortar bombs which were exploding in the area. This sudden onslaught now made me realise that the platoons, for some unknown reason, had advanced towards Point 156, without waiting for further instructions from me. It was a pretty kettle of fish!"

My own experience tells me we were very close to Point 156 and if contact with the O.C. had been patent it could have been taken. So close were we that at 5 a.m. precisely when our artillery of 25-pounders by pre-arrangement began to bombard Point 156 for 15 minutes some shells fell amongst us. Their characteristic arrival earned them the name of 'whispering death.'

Casualties on June 7th

11 killed and 22 wounded and evacuated.Many more were wounded and remained on duty. Casualties amongst my own friends:

Died of wounds .... Geoffrey Frank.

Evacuated wounded .... Terry Smedley, Aubrey
Hampson and Jo Rawlinson.

Prisoner of War .... Eddy Sayer and Henry Rule.

Wounded, remained on duty ...... Richard Platt, Bill Stevens

Nigel Downes was one of the biggest guys in the regiment. I didn't meet him on the rugby field but across a mortar base plate which if I recall weighed about 30lbs. His efforts behind a mortar at Gazala were noteworthy.

At the battle of Dadaba in Abysinnia volunteers had been called to act as pack animals to assist the support company carry its weapons and their ammunition into the fight which was at the end of a long trek on rough ground overnight. Nigel was a mortar man and I could see why he had been chosen for the job.

I knew the Downes family vaguely when I was at the age of eight and my mother had the Glamis Hotel in Florida Road, Durban. They were our neighbours; rather stuffy I thought them, in a bungalow behind a tall bougainvillaea fence. Mr. Downes was headmaster of a Durban school and very stern looking. I knew that too well when he glared at me through a hole in the fence which I suspected their cat crept through and periodically frightened my mother's pet canaries.

During home leave some of our troop were invited to a party where we had met the Downes' daughter, Nigel's sister Honor. She was a gorgeous, sedate and very mature beauty and bowled several of us over. Thereafter back in Egypt, training for tanks, Honor Downes was referred to with awe and reverence, and Nigel was always welcomed to join us for a beer and to give us an update on his fair sister. He was blessed (or cursed) with a set of Christian names which, when recited, sounded like poetic meter – Oscar Nigel Trouncer Downes, to wit!

Despite desperate attempts to retain a semblance of optimism the morale of the beleaguered 8th Army was diving. The struggles on June 7th to divert German forces from Bir Hacheim were futile. On June 10th with a suspicious calm in the northern sector of Gazala, Rommel began his final and most intense effort to possess the Bir Hacheim Box starting at noon with massed air attacks followed by ground forces assisted by engineers who were able to penetrate the box's protected minefields. Thereafter, more waves of bombers and with darkness descending the Free French were able to slip away from their positions totally exhausted but in vehicles provided by the R.A.S.C. (Royal Army Service Corps.)

Bir Hacheim had gone and Rommel headed north for the coast behind the besieged Gazala enclave to cut it off from Tobruk.

In his way there were only the various boxes like Knightsbridge, Tamar and Acroma. The South African 1st Division and the 50th English Division were about to be cut off and annihilated if these smaller boxes could be attacked by the panzers and overwhelmed. With the overrunning of boxes in the southern sector, back in the positions at Gazala Stukas attacked in greater numbers than ever. It was a portentous sign indicating the Germans were preparing for the kill. After all the same signs had heralded the loss of Crete only 300 miles across the water from Gazala.

Back in Gazala the 12th of June order groups were now very sombre affairs. Officers had long faces and didn't even bother to be jocular anymore as they gave out their gruesome info. Captain Blamey and 'C' Company had to be pulled out of the Gazala line to go and help the Tamar Box behind us, close to Knightsbridge. The Guards were in trouble there, the Scots overrun and the Worcestershires hanging on by the skin of their teeth.

"Shit!" we thought "if even the Guards are beginning to waver, what in the hell is going on."

That was the good news. The bad news was that half of our ack-ack platoon already at half strength were to take over 'C' Company's dugouts and weapon pits. That meant lugging our guns and ammo half a mile down into the flats in daylight and setting them up for action against both infantry and aircraft. As it turned out there was no prepared ack-ack gun pit at the new location and Ray and I mounted the Bren out in the open 25 yards behind the dugout.

With the fall of Bir Hacheim on June 10th the Germans, sensing victory, sped north with their panzers and began to pressure the whole extent of the allied line stretching from Gazala on the right flank through the 50th English division next to us, the string of strong points and boxes stretching two or three miles apart along our southern flank via Point B154, Elwet el Tamar, Point 187, Point 208, the Box at Acroma and the perimeter of Tobruk (See map page 198). South of this line most strong points were being overrun and the last of these were the box at Knightsbridge and a strong point on the Rigel Ridge. The German armour and its 88mm anti-tank guns had devastated the British tank complement almost everywhere. Using heavy artillery on their left flank they began pulverising the Gazala enclave where we sustained heavy casualties, and threw their motorised infantry and 15th and 21st panzers at the middle of the frail allied southern flank, hoping to penetrate it and reach the coast to cut off the two divisions holding Gazala from escaping through Tobruk. The Allied infantry from its right flank, was being funnelled into the maintaining of this stretched-out front of infantry bereft of its tanks. Still in Gazala, my diary records:-

Saturday, 13th June '42
No sleep last night (June 12th) – terrific artillery and mortar shelling. Chaps can't stick it much longer. Strain beginning to tell on me. Worked on gun positions. Heavily under strength. Tried without success to sleep. News from rear very grim.

Andrew Moorhead gives the most accurate description of armour events that occurred concurrently with the near entrapment of the 1st South African Division and the 50th English Division on the Gazala Box between June 13th and 16th (See Appendix III)

<u>Sunday, June 14th '42</u>

An hour's sleep last night. The artillery pounding us horrible. Well over a thousand shells fell on to the battalion area. Mac's section copped it. Ludlow killed.

We were all beginning to feel like lions led by donkeys ready and eager to fight but led away into retreat. If the British could only hold off the panzers using the remaining Boxes as strong points in amongst it, then from Gazala in the west to Tobruk in the east 100,000 soldiers might be saved. As it was the remnant British tanks barely held until the Boxes were evacuated…all of them except their rearguards and Tobruk defenders.

Yet, despite the vicissitudes, the eternal rounds of 'stand-to' at dawn and dusk, the choking sandstorms, the bombings and strafing, the Sidi Rezeghs, the tedium , the bugs & fleas, the summer heat and flies with accompanying desert sores, the woundings and maimings , the B.B.C. news, the poor weaponry and the food, no one in my regiment ever even in the remotest form except in simple jokes considered ultimate defeat or surrender. In our minds our families, our closest friends, school chums, business colleagues, all of them were involved in the whole hateful mess at Gazala, but surrender or losing the war was never in our vocabulary not then and certainly not after Alamein. The demise of Tobruk was a total surprise to everyone.

The cartoon 'In the Bag' circulated briefly at that time sums the situation up! (See page 198)

After June 10th news from all along the line began to get very bad indeed. Men were being withdrawn from the regiment to reinforce boxes that were under attack <u>behind</u> the Gazala line. Ray Lee and I found ourselves occupying weapon pits down on the flats to replace 'C' Company sections being dispatched in haste to the box at Elweit el Tamar and Point 181 from where the English 9th Battalion of the

Rifle Brigade was leaving to help relieve pressure on beleaguered Knightsbridge.

Again in the Gazala line, we were confronted with the necessity to engage the Stukas coming out from bombing our forward transport area with ack-ack fire and, at the same time be ready in the weapon pits to face a frontal attack by infantry should it come.

On the southern front commanding a company in a composite battalion at Elweit el Tamar was Captain Blamey M.C., an N.M.R. hero. His comments on the ensuing battle against panzers and supporting infantry adequately describe the appalling situation at Tamar (see map page 196) into which C Company had been sent with my pal Eric Gregg, surviving to this day in Cape Town.

June 13th – Major Blamey reported:

> We arrived on the outskirts of the Tamar Box at daylight…we found most of the slit trenches and gun-pits were shallow and totally inadequate for sound defence. Knowing that both German panzer divisions, the 15th & 21st, were in the area and that there would be a showdown sooner or later, 'C' Company dug faster and deeper than they had ever dug before. We were encircled by a minefield except for a section on our left flank, between us and Point 187 which was held by the Worcesters. Except for an occasional shell the enemy kindly allowed us to work unmolested until 3p.m. Then they vigorously attacked the Scotts Guards at Rigel Ridge, south-east of us about three miles away. Our artillery engaged tanks and infantry attacking that position. Visibility was poor owing to a dust storm, and through the haze the picture was distorted, but we saw enough to know the Ridge had been overrun by enemy armoured columns. Having gained that advantage, they advanced closer to us, and we were subjected to heavy shelling and machine-gunning. We felt that these attacks were largely aimed at knocking out our anti-tank guns. The 17th Battery in support of us replied to good effect. That night a patrol sent out along the mine wire running west to Point B154 brought back an officer, Capt. Maxwell of the Scotts Guards, who had been taken prisoner at Rigel Ridge but had subsequently escaped.

Author's comment: With the loss of Rigel Ridge, the panzers began to close in determined to pierce the allied centre at the Tamar Box.

Blamey continues – 14th June:

Early in the morning of the 14th – another Black Sunday – we were again shelled and our guns vigorously replied … At 10:00 am there was great activity on our whole front. Numerous tanks launched a heavy attack on the Worcesters at Point 187. A little later more tanks were observed advancing towards us from the direction of Rigel Ridge. Before long our positions were heavily shelled and machine-gunned. No.10 platoon particularly took the greater share of hammering by tanks firing from hull down positions. All these tanks, also enemy lorried infantry south of our positions were effectively engaged by our artillery. By about midday both attacks were repulsed, causing the tanks to withdraw in a south-easterly direction. There was then a lull.

On this day there were many brave acts along the besieged line on both sides, some foolish, some foolhardy and some quite ridiculous.

Eric Gregg tells the story of German prisoners his section captured at Elweit el Tamar:

"After we had dug-in on the second day, we were fired on by German tanks and accompanying German infantry. The tanks were given a hard time by our 25-pounders. We were 'attacked' by a thin line of irresolute German infantry. A few who reached our wire promptly surrendered. Jack Mason and I had two very young (+ 16 year olds) German infantry who had flown from Italy and travelled overnight from Benghazi to Knightsbridge. Apparently they had had no food since arrival and no water. They flung themselves into our trench-slit and wanted no more part of the war.

Anyway, the young fellow in my slit-trench showed me photos of his family and keeping very low in the slit-trench ate the last of my chocolate.

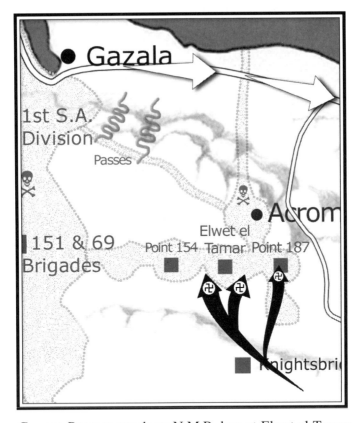

German Panzers attack on N.M.R. box at Elwet el Tamar

That evening as we withdrew from our positions, the prisoners were encouraged to bale out and find their colleagues. We were making for Tobruk and the German youths left reluctantly and very well fed."

With the Eighth Army's two-pounder anti-tank gun practically ineffectual against the panzers more strong points were overwhelmed. Early in the afternoon of the same day the neighbouring Worcestershires at Point 187 were incessantly attacked and by 5.30 p.m seemed to have been annihilated. Later Blamey had commented that the infantry of our composite battalion could do little else but keep their heads down.

Some heroics occurred when pot-shots were ridiculously taken at tanks with the standard anti-tank Boyes rifle which, even with the German monsters at close range were like 'pea-shooters' and only brought down a hail of shrapnel and machine-gun fire in response to their flashes. What the infantry did do effectively was to cover the minefields around them keeping German sappers from lifting or dismantling our protective mines. Our most effective weapons were the 25-pounders firing from behind the line or from the centre of boxes where they could be somewhat protected by infantry and the lie of the land. Even here with panzers hull down, half-hidden and with only their turrets showing, our gunfire was limited in its effect. The Germans also showed great valour in trying to recover their shot-up or mechanically disabled tanks under our mortar and machine-gun fire. Sticky bombs were handed around by the intrepid company Sergeant Major at great risk but there were no reports of any kamikazes using them under the withering fire of the panzers.

At the end of that long, harsh Sunday a sigh of relief went up when the order came, that with darkness the battalion would be withdrawn in a night-long dash for the coast road to Tobruk. Eric Gregg's summing up of the engagement was: "If only we had had some six pounders." As it was they only really arrived at the front to help the Eighth Army stem the panzers when they reached Alamein, 4 months later.

Blamey's final comment was that around the perimeter of the Elweit el Tamar box, he counted 42 German tanks give or take a few.

THE FALL OF THE BOXES

Boxes Overwhelmed

1st June .... 150 Brigade of 50th English Division.

11/12th June .... Bir Hacheim

13th June .... Rigel Ridge/Scotts Guards

14th June .... Point 187/Worcestershires

20th June .... Tobruk

Box Withdrawals

    14th June .... Knightsbridge/201 Brigade

    14th June .... Elweit el Tamar/South Africans

    14th June .... Gazala/South Africans

    14th June .... Gazala/50th Division

    14th June .... Acroma

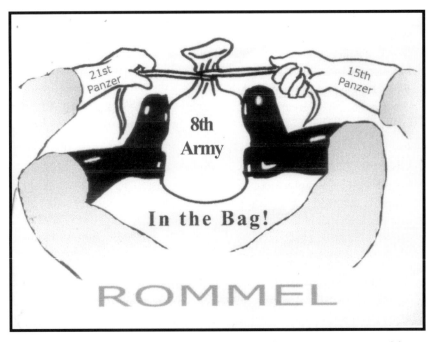

Around the 10th June '41 a cartoon drawn by someone on our side was circulating as a joke, one that very nearly became a reality.

CHAPTER XII

The almost intact South African and 50th infantry divisions on the coast could have headed west in attack long before Bir Hacheim fell while the German armour was trapped far south in the Cauldron and British minefields. Derna and Benghazi, the Italian sea ports in Cyreneica were unprotected and there for the taking. With Malta still in our hands Rommel himself could have been cut off.

The cartoon 'In the Bag' (opposite) was drawn and shown around when the news from Bir Hacheim was at its blackest. Bushey nodded his head at it and giggled and Jo and Derek showed it to me. My comment was "Too many ifs': if this, if that"* with which Derek replied "Yes, if my aunty had balls she'd be my uncle."

Despite everything we had been boxed up at Gazala for three months with all its horrors, its indignities and its monotony and were delighted at the prospect of pulling out.

Sunday June 14th brought the word through to pack up. Unclear however, was whether we were going to advance west or to withdraw eastwards to Tobruk or heaven-knows-where. Suddenly, as the sun went down and the shadows lengthened it was "Withdraw and destroy everything your truck can't carry. We're leaving tonight."

The Stukas had been knocking out trucks parked behind us for three weeks. This meant truck numbers were going to be reduced. Someone crept around telling us to scatter spare ammo when it was dark; bury or destroy breach blocks off weapons that were supernumery or un-transportable and burn any papers useful to the enemy, letters, diaries, maps. We then learnt that we were making for Tobruk on a carefully prepared overnight schedule which had to be

---

* If we had control of the air; if the navy could supply us; if Tobruk held out and if the British tank force survived...etc.

stuck to. Realising that our tanks must have lost their protracted battles in the Cauldron we were still not bothered about ending up in Tobruk which had held out month after month when besieged by this same enemy and defended by the Aussies. What did give us palpitations was that it would be a running fight with panzers closing in on us to cut the coast road from Gazala into Tobruk. Even trucks that had been partly damaged by constant bombing and shelling were to be used as long as they moved and their engines smashed when they couldn't be towed or driven a yard further. Deep down and short term, our trepidation lay in lack of confidence that our officers would be competent enough to guide us from the escarpment down to sea level in the dark via passes that would be jammed with every conceivable conveyance, packed with fleeing soldiers and in total darkness. Delay would put our liberty in jeopardy and in jeopardy we soon were.

Author's Diary:

Sunday (night), 14th June '42

After dark crept out in trucks and were not shelled. Reached rear minefields and began the greatest mess-up in S.A. military history. The whole division became hopelessly lost. Officers were not to be seen anywhere – when they arrived, they didn't know the way. After five precious hours we found the gap and reached the 2nd pass down the escarpment just before dawn.

The tendency, if not the capacity to get things into a mess when applied to a battle situation or manoeuvre was very apparent to men in the ranks. In practice very few soldiers kept diaries in any detail but when they did you can be sure that "fuck-ups" as they were commonly termed, were the item of importance most frequently noted. Bernard Montgomery knew about this weakness and made sure that the events of October 23, 1942 were not only well laid out in general orders, known both to officers AND their men, but saw to it that they were rehearsed again and again in the field by all and sundry before the Battle of Alamein put them into effect after that. Commanders and officers spent too much time congratulating each other with booze and making due obeisance to people and places instead of learning from experience and putting orders properly into effect.

This was why the platoon sergeant could assume such real importance to his men. He would usually have had the bitter experience of disaster and its causes repeated in the ranks and as an N.C.O. The fuck-ups of June 7th and the evacuation of Gazala on the 14th/15th were illustrative. In the first, the officers had become detached from the men on a battlefield and, in the second, a whole division and their equipment were at risk of being 'put in the bag' through their incompetence. The delay there meant a running fight in full daylight to get to Tobruk, with resulting disorder instead of a calm, ordered withdrawal in darkness. Some of the blame for the inability of the high command in Tobruk to organise its forces in the five days before the German assault, lay in the jammed passes leading down the Gazala escarpment on the coastal road to Tobruk.

30,000 men were lost with the fall of Tobruk on June 20th/21st. Another 10,000 might have been added to this, badly led out of Gazala.

A much applauded, regimental hero admitted his share of the blame pertaining to just his own company:

"The rest of the company, plus Support personnel, were in their trucks, following slowly behind. Bob Foss and I walked ahead of the trucks behind the protective screen. We seemed to flounder around for hours in the dark looking for the gap in the minefield.

At 2:00am I clearly remember looking at my luminous watch and, in despair, saying to Bob: "What are we to do, we seem to be going round in circles looking for that bloody gap?"

We had seen a red light but, thinking it was the enemy, we avoided it. After a while, with one or two others I walked up cautiously to investigate. As we got closer to the light I saw figures and heard a person in a low voice say: "Are you N.M.R.?" The man was a Sergeant-Major of the F.F.B. who had been posted there with the red light to guide troops through the minefield. He said he had been waiting anxiously for a long time wondering what had become of us. Apparently all the groups were supposed to have been notified of this arrangement, but that was the first we had heard of it."

JUNE 14th – WITHDRAWAL FROM GAZALA

In the passes the debris of war lay everywhere. Trucks bumper to bumper still moving jammed the roads, loaded with men hanging on to their sides, clinging on to the frames, housing kit, guns ammo, rations, jerry cans of water, brew-up tins, primus stoves, webbing, Bofors gun crews, heavy machine-gun crews mixed amongst infantry half-asleep medics and cooks, some wide-eyed with terror.

The tarmac road lay straight ahead on a narrow strip of coastline between the escarpment and the white beaches and cliffs dipping into the sea.

Suddenly shells began to burst amidst the havoc. On top of the escarpment, guns trained on the road, panzers appeared, aware of our supreme vulnerability.

Some German tanks, black blobs on the escarpment ridge in the dawn light began to probe for pathways to reach down to the Eighth Army in rout. Others plied us with ranging shells and then began to hit trucks. It was like a duck hunt and with so many sitting targets they couldn't miss. As a truck was hit, even before damage and casualties had been assessed, survivors forsaking their baggage were dashing to catch a lift on other more fortunate vehicles. The chaos was indescribable.

In the midst of it, Italian CR 42 planes arrived, sometimes in waves and began their deadly game of strafing. Partly out of instinct but mainly through months of harsh experience, fleeing trucks began to leave the road and travel on the humpbacked territory between 'Balbia' (the coastal road) and the sea. Down there, so near to the beaches, we had no tank support or protection. And so it went on. Stay in the trucks and be target practice for Italian pilots or leave your truck and stay put to become P.O.W.'s. Some, to escape, waded out into the sea and found their way via cliff faces into Tobruk only to be captured there.

Remnant British Army tanks probably drew off many panzers high on the escarpment. The rearguard company, waiting to the last to see stragglers through to Tobruk, valiantly, were overcome in the battle and lost.

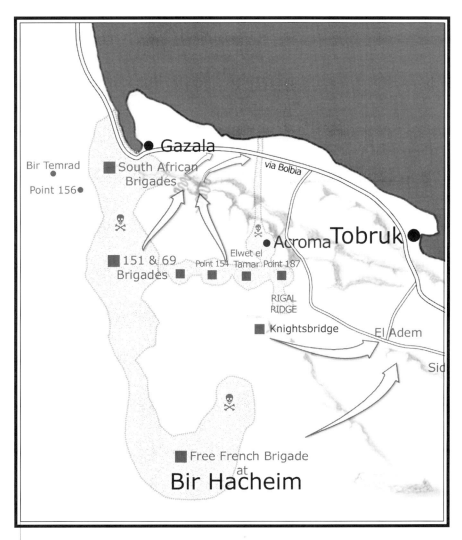

Eighth Army, 14th June, using the passes down the escarpment on the via Balbia making for Tobruk.

The struggle to get through the narrowing isthmus which was the coast road into Tobruk became even more desperate. With panzers closing in, trucks began more and more to leave the tarred road and took to the narrow strip of desert between the road and the sea. I saw the prospect of having to wade, even swim along the coastline (as many subsequently had to) an increasing certainty. The brilliant blue-green scenario of the sea revitalised my exhausted frame and I thought of how the same sea had saved my British homeland only two years earlier at Dunkirk…Trafalgar…the Armada and so on. With these refreshing flashbacks I became aware that the drivers had seen an opening, a gap in the minefield and barbed-wire surrounding Tobruk, the last of the gaps in fact, all the others already being forced to close. And so the truck I had ended up in approached the gap through the Tobruk minefields mid-afternoon. It was just as well because by then the precious water I was carefully ladling into the radiator, torn by the Italian planes' strafing machine-gun bullets had come to an end. I had ended up wedged in between the Bedford truck's engine and the right front mudguard. It was a prime position compared to those of some forty other unfortunates clinging for dear life elsewhere to the vehicle. It's drawback was the withstanding of numerous scaldings from the bubbling radiator's effusions. I must reconstruct our reception by the red caps on duty. We were also towing another strafed vehicle in far worse condition. Somehow, out of extreme concern I found myself with both drivers on foot confronting the military police at the gap. We had expected to be waved through, even greeted with some awe. At that moment whistles blew and the area, jammed with army vehicles in a bottleneck was bombed from planes at a high level. There was no shelter to make for anyway and a tank trap nearby was ominously full of drifted sand. In any case most of the men on board, exhausted, had preferred to fall asleep during the halt.

Approaching to identify us, M.P. No.1 accosted us with "And who the hell are you?" Our senior man, a farmer from Eshowe in Zululand widened his eyes – they were so covered in dust and cordite, you could hardly see them, and answered: "Well what do we look like, Ito's?"

"You could have fooled me" the red cap snorted, "What's your regiment?"

"You name it – we've got it on board, almost every regiment in the division," Eshowe replied.

The third man, Eshowe's companion, equally grotesque, broke into Zulu and fortunately a second M.P., a South African approaching with some impatience understood Zulu kitchen talk and grunting "Longeeli" beckoned us through.

But the sad state of Tobruk's outer defences disturbed me. This was not a bastion ready for siege and least of all for assault by the luftwaffe and panzers that had turned our defences in and around Gazala.

TOBRUK ATTACK (See Map page 209)

As dawn was breaking on the 20th June the desultory waves of Stukas that had harassed us at Gazala now became regimented almost into serried ranks. The R.A.F. attempts to rescue the Free French at Bir Hacheim, heroic though they were, had fooled nobody. The Allies had not had air control over the Tobruk-Gazala area for many months there and certainly had no say in the final defence of Tobruk because by then the R.A.F. had been driven off Gambut airstrip.

The Italian and German planes, Stukas predominantly, came in flights of 20 or 30 straddling the wadis and gun emplacements of the peripheral defences. Similarly the enemy artillery began to plaster the same Allied gun positions so that nobody dared move. These were not just raids but blitzkrieg, a giant monster of destruction, setting on its quarry.

Then the Stukas began to concentrate on their main target, the minefields in the southeast of the Tobruk perimeter. Rommel was signalling where he intended to penetrate the British defences. He chose a sector that was garrisoned by troops of the 11th Indian Brigade most of whom had never seen a Stuka in their lives let alone the hundreds diving with their sirens screaming and bombs hurtling. The Stukas certainly achieved their objective which was to pulverise the minefields so that the panzers could do their work. Whole chains of mines exploded together and German sappers entered the minefields to lift or neutralise paths for the 21st and 15th panzers which very quickly advanced towards these gaps with their guns ablaze. It was the 150 Brigade Box and Bir Hacheim Box manoeuvers all over again but this time against far less resolute defences.

Halting at the gaps, German infantry crept up, overtook their tanks and with mortars and smoke grenades began to obscure the battlefield ahead of them. Added to this a creeping barrage was laid down enabling the whole Axis force to advance behind it. This enabled barbed wire entanglements to be cut, mines to be lifted and the British and Indian outposts to be overrun. At points of penetration the panzers rushed through making for the Mediterranean beaches and the centre of the bomb-wrecked town of Tobruk. Very early on in the attack the C in C of Tobruk, Major Klopper had been bombed out of his H.Q. by the Stukas and as fast as he located himself in new positions his H.Q. received the same treatment. This may have given rise to the post mortem false rumour that a fifth column was operating amongst the South African forces high command.

By 8:00am most of the Indian Maharattas right and centre had been overrun and captured. From their left flank the Gurkhas, straddling the Via Balbia's eastern exit from Tobruk made an unsuccessful attack to relieve them. By 2:00pm the key points of Fortress Tobruk were occupied by Rommel's staff. By 7:00pm the 21st panzers had entered the harbour area where demolitions had been made and the remaining sea craft withdrawn. Also by 7:00pm the 15th panzers had overun the 201 Guards and Sherwoods Forresters who were without anti-tank weapons to defend themselves. At 4pm on the same day Maj. General Klopper ordered destruction of all codes, signals, documents and the telephone exchange at his H.Q. This meant that from then on the defending forces of Tobruk no longer had a central control.

Even at this stage all the perimeter defences from the Cameroon emplacements west and north to the Mediterranean were intact. These positions were held mainly by South African infantry. A concerted night attack could have reversed the fortunes of war. But Klopper had himself destroyed the central control of these intact forces. It must be said also that the option of breaking out and making for the Egyptian frontier could have been exercised. To my mind what was unforgiveable was the delapidated state of defences that properly maintained could have helped at least to slow the panzers down. Anti-tank ditches were silted up where I entered the western gates of Tobruk and this was the case too where Rommel later had punched a narrow wedge through the Maharattas.

The good night's sleep in Tobruk had filled me with new vigour. I was confident that with the old war-horse Auchinleck again in charge, the Germans could be stopped somewhere this side of the Nile delta.

But if there were any leaks of information harmful to the Allied cause in Tobruk they would have been through the detailed reports of Colonel Bonner Fellows who kept Washington informed of events at the front and who had privy to very high-up sources in General Claude Auckinleck's circles. Two British armour movements, locations and numbers had been conveyed to the Washington embassy and from there leaked to the Germans. Having contributed to the British reverses in the Western Desert Colonel Fellows thereafter added his unsolicited opinion of British prospects:

The British Army could not adequately co-ordinate with the R.A.F.

Had no armour-piercing shells to stop German tanks.

The U.S.A. should develop its own theatres of war operating separate bases and lines of communication etc, etc. and could never work in harmony with the British.*

Churchill did not hesitate to use alcohol in his own life privately and publicly and certainly recommended it for guerilla forces hidden away in Britain in times of utmost crisis. Was it offered in the desert?

Well, it certainly was on offer at Alamein but perhaps for a different reason. While we were in Libya the lines of communication were very extended. Usually from the delta it was about 250 miles and the delivery of food rations to say Gazala was hard going. Wine and spirits (especially Cypress brandy) were manageable but beer, even three tins per man was a whole convoy of trucks on its own. A daily ration of 3 tins was virtually an impossibility or so it would seem.

Richard Platt's diarised notes (post mortem) record that at Gazala the best ration was two tins a week, and that to counter this harsh rationing he and George Strachan used yeast tablets and the juice of prunes, tinned pineapple and potato peels to make an alcoholic brew.

---

* *End of the Beginning* publisher Hodder & Stoughton. UK.

During the Gazala Gallup the 8th Army bravely got its personnel back to Alamein but had to leave more than half its equipment in Libya. Reaching the Egyptian frontier before taking the Sollum or Halfaya passes into Egypt, mountains of canned and bottled beer had been dumped on the frontier because there was no room for it on Allied overcrowded and retreating transport. To prevent it falling into enemy hands each army group passing by the beer en route was offered the beer it wished. There were few, or only modest takers. It was a matter of freedom or booze. Most chose the former with panzers chasing and enemy reconnaissance snapping at everyone's heels. Strangely, no one seemed spiteful enough to delay their flight to blow up the dumps. Derek was almost prostrated with grief until he did a deal with our truck driver to dump his own kit bag for a single case of the beer.

But then at Gazala we had survived (barely) on two bottles of brackish water a day with washing almost forbidden. Sticks Firebrace, a sweet old regimental major in our early days, had always advised us at all times to keep our jewellery clean – meaning private parts – and (big joke coming) especially our hardware!

Surviving Gazala it was time to review Boxes.

Personally, as an infantryman I preferred the employment of boxes. I had helped to build the box at Acroma behind the Gazala line and on the fringes of Tobruk. (See map page 153)

I had also occupied the complexity which was the Gazala box and fought stukas and ground forces from it, and it was the same in the Alamein box.

For me the boxes gave a degree of independence which was precious to South African infantry who were all still sensitised by the tragedy of Sidi Rezegh in November of '41. It is true to say that boxes required enormous forces in men and equipment to occupy and supply them. But it is also true to say that they would have taken up huge enemy forces to subdue them. The boxes at Knightsbridge and Bir Hacheim very nearly broke Rommel's attack in June '42.

If, at the worst, a withdrawal order was given simultaneously to all the boxes and providing they had their transport there would be a

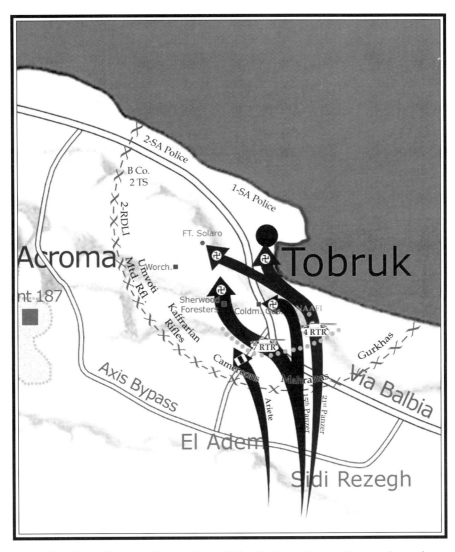

20th June: Rommel's attack on Tobruk from the south east through the lines of the Indian Maharattas.

good chance, in desert conditions of escaping capture. Such withdrawals had been made from boxes at different places – some even from Tobruk. General Ritchie may have done the right thing in getting whole divisions out of the mess of Gazala, but it was a very, very close thing.

The long, dreary periods stuck on guard duties, security and other demanding routines like 'listening post' called for endurance against solitude and boredom. I took consolation in inwardly reciting the large numbers of poems that I had inherited from high school, which had become stock-in-trade amongst the more scholarly volunteers of other ranks in the battalion. I also sang, not always subjectively the many nursery rhymes, ballads and songs of primary school. The latter gradually became transmogrified by incursions of bawdy army songs and with those that made up radio programs transmitted by both the Axis and the Allies to their troops:-

    e.g.   'Men of Harlech' became: –
           March, O march the men of Norway,
           Shooting peas up a nanny goat's doorway.'

And some terrible things were done to 'The Isle of Capri'.

Some of the 30,000 British P.O.W.'s captured at Tobruk. My friend Henry Rule taken at Gazala on June 7th shows his frustration. He is seen in the right hand corner scratching his head with frustration and posing without a helmet.

CHAPTER XIII

Falling back from Libya before the onslaught of the triumphant Afrika Corps was not easy despite the shortening of our lines of communication with bases now in the Delta becoming closer. (See map page 213).

Our infantry tasks were numerous, from fighting patrols to slogging ammunition for artillery attacks, but the number of fighting men we had left after continuing casualties was dropping accordingly.

We lost infantry men who contributed to …

Rearguard actions where there were heroic efforts to cover the withdrawal of the main body and its stragglers towards Alamein.

Artillery barrages which had to use up shells rather than to abandon or destroy them. These might assist getting our transport and troops down passes. Such bombardments were delivered at different levels – divisionally, at battalion and even company levels.

Engineers who had to be protected whilst they blew up passes, bridges and demolitions.

Anti-aircraft defence with Bren guns and Bofors to stave off strafing by German and Italian fighters which harassed any transport concentrations in retreat.

Maintaining the rear positions of the brigade with whatever was needed to keep them moving in their withdrawal…petrol, water, protection and mechanical repairs and on the spot demolition of transport that could not make the 200 miles from the passes on the Egyptian frontier to the Alamein box.

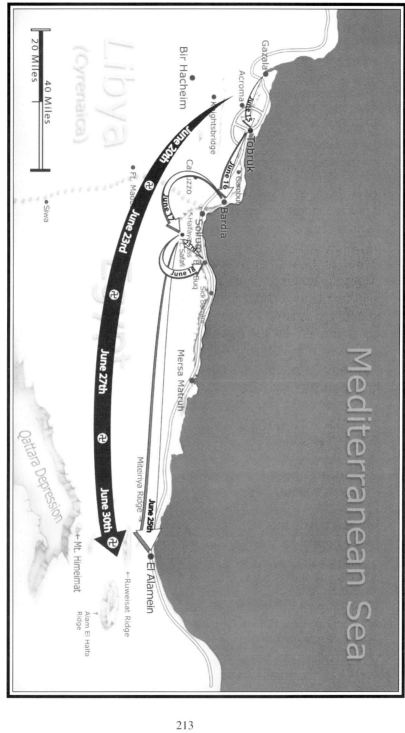

Map of the retreats of Allied forces overland to Alamein, a distance of 300 miles with rearguard actions on dated white arrows. The Germans (black arrows) reached Alamein a few days later having occupied Mersa Matruh en route (27th June '41)

213

To protecting the railway line, which accompanied the main, tarmac retreat road all the way back along the shoreline. It was bombed and strafed incessantly.

Approaching Alamein, the last line of defence, it was inevitable that we were caught up in extensive fatigues to help the frantic engineers lay minefields which, as at Gazala, had been the most reliable defence against superior tank forces.

That there was confusion in places was inevitable. No one knew what was happening. Why had we not stopped in Mersa Matruh (carefully prepared for intensive siege over many years)? Why were some forces being directed to the outer defences of Alexandria? Why had (it was rumoured) the British Navy evacuated its Alexandria base? When could we expect relieving divisions to pass thru us? Was the command of the 8th Army in safe hands? Divisional commanders had come up to the front line in staff cars just to ask whether we were still prepared to fight... Why? Major Blamey posed the matter:

> When he (Gen. Pienaar) arrived I thought he looked extremely worried and very tired. After returning my salute, he said: "How are the boys, Major?"

> I replied: "Very well, Sir, although perhaps a little tired." He then said: "How is morale, will they fight?" My reply was: "Rest assured, Sir, they will fight all right." I then told him that Col. le Roux had phoned, and I hoped he could spare a few minutes to go into our problems. He never got out of his car, but, I imagined, with his experience and keen eye for country, he had summed up the position in a few seconds.

> However, he said nothing and made no reference to my query. The General then told me to do my best and said he was in a hurry to get back to corps headquarters, and with that he drove off."*

In other places artillery had been told to stay put and if necessary to "fire over open sights," which could only mean tanks were expected. Some even felt that the German radio 'Lili Marlene' had better expectations for us than the B.B.C.

---

* From *A Company Commander Remembers* – Blamey, p.147

One thing, amidst the chaos and complexities, was clear; no one knew where exactly the final stand was to be made. The Alamein concrete bunkers prepared by the 2nd. S. African division the previous year, were now very much incomplete. They had been stripped and looted by the Arabs. The waste materials of earth (white sand) and concrete lay all around them so that they stood out like dogs' balls for the luftwaffe's attention and were sitting targets for enemy artillery, especially those 210mm Italian naval guns dragged forward from Gazala days. Uncamouflageable in a hurry, no company commander wanted any of his infantry near them, let alone in them!

We were all so fatigued I would have used them just to get a full night's rest.

There developed the fretful movement of troops from pillar to post that signalled once more the uncertainty in our armoured forces that were once caught up in the Cauldron at Gazala. In other words, 'Be prepared to move at a moment's notice, the outcome is uncertain.' This time things, we felt, were going wrong at Mersa Matruh and even Alamein was uncertain. The next moment the order came thru, 'Make for the outer defences of Alexandria!' It took us a day to establish a forward defence post on the Alexandria perimeter. An officer, new at the job, called in to inspect on the 4th. July. I asked him what were we there for? What were we to expect? Stukas? Naval landings on the nearby seashore? Or perhaps an attack up the fresh water canal, which was also close by? Should we expect tanks to approach from the front? If so could he send us out another sticky bomb or two? Where were the 6-pounders? There were rumours in Alex itself that a parachute attack was likely. He began to get cross and left with a gruff: "Just look to your front and let me know if anything approaches." What he really meant was that anything could happen if the enemy broke through Alamein and he knew no more than other ranks.

But we were adaptable. Two of us stayed on the guns that night while two went into the gay life in Alex, three miles away and despite the curfew there, had a whale of a time.

During the day, sunny of course, the other two sat alert on the guns and the rest of us swam in a fresh water tank trap risking bilharzia

Italian artillery, mainly 210mm Naval weapons or guns surrendered to them by the Germans after W.W.I. They helped to crumble Allied entrenchments at Gazala and Alamein.

and the ongoing air pageant of waves of Boston bombers flying out from the Delta to attack the Nazis' ever extending lines of communication across Libya into Egypt. We swapped about and kept this scenario going for a few days interrupted only by interludes of tickling up strafing messerschmitts with our mounted Bren-gun's fire.

On Wednesday the 8th. July we were pulled out of our Alex paradise and shunted once more into Alamein. The flap was over: the panzers had not broken thru and the front line, not yet consolidated, had held. From then on aggressive patrols were to be sent out each night to probe the enemy front, to find out what German divisions were in front of us and to maul any Italian ones. It meant that every third night fifteen soldiers from a company led by an officer would be on patrol. Sometimes a whole company would attack, always at night and take 5 or 6 hours to do the job. Only the fighting fit took part. There were always slackers and the semi-fit who had to be passed over, guys with night blindness, those teetering on breakdown, dodgers and men with poor records that could not be trusted in a crisis. You usually carried a bayonet if you were a rifleman, were always laden with grenades, the heavy fragmenting type as well as the light plastic ones which just made a loud noise that frightened the shit out of the Italian machine gunners when you threw them as a passing gesture at the end of the patrol.

In No.1 Platoon from the beginning of active service our particular role was to provide air defence for the battalion especially the battalion headquarters which were the main target of any planes bombing and strafing. Setting up the six Bren guns strategically in two interlaced triangles around the centre of regimental activity was a dawn to dusk routine with long hours of searching the skies for marauders with binoculars in order to give the battalion early warning to take cover from approaching fighter planes that would strafe and from bombers (Stukas mainly).

This constant routine of readiness we coded amongst ourselves as playing poker and indeed poker was the favourite card game throughout Allied forces anyway, American and British. But there was always the more serious side of being on call to be used as combatants in the rifle companies when they were being carved up and under strength. It meant being in and out of crisis points and almost constantly being attached to different platoons and their sections. In this way I was to meet comprehensively fellow combatants in action all over the regiment…in 'A' Company in the Gazala Box, 'B' Company at Alamein, Support Company at Dadaba, 'C' Company almost everywhere, and even the much maligned battalion cooks who were our lords and masters when a group of us were consigned to them on kitchen fatigue during rest periods out of the front line. Our arrival with Bren guns and tripods for ack-ack in different positions would evoke friendly jibes like: "What do you expect to bring down with those pea-shooters?" and… "Oo-er, meat for dinner tonight?" as if we were hunters going on safari or perhaps a reference to the pieces of pilot we sometimes collected in sandbags for their loved ones.

The N.M.R. regimental history records: 'A most successful raid on an enemy defended area was made on the night 15/16 July 1942 by 'B' Company (Captain H.B. Theunissen) together with one platoon from 'A' Company. Fifty-four prisoners were taken and a further two hundred casualties inflicted. The Battalion's losses were two died of wounds and twelve wounded, four of whom remained on duty.

'Bello' Theunissen was a real character. He had served in the First World War, had a voice like a foghorn and was well respected and loved by his men. (Earlier he had freed the author from the clutches of Sergeant-Major Herbert).

Through his wife, Richard Platt, (later decorated with the M.M.) a close friend and fellow combatant, recently left with me a graphic description of the part he played along with the rest of our platoon B9 in which most of the wounded were located:

"We headed for the enemy lines in trucks and were heavily shelled on our way in. The light was fading when we debussed, so our trucks were sent back as we dug in. With the onset of darkness we slowly moved forward. Our visibility was zero until a 'Wimpy' (Wellington Bomber) flew over and began dropping flares behind enemy lines. Whether this was part of our exercise I don't know, but it no doubt confused the enemy. We must have been about fifty yards from the enemy outposts when we were ordered to send scouts forward. Fred Knights, Jock Dickens and I were chosen from our platoon. We decided to leapfrog each other until we made contact. From the sounds we could hear it appeared that a digging party was digging gun pits and we weren't sure how heavily defended the position was. Fortunately we encountered no mines or barbed wire. I was out in front when I must have kicked a stone. Everything became dead, then the dreaded sound of machine guns being cocked. They couldn't have been more than twenty yards in front of me. Fortunately they held their fire, and I felt they must be Germans. I rejoined the others and we wasted no time reporting to the platoon. This was fortunate as will be seen later.

The order to advance was quietly given, and then they gave us a few bursts from their machine guns from close by. They weren't Spandaus, more like Bredas, so I was quite grateful. They must be Italians. We went to ground as one man. Then there was a roar from Bello, 'B' Company five rounds of rapid fire." A sheet of flame came from our side, then absolute silence. Then Bello shouted the regimental war cry, 'Wo Qowolwayo – Jii, Ulini pa', and with our reply 'Waaa!' we charged and we were in with tommy guns, Brens and bayonets. The din was tremendous and was heard from miles back. We heard the cry 'Mamma Mia' and they started coming forward with their hands up, and the order was given to cease fire. At this moment a machine gun from an emplacement to our left opened up on us. Jack Miller with the Bren, Fred Knights and I with tommy guns went for it. I threw a couple of grenades. The next moment there was an almighty explosion behind me, my head seemed to burst and I felt blood running down my neck. I was stunned and remember thinking that if this is death, it's a lovely feeling. Apparently I was walking round in circles with my tommy gun pointing menacingly. Someone grabbed me from behind and relieved me of my weapon. Jack and Fred fixed the machine gunner and the prisoners were rounded up. Two anti-tank guns were pushed back to our lines by prisoners, and about another eight were spiked by our chaps. I was delegated to escort prisoners back sans tommy gun, and this turned out to be a harrowing experience. We were heavily shelled all the way back to our lines, a few of the prisoners becoming casualties on the way. I left some of their mates to look after them not caring whether they escaped or not.

When we reached our headquarters, Jimmy Findlay gave me a good glug of neat gin, which made me feel better. We discovered that two of our chaps who were killed were scouts from another platoon who unbeknown to Bello had not reported back before we opened fire. One chap Hoffenberg died immediately, the other Fred Kirsten died in the ambulance on the way to the A.D.S.

Fred Knights was hit in the shoulder and we both were evacuated to 106 general hospital at Quassasin. Jack Miller and Phil Bullimore were also slightly wounded but remained on duty. Frank Nissen was also evacuated and Chips Ford slightly wounded."

My own account is:

Planned attacks in force, again with infantry, in platoon or company concentrations were often successful and raised morale. It was then that experienced and trusted commanders brought the best results. Captain Bello Theunissen was in charge of a raiding party on the night of July 15th, consisting of 'B' Company and one platoon of 'A'. His orders were simple, to attack a strong point and kill as many as possible. We lay quiet in the dark waiting for the prearranged signal to charge. Suddenly it was given, a great and terrible shout in which Bello's words were clear and in Zulu…"Babulale bonke!*

Richard Platt's comments continue:

It sent shivers down the spine and with bayonets glinting, as verey lights went up, we were soon amongst the enemy, tossing grenades wherever we heard frightened cries and, to our relief they were Italian 'mama-mia's.' There were loud bursts from machine guns concentrated around their field pieces and anti-tank guns and it took hand to hand fighting with bayonets to quell them. Bello strode around in the smoke and clamour encouraging us. In his report he said it was over in 25 minutes

---

* Smash them up. Kill them all!

– it had seemed like seconds and everywhere the Ito's became subdued, frightened and cooperative. The big guns were spiked and two precious Italian anti-tank guns were wheeled away by their gunners towards our lines. Tanks were heard approaching from the left and Bello ordered withdrawal.

Of the two killed that night one was Jo Hoffenberg, a Jewish boy whose heroism had long been commented on in previous actions. Rumour had it next day that our own opening fusilade had caught Hoffenberg while he was still out scouting in front of us. I seem to recall he was also at Durban High School where I had known him.

Richard Platt's final comment was:

"We were congratulated by the Division Commander for our efforts and Bello Theunissen was awarded the M.C. The day after this we were supposed to go on another fighting patrol before I was sent back. Thank goodness the job was given to another company, because the attack was a failure and our chaps were carved up."

Author's Diary

<u>Sunday, 26th July '42 – Alamein</u>

Moved up with Battalion. Now attached to 'B' Company. Took over perimeter held by F.F.B. Now in charge of No 3 section. Let the armour through the gap during the night.

<u>Monday, 27th July '42 – Alamein</u>

Rigged up barbed wire in the afternoon and cut myself here and there. Received post from home. At sunset left the positions and advanced a couple of miles to reinforce 'A' Company further along the Box perimeter. Very little sleep.

<u>Tuesday, 28th July '42 – Alamein</u>

Settling into the positions. Did the cooking for the platoon for a few meals. Had a helluva hectic night. First our artillery shelled from about 100 yards away. Then a Jerry (plane) bombed about 300 yards away with screaming bombs. Then Jerry shelled us for a couple of hours – not much sleep.

<u>Wednesday, 29th July '42 – Alamein</u>

Worked on positions and had a good nights sleep. Exit platoon officer and sergeant to hospital. Platoon severely reduced and now amalgamated with B9.

Keeping a diary has its advantages and its drawbacks. It was forbidden to the soldier at war and made you a target for over-zealous subalterns anxious to employ their newly won powers of censorship whether necessitated or not. It was a little disturbing to have a not very distinguished comrade-in-arms drinking with you and racketeering with you in poker or crown-and-anchor and then, after a mysterious disappearance of a year or so showing up as an officer with pips straight out of O.T.C* with the authority to read your mail. If it were known that you kept a diary and in long, dry psychological spells allowed it to be read by bored buddies, some of your opinions about the war effort and the goings on in such preserves, for officers, as the female ranks, or morale in general, or the politics of Joseph Stalin would have leaked. I had several reprimands for indiscreet if not militarily sensitive comments written into my letters home and censored by ferreting, eager platoon officers. Only one was referred to a higher authority who, it was reported to me, read the offending words and merely grunted 'Poppycock!' and took no further action.

Reading the war diaries of Field Marshall Lord Alanbrooke some years later I could not help feeling that what was good for the goose was good for the gander. Alanbrooke under great pressure found outlets in his war diaries for his frustrations dealing with Churchill and the myriad commanders of the divisions assembled in Britain, who he interviewed.

There is no doubt that keeping a diary can be comforting when the life is actually under threat: "Sweet are the uses of adversity."

I recommend it as therapy for anyone continuously at bay especially when threatened by both worlds, the inner as well as the outer.

The pathology of the desert sore went, according to common desert belief, that flies, in such swarms you could not entirely keep them off,

---

*O.T.C – Officers' Training Corps.

Top: South African engineers detecting mines at Alamein.
Bottom: Engineers or infantry detecting mines with probing bayonets.

laid their eggs on the skin. Bathing and showering because of water shortage was entirely out of the question on occasions and, inevitably the eggs hatched out into tiny maggots. If the skin was bruised or damaged in any way, the eggs and maggotts penetrated the skin and you had a desert sore because the pneumococcus, carried by the desert wind and dust, infected the weakened region. The ruling antibiotic of the time was sulphonamide, a white powder dusted on to the sore by a medic. Too much of the powder coating on the sores attracted other organisms.

The sores mostly became chronic and their scars, nasty blue-grey patches, could last a lifetime and be liable to re-infection. Flies contaminated the desert dust and sand. They brought infection to some soldiers who developed high temperatures with what was appropriately termed 'sand fly' fever. The psychological symptoms of this infection were appalling and soldiers with a history of it should never have been boarded back into the front line as fit for the kind of duties imposed there. Being closer to the Nile delta, Alamein was a worse area than Libya for air-borne (fly borne) contamination straight from the inhabitants' effluent.

One of the pleasant outcomes from the debacle at Tobruk was change. There were changes in attitudes at all levels and changes in command and platoon dispositions. With a powerful Allied airforce now seizing air superority over Alamein (when we had been without it for nearly a year) the ack-ack platoon was absorbed by the rifle companies. I was delighted to find myself in 'B' Company (Bello Theunisson's command) with Richard Platt and Co.

Wednesday, 12th August '42 – Alamein

Fortunate to miss a fighting patrol when the whole allied line wacked Jerry at night. Not a great success but we had negligible casualties but their's must have been considerable. Out artillery gave then hell.

Friday, 14th August, '42 – Alamein

No1 platoon is no more. We are now (Rifle Company) B9. Because of this more moving and shuffling about. Now under Corp. Bullimore, a good chap.

<u>Tuesday, 18th August '42 – Alamein</u>

Owing to some muck-up am again on an anti-tank course. Not too bad but rather hard work. Swimming and post in the afternoon. McLachlan has won the M.M.

<u>Wednesday, 19th August '42 – Alamein</u>

A good swim in the afternoon but horror of horrors, put in charge of 200 yard guard (a listening post in front). No sleep at all. Nothing of importance occurred though trouble was expected.

<u>Friday, 21st August '42 – Alamein</u>

An evening escorting or rather protecting artillery firing in front of the minefield. Terrific bombardment at Jerry from 1:45am to 3:15am. No sleep at all. Visited MacArthur in the evening and got slightly tight. Wire laying in the afternoon.

<u>Sunday, 23rd August '42 – Alamein</u>

Very busy day, fatigue in morning to build 'B' Company Battle headquarters. Wire laying in the afternoon with the result that my hands are in ribbons. Germans expected to attack tomorrow or 25th. Good night's sleep. Went to service by Nap Wheeler, quite good, who has returned.

I was with two N.M.R. platoon commanders being sent as observers of a tank battle about to ensue south of Ruweisat Ridge. At this stage on August 31st our platoon was dug in safely on the northern sector of the Alamein line, but I was happy to be part of an escort on the mission. There was an unusual air of optimism that morning. I noticed both officers chatting gaily and pointing to their map board. We were in a 15cwt. van with Bren guns. One officer was driving and stopped periodically to talk to soldiers from different regiments en route, New Zealanders and Indians mainly, there to guide us through minefields. We halted once or twice for a brew up and I began to be drawn into the picture. Several points emerged.

Firstly a trap had been set by the Allied command to draw panzers on to our anti-tank guns, but the big deal was the factor that the long awaited British 6-pounder was being employed. Usually it was transported on a Chevrolet truck allowing the gun to be used immediately. Our mission was to get into a good viewing position on Ruweisat Ridge to observe the approaching battle at Alam Halfa about 3 miles away at Point 132. The N.M.R. knew that they themselves were destined to be converted into an armoured reconnaissance unit and this mission would be valuable experience. From a high point on the eastern tip of Ruweisat Ridge we were able to watch the antagonists spread out into the distance below us. On the extreme left 3 miles away on our left flank was Point 132, the highest level of Alam el Halfa ridge with what we were told was the 10th Armoured Division on its South-western shoulder.

31st AUGUST 1942

Down on the flats, clearly visible 4 miles to our s outh was the British 7th Armoured Division. Immediately in front of us was the 2nd New Zealand Infantry Division also on the flats. On our left occupying the Western tip of Ruweisat and extending northwards to the South African 1st Division was the 5th Indian Division.

Four enemy armoured divisions were advancing eastwards, south of Ruweisat. Beyond them lay Mount Himemat and a little further was the Qattara Depression. The enemy formations attacking on the 31st August were:

> 90th Light Division (German)
> Two Italian Divisions
> 15th & 21st Panzer Divisions
> German Infantry Division

Our observations began in mid-afternoon and, at first, there was not much to see as these columns slowly penetrated our minefields. Artillery fire seemed continuous, and, in the distance tanks and trucks were brewing up. With the occasional assistance of the officers' binoculars I was able to see that the panzers had turned north-east and were engaging our forces in front of the eastern tip of Alam Halfa.

The panzer attacks were repulsed and the British 6-pounder was at the heart of the German reverse. The new six pounders must have accounted for more than a dozen tanks on that day. Our party returned

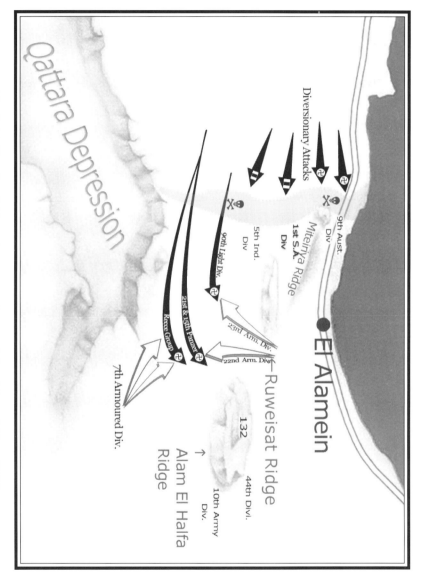

The initial battle of Alamein occurred around the ridge of Alam Halfa

to the N.M.R. and spread the good news about the 6-pounder but not before we had witnessed another spectacular. The panzer attacks continued for three days and on the first night were spotted by the R.A.F. using flares.

"At 12:30am our bombers returning from Tobruk found his whole strength had moved eastwards and located him with flares in the valley below us. It was one of the most awe-inspiring sights I shall ever see, I think – there were seldom less than twenty flares in the air at any one time and the whole valley with its mass of Afrika Korps stationary was lit up like a huge orange fairyland. All the time, red-orange, white-green tracer was darting hither and thither like little 100-mile-an-hour coloured fairies. The huge flash of the bombs, which included two 4,000 lbs., also inspired the whole thoroughly warlike scene, with little figures silhouetted against their vehicles as they tried to find cover from our bombs. The bombers were so accurate that they bombed right up to the minefield beyond which, 2000 yards away, was another of our companies."

For days afterwards a tally of German tanks lost in this battle of Alam Halfa was kept by us, and we knew then that with this kind of prestige building up, the resolution of the impasse at Alamein would be resolved in Montgomery's favour. I had witnessed for the first time the power of coordinated forces, of artillery, tanks and bombers meeting up with Rommel's expertise.

Passing through the lines of the Indian division we learnt that they too had counterattacked with success a thrust made at their lines by the Axis forces and there began a new spirit abroad in the Eighth Army which I always traced back to Ruweisat. Both the Indians and ourselves could now consign our mutual sorrows over Tobruk to the past and look to the future.

Author's Diary

Saturday, 5th September '42

Had my hand dressed at M.A.P (desert sores) erected tent next to the truck and expect to stay here several days. Official figures of the tank battle which has been raging, 96 German to 50 of ours. Many muck-ups by the tank regiments. Ito brigade succeeded in repulsing two of our brigades (N.Z.).

<u>Sunday, 6th September '42</u>

After breakfast large force of Hurricanes attacked German positions. On their way back ME.109's tore into them. I pumped 300 rounds at them without effect. Two hurricanes downed within 400 yards. Ran and helped pilot and saved parachute from one. Other a total wreck and pilot killed. Score for day 6 of ours down.

News came through that Corporal Archie McLachlan M.M. had been wounded, but not seriously, while on a fighting patrol at El Alemain on 31st August '42.

At age eighteen, nineteen, and twenty, sixty years ago, you don't ask too many questions about the Geneva Convention, either on behalf of yourself, or for those you are fighting. Nevertheless, in a volunteer army, such matters did come up in W.W.II.

English born I was subjected directly and indirectly to air attack and was, serendipidously positioned to answer back both directly and indirectly.

Directly in 1941/2 my regiment was bombed and strafed in East Africa and in the Western Desert where, at the time, Mersa Matruh, for instance, was the most bombed place on Earth.

Indirectly, my elderly relatives were being blitzed out of their homes by incessant enemy action in England, during that period. Directly I was an infantry anti-aircraft gunner in the front line firing at marauding German and Italian aircraft, Stukas and Messerschmidts, mainly overhead. Occasionally I was confronted with enemy pilots parachuting down from their burning aircraft. There was a good chance, many times, of their landing in no-man's-land, or even in enemy lines, free to fight again.

Though by nature a compassionate being, I felt compelled to fire on escaping pilots to prevent their furthur participation in the brutal war which had been the result of their own nation's aggression.

I was not popular amongst my own comrades, particularly when I had kept in reserve a specially extended magazine loaded with incendiaries and tracers for that purpose. In Northern Italy, long after her surrender, and we were in tanks by then, the question arose again when fifteen-year-old Hitler youths firing from trees became the easy targets. I personally, did not fire back.

The Six-Pounder anti-tank gun arrived almost too late to save Allied forces from ultimate disaster and in practice did not appear before the battle of El Alamein. They were carried on a Chevrolet portee and evened-up the odds against the Africa Corps.

CHAPTER XIV

The policy of the Allied forces at Alamein from July to October was to maintain aggressive action against the Axis. Patrols often took up almost all the hours of darkness, the patrol leader requiring to act as a listening post or silent observer of phenomena occurring in enemy positions. As an accompanying rifleman (or tommy gunner) there was not much else to do in the dead of the night but lie there for long hours staring up at the stars, at the heavenly blaze. The clear desert air seemed, not only to emphasise the celestial display but also to imprint your mind with the inevitable conclusion that as there is life on earth, there must be life somewhere else in those billions of points of light. And if there is life surely some of it is conscious. And then the question becomes 'How conscious?' Even the modesty of the average human would accept that earthly consciousness in such a speculative area is about half way developed in its possibilities and if we have our da Vincis, Platos and Mendelssohns there must feasibly exist such beings elsewhere especially in what appeared to be an infinite universe.

The conclusion of such patrols was inexorably a shoot-out of some sort, to excite the enemy to show himself in his response, to bluff him we were in great strength by firing at him from different positions out of darkness and hurling lightweight plastic grenades with loud bangs.

The idea was to activate an enemy machine gun crew, spot the position of the gun flashes in the dark, charge it, grab one or two prisoners, kill everyone else and get out. If a prisoner was unruly or aggressive the patrol leader might shoot him and snatch off badges, epaulettes, letters or other means of identification.

If there was barbed wire and no one could get through it you just blazed away with a tommy gun to give the Itos an impression that some of you were close and penetrating their wire. You had to be big and tough to carry a Bren gun that far or have rickshaw legs like Pooch Marais.

If you were a survivor you finally headed east towards the paling skies, the Allied lines, dawn with its grey fingers sweeping night's cobwebs from the skies and friends welcoming you and your password at minefield gaps in the barbed wire. Then precious sleep until the warming sun was high and unpleasant once more. The dreams that came at these times mixed Plato with Florence's David and with the nightmares of the previous night and dead friends beckoning half alive in impatient dreams and out of disordered patrols from Gazala to Buq Buq and Mersa to Alamein. Civilised life on earth? This? Well, really!

Patrol story – Not surprising, in the long gaps of desert idleness and boredom, questions arose out of thought's wildernesses like Who are we, here on earth? Where do we come from? Why are we here at all? And, of course, in the precarious situation of desert warfare sensing immortality, Where do we go to after death? After burying mother I had read a book "The Dead Have Never Died" and had, even in dugouts during bombardment, learnt to sing in my own words to the tune of "Home on the Range"...

> *"O give me a home*
> *Where the bright diamond sand*
> *Rolls eagerly down to the sea*
> *Where the graceful white swans*
> *Go gliding along*
> *Like a maid in a heavenly dream ."*

Did I believe in God? I had to…then!

On one patrol which kept us out from the allied line for many hours, I had watched the constellation of the Great Bear, or Plough as we called it partly rotate around the North Star, its two pointers so faithfully giving direction to the lost and comfort to the threatened. It was a terrible denouement to fall asleep lying out there during long waits when you should be alert and then to discover on awakening that the patrol had slipped away and you had to find your own path back to the allied wire alone and without a compass.

The North Star just above your left shoulder kept you safely orientated moving eastwards. Sometimes the same stars in their rotation around Polaris suggested the similar strange effect as that conveyed to a whirling dervisher and then I seemed to enter a different dimension.

And there were others out in the desert at such times, other patrols, friendly and occasionally sudden German raiding sorties. Someone in the platoon had a ghastly experience lying out on the extreme of his patrol, half asleep no doubt, when a hand clamped over his mouth and another pressed him to the ground and felt for his epaulets. In horror he turned his head to the attacker who was holding a knife between his teeth that glinted in the full moon. It was a Gurkha on a fighting patrol out to get prisoners for identification. The Gurkha's hand had felt the epaulet for insignia and locating the red flash, characteristically on the shoulders of South African volunteers, then patted the terrified private saying "O'right Jonny"… and was gone.

Sometimes heroes are born with courage shining in their eyes and eventually gleaming in everything they do. Other times the vicissitudes of life draw their courage from hiding.

Early in its W.W.II. manifestation the regiment was cursed by an appalling epidemic of meningitis. It was soon thrown off because of measures taken at responsible levels. In the various training camps for instance, where the danger was most serious, the men in barracks were made to sleep head to foot in their beds. Nevertheless there were casualties. The effect of this condition, an inflammation that attacks the membranous coverings of the brain, leaves the most debilitating results long after cure or successful treatment is over. The courage of military survivors of meningitis to return to active duty can only be appreciated when you have lived with them in the awful conditions that war can subject you to. Amongst the officers, Captain Dixie Adams was one such hero who struggled many times after meningitis to play a significant role in the regiment's affairs. After the war Dixie became a good friend. I began to write books and he gallantly carried them in Adams & Co., the best bookshop in his and my hometown.

Ted Borchart was another heroic character that returned to the line bearing the notorious psychological scarring of the meningitis condition. In 1942 he was drafted to my platoon and lived with me in my dugout. The dreadful effects of the condition would show themselves whenever situations were beyond the control of everyday routine but most especially during bombardments, Stuka attacks and strafing. Ted was by nature a kind, gentle person with an extraordinary sense of humour that was certainly a delight, but only too dreadfully emphasised his garish, one should say pathetic (in a non-pejorative sense) manner during the stress of front line exposure.

One moment he would have you in fits of laughter with pithy comment and sly innuendo as either of us went through the daily indignities that living two in a hole 24 hours a day entails, and the next moment as you and he went through the embarrassing behavioural antics that were your response to some of the most devastating tortures of modern warfare such as bombardment.

Ted Brochart stuck it out like a true Desert Rat, when others better equipped and with less excuse than he, would have fled. Ted was there in the opening days of the Alamein battle and was carried off wounded in the legs three days later and survived the war, not decorated.

AUCHINLECK

Auchinleck was always in demand especially after Japan attacked Pearl Harbour and India became vulnerable but he was heavily involved in the Crusader operations.

Auck was a professional amongst many amateurs who under estimated the psychology both of his own men in the line and of his enemy as well. Before the gates of Egypt with the Eighth Army desperately trying to recover and reorganise, he did not need to search for Rommel's weak chink. It was the Italian components of the enemy colums moving in for the kill and Auchinleck ordered his beleaguered men to mount attacks specifically against Italian regiments. An ongoing series of Allied fighting patrols ensued nightly, and they were meant to be, successful or fruitless, a menace to the cohesion of Rommel's front. Time and time again Rommel had to thrust elements of the Afrika Corps in to counter the havoc caused to the demoralised Italians at the receiving end of the Eighth Army's persistent attacks.

For weeks on end you were either on patrol yourself or preparing for the next one, or taking up positions weakened by casualty losses. There seemed to be no end to it, but it was the best thing to do while the front was being re-supplied mainly with American planes and tanks. Auchinleck's intent at this desperate stage was to give up land, even fortified positions in order to maintain the Eighth Army as a coherent active unit at all costs.

It should not be forgotten that although the Western Desert had consistently acted as Britain's second front, the entry of Japan into the war had diverted large supply convoys from the Middle East to India.

Everyone hated the menace of having to go out on patrol, for most of us something like once every four nights. Patrols were successful when they killed or took prisoners. They were unsuccessful if there was no response from the enemy even after blasting off every single one of the patrol firearms and the hurling of grenades over the enemy wire. In its distress the Eighth Army focussed infantry attacks on Italian regiments, which was the best policy while our armour was refitting and for the most part unaggressive.

Amongst the officers' real heroes in the battalion like the Captains Blamey, Theunissen, Paul and Lyster, many knew the hell of night patrols and accompanying aggressive actions and they had their own opinions about the cheeky new subalterns who came up to the line anxious to 'join in the fun' and too often soon left on transfer or in disgrace, respected by no one for their ineptitude or excessive enthusiasm.

Sergeants promoted from the ranks did their best to protect their men from mad officers out on patrol for the first time. The rank and file saw patrols only as one more pest like dust storms and as an opportunity only for officers to make their names.

The changes in command of the Eighth Army were bewildering. Bernard Montgomery was the fifth change in less than one year. One must go to the War Diaries of Lord Alanbrooke to find some of the reasons for change but probably the majority were directly through rank incompetence.

It should never be forgotten that in 1940 and 1941 there was always the threat of invasion directed at Britain and it would be ridiculous to pretend that in regard to planes, tanks and other weaponry Britain herself should not have the lion's share. Nevertheless it meant that the North African desert, the only continuous front line of the war for four years, would suffer from alarming shortages away from the Home Front because of the length of the lines of communication with it.

No sooner was the threat of invasion of Britain removed but the build-up of an army in the Middle East to accompany the American invasion of Europe began and diversions of material were made there. Under these circumstances planning of tactics and execution of advances from Alexandria to Tripoli were fraught with difficulties and changes in command inevitable. In review, I believe, along with many others, that Claude Auchinleck suffered most from injustice and was given the least credit for the sound tactics he adopted. For instance, his determination to preserve the 8th Army at all costs, and thus being prepared to sacrifice fortress, equipment and ground by retreating to the 'safe' line at Alamein was a courageous decision, which saved the day in 1942's terrible retreat from Gazala.

TWO & SIX POUNDERS

In the re-equipping of the Eighth Army at Alamein, it was recently suggested* that each infantry battalion was provided with eight two pounder anti-tank guns in order to protect it against any breakthrough by panzers (which were the main infantry predators) and against armoured vehicles in general. This was certainly not true of the N.M.R. which held positions vulnerable to tank attack in the line at Alamein almost continuously. For the few months before October 23rd we held dug-in positions by day and night and on several nights a week went on patrols. Our own anti-tank platoon had been disbanded, and its men transferred to rifle companies. Its weapon, the Boyes anti-tank rifle, was derisory in its effectiveness. It could have been that 6-pounder and 2-pounder artillery units had been attached, but we never saw them and they were certainly never dug-in with us in the front line.

The infantry's concern about the matter of adequate anti-tank guns ran deeply in the mistrust it had of the competence of British armour to defend their infantry divisions drawn as they were mainly from the white empire.

When Alexander and Montgomery took over the Eighth Army there were all kinds of deals and shareouts of the new equipment arriving in vast quantities in the Middle East. The New Zealanders, Australians and South Africans had all been mauled many times by panzers when British armour had failed for various reasons to perform. The three commonwealth divisional commanders became alarmed at the plans Montgomery was preparing and in the last days before the start of the Battle of Alamein, internecine war broke out again in the Eighth Army over this old irritant. Put simply the three generals commanding the infantry from the white dominions did not trust the British armour to provide an adequate screen for its infantry once it had smashed gaps through the German lines and the latter could be expected to counter-attack with its panzers at a time when the allied infantry would probably be exhausted if not decimated by its onslaughts on the first night. Indeed, it was a weighty argument because the plan of the battle of Alamein was to send the armour straight through the opened gaps hell-bent for Tripoli. The argument was countered by Montgomery in two ways. Firstly he increased the planned intensity of the opening barrage to include nearly a thousand field pieces and secondly, he seems to have softened about slamming the armour through the gaps poste haste. As it turned out Montgomery was blamed for the slow breakout of the Eighth Army from Alamein. To his credit, he defied Churchill and other hotheads out of respect for the advice of the three Commonwealth generals knowing full well he would need the infantry to open up gaps in German front lines all the way to Tripoli.

TRAINING FOR ALAMEIN

In the weeks and then days before the Battle of Alamein it soon became clear to the infantry what the manoeuvres they were practising were all about. We were to conduct a frontal attack on Germans dug-in behind massive minefields with layers of barbed wire surrounding them with mortars, machine guns and heavy artillery as their back up. In case there was any doubt about the effectiveness of our artillery barrage, a creeping one behind which we were to advance on foot was planned. We were to undergo further training in bayonet fighting so that this 'coup de grace' could finalise our do or die effort. As Phil

Bullimore the corporal of our infantry section (one of the bravest men I ever met) put it after covert information had come from his elder brother, an officer of some rank: "You fight your way through the barbed wire and avoid treading on mines in the dark, you kill any German still alive in his trench after the barrage lifts. You use your grenades, your bayonets, pistols, sticky bombs, anything because there is going to be hand-to-hand fighting to get these swines out. Engineers will follow you, lifting mines and laying white marker tapes to create a track for the tanks."

Bully had had to take a few gulps of cypress brandy before it finally emerged. He pulled constantly at his right ear as it all came out. It seemed we had been going through practise manoeuvres of the plan for ages, but only when he blurted it out, finally, dancing on his bedroll with annoyance that we really understood what we were in for.

Bullimore had been holding something back. A few more swigs of the cypress and he broke into his military vernacular, preceding each utterance with a protracted, confirmatory "ye-e-s." The arrangement was that infantry would hold open the gap they had created in the German front line at all cost and let the 8th Army tanks through. The "ye-e-s" signalled "I know what they're going to do!" His tirade spoke for our own feelings. "Yes! The P.B.I.* will take all the stick and get shat on and then the armour will break out and leave us behind to fend against the panzers unprotected."

We had seen it happen before in the boxes at Gazala and the siege of Tobruk.

"Hell!" I said to myself "Have we really not progressed at all since Thermopylae when we killed each other with swords and spears?" I remember shouting at Bully who was himself hardly as tall as his rifle, let alone with a bayonet fixed to it.

"Bully, what do I do with my Bren gun while I'm carrying the fixed bayonet?"

It seemed petty to raise such an old anguish that had troubled the desert armies before, that British armour was no match for Blitzkrieg.

---

*P.B.I. - poor bloody infantry

At a high level of command the same fears were being repeated. Oliver Leese our Corp commander, with no knowledge of the desert had been confronted by three of his commonwealth generals who were unhappy at some of Montgomery's plans too and were to express the same fears that our midget corporal had voiced. The gaps that the infantry were expected to make in the German lines, were unlikely to be completely created in one night. As it happened Montgomery did amend his plans somewhat so that some of the British tanks would come through the gaps as they were created and remain outside them to take on the panzers in a defensive screen.

Saturday, 19th September, '42 – Alamein

Bayonet training first thing, – then platoon manoeuvres – wrote letters, saw doctor – played football for B9 against Support 2nd. We won 1 – 0. Had a binge up in the evening.

Saturday, 3rd October, '42 – Alamein

What a day! Our (canteen) order arrived consisting of 19 bottles of wine and 120 tins of beer and with it came McLachlan from the R.D.L.I. who we are relieving. Talked over old times (at Dickinsons) with him and got him drunk. Drove him home. Got drunk myself, played poker and won five shillings. To bed early but slept badly because of earache.

Sunday, 4th October, '42 – Alamein

Drank in the morning. Packed up my kit. Left on truck at 2pm for the front line. Acted as guide to the company which arrived after dark. Fortunate in securing a fairly good dugout which I am sharing with Richard Platt. Slight artillery activity. On guard and saw much machine gun tracers.

WATERCARTS

Nobody liked the authorities that distributed the regimental water, which on most occasions was strictly rationed. In practice, until Alamein this was one gallon per man per day. Ideally, given sufficient water in hot desert conditions, it should come out of a canvas bag (traditionally a goatskin). The canvas allowed a dampness to percolate through to the surface so that evaporation was continuous. The bag was hung in a shaded area and given a very slight breeze, cooling was ongoing.*

Alas water supply was a tenuous procedure and broke down frequently which meant the soldiers on the watercart were targets for obscenities. However there were always men who preferred any kind of insult to night patrols and frontal attacks who became water truck stooges. After rough engagements at the front Bully would single out the water wallahs for attack. Being a shaving type, he had as it were with daily shaving, vested interests and noted with alacrity any sloppiness amongst the gunga-dins. One of them was a Johannes Factotum, a butcher boy at the start of the war who had been useful in the regimental kitchens in the early days when fresh meat was on the menu and later when we had fallen back to the Delta and meat had come in bulk frozen from New Zealand. Johannes had made several attempts to join combatant units but always ended up on the watercart. Bully was scathing after he heard Johannes crowing, magpieing to new recruits about how many prisoners he had taken in recent fighting.

"Y-e-e-s! And you know where he was at the time…fucking miles away bringing up fucking brack water!"

Shorty Carneson was a dumpy, bald-headed alcoholic who tagged on to platoon B9 after gravitating from the group of cooks who ran the company kitchen. He had a special affinity for Richard Platt and I and was a guy that followed us through the period of 1942-44 uttering Cassandra like prophecies about my future, which unaccountably came true.

Fred Carneson, Shorty's brother was a young communist soldier in the South African Army hovering over the precincts of power during the war years. After the war he became a communist MP taking his seat in the legislative assembly in Cape Town. He was a remarkable, extrovert young man who with great determination had taken up the cause of communism at a very opportune moment. He had joined the forces of the Union of South Africa at a time when Jo Stalin's name

---

*At the beginning of the war water came in 4 gallon square drums, then, the same but in 4 gallon tins and finally in jerry containers. It might also be dumped in 40 gallon cylindrical drums.

was on every Allied soldier's lips because from the moment the USSR had been attacked in June 1941 he had seemed to be the only good news on the European war-fronts. The heroic struggle of the Russians had caught the imagination of Allied soldiers to such an extent that in my own regiment and many others that I can speak for, Stalin was called Uncle Joe, which in the English dialect of South Africa meant senior friend. Field Marshall Jan Smuts was also called 'Oom Janie' meaning "our Uncle".

A while later with the accession of the National Party to power in South Africa, Fred Carneson had become a Member of Parliament representing the Natives, as I recall it, one of six native representative seats. I met up with him in the N.M.R. in 1942 when he would visit our lines, he being then in uniform. He came to visit because his elder brother was a private in the regiment and he held a series of conversations, in which he quite overawed several of us into becoming the nearest thing to communists, as the army would allow. After the war, quite a few of us joined the Springbok Legion.

Shorty Carneson was the exact opposite of his young brother Fred. He must have been in his early forties or twice the age of the rest of us and he looked it. He was very sloppy, bald and almost toothless. He was absolutely terrified of any show of force by the enemy. The further he could get from the site of any action, pleased him most. He was happy to accept various fatigues if it meant him not having to approach the actual front line. He became like the cooks of the company, oversensitive to the frequent air raids that South African infantry experienced in the desert. Air raid procedure usually meant a warning whistle blown at the sight of a possible enemy plane which with its strafing could be very dangerous to men behind the front assembling at the kitchen for an evening meal or breakfast.

When possible the procedure at mealtimes was for active personnel like myself taking turns to leave the front line and queue for the meal out of thermos trays at the squadron or company headquarters. Many like myself had been trained in aircraft spotting which meant that we had tuned our ears to the very characteristic sound of axis aircraft, long before whistles were blown in warning. As active combatants perhaps we could be forgiven occasionally whilst standing in a meal queue for misinterpreting deliberately the sounds of approaching hostile planes. When we let out our warnings they were usually focused upon words like, "Hello, hello, hello, hello" which meant, "We can hear hostile planes coming". Any kind of warning like that scattered the army chefs and their helpers who would run for cover in shell slits previously dug close by leaving the food trays open and exposed for whoever cared not to take cover. This would happen serendipitously more often on the days when the menu was unusually good. Combatant soldiers rarely took cover and instead helped themselves to the kitchen fare. Shorty was never upset at being classified as virtually a non-combatant.

I sometimes fell into his disfavour through being one of the 'edicated' but usually a commendation of me in a letter from his brother restored me and at such times if Shorty was on kitchen serving duty I would be helped more than generously if there were any prime cuts.

All this changed when Bernard Montgomery took over command of the 8th Army in October 1942. It was his instruction that he would assault the German line at Alamein when the Allied troops were ready. His instructions made it absolutely clear for the whole of the 8th Army that when the day arrived for the battle of El-Alamein to take place, everyone would have to carry a weapon. The army postman, the hygiene staff, the medical stretcher-bearer would all be armed and drafted into the fighting line. There were many like Shorty who trembled when they read these advanced orders. Shorty was one of the non-combatants who were drafted up to fill the empty places in the ranks of forward troops. Our own regiment badly mauled had shrunk from 1200 to 250 fighting men and was sorely in need of reserves of any kind. That's how Shorty joined our platoon, 'B' Company platoon No. 9. The two weeks before Oct. 23rd 1942, which was, the day of the Battle of El-Alamein were crowded with manoeuvres.

Manoeuvres in this instance were battle procedures. We literally rehearsed every night, formulae in which we penetrated, as fighting infantry, German minefields, laying down tapes to indicate gaps we were going to create in the minefields when the battle was to begin. Sappers would then follow up and lift German mines from the gaps that we had indicated with tapes. The purpose of the gaps was to let tanks through once the infantry had taken the forward posts. I carried a Bren gun and amidst my equipment a hundred round circular ammunition magazine.

Shorty was one of four supporters of my machine gun element, carrying 28 rounds of curved .303 bullets in 6 magazines in Bren pouches. All these preliminary armings and manoeuvres were observed by the non-combatants with increasing alarm. Shorty himself was always in a state of near panic mainly because being illiterate he never understood what was expected of him. Monty's battle plans were learnt by the troops as if they were laws of the Medes and Persians, all of which passed Shorty by. Shorty was quite happy to go along with everything on the instructions that I had given him. "When the attack starts, keep me in view, that's all you have to do, and if I need ammunition I'll signal for it". Came the 21st and 22nd of Oct and trucks bearing Cypriot brandy, Australian beer and an unnameable wine arrived for distribution. Many men had two water bottles, one with an alcoholic beverage in it. Shorty's dark secret was that he was alcoholic and whilst he conceded that this last measure was highly remedial, his terror at the forthcoming engagement still knew no bounds. Hostile aircraft he had learnt to cope with, but full battle procedure, never before by him experienced, was something that horrified him. It cast no reflection on the courage of the young men who risked their lives on the night of the 23rd that they might have had access to bottled courage. Our own barrage, when it began was one of the most staggering experiences any of us had known. The cordite fumes, the explosions ripping the earth open every few feet was more than anything we ever expected. Occasionally our own shells were landing amongst us. German mortars added to the maelstrom.

One of the first casualties was Shorty Carneson. An explosion at his feet had sent a piece of shrapnel ricocheting into his chin. In the sulphurous hell he rushed over to me, forsaking for the moment the many and widespread booby-trapped foot mines that could be observed in the light of the full moon. I looked at the wound, sticking a finger into it and realised that it was not going to haemorrhage excessively.

Shorty began to waver and look around him. He didn't like what he saw and his eyes started to bulge. I grabbed his water bottle and thrust it into his hands and shouted in his ear "Drink and be merry."* He took a good glug of it and shouted back "Gee whiz!" I straightened him out and pointed him to a gap in the advancing line of our platoon. Thirty minutes later I myself was wounded very badly and did not see Private Carneson again for some months. He had bravely carried on; joining the platoon, despite his wound and was amongst the very few who were mentioned in dispatches.**

When Shorty Carneson became drunk, he became prophetic and, like Cassandra, no one ever believed his prophecies but there were a few who discovered their reality. They came true in individual instances and I was one of these. Prior to El-Alamein when the company was resting behind the lines there were frequent booze-ups. Shorty liked the hard tack and as he slowly became drunk he would team up with a mate who played the guitar and the evening would be given over to mournful singing with commentaries on passers-by provided by Shorty. The old resentment resurfaced. He liked me because I was a friend of his brother's but he held it against me that I was "edicated". On this particular occasion just before the big battle, he singled me out and told me that I would be struck down in the coming battle as he would himself and wove into the forecast all kinds of melodrama that became only too painfully true. We had both been hit at the same place within minutes of each other. After the remnants of the regiment returned to South Africa to recover from its mauling at Alamein, they were transferred from being infantry to cavalry and were, in fact, retrained to take on the Germans in Italy. Just before commencing the protracted assault on the Gustav line, Shorty surfaced once more, forecasting again that in the coming blood-bath, this time in tanks, I would be cut down and it was doubtful in his mind whether I would survive.

He would have gone on with his melancholic reading of the future, had not Richard Platt and some of my friends halted him being greatly concerned that they themselves would be named in the uncanny

---

* "Eat, drink and be merry for tomorrow we die."

** HONOURS & AWARDS

predictions in his alcoholic semi-stupor. I was concerned enough by the prophecy to discuss the matter with some buddies in my troop and spoke to Richard Platt as to what steps I could take to avoid these portents of doom which again proved accurate. I remembered the conversation so well. It was in a vineyard on an Italian roadside and the unpicked grapes hanging overhead were purple and bursting from recent rain. Shorty survived the war and I lost touch with him. In one of his worst melancholic outpourings he told us about his family concern for Fred who was the intelligent one. They had high hopes of him becoming well educated so that he could put into effect some of his yearnings and ambitions. The family was poor but somehow or the other, they had scraped the money together to equip the young Fred with the necessaries for attending High School. It was with great pride and joy that they had sent him off to school dressed in blazer, grey flannels and school badges. Two or three days later it had come out at school that the family was poorly placed and Fred accordingly was relegated in the pecking order in his class. Some older boys had picked on him and roughed him up. They had torn off his new school jacket and stamped it into the ground, smashed his suitcase and spilled the textbooks calling him all kinds of disgusting names. It had broken the family's heart when the boy got back home and it had cultivated in Shorty a deep hatred of anyone privileged. For instance, in the long retraining programme of converting infantry to tank men, we all had to undergo class tests. Poor Shorty had to struggle to stay in the regiment because his scores were so low and he seethed with disappointment and resentment.

Chapter XV

On leave in Cairo, ranks below sergeants usually found themselves in cabarets after a long afternoon siesta. Usually with your combibones you chose one out of several cabarets as your favourite meeting place to start the night's revelry having wined and dined at some modest cafe or restaurant. Soldiers' cabarets began quietly enough. The drill was that you and your mates grabbed a table and covered it with drinks, usually iced beers and then surveyed the scene, meaning the cabaret girls. Dancing on the floor by couples mostly female was then the order. When you decided on a young lady she would come to your table and order a drink from a waiter. The catch was that her drink was usually just a cordiale but the price was the same as a soldier's double whisky. If you then, continued to become unsteady, the price of the drinks would go up steeply and your courtship was certain to be short. If the girl liked you, she would settle in at your table especially if some of her own cronies were already there. Several nights of this routine with the same girls meant that your name was on most of the cabaret women's lips and they would regard you as one of **their** comibones teasing you, flirting, cursing you, sharing girlie talk with you, and making the waiters bring them something stiff like cypress brandy or a parfait amour liqueur for which you paid handsomely and if you didn't you were scolded loudly, even sworn at like "Hey Tosh! Don't be a bloody cunt, pay the waiter!"

It was all a laugh and went on for hours. As the drinks flowed your girl would probe into the state of affairs up at the front and if she didn't like your answer would warn you that her Franz or her Fritz would soon carve you up in the next battle or, worse still make you gallop*. They became very friendly at the table with wandering hands that sought amorously for your wallet or paybook which both had a

---

* Retreat

246

price on the Cairo black-market. It was through this sort of familiarity that soldiers arrived back at camp fleeced of everything. If your friendship tugged at a romantic cord in her you might be given her card and told when to come to her apartment perhaps next day and so on. But you still had to pay.

Things would get more and more hectic as the night came to a close. Some of the girls followed you into the urinals and had the knack of drawing up their clothing to let go a stream standing next to you. They did not find it revolting as we did. Some nights finished more dramatically than others. Suddenly the cabaret would empty of girls and a few tough looking fezzed Arabs would take their places. It was time to close. If you did not wish to end the revelries and there were plenty of soldiers around and especially from your own country...Australians, Tommies, South Africans you might give the cabaret staff a hard time. It was really quite disgusting, as if we were more an army of occupation than allied to Egypt.

One of the favourite cabarets was the Grand Trianon, a first floor business with entrance and exit up a long, straight flight of steps from the main street. At the close of one particular night there, our party's slowness in winding up proceedings brought the chucker-outs to our table which they proceeded to wrench away from us.

A struggle ensued with the table, very large and ebony black being upended and dragged to and fro, ending up at the exit steps. A helping hand from the diggers*, about to leave, who with great esprit des corps, drove off the staff and with a final flourish our party boarded the now capsized table and tobogganed down the cabaret steps into the street.

After a long day at Heliopolis, swimming and skating, I went that night to the Washington Cabaret. I was in a gloomy mood pondering the long journey back to the line next day, when I became aware of a girl who had silently slid into a chair opposite me. I expected it to be the typical floozy anxious to earn her keep getting a feller to buy her a drink. But she must have been in her forties. The olive complexion was grooved with wrinkles like a piece of desert and its wadis seen

---

*Australians

from 20,000 feet. The nose was a talking point on its own, long and inquisitive. The eyes were dark brown and ringed with those dark circles that suggested a Lebanese.

She was what Shaw might have called a venerable grotesque, a Fatattateeta to Cleopatra, a well-used servant girl who had seen better days and was about to complete her drying out into an old prune. But the eyes were bright, even compassionate and they had fixed themselves on me expecting derision.

She was a Madame Sesostris in the wasteland of a country quickly losing its soul, but she was female and respected. A waiter brought her a well-set tray with a cup of coffee. She expected to be slagged off and started the conversation. "You are the handsomest man here tonight and you sit dejected in a corner." Her English betrayed its levantine connections but was word perfect. "I see you are curious as to why I am here," she continued. Her turkish cigarette matched the coffee and she was quite at home and I wanted to know how such a jolie caide* could sit so sedately in a place of such iniquity without losing her well trained poise, almost sophistication.

The guys came off the dance-floor. Some were tipsy and raucous. She offered them her packet of turkish cigarettes and was unruffled at their side comments. When the music blared again and we were alone she told me her story in her deep, firm voice, "I come here every night for a specific reason. No, not that, never that. I come here to watch over someone. A long time ago during the Great War, I was one of the girls here when Allenby's boys were everywhere. They went off to fight the Turks and left me with child and a little money. With it I bought a small share in this cabaret and worked here for a time. The one I watch over is my daughter, the little one that the English major left me with. When he was killed we moved to the Lebanon. Soon I shall return there. There she is now!" She called across the room as the music ended and a slim girl, with a skin paler than her mother's came across the floor and sat next to her. She was my dream girl, a Hedy Lamarr but twenty years younger, her English was less polished than her mother's but her teeth and her complexion were exquisite and radiant.

---

*Ugly women whose fascination lies in their gross features

<u>Tuesday, Sept 15th '42</u>

Went out to Heliopolis to skate and swim. Succeeded in the latter but not in the former. Had photos taken.

Went to La Americaine for lunch and the Royal for the afternoon show. Had dinner with three hags and an extra. Ended up with meeting my dream girl in the form of the extra's daughter.

Home 1a.m.

The mother's name was Marcia. Other guys had met her and spoke of her kindly. In the long hours acting as chaperone to her beautiful daughter she did odd jobs for the soldiers – darning, sewing on buttons, badges and flashes. The glory bag she carried was a marvel to see with its nail file and clippers, elastic, thimbles and there were dress buttons from many current army units.

Marcia was no Mata Hari and carried a clearance letter from the British Embassy in Cairo. Before I said a final goodbye to both, a month before the Battle of Alamein, Marcia had taken me by the hand and said "My son, you are a Capricornian and will suffer long and cruelly from this war. They have given my little one many names. Her real name is Tassia. She will answer to it always. Write to her when you can." With that she pressed her daughter's card into my hand.

Medium height, Joe Rawlinson a pleasant, refined person played ding-dong to Bullimore. Bully could bounce ideas off him, use him as a confidante, ally, nurse and companion on leave and stalwart supporter in mundane military affairs.

If Joe demurred over some matter Phil Bullimore looked at it again to see where he had gone wrong. Phil was careful in his decisions partly because he was small and couldn't throw himself around without looking ridiculous. Rawlinson set himself high standards. His enamel mug was always clean. He enthused if the niceties of life occasionally held sway… glasses for the wine, cleaning fluid for spectacles, clothing somehow always immaculate. In the group he had the reputation of being straight out of Poona with the manners of a benevolent colonel or major who had seen service with the Indian army… hated anything

The Author at Heliopolis

shabby or not quite above board. He would tell Bully immediately if something was not quite pukka and chose all his words with care, never swearing or being rude if he could help it. Joe's language, 'Poona' of course had lots of hums and ha's, with narrowings of the eyes, clearings of the throat, adjusting of his clothing.

The Army life we were leading, hazardous as it was still, taught us many useful facts about ourselves and how to deal with the precarious as well as with the entrenched. I suppose there emerged a psychology of army life, which you either accepted and got along reasonably well with or you rejected, preferring a more independent even existential way peculiar to yourself. With the onset of team spirit through having to complete missions together like kitchen fatigues, night patrols, laying mines, driving in convoy, packing the section vehicle, mounting Bren guns, digging your own daily lavatory or a communal one and sharing dugouts you adopted the psychology of sharing or being prepared to partner every event that presented.

Obtaining leave in Cairo and Alex were events that were precarious because they came under rotas that were unreliable, broken by the vicissitudes of military campaigns or replaced by drawing names out of a hat. Suddenly out of the blue you found yourself going on a five-day stint with say four comrades sometimes even strangers. You might be fortunately endowed with money or your pay book might be a disaster area. You would be altogether, doing a night club or having a meal, or buying this or that. The only way to handle the situation and avoid shutting out a buddy was to stick all your money into a common pool and give it to an acting treasurer who was the most reliable of all of you under all circumstances and he paid out for everything from the common purse as the expenses occurred.

Except for rare occasions the method worked admirably. It was a good leveller. Alcoholics like Shorty Carneson or sex maniacs or pot smokers operated independently and just faded away into the kind of environment that suited them best and you didn't see them again until you were on the truck taking you back to the regiment. Sometimes there was money over and you shared it out on the last day of the leave to wallop on anything you fancied. I usually bought a sandbag full of onions and a couple of tins of jam to make the bully beef and biscuits, the every day fare, more palatable. Occasionally, as

Alexander, Churchill and Montgomery

circumstances provided, you went off with a pal who had the same predilections and just one of the two held the purse. In Alex, Len Clark and I took sailboats out on the extensive harbour, played tennis, hired bicycles, did the various sights etc. After the war, soldiers who had adopted this army psychology of sharing habits, habitats and purses, adapted easily to business situations that required associates.

Occasionally the method backfired.

Cowboy Brennan was a carefree short-sighted extrovert. Blond, aquiline features and ruddy complexion made for distress in the sun, and the Western Desert could provide many variations on its notorious central theme of heat and dust in summer, and cold and khamsin in winter. There were eight variations – flies, boredom, brackish water, flash floods, bully beef and biscuits, ticks, fleas, fatigues and masturbation. But there was one more, alien to the desert and brought in by mischance and the gracious consent of its host. Its name was acaris…better known as crabs.

The ladies who donated them in the brothels of Cairo and Alex were not wholly to blame. They were indigenous to Delta dwellings, the Delta climate and the Delta temperament.

To be forewarned was to be forearmed, but to be short-sighted was to be vulnerable to attack. Cowboy was a newcomer to the desert and was regarded as a "Tobruk Avenger", arriving in a group in time for Alamein which heroically decimated them. They had not had the early indoctrination of the whore houses of Addis Ababa and the streets of shame in the Delta known as Sister and Burka, and inevitably their first intimations of this special kind of torment was a crotchety itch. Now itches are not uncommon in desert circumstances and the Medical Aid Posts were sometimes overrun with young soldiers back from leave seeking help for their itches and a diagnosis where possible. Bully was always a kindly adviser of lame ducks and had through incessant consultations earned for himself a reputation, by spot check of the exposed soldiers' genitals. His opinion was that of an expert, almost specialist. Cowboy, a fortnight back from Delta leave had approached him and lowered his trousers patiently. Bully didn't need to put on his reading spectacles to give an affirmation out aloud that was the dread of the victim and a trigger for either laughter if you had not suffered the experience yourself or grunts of compassion and consolation if you had, from anyone around. Bully's version was: "Y-e-es, my God y-e-es, everywhere. They're laying eggs and they dropping off you. Go to the M.A.P. and get some blue butter, and for heaven's sake take your own razor!"

Early in October I had trouble with my left ear again. 'Otitis Externa' the medical aid post had written down on my card. I was one of a long queue that got longer, as we laid more and more barbed wire and fingers, gloved or gloveless, got further torn and with the help of the flies became quickly infected. Desert sores had become epidemic and even grown on us as part of social life. You discussed them with friends, unwinding your owm filthy blood and pus stained bandages to compare notes, even helping to replace somebody's who had sores in delicate sites and sometimes holding mirrors at difficult angles to show them up. Everyone agreed that if you could see the sores you helped them in some way. I quoted "Energy follows thought" as a Buddhist-yoga axiom. You had to be careful if you let your sore stay uncovered too long. Even if you were in a dugout, flies would settle and lay their eggs on your sores. Some soldiers were of the opinion that the maggots hatching from the eggs would do a better job at cleaning up a sore than the M.A.P., but I wasn't ready for that. The long sick queues were more of a breeding ground for alternative methods of healing than a place you could swap maggots. On occasions with the passage of hours and inattention the queue would fade as the disheartened left. It was during such a period that I had missed my injection and the abscess in my left ear became acute. I had terrible attacks of pain and earache. Some bought painkillers in desperation, freely available on the Cairo market when we were on leave.

It was coming out of one of these episodes in the middle of the night that I had a vivid dream of the Rogers boy. Michael was the youngest son of a family of three brothers. A boarder at Durban High School and in my own class he had cheeked the teacher and become implicated in a petty classroom scandal of altering the teachers' marks in the mark book. He had, it was said, changed the marks of several pupils to a higher level. His was one of those changed and mine was another, but we all had a rough ride while the matter was investigated, the innocent and the guilty.

In my dream I saw Michael staggering and clutching at his body fearfully as if he were trying to hold it together and then a phantom figure leave it. I awakened shocked but with my earache gone. There was a clatter outside the gunpit and a shout. Bullimore had brought up a replacement because I was short of a tommy gunner. It was an old friend, Richard Platt, one of the heroes of June 7th just discharged from the 106th. S. African General Hospital where his wounds had been cleaned up and he had survived a bout of sandfly (tick?) fever. Almost coincidentally the news came through that Captain Noel Rogers, the eldest of the three brothers had been struck in a shell burst and died in hospital. Noel had been a highly respected figure, role model of courage and elegance. A few months later on home leave, I ran into the middle brother who was in a pilot's uniform of the S.A.A.F. and had the opportunity of talking to him about his paradigmatic elder brother Noel who remains as a symbol in my subsequent dreams of valour and elegance. I noted down somewhere that when you had known three brothers in life, invariably they provoked dreams. The brothers Platt, Frank, Smedley and Rogers of the N.M.R. were examples for me.

Churchill visited the front on August 5th. It was a surprise and there would have been no chance to put together a cheery reception by our regiment. He saw the divisional commanders however and that was important because Smuts was about to meet Churchill in Cairo in private discussion as to the future of the first South African Division already decimated in the desert. It was important for developing events to keep South Africa in the war and Smuts needed reassurance that something else than infantry disasters would befall the forces of his small country remembering those events at Sidi Rizegh and the fall of Tobruk. He knew that his division had been on active service unbroken for two years and needed rest at a time when a new commander of the Eighth Army was hell-bent on a frontal attack by infantry to break out of Alamein. Smuts, Alanbrooke and Churchill solved the problem by deciding that the South African division already decimated in the desert, would be converted to an armoured force* and the ensuing training in tanks would be part of its 'rest'.

---

* Eventually the Sixth South African Armoured Division operating in Italy in 1944.

And that was how it was to turn out. In the event the conference of the big knobs in Cairo conveyed the intelligence that the Americans were going to land in North Africa and pincer Rommel between their armies and those which Montgomery would break out with from Alamein. The implied preliminary was that the U.S would send massive reinforcements to Egypt to help this plan.

"One other thing – out of the mistakes and the failures there was good metal coming to the top. With every campaign a larger and larger group of men was emerging.Our pyramid had been misshapen and badly built before.Now some of the misfits had been removed. Little by little the pyramid was being groomed and adjusted. Inevitably it was going to be a better pyramid in the end than the German one, and at its top it was going to have a better general than Rommel.

When I got back to Cairo the best energy and brains among the Allies was being put into the job of reorganization. We had had a bad shock. The old business of holding the Middle East on a shoe-string was going to cease. There was going to be no more bluffing. So Churchill flew in from London one morning to hold his conference in Cairo. He had with him Averill Harriman, the American Lease-Lend administrator; General Sir Alan Brooke, Chief of Imperial Staff; General Ronald Adam, the Adjutant General and one or two others. Wavell came across from India. Smuts flew in from South Africa. All the generals, the senior Admirals and Air Marshals of the Middle East were gathered. It was a momentous conference, one that was going to change the course of the war. It meant that at least we acknowledged that we had a second front right here in the Middle East, a place where we were immediately in contact with the enemy and able to buttress Russia's left flank.

There was the usual purge of generals – Alexander, a dynamic little man who had done well at Dunkirk and as well as possible at the fall of Burma, took the place of Auchinleck. By giving General Maitland Wilson a separate command in Syria and Palestine, Alexander was free to devote his energies to the desert. He had a new subordinate in the field – Montgomery.

Several other generals were replaced and reshuffled. This much was announced. But the changes went much further. They have not even yet been completed or felt. At this conference a new army of the Middle East was given birth, an army that for the first time was going to include Americans as well as British. A tide of reinforcement such as the Middle East had never known before was going to come in, and from it a better army will be built.

— *A Year of Battle* – Moorehead

Another family that had contributed its sons to W.W.II. was the Cowleys. Joe Cowley was a Durban lawyer living on the Berea in pre-war days.

Some years ahead of me at Durban High School, his family traditions were embedded in our early regimental history. His younger brother had been in my class at school, wherein he had been more noted for his appalling handwriting than for any other talents. Nice guy, he had joined the Air Force at the outbreak of war and was soon invalided out with dreadful disfiguring wounds. Joe Cowley was a sturdily built uncomplaining stalwart who braced every military process he was part of, from kitchen fatigues, through patrols to bayonet fighting on the Miteirya Ridge at Alamein. He was a good companion, reliable when given a project, obedient to orders, consolatory to the downcast and very lucky at poker. He had his faults, and one was his tendency to view every argument, internecine, public or political as if it were in a courtroom. Facts and figures, statistics and performance were his mediators. He had a heart of gold and a determined patriotism that was infectious during the vicissitudes of desert warfare. His weaknesses were understandable… unforgiveness towards those who wavered or showed lack of moral fibre and despair over his premature baldness.

Going to Joe Cowley for advice usually involved you in a third degree which he put me through when I was charged with a minor offence by the regimental sergeant major who had overheard my frank descriptions of him while he was eavesdropping on our rifle section.

In our final attack with hand-to-hand fighting at Alamein he was shot through the neck and found by Dick Platt after the battle, groaning in a slit trench covered in dead Germans. Some years later, describing to me the German defence of the Miteirya Ridge, Joe said the discipline of the enemy bombardiers staggered him. Even while he was bayoneting them they continued to feed their bombs into the mortar barrels.

BUSHY BERMAN

Occasionally when conditions would permit it, some of us would join forces and share our meagre talents in impromptu communal sing-songs and poetry readings; small consolation, but anything was a welcome interruption to the ongoing boring episodes that contributed to desert warfare.

It was in sharing one of these sideshows with Bushy – that we became firmer friends and sought each other out, tattered poetry books in hand or in mutually seeking solutions to crossword puzzles.

The nickname 'Bushy' arose partly through his surname which was given to a famous drive through bushy country in the north of Durban called 'Burman Drive.'

Bushy had one great enemy, the platoon sergeant. The two of them had both joined the regiment before the war and had quickly become corporals in the same platoon but, according to Bushy the latter had been promoted sergeant by stealth. There had been, ever since, an intense mutual loathing.

Sergeant Beardsley was an ignoramus and I faintly remembered, as a schoolboy out shopping with my mother, being fitted by him with a pair of shoes at Cleghorns in Durban's West Street.

In our volunteer army there was nothing wrong with counter jumping but the level of intelligence in our regiment was high and generally so was the standard of education. Alas, apart from being spit-and-polish always immaculate, Sergeant Beardsley was thick and soon found that superior rank did not always defend him from the sharp-witted who were intent only on winning the war. The only defence he could muster was an indescribable frigidity towards those who outranked him in such intelligence and wit.

Beardsley was widely unpopular, arrogant and unfair. He could not take his alcohol or the backslapping, old-pals routine that levelled everyone in periodic army booze-ups in the canteens. Countering Beardsley's privileged superiority, Bushy went intellectual and assumed it in his relationship with his sergeant. Very subtly he marshalled rank and file behind his vendetta.

The feud between Bushy and Sergeant Beardsley at one stage had become so intense that they avoided each other even to the extent of it affecting military considerations. Bushy walled himself around with his resentment and was virtually in a self-imposed Coventry. He was, in practice, refusing to take orders from his sergeant whilst being totally obedient to the platoon officer Vic. Knott and the company sergeant major. This clandestine mutiny was, for some reason, covered up by Sergeant Beardsley who soon began to have increasing difficulties in his relationship with his platoon's rank and file. Bushy's influence worked insidiously against that relationship in the background.

At my own humble level I began to find some of Sergeant Beardsley's orders unfair and even unfathomable. Some of us, privates in rank, became targets in excess for fatigues…water hauling, kitchen duties, hygiene fatigues, ammunition fatigues…every fatigue imaginable, from digging lavatories and officers' trench slits to peeling potatoes and manhandling quartermaster stores. Even the pleasantries of going on Cairo leave and getting your teeth fixed could be proscribed by Sergeant Beardsley. Complaining privates, acting through their corporals (and especially Bushy) communicated the dissension to the Sergeant Major who eventually launched an enquiry into Sergeant Beardsley's conduct and I, with many others were called to give evidence during the occupation of Mersa Matruh. Bushy was gleeful and insidiously tampered with witnesses which eventually militated again Sergeant Beardsley's future in the regiment so that between the two battles of Alamein he seemed to disappear on transfer or, more likely officers training!

Bushy had reacted to all these investigations by keeping a low profile. In terms of the war effort his deliberate withdrawal and isolation earned him the temporary reputation of being a slacker at a time when the battalion was undermanned and had to provide frequent night patrols. Bushy was absent from these as part of his very unofficial protest against Sergeant Beardsley who helped pick men for patrol.

But events turned critical after Gazala when Sergeant Beardsley departed on O.T.C. and a new sergeant replaced him, when suddenly Bushy became reactivated. He volunteered for every patrol that was going and endeared himself with his persevering gallantry and resilience faced with the superhuman demands of almost nightly dangerous patrols. As contributor to events, if not manipulator, I never heard Bushy ever brag or eulogise his unflinching activities under fire. He was never to be considered for promotion after these events and presumably Sergeant Beardsley was able to put in the last word.

Corporal Bushy Burman was by far the most complex if not eccentric character I ever met in the Eighth Army. First of all, he was, as his sobriquet indicated, a study in hirsuitism from head to foot which gave him a fierceness that was just not there once he was off the parade ground. Slenderly built, his bushy eyebrows and tufts of hair sprouting above his vest or collar gave him such a fierce demeanour on parade that the obedience of the drilling squad under his ferocious commands was both implied and exacted. I thought his bloodshot eyes were part of his apoplectic parade ground performance. In fact it was because he read poetry half way through every night, with an occasional romantic novel thrown in. It was at being past master as squad-drill instructor that had earned him his peacetime stripes. He would be so demanding of the platoon he was drilling that even the execution of the most complex manoeuvres with perfection was not enough, but at the halt you had to stand there at attention without the slightest movement of a whisker as he barked "Not a man move!" With that, he would walk down the three ranks as if inspecting them and giving each volunteer a baleful look as if challenging him to bale back.

Yet he was, when you and he had suffered together, in some flea-bitten, desert hell hole, one of the kindest beings imaginable. Weak sergeant majors would get him to do their drilling to stiffen up discipline in base camps, but it was to Bushy that many a raw recruit turned in anguish and secured comfort and advice. I remember once, during an 'at-ease' break complaining about an order frequently given by him during squad drill, "Squad will advance. About turn!" I suggested it was a contradiction in terms and an assault on rational thinking and bad English. Uncharacteristically he replied very quietly "Baker, on parade I disagree with you but off parade I'm on your side. The command is an offence to clear thinking. Unfortunately it's in the army manual."

As the war developed and disasters in leadership abounded Bushy found his role harder to fulfil. Forced by active service conditions to use subterfuge to read at night he took to using a torch (flashlight) underneath the covering of his sleeping bag, which gave his daylight apoplexy and bloodshot eyes a sound basis. He thought danger of attack by enemy patrols at night so real that, out in the desert, he would sleep away from the madding crowd in the blackness alone, with only a revolver as company. There, undisturbed he read and read. He was almost a law unto himself. One or two bosom friends knew how to reach him, and when close, in the dark, would warn him by tossing pebbles noisily ahead.

Just before Alamein he was badly wounded by shellfire and I lost track of him. The moment Beardsley disappeared from the platoon Bushey emerged and volunteered for everything to the point of exhaustion.

CHAPTER XVI

POOCH MARAIS

Everyone loved Pooch Marais. He was a little guy but built superbly with muscles that bulged especially his calves. His movements were very purposeful, both on the sports ground where he joined in almost any team endeavour and on patrol or the bloodiest attacks. These attributes earned him the nickname of "Rickshaw" or "Shaw" for short. Pooch disliked the allusions to both the little dog and the sturdy rickshaw boy, but coming newly, as an Afrikaner youth to a very English (Durban) regiment he soon accepted them. His closest friends (and he had many) would oft times hail him with a short whistle, as you did when you called for rickshaw help in the Durban municipal market.

On the hockey field (and I was fortunate to play with him for 'B' Company, rather than against him) you could hear the hammering of the soles of his feet as he approached a melee. He was the same carrying a Bren gun or a mortar plate, determined and intractable. Pooch was bilingual and his coterie of friends from neighbouring regiments would carry on conversations with him in the language of his Boer ancestors using the Afrikaans idiom and the English side comments with staggering fluency. If you said something disagreeable, he would turn on you fiercely but would just give you a look that was both pained and quizzical as if to say 'I've suffered you for so long, now what is it?'

Phil Bullimore dreaded a look from Pooch and would do anything to placate him. Pooch could rag hell out of you. He could act quietly and methodically first on his own habitat and then more menacingly on yours…straightening, correcting, inspecting anything that was out of place in his kit giving you a chance to revise your remark or jibe. At his worst, I had seen him turn his backside on you, bare it, and posing it invitingly as a supreme or final insult. Before my army days I had only seen baboons do it. Pooch filled in his days reading and doing crossword puzzles. He had a very forthright attitude to the war. Comrades killed in action or wounded did not deter him. He would go on fighting, wielding a Bren gun from position to position as if he was in a hockey bully always getting the first shot off.

Pooch tried to keep a precise routine and taking a shower was part of it. If swimming in the Med. was feasible and a truck had been made available, he would be there often fitting it in with his many sporting involvements. There was always the danger of the Messerschmitt catching the naked swimmers in the enticing blue-green waters. Some German pilots even flew home that way, just thirty or forty metres above the waves. If they strafed, even if they were seen to swoop, it seemed silly to have to dash madly through the breakers and fling yourself flat on the beach and the miles and miles of coastline was hardly worth posting with air sentinels. The trouble was that even while you were fully clothed and armed you felt so naked to assault in the desert anyway. Some others waved at the marauding planes and occasionally this may have decided the pilots whether to open fire; some bathers just stood like a Venus de Milo and did nothing; others ducked beneath the glittering waters. Pooch Marais on one occasion caught out in calm shallow waters not far from the shore, would have none of it. He had lost his best civvy pal, Johnnie Chowles on June 7th at Gazala and made one of his totally indecent gestures at two Messerschmitts, turning his naked rickshaw bum to them and bending over patted it at them as a target. Either the pilots took the joke well or were out of ammo and Pooch survived. Bully had heard the story and had insisted Pooch give a demonstration in the section tent that night. Fortunately Pooch was in underclothes and obliged on the spot. Joe jerking about in laughter had to add his comments: "Hell no Bully! Let him keep his pants on…Dash it, a man is entitled to privacy." Richard Platt did a 'Hmm, ha-a-a, gerr, swish, not cricket' and I shouted 'poonahs and Khyber passes.' It was a pleasant evening and someone produced hidden bottles of cypress wine long before his birthday and we murdered them.

The Alamein line at the narrowing of pathways into Egypt from the west had been worked on sporadically since World War I. It had not been considered as central in the defence of an attack from Libya as had Mersa Matruh which had become a point of stability as the British began to build up their mobile forces to counter Italian aspirations and later, those of Italy's important allies, the Germans. After the fall of Tobruk on June 20th, General Auchinleck had taken over command from General Ritchie and his aim was to preserve the Eighth Army at all costs, to extend the German lines of communication to the maximum, and to gain time to integrate all surviving components of the Eighth Army retreating into Egypt into an effective and lasting front line which could defend itself under the immediate threat and from which to attack again as reinforcements of tanks, guns, aircraft and men arrived, now mainly from America.

But the momentum of the gallop from Gazala had been maintained because of the effectiveness of Rommel's forces now using captured British equipment. From Tobruk on to Alamein was 300 miles but on the 27th June, only a week after Tobruk's fall, the Germans were in Mersa Matruh. We never heard what had really gone wrong but felt the loss of our desert bastion keenly. There were a few noteworthy physical features between our right flank, (the Mediterranean Sea) and the left flank anchored to the Quattara depression. These were Tel el Eisa a knoll in the north near the sea and which became almost the domain of the Australian Infantry Division. Moving southwards slightly to the east was the Miteirya Ridge just in front of the Alamein fortifications which were mainly unoccupied. The attacks against German paratroopers on this ridge were practically to wipe out my own N.M.R. company on the night of Oct. 23, in the Battle of Alamein. South again was Ruweisat Ridge which was the main feature of the Alamein line giving splendid views of the desert battlefields in all directions. To its south and a few miles further east was Alam el Halfa – another prominent ridge where Rommel's panzer attack was smashed in the first battle of Alamein. Much further south and to the west, close to Quattara was Mount Himmamat, marking also the limit of Rommel's advance in that region.

Military actions at Alamein can usually be traced to one or other of these geographical features, but the final victorious battle at Alamein embraced them all with coordinated efforts between the infantry which needed primarily to create gaps in the enemy minefields, the tank regiments which passed through them, a very aggressive airforce that harassed ground formations night and day and last but not least the artillery which progressively crumbled the enemy wherever he lingered.

VIC PAUL

Captain Vic Paul was another of those rarely born heroes that blessed 'B' Company in the steps of Bello Theunisson. Big but not ungainly, he seemed to shoulder his responsibilities with equanimity showing his resilience in every kind of fight. I was with him on night patrol on 14th October just before Alamein and remember well his steadying voice with its deep timbre, coaxing and comforting through the long night. On this occasion the patrol was made up of two sections instead of one to bring back a load of mortars that had been lost in earlier actions in no-man's-land in front of the Alamein line. One section acted as a protective guard, myself with Bren gun and the biggest guys in the second section lugging the mortars. It was the confidence that Vic instilled even in this filthy job. He did the job, and knowing we were nigh to exhaustion and had been exposed to front line conditions for weeks on end, did not look for trouble. With a man like that, a bulldog countenance scarred with battle you could trust him. No wonder when the patrol lists were being prepared you squabbled with each other to get him as your leader. The respect he won added to his prestige among commanding officers. At the coming battle of Alamein he was to be given the most terrifying of objectives, leading once more, the depleted ranks of his battle-stained worn out company to victory. Even when you were broke and most were always so, as company commander he would over-rule the paymaster and get you extra money for your leave.Having Norman his younger brother as a buddy in our ranks cemented our goodwill towards him.

Just before the Alamein battle B9, our platoon had a new commander appointed. His name was Dennis Platt and, at first, we all assumed it was another of Richard Platt's brothers. Family associations with the N.M.R. were frequent and generally favoured, and Richard's two elder brothers, Geoff and Cecil Platt had already passed through the regiment when the third brother, the youngest Richard had become prominent.

Affectionately Richard had been known therefore as 'Dick de Turd'. In actual fact, there was a fourth brother who had joined the airforce as a pilot. Richard hotly denied that Dennis Platt, the new commander was related. It turned out that he, Dennis, was an 'Isipingo Platt', hailing from a coastal town ten miles south of Durban. Dennis Platt was proud to have been given command of B9 whose reputation was already highest in the regiment for its battle honours. He couldn't get into the line quick enough to be with his own seasoned men even though, until then, none of them had heard of him. We were all impressed with his youthful and fresh qualities. Fair-headed, with peaches-and-cream complexion, he was an antidote to our grimy, weatherbeaten countenances and desert sores. And he always saw to it that in his get-togethers there had been some sort of alcoholic advanced goodwill.

Gunboat Smith did not earn his nickname because of his appearance. A less soldier-like figure you could not imagine. He was runner to Lieutenant Marcus Frank, one of the N.M.R.'s families of combatants that, like the Smedleys were practically wiped out. Gunboat used to look awful because of the loads of equipment he carried around related to his platoon officer. The 'gunboat' name arose, I supposed, from the gunboat diplomacy of a lost imperial era. He was always there with his officer when trouble was brewing, guarding the water supply in Berbera Somaliland, in front of the line on June 3rd 1942 at Gazala when the platoon sustained casualties on patrol. At the front, whenever Gunboat would come streaming across our company lines following Marcus Frank, fully loaded I would sing out to the chorus of 'Steamboat Bill' the lines

> *"Gunboat Smith!*
> *Riding down the Mississippi,*
> *Gunboat Smith, mighty man was he!*
> *Gunboat Smith, riding down the Mississippi*
> *Out to break the record on the Robert E. Lee."*

Marcus Frank use to think it was a hellava joke.

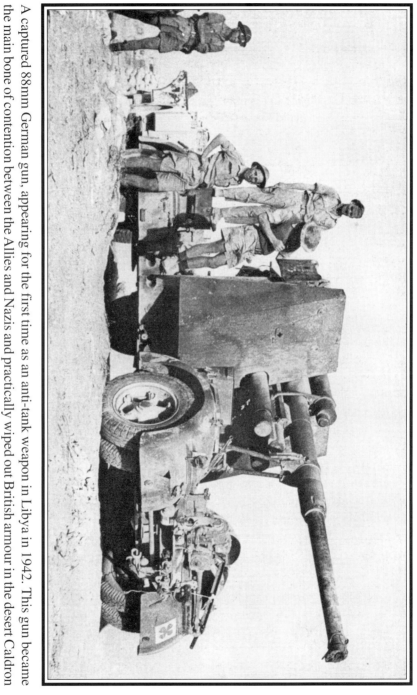

A captured 88mm German gun, appearing for the first time as an anti-tank weapon in Libya in 1942. This gun became the main bone of contention between the Allies and Nazis and practically wiped out British armour in the desert Caldron as the result of which Tobruk fell. Both in Italy later and in Normandy it destroyed hundreds of Sherman tanks.

On the night of Alamein both Gunboat and Marcus Frank were killed by a shell in the opening barrage. Some believe that Gunboat had been carrying the platoon's sticky bomb and the culprit shell had triggered it off killing him and Lieutenant Frank instantly.

Gunboat's sobriquet may have come to him also in his close association with Lieutenant Frank who, to put it mildly was also accident-prone, or worse, even a calamity prone soldier. At Gazala his dugout had been completely destroyed under bombardment whilst he had been out on some operation. Two weeks later his trench slit sustained a shell burst only two feet from it when again he was unhurt. As his runner, Gunboat would have been nearby both of these. (see Photo 210mm Italian Guns, page 216).

Where there was any position in the line that had become static, the Italians might draw up their naval guns especially at Gazala and Alamein where these monsters would persist in crumbling our positons.

RICHARD PLATT AT ALAMEIN

Richard Platt had been in hospital with his wounds from our attack on July 15th against the Italian outpost. His return in October was like a breath of fresh air. We were all stagnating with boredom and his latest news and bullshit straight out of the South African 106 General Hospital was refreshing. At Gazala he had lost friends killed in action and here in the line, at Alamein had sustained more than his fair share of the ongoing slings and arrows. Until now the pressure on our part of the line was traumatic and sustained enough for us to have to man our weapon pits for weeks at a time usually night and day. We were half strength in manpower, malnourished, weary of the war, infected with desert sores and exhausted by patrols and night guards in no-man's-land.

Richard was returned to the line by Phil Bullimore. My gunpit was one of two arms of a right-angled triangle. I showed Richard the areas in no-mans's-land that the arm of his gunpit covered, the variety of machine guns it held, most of them captured from the enemy, where the small primus stove was strategically placed for both of us to get a hot drink at night and away from the ammunition and grenades. He was impressed and as if to rubber stamp his approval immediately pinned up a couple of Varga girls on the part of the sandbagged wall we could both see. To demonstrate the reformed attitude of our commanders under the new Montgomery, I fired off ten rounds from my Bren at some beer cans posted on patrol by me as a target about 300 yards away in no-man's-land. The tins clattered with hits and he had a go himself. There was no clatter and he said "Fuck you" to the gun and laughed.

We became even greater friends and we shared everything...our sorrows and joys. I had earache that kept me awake and he dripped warmed oil into it; he had recurring bouts of sandfly fever and wouldn't report for treatment at the M.A.P. in case he was sent down the line again. We both esteemed the two medical orderlies at the M.A.P. especially Folkey, with his marvellous torso and frowning concentration as he worked on your desert sores. He was already cited for decoration after June 7th. The other was Monkey Jankowitz who was a noted rugby player. Nonetheless, he had a positively hominid appearance and acted like one when he walked. As a therapist he was a mother with a child. He would cluck around you as he bandaged, keeping a concerned dialogue about how you should take more care of yourself. Back from the M.A.P. Richard would go into hysterics giggling at the methods of the medics there and the way Monkey had dug into my ear with a cotton-bud like an ape in a forest digging ants out of the tree bark with a twig. Jankowitz was shocked at what came out, bits of Abysinnia and Kenya. His comment was "What you been putting in your ear? Fag-ends?"*

In the army Richard was always alert and an early riser. Next morning before getting me up for stand-to I heard him at the primus stove making coffee. The stove gave its usual awful performance and presently I heard Richard singing frustratedly half in Afrikaans:

"Wat mark yo pricker in my primus stove" and more giggles.

In those days I was totally extrovert whereas he was spasmodically so. He had evolved out of Hilton College where the decorum of his boarding school was paramount. Richard, had not yet worked hard for a living whereas I had already been an office boy, customs clerk

---

*Cigarette butts

and salesman by the time I was mobilised. He liked my openness and
frank expressions which oftimes were a cause of controversy and he
would sometimes in the background hum, sometimes sing…

> *"There's no highbrow etiquette*
> *Just plain people and when you've met*
> *They will never forget*
> *Down forget-me-not lane."*

It was not just when he was troubled, but sometimes, for no reason,
he would become tense and sit by himself, almost unapproachable. I
realised after some days, especially when we were under the intensive
gunfire of 210mm shells, that he badly missed his comrades killed at
Gazala and felt partly responsible for the death of one of them. He
had a very vivid imagination and could sense trouble a long way ahead.
Richard was rarely scared for his own safety. I saw it once in the
coming Battle of Alamein when our own creeping barrage overtook
all of us. But he could anticipate hurt for those he loved or for whom
he was responsible.

When the shells were coming down fast and furious we would
meet head-to-head in the weapon pit at its right-angle screwing our
heads into the blanket rolls there. It was while waiting for the next
close shell burst here that he told me about the tragic death of George
Strachan. It is better to quote Richard Platt's own version of Private
Strachan's demise:

> "The battalion had moved into positions in the Gazala line on
> the 15th March '42, taking over from a Polish battalion. Before
> we could occupy our dugouts, the engineers had to be called in
> to lift mines which apparently were planted round the dugouts
> by the Poles. Obviously they weren't encouraging visitors.
> George Strachan and I shared a dugout, which although
> fashioned in solid rock, was quite comfortable and appeared to
> be relatively safe. We were settled in for what turned out for
> me to be a long tedious period. The regimental records show
> that two cans of beer per man, per week were to be made
> available. We weren't going to get pissed on that. So we saved
> all the yeast tablets we could lay our hands on, together with
> prunes, tinned pineapple, potato peels and such like and

concocted a brew that had, when matured, the veritable kick of a mule.

Not long after we had settled in, an incident occurred which resulted in a tragedy. We heard one evening a scuffling noise outside the dugout. It turned out to be, not an enemy patrol, but a wild dog. We immediately gave chase pelting it with stones until suddenly I realised it was heading for a minefield. I was on the point of shouting to George, who was in front, to stop, when an 'S' mine exploded.

An 'S' mine, known as a 'crow's foot' or 'jumper' mine was of German origin. It consisted of a metal cylinder full of pieces of metal, set in a metal sleeve. To this was attached a metal prong protruding above the ground. When depressed the crow's foot set off a cartridge that sent the mine to above chest height when it exploded projecting bits of metal fragments in all directions, an ingenious, diabolical piece of ordinance but very effective. George collected a piece of shrapnel that severed his femoral artery. Help was soon at hand, and he was sent down the line to the safety of a field hospital. A week or so later I saw a very dejected looking Ken Frank heading for our dugout. I knew immediately that this was disaster. George had died on the hospital ship Ram IV that had been sunk in Alex. harbour. I was devastated. It was the first time I had lost someone so close and it filled me with a sense of remorse and guilt. To have lost a friend so full of life, so full of nonsense, so friendly in that way, seemed so futile and unjust. The Ram IV was an Italian hospital ship captured by the British in the East African port of Mogadishu. The Italians apparently threatened to bomb it if the British did not hand it back. This the Italians did and the ship apparently sank with no survivors."

[Privately I thought the Italians had, in quite a few instances, shown a strong will in various heroic and determined acts … the sinking of the two British battleships by Italian midget submarines in Alex. Harbour, the destroying of the Ram IV in the same harbour as they had warned they would, and even in the desert had on several occasions repulsed allied infantry attacks and stood up to their bullying German allies].

Montgomery's plan was to attack the Alamein line in the North with infantry, lift mines in lanes behind them as they gained their objectives and then to press with British Armour through the cleared lanes of mines, consolidate and protect the infantry whilst it recovered and reorganised. The armoured divisions would then break out into the desert and drive the enemy all the way to Tripoli. The plan required a full moon and repeated rehearsals. The night of the Full Moon of September would have been appropriate but there were delays in training and Montgomery was forced to go for the Full Moon of October 23rd & 24th 1942.

The original plan was for the British armoured divisions to use the lanes cleared between the Australian Division on the extreme north of the line at Tel el Eisa and the 51st Highland Division on their left flank facing the enemy. In fact much of the penetration went through the sector captured from the Italians and Germans by the South African and New Zealand Divisions which were on the 51st Division's left flank as the 7th Armoured Division struck at Kidney Ridge lying beyond the Miteirya Ridge which was finally overrun by N.M.R.'s Platoon 'B9' on the first night of Alamein (23rd/24th October. See map page 276).

My own part on the first night of Alamein must be supplemented by the testimony of four of my closest friends who with me were survivors of the desperate charges made by the N.M.R. to secure the Meteiriya Ridge enabling mine lanes to penetrate the enemy positions. I personally was involved in the initial attack in securing the main objective which was the entrenchment of mortars, machine gun and sniper emplacements dug in on the ridge. Survivors' accounts are given here successively by Cecil Ritson, Richard Platt, Lenny Clark and Eric Gregg, all of whom progress through these diary leaves. They were part of the company's 28 men and one officer who reached the objective, the rest were killed, wounded and evacuated or died of wounds; i.e. 28 out of less than 90 men of 'B' Company who began the attack.

Testimony of Cecil Ritson — Living survivor (Platoon B9)

"I was a member of 'B' Company of the Natal Mounted Rifles and in October 1942 we were holding forward positions, facing the enemy, who were entrenched on a ridge to the south-west. About 1500 yards separated the two lines. Over several days there was a build-up of armaments in the area behind us. A big attack was being planned. On the 22nd October we were given the details of this attack which was to be on the following night.

On the night of 22nd I was picked for a patrol along with two other comrades whose names I cannot remember. Our task was to find out if anti-personnel mines were laid in the enemy's minefield. I was very concerned about this duty, because, firstly, this was full moon and it was a clear brilliant night, and, secondly, we had knowledge of the following days plans, if we were unfortunately captured. We achieved our objective by crawling for hundreds of yards over hard stony ground. The gun emplacements were close by in the rising ground above us. However we were able to see the trip wires and mines in place and crawled away without detection. On reporting back we were informed that, at this late stage, not much could be done about the anti-personnel mines except to warn all concerned to take care. (In the event, these mines produced casualties in our ranks on the following night.)"

AUTHOR ON 22ND/23RD OCTOBER

The N.M.R. now knew exactly where the regiment was to join the infantry frontal attack on Rommel, keeping close, but not too close to a creeping barrage laid down by a thousand guns slinging 25-pound shells. In the last two days before this giant armageddon stretching 25 miles south from the beaches of the Mediterranean to the swamps of the Quattara Depression, the immediate area behind the dug-in infantry of the line was literally filled with artillery pieces and the crews that were to apply the barrage. Everyone knew exactly what to do. No one was exempt from the great concourse gathering together so tightly knit that at the very moment the first guns flashed, the whole inferno of men and their instruments of war would begin as a single being initiating the first real victory in the long misery of defeat between 1939 – 42. Everyone was there, backing in vehicles loaded with

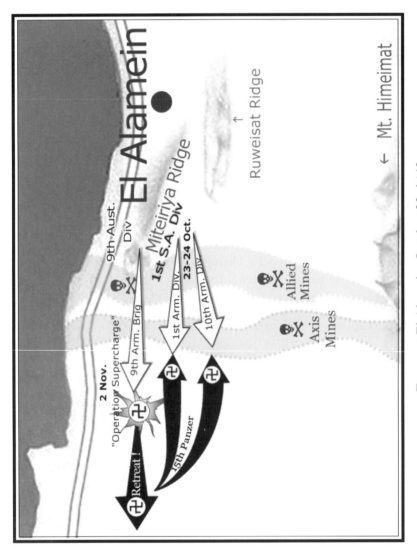

Forces at El Alamein, October 23rd '42

thousands of shells, heavy and light machine guns, mortars, boxes of sticky bombs, cases of grenades, familiar small arms ammunition boxes. Infantryman from New Zealand and Australia, South Africans, Indians and of course the Tommies, Highlanders with their pipes, Guardsmen slick and staccato, progressively took up their positions, quietly almost reverently. No one was exempt, cooks, postmen, medics, engineers and tank men and their gunga dins — 220,000 men, unflinching, dressed for battle and armed, singly and in units, in companies and battalions, bombardiers, troopers, staff and stretcher bearers.

The sensations one experienced waiting for the start of the barrage seemed strangely similar for everyone. It was that a change was going to be undergone in all our lives during the next hour. Our destinies were going to be realigned by unfolding events. I saw it as something inevitable, ghastly but uplifting, awesome and revelatory like a leviathan entering metamorphosis. Fears? We knew what to expect, a man-made hell mainly taking the form of broad fields of mines that had to be walked or charged through whilst they were being straddled by machine gun fire, mortar bombs and artillery.

The Alamein scenario on the night of the 23rd turned out to be everything that Montgomery promised and it was the giant metamorphosis of the British army which came out of its pupal case of defeat, a new creature the imago of victory for democracy.

MY ALAMEIN (BY AUTHOR, LIVING SURVIVOR, PLATOON B9)

Somebody had worked it out that with a thousand guns each firing a shell a minute, shells would be exploding along the line at sixteen per second. In the event they came down detonating in front of our eyes with the rapidity of an ongoing non-stop machine gun. It just took your breath away to see the ground boiling and writhing with an unspeakable din. This barrage went on for 15 minutes. I did not find it frightening but very sobering for there was hardly a man in our ranks that had not had a chance to take a welcoming appetiser for the trials that lay ahead.

I felt elevated and while we waited for the fifteen minutes of torrential explosions to do their work, in the brilliant light of the full

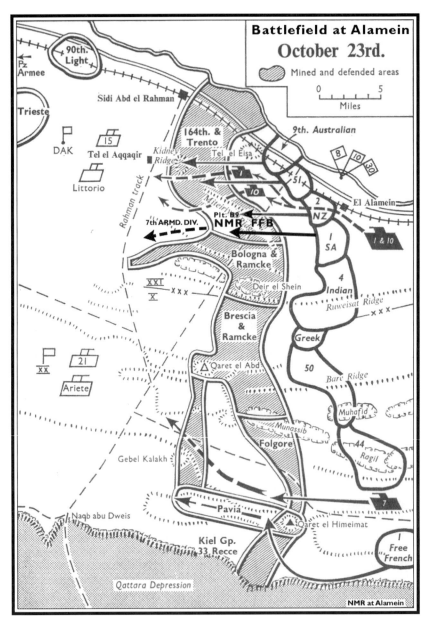

Battlefield at Alamein
October 23rd.

Mined and defended areas

0   5
Miles

90th. Light

Pz Armee

Sidi Abd el Rahman

Trieste

164th. & Trento

9th. Australian

DAK

15

Tel el Aqqaqir

Kidney Ridge

Tel el Eisa

8

10

30

Littorio

Rahman track

51

10

El Alamein

7th ARMD. DIV.

Miteiri

Plt. B9
NMR FFB

2

NZ

1
SA

1 & 10

Bologna & Ramcke

Deir el Shein

4
Indian

Ruweisat Ridge

XXI
X

X X X

Brescia & Ramcke

Greek

50

Bare Ridge

21

Qaret el Abd

Muhafid

Ariete

Munassib

Folgore

44
Ragil

Gebel Kalakh

Naqb abu Dweis

Pavia

7

Qaret el Himeimat

Kiel Gp.
33 Recce

1
Free
French

Qattara Depression

NMR at Alamein

The N.M.R. achieved its objectives on the first night of the Battle of Alamein which allowed a pathway through the extensive German minefield to be cleared and for armour eventually to pass through. The badly mauled F.F.B. called for N.M.R. help and Platoon B.9. headed the final penetration.

276

moon, Montgomery's Moon, I called it later, I stared into the distance on my left and right observing the unending row of soldiers. South Africans to the left and right and beyond that out of sight but also trained and ready for the job, ANZACS, Scots, Hindus and Moslems, Poles and Free French. Surely this was the epitome of democracy and it stirred me deeply. On the stroke of 11pm the barrage began to creep, a steam roller replacing the monsoon of static bombardment. Then the long, miles long, line of allied infantry moved forward.

Now you had to have your wits about you. Soon, with your eyes studying the ground for mines and both eyes and ears taking in the positions of the men next to you, Shorty Carneson on the left and Roy McCartney on the right, you became aware of trip-wires everywhere. Worst of all, a gun was firing short and shells were landing amongst us. When the missile came close, amidst the hullabaloo, it gave off its own note and you flattened. My face "kissed the deck" several times and it was then I became aware of nasty three point prongs sticking up out of the earth and I was grateful for the Ritson patrol's warnings of the previous night. Messages came down the long line to withdraw 50 yards to give the creeping barrage the chance to get ahead of us instead of amongst us. Then the high point of the ridge loomed. In the misty grey of smoke, cordite and moonlight the knobs of enemy groundworks took shape. The grenadiers were distinguishable coming out of their dugouts and jumping into their weapon pits. I flung myself into a shell hole and switched the Bren from single shots to automatic and engaged the machine gun nests.

The next moment Shorty Carneson rushed up. A piece of shrapnel had hit him in the jaw. He was wide-eyed and scared stiff. I used a handkerchief or piece of two-by-four to staunch the blood flow, told him to take a pull at his side bottle, grabbed some Bren magazines from his wobbling pouch and sent him on his way. I jumped back into the shell hole and fired the magazines taken from Shorty. Machine gun fire came back in reply. Another rush forward and we began to overrun enemy pillboxes. Few prisoners were taken. Occupying the main objective delighted everyone and the memories of the Gazala fiasco deadened. It was dangerous to leave gunpits and dugouts uncleared and cleaning them up was easiest by dropping a grenade in or using a pistol. But there was a rogue gun still firing short, right on top of us, and I took cover in a 25-pounder shell hole. I had just raised myself to observe when there was a huge bang behind me. It was as if something nasty, jagged and burning tore up my back and knocked my tin hat off. I was dazed for several seconds; and feeling the back of my bared head my fingers sank into the huge hot mouth of a five inch gaping wound. There was worse. My right arm was paralysed and the fingers of my left could only trace the top end of a second, much larger, broad wound that had in fact removed most of the muscle from my shoulder blade.

I was now lying in a welter of blood, a smashed Bren gun sprawling on its side and its magazines spilling out from torn webbing pouches. From the right McCartney shouted "Are you all right?" He approached shocked at my state and above the roar I answered "No! I'm hurt. I'm useless" I nodded at the Bren gun and said "Take it" . McCartney shouted something to the effect the gun was shattered, took a look at my back-wound again and shouted "I'll get a stretcher-bearer, stay here."

I staggered to my feet looking for my tin hat. It was ten feet away, holed. As I did so in the moonlight I saw a movement to my left. The chaos of my thoughts suggested it was just the moonlight acting on a piece of scrub but it came closer and it was no stretcher-bearer. I tore my .45 revolver out with my left hand and shot at it. Only a few feet away it whimpered, threw up its arms and fell flat. I put another shot into it and sank back into the shell hole. Exhausted, I began to feel very cold and soon the stretcher-bearer arrived. He had already opened up a large shell-dressing. He was a black man and his English was poor and he showed his concern not by words so much as by clucking, comforting and mothering noises as he struggled with the awkward task of staunching the blood and applying a dressing to the massive wound. Then he did the head wound and kept repeating the word "solly, solly' as he bandaged. I began to feel less isolated and asked him what part of South Africa he came from. It could have been Basutoland or Swaziland or even Zululand. He got me to my feet and as he did so Ernie Coleman from H.Q. approached and took me over and the stretcher-bearer went on up the hill to treat others.

Testimony of Cecil Ritson continued...

"At 21:00 hours we silently moved through our minefield on premarked routes, and then spread out in a straight line facing the enemy. The Cape Corps drivers assigned to take charge of P.O.W.'s formed a second line behind us. We lay down on the hard ground awaiting the zero hour. I remember feeling very tense wondering what would happen in the next few hours, as the promised battle was about to commence.

At 21:40 hours, hundreds of guns behind us opened up an artillery barrage intent on softening up the enemy. The ground shook; the noise was frightening; and, the sky behind us was aglow with gun flashes. It was an awesome show of fire power. At 22:00 hours (Zero Hour) our long line of infantry moved forward as the artillery bombardment changed to a creeping barrage ahead of us.

The advance was going steadily according to plan, but then out there in no-man's-land something went awry and part of the creeping barrage descended on our own long line. We were forced to the ground as shells were bursting all around and shrapnel whistled in all directions. This was a most frightening time as the shelling was very heavy. This helpless situation seemed to continue for ages, but it was possibly only a period of five minutes or so. I was to learn later that many casualties had occurred in this period.

After passing through the enemy's minefield we were called back into the minefield to adjust the line and wait for a coordinated final attack. We overran the emplacements on the ridge, rounded up prisoners, and took up defensive positions for a possible counter-attack. We now came under sustained shell fire, and a mortar crew just behind me suffered a direct hit. I was to learn that Ted Harrison had "copped it" in this incident. He had been a fellow student in my 1939 Matric class.

Although a counter-attack was not forthcoming, 'B' Company's duties were not over for the night. In the early hours of the 24th October, 'B' Company was assigned to attack positions held by German paratroopers. Apparently this defence area was set back from the front line in a depression, and the Field Force Battalion on our left flank had suffered heavy casualties in attempting to capture the positions.

We passed back through the minefield on a cleared gap and moved left to join the F.F.B.'s positions. Here we were given an appraisal of the conditions ahead, and I remember that we were told to beware of injured and dead F.F.B. men in front and also of German snipers. Our Company Commander, Capt. Vic Paul, called for mortars to lay a smoke screen and we advanced as the dawn was approaching. In the charge, I remember having to negotiate a fence, and then there was a blinding explosion next to me. I must have passed out, because when I gathered my wits, I found I was lying about 15 paces in front of an enemy machine gun pit. Our platoon officer, Lt. Dennis Platt, was lying on my immediate left. At that moment he raised his body possibly with the intent of charging and he was shot through the head. I "froze" in my exposed position and I could clearly see the gunner pointing his spandau in my direction. It was a terrifying moment. Then I was aware of Jimmy Shrimpton closing in from the right and being shot as he jumed in among the Germans. I then rushed at the gun pit as other comrades converged from the left. The positions were taken and prisoners rounded up.

It was now dawn and I was guarding the group of prisoners from a stand-off position. One of the paratroopers decided to make a break, and with head down, he dashed to my left front. I shouted to him to halt, but he still continued. My Bren gun was set on single shot, and I fired from the hip well ahead of him. I was amazed to see him drop like a log, hit in the head by a single bullet. This action appeared to put paid to any further attempts at escaping.

Friendly tanks and support trucks, etc., started to come through the area. Suddenly a shot rang out near us. Apparently, a German soldier hiding in a hole had jumped up, and shot a driver of one of our vehicles and attempted to make his escape in the vehicle. We rushed across to the scene of action and, to our amazement, a whole company of German soldiers rose out of "dug-in" positions and surrendered to us. We were fortunate that they had elected to surrender, because they greatly outnumbered the weary survivors of our 'B' Company."

CHAPTER XVII

Testimony of Len Clark – Living Survivor of Miteiriya

"The news came through to Company H.Q. that one of our regiments, the F.F.B. (Field Force Battalion) had struck severe opposition in the form of Panzer Grenadiers. They had pressed home a Company attack which had been repulsed and then persevered with a two-company attack, again to no avail. The order came through for N.M.R. 'B' Company to take up the assault. I informed the Platoon commander, and we picked our way through the spasmodic enemy shellfire to meet up with "A" platoon and prepare for the assault. We did not know at the time, but the enemy was split into three forces – one each dug in on two knolls, and the third force (which was the target we knew of) – dug in, in a saucer-shaped hollow at the foot of the two knolls. As the sky began to lighten slightly from the east behind us, we took up our positions – we were provided with a Dingo armoured car to support the assault; The enemy was firing from a few hundred yards ahead. Mortars joined us to lob bombs ahead of our advance. We lined up in open order and then with a burst of inspiration – our Company O.C. Vic Paul – called for three minutes smoke from the mortars, this undoubtedly gave us a breathing space. The night and early morning were quite chilly – I remember that I was wearing my Army-issue jersey as I think most of us were, but otherwise we were clad in shorts, shirts, stockings and tin hats.

The smoke from the mortar bombs formed a hazy screen with the early morning mist and we moved forward at a brisk trot against the enemy fire, the spandaus with their staccato rapid bursts were most intimidating. The armoured car proved of no help, being blown up on a landmine after only a few yards progress. As we ran, we were conscious of the bodies of our F.F.B. comrades all facing the enemy, and all in various grotesque positions as they had made their final sacrifice. We came to a barbed-wire barrier, and as I leapt, my right stocking was hooked in a barb, I felt as tall as the Empire State building as I struggled to free myself. The more I struggled the more I became entangled!! After what seemed an eternity, I was loose and flopped down next to Brian Keal and the others in a slight fold in the ground; just sufficient cover to allow us to catch our breath. Dennis Platt was a few yards ahead of our line. He rose up shouting, "Up the N.M.R." and it was then that he was killed and I saw him crumple. As we were again on the move, firing from the hip, I could hear one of the enemy shouting "English Schweinhund", and one of them trying to clear the breach of the Spandau which had probably jammed in all the sand and dust. On the charge, a machine gun caught four of us. On my immediate right Brian went down with a shoulder wound and on his right Joe Cowley was hit through the throat; on my left Pooch Marais was hit in the same place as I was, i.e. right arm between shoulder and elbow. The warm sensation of the blood coursing down the sleeve of my jersey caused me to test for finger movements. Happily they were functioning normally. Brian said he was O.K. and that I had better take the Tommy-gun – I picked it up only to find it completely useless from all the dust and grit, so I stuck to my old Lee-Enfield and bayonet.

Then we were in among their slit-trenches. I saw one slit-trench explode in a sheet of flame from a well hurled handgrenade – Jimmy Shrimpton grinned at me through his agony and said: "The bastards got me, but I got him"; Jimmy had a bullet in the knee. Joss Deacon on my left disappeared in another sheet of flame as a German potato masher grenade exploded on his midriff. I felt sickened not expecting to see him alive again. To my amazement, the next moment he rushed up to our Sergeant, the late Ken Frank, and said: "Ken, can I go back, I've been hit!" Ken looked at him askance and asked, "Where?" Joss replied "Where it hurts most!" Ken gave his permission! At last the enemy had had enough and came out in surrender. In the heat of the battle it was difficult to restrain some of our comrades from committing mayhem; I recall that "Cowboy" Drennan was all for forgetting about Geneva Conventions!

It was fairly light, and the Cape Corps (non-combatant) took over our captives. A Bofors gun arrived on the scene to lend ack-ack support when to our consternation we were fired on from the two knolls of which, until then, we had been unaware. The Bofors gunner started to traverse the gun onto the new targets but was wounded before he could get off a shot. One of our number took over his seat and started to continue where the gunner had left off. But suddenly a white flag of surrender appeared on the knolls. Whether it was the barrage or the sight of the gun barrel of the Bofors menacing them, we will never know, but ninety to a hundred Jerries came down from the knolls and surrendered."

Testimony of Richard Platt, El Alamein– The final assault on Miteiriya RidgePlatoon B9

"I rejoined the regiment at the end of September after enjoying a month's rest at 106 General Hospital, and was greeted by Doug Baker with whom I was to share a dug out. One new platoon officer Dennis Platt had just arrived fresh from training in Palestine. He introduced himself via a few cases of Aussie beer which was a good way to meet men.

Early October saw feverish activity behind the lines with the digging of gun pits and bringing in ammunition. On the 22nd, the day before the battle we were briefed where it was stressed that success depended on our following the creeping artillery barrage as closely as possible, in order to achieve the element of surprise. We spent the rest of the day checking and cleaning weapons, writing letters, and cleaning ourselves up for it would be some time before we would be able to wash again.

At 19:00 hours we were in position, and at 20:00 hours we were given the order to advance as approximately 800 guns opened up behind us. It was full moon. As far as the eye could see to left and right there was one long line of soldiers with weapons at the high port.

The effect of the blast from the guns was as if one was being thumped on the back by a heavily gloved hand. It was impossible to hear orders, which were passed on by shouting in the next man's ear. Every now and then we would go to ground as we came too close to the barrage. Dennis Platt was an inspiration, continually walking up and down the line shouting words of encouragement to his men. Suddenly the barrage in front of us ceased, and to my horror as I looked back the bursting shells were creeping towards us from behind. I ended up in a shell crater blocking my ears until the shells were bursting in front of us. Shrapnel clinked against my tin hat and tommy gun, and a red hot piece burnt my leg. This must have been when Doug Baker collected one in the back and head.

We encountered no opposition on the way to our objective. As we came across dug outs we simply fired into the entrances and moved on, and it was impossible to know whether shells bursting around us were theirs or ours. We dug in for fear of a counter attack, which never came as we had Italians in our sector.

At about 2:00am we heard a runner calling for Capt. Paul our O.C. of 'B' Company. This was trouble, as we knew we were reserve company to the Brigade. We were led to the F.F.B. Sector opposite Miteiriya Ridge, where it transpired that two attacks on the position which was manned by German paratroopers had failed to take the ridge. The F.F.B. casualties were heavy, as the first was a two-company attack, and the second a company and two platoons. Capt. Paul ordered the F.F.B. mortars to lay down smoke on the position as the mortar crews had suffered heavy casualties from a sniper. We eventually captured the sniper's rifle complete with telescopic sight.

We were lined up on either side of our company commander, then came the order. It was more a growl than an order! 'B' Company Charge! We charged – slap into a wall of triple Dannet barbed wire. We could hear the German fire orders whilst the Spandau was firing continuously. Somehow I found myself on the other side of the wire. There were bodies everywhere, some shouting "Don't shoot." As we came nearer to the position I threw my two bakelite grenades and fired short bursts from the hip. I found cover behind a small mound which seemed to be close enough to the mortar pit so threw two H.E. grenades. I felt someone pulling by my shorts. There lay Shorty Carneson, the smallest man in the Platoon. "Two bricks and a piss-pot high", as Tom Patterson described him. Tom wasn't much taller himself! Shorty had been a Checker on the Railways at Rosetta in Natal before the war. "Richard", he said "throw my grenades, I'm too small." I took them from him and threw them. After the scrap was over I went back to where we were lying and found my way to the mortar pit. There on the edge of the pit, I found two grenades with the pins still intact. In my haste to get rid of them, I had neglected to pull the pins.

I must have been operating on "Automatic Pilot", for my next recollection was landing up next to Pat Lyster who shouted "get him", pointing to a Jerry emerging from a dug out. I fired from the hip, one shot and the tommy gun jammed. "Hande Hoch", I screamed, fortunately he obliged. The idea caught on and they came out one with a white flag. We lined up about twenty of them, the remnants of the force that had decimated the F.F.B. Some were still armed so I shouted "drop your arms". From behind there was a shot, whilst a German in front of me held out a blood splattered arm. Behind me was a snarling red-headed "Cowboy" Drennan. I think he must have reckoned the Jerry was going for his gun.

I remember seeing a German running away and Cecil Ritson shouted "halt". No response, a burst with the Bren from the hip and the man was brought down. We heard groaning coming from a slit trench where a dead German was lying. Underneath the body we found Jo Cowley who had been shot through the neck. Although temporarily paralysed he recovered, going away with the Natal Carbineers in the 6th S.A. armoured Division to Italy.

The Cape Corps stretcher bearers did a magnificent job. The area was heavily mined with trip wires everywhere. There were constant calls of "Pas op vir die wiretjies", many of them ironically becoming casualties whilst helping the wounded.

The regimental history records that 'B' Company strength at the end of the show was one officer and twenty-eight men able to report for duty. The one officer, Pat Lyster, who was awarded the M.C., was subsequently evacuated with a wound across his chest. We learned with great sadness that Dennis Platt our platoon officer had died in an A.D.S. He had been shot whilst leading a charge on a machine gun nest. Had he survived, he would surely have been decorated. What a waste of such a likeable and courageous man."

(My own post mortem to the final casualty list of which I was a part supported the rumour I had heard while in the casualty stations that, Dennis Platt had been shot in the spleen on Miteirya Ridge and had died in a C.C.S. from blood loss. – **Author**)

ERIC GREGG AT ALAMEIN

Eric Gregg was again involved with Italian prisoners on the night of the 23rd October at El Alamein. He was the section Tommy gunner used when close up to an enemy trench. After firing a few rounds his Tommy gun magazine drum was hit by shrapnel. It didn't explode but the Tommy gun was out of action.

With this 'lethal' weapon Eric Gregg sitting on an armoured car escorted about 60 Italian prisoners' back to the rear. Eric, in 'C' Company paid this tribute to its commander: Alamein was Captain Blamey's last appearance at the head of his men and it should be reaffirmed here that his men trusted him because he always kept his word and would not allow them to be abused. I always remember the charming way in which he saluted, his hand coming up to his right ear as if he were hard of hearing which he was not. He genuinely thought that it was sweet and fitting to die for his fatherland and on several occasions I was there when he very nearly did.

Author's Diary

24th October 1942 (starting 1:00am)

'Went through many M.A.P.s and casualty stations. Slept for a few hours then to a N.Z. C.C.S. where rested all day in a dustbowl without attention. Many wounded – not enough stretchers or blankets. By ambulance to British C.C.S. at Burg al Arab. Dressed and injected and herded on to a truck like animals and sent to Amoriya.'

ARCHIE McLACHLAN

Further up the line on the right flank of our 23rd/24th October attack, Archie McLachlan M.M. now a Sergeant was involved in the Grand assault in No. 6 platoon of the R.D.L.I. at Alamein.

DUST BOWL NURSING

It was lying almost uncared for in that dust bowl for all the hours of daylight on the 24th, that began to plant doubts about whether I would pull through. I knew I was bleeding because my khaki clothing was clinging to me, matted and drying everywhere. I had heard that the famous New Zealand general Freyburg* had often complained about British unconcern for their infantry. Now, in a crisis the New Zealanders had no clout behind the lines. As the barrage began they had opened the doors of their Casualty Clearing Stations to anyone wounded and rendered the primary essentials of dressings and morphine expecting a flow of ambulances to carry away the wounded. Coming seven thousand miles to fight for their mother country they could hardly be expected to provide extra ambulances when the English Commander-in-Chief had ordered such a big push that all the infantry of the Eighth Army was involved on the first night under creeping barrage conditions.

The advice of the experienced commanders and generals had not been fully listened to. The roads, pathways and tracks up to the front were already jammed with tanks and support vehicles and there was no room for ambulances to get back to the N.Z. casualty stations even if they were coming at all. Three infantry generals had emphasised that the infantry would need time to recover.

It was almost dark on the night of the 24th, when the ambulances did arrive. They had had to make the last part of their journey across the desert which was severely hump-backed in most areas. The cursory investigation by the casualty station had put me on the D.I. list. Dangerously ill meant something more threatening than S.I. for Seriously ill. Wounded early I was furthest from the entrance to the dust bowl and was carried out past the lines of men lying patiently resting and awaiting their turn. Many were covered over and would fight no more. By then the dust had abated. I would have walked to the ambulance but the big D.I.L. label pinned to me and unsteadiness from loss of blood prevented it. The ambulance men were kindness itself, a race apart in tenderness and compassion. Deciding that fighting

---

* 2nd. New Zealand Infantry Division - Commander Freyburg, Sir B., Lieut-General V.C., G.C.M.G., K.C.B., K.B.E., D.S.O., later, Lord Freyburg.

was not for them but nursing the wounded was, they were experienced. In a few moments the ambulance was full with no time to tend individually to wounds. Bang-bang on the cabin of the ambulance wall and we were away. I was stretched out fully and the single attendant had stationed himself next to me and was agitated about something. He was in his early twenties, a Tommy and fresh faced. I called him Johnny. Then he announced his grave concern to the wounded on board. He said that because of the tanks using the roads we would have to go overland and because it was dark and we had no headlights the journey was going to be bumpy. Not much of a problem except with all occupants liable to haemorrhage in even minor jolting it would be hazardous.

The ambulance driver did his best shouting a warning when obstructing hummocks threatened. It was a protracted nightmare not helped inside and outside the vehicle by the blackout. The many ambulances had to stick together because more dust was being generated by them too. It was a hell ride with every jolt, even minor ones evoking screams from the severely wounded. My problem was I could only lie back downwards. I came off the ambulance having learnt what the medical term "guarding" meant and for months I could not allow anyone to approach me in a rush without trying to protect myself from impact. Forced to lie on my side in the mayhem I was nearly thrown to the floor from the bunk. Johnny had to hold me firm and it helped and from experience he knew it. I understood then why so many injections of morphine were given; it was because wounded men had to be shuffled around getting back to hospital and given the opportunity the drug could make the whole body 'sing' inwardly almost euphorically in the face of pain.

It seemed to go on for hours before we reached another casualty station beyond at Burg el Arab, and I said goodbye to Johnny who had been my faithful nanny and shown such empathy. Then more dressings and needles and we were packed into army trucks and sent to Amiriya. I do not recall being offered food up to this stage.

The problem now was retaining consciousness. At Amiriya I was put on to a train crowded with Tommies making for the Suez Canal zone on what proved to be a 14-hour journey which took us directly east across the spread of the lush greenness of the Delta. As dawn

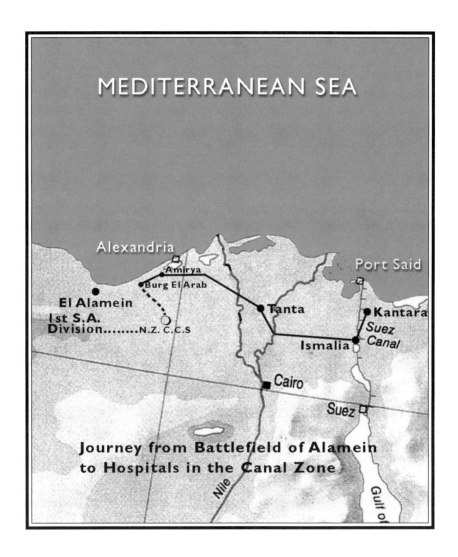

MEDITERRANEAN SEA

Alexandria

Port Said

Amirya

Burg El Arab

El Alamein

Tanta

Kantara

1st S.A.
Division........N.Z. C.C.S

Suez
Canal

Ismalia

Cairo

Suez

Nile

Gulf of

Journey from Battlefield of Alamein
to Hospitals in the Canal Zone

broke I came out of a deep sleep, no doubt morphia enduced, very hungry, sitting up in a well appointed compartment full of wounded men as was the whole train. They were friendly but solemn. I was regarded with a little suspicion at first and as the Delta villages rushed by and conversation with them became less stilted, I realised what it was. They thought I was an officer because of the red tabs I wore as a South African volunteer. I disabused them of that and someone offered me a fag. After that it was easy. One or two Tommies climbed up into the compartment's luggage racks and fell asleep and the crush was reduced. I was able to stretch my legs and from somewhere a Tommy produced a bandage roll and added it to the one on my head wound which was oozing blood. Suddenly the train pulled into a station full of women serving chow and doorstep sandwiches. "Corn in Egypt" I remarked with satisfaction. A Tommy looked at me strangely and said "You alright mate?" Another handed me a large breakfast cup of tea and a doorstep…spam of course. Everyone wolfed the sandwiches down; most had, like me, not eaten for two days. I managed to get to the window and I must have looked a sorry sight with head and chest swathed in bloodied bandages. Two of the women came over. They were English and from the local Toc H or some such. They handed us chocolate and the Tommies chaffed them. The next station was Tanta at sunset, half way to Kantara on the Canal. The platform was crowded with every kind of Egyptian, peddlers, fedaheen, businessmen and war correspondents who were desperate for news direct from the front. They had heard the guns thudding endlessly for many nights and news was strictly censored. M.P.'s kept them from talking to the Tommies and whole train loads of wounded alarmed some of them.

Perhaps it was the rhythm of the train that started the scapula wound haemorrhage again. First of all the dressing soaked through. Then a definite trickle down the back. Turning to an awry side-sitting position only diverted a flow round the front into my pubic hair. I must have passed out. The Tommies said I went white and fell asleep. They called an orderly and I was quickly taken to the front of the train where the soaked dressing was removed from my back and I was re-bandaged and given a place to stretch out and with another injection slept the remaining four hours to Kantara.

Sunday, 25th October '42

Entered English C.C.S. in early morning. Still bleeding. On to train after a little sleep at 12 noon. Put as sitting patient and bled badly as a result. Into (train's) hospital truck where redressed and then managed to get sleep. Travelled for 14 hours. Train full of Tommies.

HOSPITAL 101

We got to the 101st British General Hospital in the early hours of Monday morning. It had been my longest weekend with each drug enduced sleep making the two-and-a-half days from the front to the hospital seem like an eternity. The reception area could barely cope. There were what appeared to be hundreds, certainly scores of soldiers filthy dirty, hair matted and clotted, limbs bloodied or bandaged, hobbling, some with foot blown off by shoe-mines and of course those on stretchers. The nurses, some of them looking fresh from England did their best. The one wheeling me in said "Good God you look like my young brother in England. He's only nineteen." The head bandage had slipped covering one of my eyes. I must have looked heroic. "Spot on" I answered. Two embarrassing moments occurred; one was waiting for a male orderly, to ask him for a bottle and not a nurse. The second came minutes later. The hospital had got help from Palestinian women volunteers who contrasted markedly in their smart khaki blouse and skirts from the English nurses in white and their skins bronzed or middle-east browned. A very attractive one advanced on me with a pair of large scissors and cut the remnants of my uniform off me, and my socks. I showed some embarrassment and she threw a towel across my waist and still with my lying on the stretcher bathed me, struggling with the dried and clotted blood in the pubic region. The memory of her tenderness and compassion never left me.

Then I was given breakfast and put into Ward 87 and had my first treatment. It was decided to apply fresh eusol dressings five times a day, including those at night. Eusol was short for "Edinburgh University Solution of Lime." It turned out to be my heaven-and-hell. The lime solution had been used extensively in England. Through soaking dressings in it and applying them to the horrifying civilian casualties of the Blitz, they warded off infection. Laid on to large wounds and held firmly in position they acted through their lime content as an antiseptic. As such the dressings were very effective. They also removed destroyed tissue. I liked the smell of the eusol and the soothing effects of its cool application. That was the good news. The bad news was that dressings in the hot desert climate dried out quickly and stuck to the traumatised flesh.

It was then bad enough having a ten-inch dressing dragged off your back by day, but to be awakened by a determined but exhausted nurse twice a night was the hellish part of the heaven. But you did it and bore it day and night, day after day.

X-rays also brought heartening results, no fracture of the skull and no penetrations of the chest. The young doctor in charge of Radiography, a Dr. Hodson, took to me and we talked rugby. He was a naturalist and we had common attitudes about war, heroism and things like dreams and aspirations and savage tribes like the Zulus. He visited me each day ostensibly to check whether I had any signs of concussion because the gash on the back of the head had been severe and left a gaping laceration.

For days I did nothing but sleep, write letters home and complain about the food. The daily menu was built around the buffalo. I had seen these surly creatures at work in the Delta fields and didn't appreciate their smell either, not in army skilly or in situ, not even roasted or as chops We had been spoilt at Alamein since Montgomery's arrival and shorter communications had brought us beef frozen, from New Zealand which even the army cooks couldn't spoil and which Derek and I on kitchen fatigue purloined and ate raw believing it would reduce our desert sores.

Then I began to show interest in my hospital surroundings. The wards were made up of E.P.I.P. tents, huge things that let heat and flies in. The temperature always seemed to hover around 100° F and sweating was the only way of cooling down. Central heating was unheard of and there were no fans. I couldn't even use a straw fan with my right arm not yet able to motivate it. The tents were half below the ground surface as a protection against air attack and this shut out sea breezes and enhanced the effects of dust storms. Just outside the tents were deep shell slits to be used by patients while air raids were in progress. The scenery changed with each influx of wounded from the front. There were always one or two beds going spare vacated by the dying. Penicillin had not yet reached the troops. It was still a product only for the very rich. Sulphonamides were still in use and deaths in the wards were not infrequent especially after a push. The time for the back wound to be sewn up began to draw close and it became clear that I would have to be transferred to another hospital for it to be done.

<u>Saturday, 31st October '42 – 101 Hospital</u>

Allowed to walk about a little but feel very weak still. In the afternoon packed off to No. 92 General (Hospital) some 10 miles away at Kantara East. This hospital is a new one and very ill-equipped. Nurses here are very much better though food is putrid. Met several of our fellows from the platoon and was cut up to hear of the deaths of Dennis Platt, Stanley George, Brian Lloyd and many others.

<u>Sunday, 1st November '42 – 92nd General</u>

Quite enjoying my stay here. Ward full up with Tommies and other Imperials. Fretting for a South African hospital. Derek in bed next to me. Nap Wheeler killed by a shell.

<u>Monday, 2nd November '42 – 92nd</u>

Nicknamed one sister 'Battleaxe'. She's not too bad but a tiger for red tape. The other nurses very nice. Back wound is very clean I believe.

<u>Tuesday, 3rd November '42 – 92nd</u>

Lack of equipment makes work hard for sisters. Many chaps and self included haven't had dressings for days. Not the fault of the sisters.

<u>Wednesday, 4th November '42 – 92nd</u>

Doctors will sew my back up tomorrow, and also my head. Chaps in the wards are very good fellows.

HOSPITAL 92

As I recall the 92nd Hospital was not much different from the one I had just left…E.P.I.P.'s sunk into the desert sand, air raid slits, flies and dust. The wards were crowded with Tommies. Surprise, surprise, Derek wounded and sober was put in the bed next to me. I gave a long whistle. He gave a giggle and drew out a pack of four tins of U.S. beer from his kit bag and hid them under my blankets. At dressing time Derek had a view of the gash on the scapula and gave me the first honest outside opinion. He was shocked by its size but said "It's clean, very clean – I could put my head through it and have a look around inside."

The nurses at 92 were charming but the fly in the ointment was matron who endeavoured to run the wards neat and tidy, with the tidiness of your locker coming first and its patient thereafter. The Tommies fell prey to this nonsense and were ordered about until I felt I had to intervene on their behalf. Matron decided to wait for her revenge. Derek took over management of my locker and a cousin wounded at Dunkirk and transferred to the local N.A.A.F.I. promised by letter to visit and ease the food problem and our duel with matron shifted to the harassed ward orderlies. They were nice guys and would 'do' for you for a few fags. Neither Derek or I smoked in any shape or form and had rationed cigarettes to burn, dreadful things called Woodbines. A few of the orderlies would get underclothing laundered and even a shirt ironed.

The boredom of day to day living had to be dealt with under the restriction and routine imposed by my wound dressings still 5 hourly eusols. A complication arose when something went wrong with the bread supply. Everyone got a touch of gypo-guts (gastro-enteritis) and the bed pan ruled supreme. Orderlies had to fly around the wards answering despairing calls of "Orderly! Orderly bring me a bedpan!" The orderlies, often a bedpan in each hand, sometimes couldn't quite make it and then there were screens, clean sheets, loud words, tummy eruptions and other commotions. Derek and I found it huge fun. The former had been a nifty scrum-half in his early days and was able to make the toilets in good time. He had to help me in travail to the toilet and my times were nearly as good as his. It was much worse at night and as a diversion during a lull I had let loose a stifled shout for an orderly into my pillow, just for fun. Chaos ensued with hoaxers joining in elsewhere adding agony words to the basic clarion call like "Orderly, hurry for godsake!" and to this there would be the response "I'm cooming choom!" Less said the better.

The inevitable happened and I met my Moses when I was ready to be sewn up. The radiologist, I called him 'Hoddy' had joined us again with his surgery team at the 92nd. He examined me and pronounced the three-and-a-half inch by eight inch cleft (one of the Tommies called it the 'Watford Gap') ready for sutures. Hoddy had explained that with such a wide wound the operation might have to be repeated to get sufficient closure for it to scar effectively. All went well though I awakened cursing from my 'twilight' anaesthetic. I was that night lying on my back with giant stitches pressing and pulling that I knew pain at its worst and for so long.

Two days later I was up and about and dressed in the gaudy hospital blues, went with Derek into Kantara to see a show. He had rigged up a dummy in my bed to fool the nurses. A sister Page came to renew my eusol and nearly had hysterics confronted with an immovable form. News came through that Nap Wheeler, the regimental chaplain had been killed by a shell near Alamein. He was from my church (St. Pauls) in Durban and had taken me for some of my confirmation classes before I volunteered in 1939. Streams of casualties kept flowing into the 92nd. Derek helped where he could. A very sick looking Scots boy occupied the bed opposite me. He looked a 'goner' to me, almost olive green in colour but he clung on. All of us were now in difficulties with the nurses struggling to absorb each new flood of wounded men. Their accounts of happenings at the front were always disturbing making you wish to rejoin your own buddies in the Regiment.

CHAPTER XVIII

My cousin Ken Haslewood finally came to see me. He was a real base-wallah, an overweight staff sergeant at N.A.A.F.I. Shocked at my appearance and loss of weight, he got permission to take us over to his den in Kantara. I had met him in 1934 when he was a waiter at a large hotel in Folkestone. He was then eighteen and took me to the funfair on the beach front. He was a good-looking youth then and as randy as a fiddler's bitch. His joie-de-vivre was infectious and his attraction to the fair sex alarming. Now, eight years later, the libido was still there but his looks had gone and his undercarriage was beginning to buckle. He fed us sumptuously and loaded us up with luxury items to provide relief from the buffalo skilly. But he gave me a word of warning that I was not to mention, in any shape or form his shenanigans in Kantara when I wrote home to England. By these he meant his amours amongst the hospital staff at 92, one of whom was a staff nurse in the same surgery that was handling my injuries and gave light-hearted hints that if when I recovered I wanted some fun …? I said nothing and moved him over to Derek who nearly choked over his double Scotch. We paid many visits to my cousin whose 'goings on' never abated; his wife knew nothing of them; he became a very successful restauranteer in the Midlands and died young.

My back wound was reinforced by two 9-inch straps of thick elastoplast running down its length overlapping the replaceable eusol dressing between them which was covered with cotton wool padding to ease the pressure of the stitch knots. A rubber tube draining the whole was permanent and smelly. Dressing time attracted a few onlookers and even the 'goner' in the bed opposite, during a remission, got a good look. Rarely, matron did the dressing. She raged at me, a bed patient, for stealing out at night with Derek for a snort at a nearby bar and made up for it at dressing time. Normally the dressing came off gingerly and piecemeal. On this occasion matron putting her nose to it in advance, decided the whole should come off. I gave a few 'ooos-and-aahs' as she took hold then without warning she wrenched downwards and I did a 'John Herbert' on her letting out a huge roar "aaah, you bloody bitch!" There was an appalled silence for a few seconds. Then she said with protracted satisfaction "Yeees", turned to her assistant and ordered her to "Carry on Sister!" and strode off, the victor. On another occasion a soldier from the 50th Div., Durham Light Infantry, seeing the wound bared for the first time uttered, wide-eyed at the two uprights and criss-crossed black stitches, "Gor blimey, looks like 'Anley Park gates!"

We cursed the flies of course, but some bed-ridden pervert, with nothing better to do, had observed a certain fly phenomenon and swore to his hypothesis, "These little bastards can scent death and gather on the beds of those who are about to snuff it." I had quickly glanced down at my own bed and gave it an 'all clear.' But when I looked at the bed opposite, Oh dear! My worst fears were confirmed, there was somewhat of a gathering there. The nurses had given the patient what attention time would allow. The hospital was hopelessly ill-equipped and undermanned for a big offensive like Alamein. The Scot opposite was an example. I think his name was Palmer but I called him Scotty.

At his best he was bright enough and catching me out coming in late from a night in the town warned me "For Chrays sake mon, ye dinna ge yerself a chance!" Poor guy, he had not responded to treatment. Scotty had two small flesh wounds on the front of his abdomen which the C.C.S.'s had patched up, but two or three days after hospitalisation it was discovered that these were penetrating wounds that had come out his back. Yes and a few days later flies did gather on his bed just before termination.

Nine days after suturing, my stitches were unceremoniously taken out. The next morning where the wound still gaped, more were put in. Didn't need an anaesthetic this time and was told there was always a danger the scarring could break down. The head bandage came off and my favourite ward sister said I was better looking without it. So much for heroism!

PAIN AND WEEPING

During the long days in the 92nd with wounded Tommies all around me I had time to ponder on Pain and Weeping. In the line, a few men sobbed without their women; sometimes in the corner of the dugout with only reddened eyes to show their shame; it might be with an uttering of the mother's name if there was real pain, the pain of physical hurts. Some wept for their wives, girls or fiancees if they had been naughty in Cairo and now alone could shed a tear reading over the beloved's letters. Some cried naturally of course, over bad news from the paradise they had called home and especially where they were patients in an army hospital seriously or dangerously ill confined to their beds and with sheets to hide their crying and where there were horrifying wounds to be dressed interminably with eusol through the night and... O dear! Those awful, prolonged cries of the badly burnt and the stench that went with them.

We all delved into a little astrology out of boredom and now and then with head turned aside and staring hard at some distant point I tried for distraction to identify their agonising calls with appropriate correlation to their zodiacal sign.

In Aries, head wounds and lambs bleating their discomfort; in Capricorn the broken staccato of severe hurt afflicting an isolated kid goat, and even patient Ellis at the 92nd General with his Scorpionic, hurt-animal outbursts; and finally the Catholic calls of Pisceans to their Virgin Mother. It was all there; true or false it shut me out behind my own screen of "maddening freedom and bewildering light,"* from the terrors of men wounded grievously in battle and reminded me of Hecuba, queen of vanquished Troy calling to wailing Trojan women being driven into enforced conjugality:

> O mothers of the brazen spear
> And maidens, brides of shame,
> Troy is but a dying flame...etc., etc.**

Troy for me was the symbol of my youth betrayed and defeated by the war and I would weep a little too. Bill Stevens used to evoke

---

* 'The Land of Heart's Desire' by W.B. Yeats
**'The Trojan Women' by Euripides – translation by Dr. Gilbert Murray.

tears if left to himself to choose the songs and eventually with his own loss of innocence he could orchestrate a platoon's sad moments after there were casualties, or the Padre's penetrating sermon.

No.1 platoon, so often had to split up on different anti-aircraft ventures. It had its own song, a Negro spiritual which would be sung through with gentle reverence:-

'Tell me the story of old Missouri
That my dear old mammie told me;
Just let me picture once more
That old sunny shore,
Where I played round the old cabin door.
I remember the day she taught me to pray
When I was a child at her knees;
I've been a rolling stone
Since I was eleven
And if you want to lead me
Right back to heaven
Tell me the story of old Missouri
That my dear old mammie told me.'

Some diary notes:

Monday, 16th November '42 – 92nd Hospital

N.M.R. regiment and all South Africans withdrawn from the Alamein Line to Quassassin

Saturday, 21st November '42 – 106 Hospital

Transferred to 106 South African Hospital. Travelling by truck & train arriving 7:00pm

Tuesday, 24th November '42 – 106 Hospital

At 106 Hospital – still being treated for concussion (suspected skull fracture)

With the regiment coming out of the line there were now many visitors, old regimental friends mainly but officers you had served under in the last three years. A trio of Bello Theunissen, Vic Paul and a Captain Pat Lyster came and talked briefly. They had come for some specific purpose but at that stage I could not tell what it was. The two first mentioned knew me and my army record very well but they were more interested in my physical condition and came to the conclusion that the nature of the wounds meant I would be invalided back to South Africa and boarded out of the army. They had already spoken to the hospital authorities and examined my medical papers. Only when they left did it occur to me the purpose of the visit, friendly and comradely though they were. Even if a citation would have been forthcoming the fact that I would play no further part in the regiment would have decided the matter for them. Nevertheless I was pleased that Shorty Carneson was mentioned in dispatches.

Three days later the awards of medals and honours for Alamein were announced. It was surprising how few there were for such an important victory. Now the regimental ranks began to fill rapidly. We were going home. The regimental ship was not going to sink and guess who were returning in large numbers from the four corners of the middle east. I began to see faces I hadn't met since the first shots in Egypt were fired. Men from officers training, extended leave, abstruse medical conditions, A.W.O.L.s, basewallahs, seconders, reserve adjutants and quartermasters, drop-outs and the shell-shock, the lame and the lazy, the rats and the mice.

Parties of men were going off to Palestine and Syria on a week's leave. Derek and I decided to go to Cairo. I had a special reason and Derek's reason was always the booze but he was good to have around in case of trouble and I was still 'winged' with a shoulder wound in bandages producing proud flesh.

Derek turned paternal and demanded that I take my great coat because in mid-December the evening air could turn chilly. I refused and the compromise was that he took his. In it he looked like a Grant tank minus the 75mm and drew some giggles from the girls in Cairo. The hospital had no idea I was going on leave and I would be crammed in on the truck that took the score of us into the Delta. I was a little alarmed when I felt a tell tale trickle of you-know-what run down my back as far as my webbing belt. We booked into the New Hotel and later had a gorgeous dinner for four. I had promised Derek a luscious blind date and he agreed to keep sober. His date was Tassia's mother

Montgomery in front of a Grant Tank

We all welcomed the Grant tank to the Allied stand at Alamein. It seemed huge but with its main gun sited on the hull instead of being mounted on a rotating turret its effectiveness was nothing like that of the Sherman tank that succeeded it.

Marcia, the venerable grotesque. His only comment was a question about her preference in Liqueurs. I said "Grand Marnier." He said "Fuck you, that's the most expensive hooch on the market." I consoled him "At least it's French." He grunted and went off to buy it. One of the consolations of having Derek for a friend was that the Wool Market which employed him in Durban paid him in full while 'up North,' and he was never tight when money for liquor was required.

I suggested he pour himself a good measure of the Marnier before the girls arrived.

Tassia was loveliness herself. She fluttered in ahead of her mother and Derek's hopes rose. The mother was smartly dressed and veiled as usual. I took her hand and kissed the agate ring, a symbol of my own sun sign Capricorn. "Tassia said you were badly wounded and you are not even in hospital clothes," she purred as she looked me up and down. I smiled and took her over to Derek. Then she flipped up her veil and fixed her steely eyes on him. Derek took a step back to steady himself. It was not the Grand Marnier but the sight of the Grotesque's clefted features that had set him back. Derek's mouth had dropped open and Venerable smiled sweetly at him, "Mr. de Madillac, I believe you are still in mourning for France," and she gave him a sympathetic and encouraging look. "You see, I was born in Syria and love Frenchmen." "Madame I'm not French" Derek spluttered and took up the bottle of Grand Marnier defensively and filled two liqueur glasses. Grotesque took one and I took the other, sidling over to Tassia.

Derek and Marcia began chatting and got on like a house on fire. Talking to Tassia was like dashing my face with ice cold water from a bubbling stream. She refreshed, renewed and sweetened my cheeks after all the harsh miseries and tensions of confrontation during '42.

I drew her out on to the balcony into the cool evening air and sat her just where her mother could see and we talked and talked and held hands and she felt for the healed red furrow on the back of my head. She smelt of Jasmine.

Back in the room we all had another liqueur and Marcia began to sing. She had a compelling throaty force and sang Mandalay and one or two other songs she had learnt from her husband. Derek and I responded with 'The Legion of the Lost' and the 'Song of Old Missouri.' Then for encores I sang them 'My Sweet Comanche Rose' whose words went something like:

> 'You're my sweet Comanche Rose
> The fairest rose that grows
> And you're the sweetest of them all.'

I laid my hand on Tassia's wrist as I sang and Marcia blinked away a tear. And again:

> 'May your love go on for me
> For all eternity
> And may we never drift apart'

And then the mood became sombre. We were seated at a round table and the Grand Marnier was on its last legs. Marcia, looking at me said darkly "My son, your travail is not yet over. I have looked closely at your birth chart. Because your time of birth is so accurate I can even read your present situation and there is something pending." I laughed gently, saying "But the big battle is over and I'm now out of it for good." Derek had got to his feet adding "Madamoselle for Douglas, the war is over," and standing behind me with both hands gripping the lapels of my unbuttoned tunic he drew it off gently. Mother and daughter got up quickly to look. A small dressing put over the granulation tissue in the centre of the wound could not hide the huge red gash and Tassia, with her hand to her mouth concealed a scream. Grotesque nodded her head "Saturn in Libra," she muttered, "scarred right shoulder. Yes, the chart is accurate and it says you are now, even out of the fighting, in extreme danger. Yes! Right now." She was quite emphatic. Short term and long term, there was still some threat. I drew my tunic back on and buttoned up. The magic had gone out of the night. I felt suddenly weak; possibly I should not have been out of the hospital so soon and possibly I had reacted to the look of horror on Tassia's face, even of revulsion. The party broke up; I asked Derek to take them home in a gharry, smiled at them both and went into the bedroom closing the door.

Bike rides in Ismalia, December '42
(from left, Colin MacArthur, the Author and Richard Platt).

<u>Monday 14th December '42 – Cairo</u>

Into Cairo on leave with Derek. Had a wonderful time – saw cinemas and met Tassia in the evening. Drank and gorged – stayed at New Hotel.

Returning to Quassassin from Cairo on a crowded army truck was not something to look forward to. As expected early signs were not encouraging. When we reached the parking ground…the driver was late, several passengers were staggering drunk, two others urinating uncertainly on a young flamboyant tree and one had passed out in the bed of canners. Five were A.W.O.L. Otherwise take off would probably not be delayed more than an hour.

It was dark when we left and the driver was almost sober. In any case, most of us had, as usual, spent all our money and had no option but to return to camp. Derek wore his great coat and was not greeted happily by the overcrowded passengers and we had to stand for the three hour journey. Fortunately, I spied Joss Deacon in the corner of the truck and he made a place for us. Outside of Cairo the road was straight all the way. The desert air turned freezing and Derek gave me his great coat. I accepted this canopy with some reluctance. It hung on me absurdly. But I settled with a compromise. Joss, recovering from his wounds was also freezing and sufficiently slender for him to share the coat each of us with an opposite arm in the sleeves. At least we were warm and began to join in the risqué army songs. I recall only one of them:

> 'Way down in Arkansas where the bullshit lies thick
> I lay for an hour with my hand on my dick,
> A-dreaming and scheming of the girl I adore
> Sharlot, the harlot, the cowpuncher's whore.
> She was easy, she was greasy, she was always on heat
> As often as not she was out on the street,
> For a dollar, a sixpence or tuppence or more,
> You could have Sharlot, the harlot, the cowpuncher's whore…'

The song went on and on with its unspeakable verses. Joss shook with laughter but I couldn't. It hurt too much.

We must have been ten minutes from our destination and the road became crowded. Just before midnight we collided with another army truck and rolled over. Inside the truck we were bodies all rolled up and there were a few shouts and screams. We had managed to get one great coat button fastened and this had not given way. Joss, with his injured gonads, was protecting himself like a soccer player and I had my back jammed against the metal bodywork for protection as a mad rush to get out was prompted by a strong smell of petrol. Unbelievably, an argument firstly between the drivers ensued and then it was taken up by both trucks with some fists flying. Derek strode into the thick of it with "You chaps are fucking about arguing and there are men lying hurt and needing help." There was a general sobering up with broken bones, cuts and bruises but no one killed. Venerable Grotesque had been right in her forecast.

My diary of that day reads:-

Tuesday, 15th December '42 – Cairo
'Did some shopping and loafed around. Saw a show. On the way back to camp piled up with another army lorry just before midnight. One chap's arm broken and another's skull cracked and many bruised and cut. Back slightly hurt and bleeding. Reached camp at 2 a.m.'

It took only a day to visit the local aid post and get the wound dressed and recoup, and then a happy day with Richard and Colin MacArthur:-

Thursday, 17th December '42 – Ismalia
'Into Ismalia with Richard and Mac and had a perfect day. Plenty to drink (non- alcoholic) and eat. Bought some odds and ends and hired bicycles and had photos taken.'

The problem with my shoulder wound had been that it had gaped so profoundly that even the first and second suturings were not able to bring both edges together and healing by first intention had not been possible. But now granulation tissue (proud flesh) nodules began to appear which were later to produce scar tissue successfully. At this stage it was necessary to reduce excessive exuberance of this tissue by burning it off with a silver nitrate pencil. This procedure went on for some time and had required periodic dressings. Some of the stitches were also left in where gaping was maximum.

Monday, 28th December '42 – Suez area

Seem to be leaving (Egypt) very shortly now. To 106 (hospital) to have back burnt (silver nitrate) and dressed.

Tuesday, 29th December '42 – Suez area

Kit inspection. To 106 again for dressing. Packed up all kit ready to move.

The inspection was held mainly to check whether soldiers were carrying souvenir Italian grenades back to South Africa and in danger of exploding en route.

STRETCHER BEARER

We were all now getting ready for the voyage back on home leave to Durban. I felt strong enough to undertake the very special mission for me of locating the black stretcher bearer who had first found me on the battlefield at Alamein. It required a long search through many encampments in the midday sun of the Canal Zone.

My recollection was that he was either a native of Basutoland tucked up in the mountainous area of the Drakensberg Mountain range or from Zululand. I had just given up the search when there was a shout from a group of tents on some high ground. It was my rescuer who had so lovingly applied the shell dressings to my back and head. He came running up to Derek, Richard and me. I embraced him and a crowd of his friends stood staring unbelievingly at this extraordinary scene for them, a white South African soldier embracing a black one. The medic was weeping and begged me to show him what he had remembered two months before as a mortal wound which he had dressed with such loving care as I lay across the shell hole with shells and mines still bursting around us.

DIE NIEUW AMSTERDAM

Though the size of Nieuw Amsterdam was impressive we knew that the seas in the Atlantic and now, even the Indian Ocean were not cleared of the U-boat and surface raider-menace. The *Ceramic* a large British liner had been sunk in the Atlantic during 1942 and there had only been one survivor. The British had by now, of course, cracked the *ENIGMA* German code in U-boats which had put them out of communication directly with Admiral Donitz, the Nazi naval supremo. We were sailing without convoy which was not comforting. But alone, we would be able to travel at full speed, too fast for a U-boat, or even a Nazi raider to overtake us. There were also further risks. The Japanese had access to the Indian Ocean both by sea and by air. Japanese planes were already raiding Calcutta, and the Horn of Africa which we were soon to round was not that far from India. As a final security measure, the Nieuw Amsterdam zigzagged her way on the open seas to make her position impossible for U-boats to calculate.

About 7,000 troops were reputed to be on board and probably a crew of more than a thousand, mainly British. The voyage would pass through some of the hottest parts of the world and would cross the equator. Sleeping in the crowded conditions four or five decks below, possibly even some decks below the water line was uninviting.

The food served at meals was excellent and surprisingly fresh. Our destination was Durban non-stop from Suez. The whole day, every day was taken up virtually queuing for meals. You no sooner eat one meal than it was time to stand for two or three hours in a queue for the next because feeding 7,000 men and crew three times a day was a logistical nightmare. Queues took all of the outer decks' space. Very little promenading was possible. Boiling hot food had to be transported in trays and open containers, including tea, to the heads of the queues, which were three or four deep and perhaps 50 yards long extending down into the staircases. It seemed ridiculous to spend ten days standing in the queues but there was no where else to go and you might just as well be there as anywhere. Delivering the food at the right moment was heralded by the hard-pressed chefs shouting "Red hot! Watch it! Red hot!" The crew were charming, not necessarily sailors at all. They thought we were bloody mad to risk our lives and we thought they were bloody mad to take on such tasks.

The atmosphere was excellent. We were going home. What the hell else mattered… trying to sleep in hammocks, resting on the deck floor below them, and rooms heated to more than 100° F, enemy subs, the twisting and rolling of the giant ship as it changed course zigzagging and so on made for restless nights. Then there was the plumbing which just gave up under the heavy duties imposed on it. Lavatories and wash basins overflowed and waves of sewage raced across some of the deck space deluging unwary sleepers like a sudden turn of the tide catches people in their deck-chairs on the beach.

Wild horses would not have dragged Richard Platt and I down below to sleep. We preferred to sleep out on the top deck in the blackout under the stars hugging our life jackets come rain or hurricane. Sometimes we were fortunate and secured shelter below the bridge on the promenade deck. The officers, of course, had the cabins and were rarely seen out of them. In the course of those long nights it was a good time to review the events of the last two years on active service, to lay plans for the post-war years and so on. Jokes flew around and awful speculations. Richard thought that for the first few nights after arrival, the ten days of hopes, wishes and frustrations would turn our destination Durban into a sea of heaving bums. The current circulating pick of the bunch was the story of the married soldier arriving home after two years:–

"What will be the first thing you do when you get home?"

The soldier answers "I'll be up those stairs and fling her on the bed and do her."

"Then what will you do?"

"I'll take my pack off."

On the 1st January, '43 we set sail on the New Amsterdam for Durban and at 8am, ten days later, the ship docked unscathed in Durban with the 1st South African Division on board with large crowds to greet her and Mrs. Perla Siedle-Gibson, the Lady in White to welcome them with joyful and patriotic songs.

Chapter XIX

'Home again' was farcical for me in the main sense. I had joined the army in 1939 from the YMCA and had left a few belongings and the family piano with the kindly old housekeeper at the Y.M. My two elder sisters were both entering second marriages and my younger brother was away in the Royal Navy. I had several offers to stay from my buddies but chose to stay for our short leave with Richard Platt whose home was but a block away from my own home on the Berea where my mother had died the year before the war. Richard was restless; I was restless, and after the usual run around the night-clubs in Durban decided that after the years of flat desert we would go up to the Drakensberg Mountains on the Northern borders of Natal. Try though we did to miss family entanglements, both sisters were not going to miss anything if they could help it and the thing began to snowball. Soldiers from 'up North' on home leave had a bit of gloss and the gilt was petrol coupons in a gasoline-starved war impacted country.

The sisters and their associates took the biggest car (and the petrol coupons) and drove up to Cathedral Peak and Richard and I took the train. It was a bracing ten days which I wouldn't have missed. Dick and I would take a mountain trail as far as I could walk and just sit some distance apart and stare into the foothills which undulated out from the inner and outer Horns of the Drakensberg range. The scenery seemed to engulf me and fill in the nasty vacuums which cruel desert warfare had left in my nature.

Back in Durban the impact of the First Division's return on leave was not always met with goodwill. There were many other troops in transit through the city. Massive convoys were en route to the Middle East. Sometimes more than a hundred ships would choke the harbour and its approaches. Beer in the pubs would be sold out by 5 p.m. daily. For Durban's returning soldiers organised dances especially at R.D.L.I. Regimental H.Q.'s at Greyville were oases in a city somewhat in chaos. I attended one-such with my sister and her husband Cecil Wheeler and immediately ran into trouble. We were dressed up and I in uniform. Having parked the car and while approaching the R.D.L.I. hall entrance, we were barracked by a group of Royal Navy sailors from one of the cruisers in the harbour. Sour comments were made like:

'Pretty boys from up North…!
Nobody wants us anymore…!
Who the hell do you think you are?'

It was OK by me but we were being confronted. I certainly wanted no trouble with a back still in bandages. My brother-in-law pushed one of the sailors out of the way. His mate took a swing at me and knocked me flat on my back. Cecil hit one of them with a punch to the jaw and got a black eye in return. My sister in a long flowing, well-filled evening dress, seeing me on the ground in distress, ran at the sailor. He had his sailor's hat stuck on the back of his head and a shock of hair in the front of it like Frank Sinatra and wasn't that tall for all his cheek. Margaret grabbed his hair with one hand and swung her sequinned bag at his head screaming "You dare to attack my brother, wounded and in bandages…!" The sailor was either too surprised or too much of a gentleman to take much action on this female wildcat. He backed off shouting "Sorry missus, sorry," picked up his hat and ran off with his mates as M.P.'s closed in.

That meant a series of visits to the soldiers M.A.P. in Springfield Road. Margaret, the only unmarked participant in the fracas was the sole victor of the evening, but there was a charming outcome. I was called to the Hall entrance an hour later. The sailors had come to apologise and I got permission to invite them over to our table where we all joined in the hot favourite song of the night which was Perry Como's "In the Mood." I couldn't dance that night but the sailors did and the girls in the party didn't mind dancing with them.

My sisters , it should be said, had spent all their spare time, during the two years I was away, frying eggs at the Victoria League Club for the thousands of Sailors and Tommies passing through Durban. My older sister Kay once calculated how many eggs she had fried during the two years and it was more than one hundred thousand!

On home leave I went out with Archie McLachlan several times and a rather alarming episode occurred when we both attended a film matinee at the Cameo Theatre. The theatre was dark and we had someone seated in front of us. In a loutish mood, I put my feet on the back of the seat in front of me which was vacant. During the introductory filmlets, before interval, the figure in front of Archie turned round and barked at me, "Take your feet down, please!" I leaned forward and said, "My feet aren't worrying you" and left them in position. In the interval, I was surprised to find that Archie McLachlan had left his seat before the lights came up and I was shocked to see a military figure, in fact a colonel, getting up from the place in front. It turned out to be Colonel Butler-Porter of the Durban Light Infantry who gave me a hard look, examining my regimental badge in case I was in his own regiment. Outside I found a trembling Archie McLachlan, much embarrassed but not in anyway blaming me. Being now an officer in Butler-Porter's regiment he had decided not to argue the matter out during the interval.

Slowly but surely I was recovering my good health and vigour with dressings coming to an end in the beginning of March ('43). I was ready to face the great question, did I really and truly want to say 'Goodbye to all that' or should I morally, ethically and now, dare I say it – spiritually return to the front?

Having examined the advice given me; Dr. Hoddy in the 92nd had advised that I should accept invalidism and be returned to South Africa: Clem Woods my civilian job boss at John Dickinson's had again said "Douglas, your job is still open. We need you." A strange voice within me seemed to say "You've done enough." I had grabbed at my lost youth whenever I could on short leaves, did I really want to go back into that frightful mess coming up in Europe, especially as it would be this time in armour?

In the end I left it to the doctors whose advice was simple. We will board you 'D' which means your health status is deferred to a later date. Your scar may break down with hard work. If it does you would have to leave active duty immediately. You need a year to recover fully. I was allowed to rejoin the regiment, but it was made quite clear I would have to prove my competence to be reboarded A1 by my ability to fulfil the demands of the stiff training imposed on the newly-constituted N.M.R. regiment which was now in the South African 6th Armoured Division preparing for Egypt. I accepted the arrangement.

I had a dream that night after reading poems of Gerard Manly Hopkins, in which I was standing in a high place and someone in the valley was trying to sing:-

> *'There'll be bluebirds over*
> *The white cliffs of Dover*
> *Tomorrow when the world is free...*
> *There'll be love and laughter*
> *And peace ever after*
> *When the world is free.'*

The symbols of my inner life were scanty, but birds flying high over white cliffs nourished me in the difficult years ahead, especially the falcon portrayed in Hopkin's poem 'The Windhover.'

My new found vigour took me back to Durban's gorgeous beaches and with old civilian friends and army friends we surfed the brisk waves often muddied by the flood waters of Zululand's Umgeni River. I thought the Tommies on the Durban beaches were great chaps despite their awful accents and laughable attempts to deal with the rough seas and formidable breakers on the Natal coast. We were now troopers in the cavalry and squadrons of an Armoured Division back at camp.

Tuesday, 13th April '43 – Durban

'Our squadron on duty. Broke bounds again. Went with Mousie and Cecil Ritson for a swim and watched Tommies being dumped (by the breakers). Home (Clarewood Camp) for dinner and thence to Playhouse for a few drinks – a grill and then home.'

FRED CARNESON

Soldiers were practically untouched by communism during the early stages of the war. My friendship with Fred Carneson, Shorty's brother had got some of us interested in the Springbok Legion which, as I took it, was a band of soldiers serving in the South African army with the common interest of striving for better conditions. A monthly pack of Springbok Legion propaganda arrived by post each month which I shared amongst the interested few. While in Durban, mainly as a friendly gesture to Fred I attended a meeting of the Legion in the City Hall. About 300 people were present and several good points were lobbied but it was not for me. It was plain even then there were those behind the movement who were aiming to turn it into a sort of soldiers' trade union and that meant politics. I had my own idea about the political scene and though sympathetic at that stage towards the U.S.S.R. and its magnificent stand against national socialism, it was counter to my own aspirations.

After the war there was a slender chance that returning soldiers could have a political voice when 'Sailor Malan' led a large group of ex-servicemen in torchlight processions against an apartheid government. If anything that movement was right wing. Poor Fred Carneson became involved more and more with communism and out of that kind of thinking emerged the African National Congress and agitators like Nelson Mandela with his liberating ideas. I had long talks with Shorty about his brother's leanings. He was loyal to the end and never forgot Fred's traumas in adolescence. But I was doubtful.

Early April saw me back at various camps sweating it out on daily route marches and squad drill and getting fitter by the day. Our impending departure for training in tanks in Egypt and armoured fighting certain thereafter in Italy we were anxious to have last minute flings, partying around Durban:

Thursday, 15th April '43

Route march to Reunion Bridge. Drew some pay and went into town with Joss. Borrowed Margaret's car and went swimming. Dinner at home (Margaret's) and thence with Lenny Clark and

Joan Anderson and Sheila to cinema and a grand evening. Home in George Scott's car.

<u>Saturday, 17th April '43</u>

Squad drill and am stiff as a poker therefrom. To lunch at Mayfair with Kay and Joss. Thence to cinema. Home for a bath and out to Kew (dance hall) in a party of twelve for one of the most enjoyable evenings of my leave. Gave it a big thrash with 6 bottles of champagne and much other hooch. Took Sheila as partner, pretty but dumb. To Honor Downes' place for the rest of the evening and had a wonderful time. Back to camp by taxis around 3:30 a.m.

This party at the Downes' home left us with a final and lively memory of home leave. Richard Platt, Joss Deacon, Lenny Clark, Jock Dickens and myself were to share a tent together in training with Phil Bullimore, Pooch Marais and Joe Rawlinson… lovely girls, a great night and then, the next day, embarking on H.M. Troopship "Ille de France", once more for Egypt.

Another twelve days at sea, all of us arseholes broke, depressed at our prospects, and the Lady in White on the pier's end singing "Bluebirds Over." The numerous storms en route with squalls thrown in seemed to be warning us of the perils ahead.

The Ille de France gave me nearly two weeks to resolve certain disturbing inner queries that had pestered me subjectively. The war was bringing an end to Axis domination in Africa. Fascist and Nazi aspirations would soon be driven completely out of the Dark Continent. It was time for a new thinking. Churchill had been an emotional firework, a sparkler at a time of great darkness. More than three years of war had made me review the role of my native land which was England. It seemed to me, standing aside from the jingoism of my youth, that Britain's aspirations should greatly broaden. The truth of the war so far had been obscured. Hitler was targeting Russia as his primary aim. The wars he had initiated in Western Europe had been undertaken to secure his rear before attacking his arch enemy which was Russia's brand of communism and to extend German dominance into the Ukraine where there were unlimited wheatlands and the Caucasus where there was unlimited oil. The real truth was that, with the fall of France, his threat to England was only the military threat of a feinted attack to detract attention from his machinations against Russia. The most relevant part of this strategy to the 10,000 troops on board this giant ship was whether say for another two years the lion's share of equipment was going towards this diminishing feint of an invasion of Britain or whether it would really come to the site of the impending attack on the soft underbelly of Europe which was Italy. The Commonwealth armies had had enough of fighting battles without appropriate equipment. It now looked likely that the U.S. could well equip a second front in Italy or even Southern France, but if it was to be across the channel to Northern France, would we again be left high and dry like a beached whale in Italy?...as we had in the desert earlier. The heroism of Britain was beyond praise, but the issues were no longer Churchillian, they required appeals to the mental attitude of the allies and to my mind Franklin Roosevelt was the only one who could press for a New Order on the planet. The matter of Japan and how to destroy her as an ongoing aggressor was also an issue, even in '43. I used to pull down a screen obliterating that area of the war. There was not the slightest glimmer of any new weapon to destroy Japan at the time and the loss of perhaps millions of men in the process was too awful to contemplate. On the Ille de France I had strange feelings as if, in extreme contemplation of these problems, the thousands on board were sharing their thoughts with me.

Our arrival in Egypt this second time was without frills. From Suez an overnight cattle truck journey took us to Khatatba, a training camp of tents, shower baths and open mess rooms scratched out of the arid, barren desert 20 miles down the Nile half way between Cairo and Alexandria.

The frills began almost immediately. The late commanding officer of our division General Dan Pienaar had told his junior officers "When these boys get back I don't want them buggered around. There are to be no parades, guards or other duties, only essential kitchen fatigues such as peeling potatoes and keeping the camp clean. Unless they ask for it, don't even make them play games. They are tired and need lots of rest. Give them lots of beer in the camp but try to keep them out of towns where they could get into a lot of mischief". His great admirer Captain Blamey had reported his words spoken a fortnight before Pienaar died in an air crash returning to South Africa.

The advice had taken credence of the two years of harsh active service in the desert and having proved themselves in battle his men no longer needed British army spit-and-polish.

Khatatba tried to prove him wrong. Training we could accept and there were endless classes of it, but the squad drill and route marches, the kit inspections and the red tape were derisory for veterans of more than 3 years in war service. But the nonsense went on and on. It was mid-summer madness.

Apart from an ear infection picked up in Marsabit forest I was fit as a fiddle and pleased to be medically boarded A1 again. It was my Rubicon and I threw myself into the tank training.

Church parades were now becoming intolerable sometimes with a march past anachronistic.

<u>Sunday, 16th May '43 – Khatatba</u>
Abominable church parade, (played) crib and read, the band played "Bless 'em all" on march past in protest.

I might note that few used the word 'Bless' – most used a four-lettered one. The next day the F.F.B. was used as the band in a practice march past, ours being in disgrace. This was all for a build-up to Empire Day, on 24th May. We were furious. We had a new Colonel which didn't help matters, who joined the regiment with personnel from his armoured car reconnaissance unit. Elements of the South African Air Force were also transferred into the battalion which ended up with a totally unwieldy name which no one liked. As volunteers we also felt hoodwinked into giving obeisance to such things as Colonel's kit inspection, church parades and ballyho. We wanted to fight, not fiddle with the frills of buttons and bows.

The first thing you noticed settling in at Camp Khatatbah was the number of new faces. To bring up our numbers after the decimating battles in the Western Desert, other regiments had been disestablished and amalgamated with the N.M.R. It is well that the name Natal

Mounted Rifles which had only been confirmed by the state in 1932 was retained or most of us wouldn't have known who the hell we were. There were strangers in our ranks now from every conceivable source deriving from a nation that was already multiracial and multilingual. Men living together like chickens can be very cruel to each other. Pecking orders are inevitable. That imposed by the Army under the name of 'Officers and Other Ranks' had military law behind it but there were many others and you had to accept what was politic even if it was not appropriate.

Borrowing from the British Army, the label 'Officer' had the word 'Gentleman' added to make 'Officer and Gentleman' which was not always true, certainly not at some of the Officers' Mess tables I served at while on army kitchen fatigue in 1940.

Now experience counted and cliques below the rank of sergeant formed. If you had years on active service you mated together and took over one of the tents at Khatatba, usually eight strong. My clique was such and it had been consolidated by fellowship on the recent home leave. Other tents grouped according to areas of derivation e.g., the Isipingo or Pinetown group and later as cavalry in Sherman tanks a group or platoon was called a 'troop.' Sportsmen, boozers, smokers and nondescripts sorted themselves out into tents according to their predilection and despite a few scuffles the camp became reasonably harmonious and where friction became a threat 'Aga Kahn', the new Sergeant Major (himself an 'alien' from the abandoned 3rd Reconnaissance Unit) intervened after a session of prying. Sterzel was an example in point.

Sterzel was a romantic, which was tough going considering the crew he joined the army with. He was good looking enough to wear silk scarves and an earring without eliciting whistles or wolf-calls from bemused comrades and possibly because he packed a ferocious punch. He was charming without being a show-off and his demeanour was introvert. Beneath the charm you suspected the loneliness of a fractured relationship or even withdrawals within himself that might become psychotic.

He was best remembered when the squadron was in harbour or encamped at base. These were the occasions he chose to go off on his own, or possibly to visit a nameless friend in a neighbouring regiment.

Hardly forgotten rather than remembered, were his returns in the dead of night well-oiled and singing out as loud as he dare in a mournful serenade, songs like "She's only a Paper Doll." He ignored the comments, insults and catcalls from each tent that he stumbled past. But Sterzel had a secret enemy that boiled his German blood. His antagonist, a burly Afrikaans miner from the Witwatersrand, head shaved and florid from excursions into the red wine, had felt flaunted by the presence of someone with a German pedigree, so neatly attuned with handsome hairstyle and said so loudly on several occasions. The two had twice been pulled apart and Aga, the company Sergeant Major, on behalf of the squadron suggested they meet in a properly organised boxing match to settle their dispute.

The patched-up ring was not really needed; the crowd thickened into its own surround and an officer reffed the proceedings. To be honest, the miner was the more popular, but with false teeth out (no gumshield) and face greased, he was hardly the candidate for crowd acclaim. Sterzel, an inch shorter and slightly contemptuous of his ugly opponent looked much the better stripped to the waist, handsome even in boxing gloves with knees bared and slightly bandy.

In a regiment that had been blooded in battle and subjected to crown-and-anchor and poker schools on troopships plying north and south of the equator, bets were bound to be placed and Sterzel gaining consensus edged into favouritism. The way he pawed the air before the cheering onlookers added to the growls of the Afrikaner. The first two rounds were pretty even. Sterzel sprightly on his feet, danced around his opponent who quite unconcerned merely kept edging forward accepting the accurate punches of his assailant with surly looks and grunts. It was in the third round that Sterzel, closing in, took the first punch of any sizeable impact full on his chest. You could hear the air forced out of his rib cage and the snap of its cartilages as they attempted to straighten.

From then on the fight was really over, and as the slaughter continued you knew that Sterzel was no longer there. That he had had the physical guts to stand up to the persistent bully there was no doubt but physically now he was finished and his sovereign consciousness was hovering uncertainly a few feet above the massacre. The Sergeant Major, 'Aga' Kahn judged that both sides of the gathering had had enough and made the referee stop it. Sterzel's eyes were now nearly closed and he had to be led to the centre of the ring. The referee held up the arm of the winner and there was hardly a note of praise. When he raised Sterzel's arm there was a roar and I was reminded of Horatio and the Tuscan's "And even the ranks of Tuscany could scarce forbear to cheer."

Despite the thrashing he had received, 'Sterze' had considerable panache. He believed that style came before experience and when we took him yachting in Alex. harbour he demanded to sail the boat before he knew precisely what things like 'tacking' were. Eventually I handed over the tiller and left him to it. The result was we nearly sank the battleship Queen Elizabeth in a collision.

One can't spend more than four consecutive years in a group at war without being at least partly conscious of changes in its protean existence as it adapts to the demands of its purpose and its environment. The regiments of South Africa, drawn into the defence of its motherland in the fight to the death with Hitler's Germany were called upon many times to reinvent themselves when practically wiped out (at Sidi Rezegh), captured at Tobruk, retrained from infantry into cavalry and from mechanisation back into infantry as aggressive Germany went over from attack to defence.

British guard's regiments were also wiped out or so severely mutilated in the Western desert and Italy as to require total replacement, but they had centuries of tradition in name, battle honours, flags and colours, around which they could rally and return to the fray. The re-assembly or strengthening of a decimated regiment in the South African part of the Eighth Army required sensitive expertise as it called for replacements only from volunteers and from a multi-racial nation that would only allow its tiny white minority, itself bilingual, to engage in actual combat. Time and again regiments were merged, their names changed or soon dropped. Traditions were lost, new arms and strategies had to be employed, supreme commanders were suddenly bowler-hatted, lines of communication were overextended, whole regiments lost in dust storms lasting days, plagued with desert sores and exhausted from imperial retreats or stricken by heat and lacking reserves. Entries of personnel into and out of the Natal Mounted Rifles were so numerous per misadventure, that some thought of it merely as a transit camp. At one stage name mergers had temporarily endowed the regiment with the title N.M.R., 3rd Recce, S.A.A.F., a polyglot that when spelt out in full ran to two or three lines.

In the worst times the battalion numbers would drop to a few hundred as battles raged, but in happier moments such as embarking for home leave at Suez, the personnel would swell. Montgomery's order that everyone … cooks, postmen, quarter-masters, headquarters rats and mice were to be in the frontline when the barrage began at the final battle of Alamein was not just a gesture but an absolute necessity.

It is not surprising that with such diversification we began to resemble the French Foreign Legion famous for anonymity in its rank and file. Men appeared and disappeared inexplicably, travelling to and from hospital, compassionate home leave, short furloughs in Cairo, Alex, Rome and Naples or even the Holy Land, training courses, fruitless recruitment campaigns, technical workshops, manoeuvres and officers' training or were simply deserters and A.W.O.L. Nobody checked absences with roll calls or military police. Occasionally there were disciplinary hearings, but absenteeism was always in time of crisis, a deleterious factor that worked on morale and contributed to the exhaustion of responsible fighting men. During the occasions when infantry reverses in the desert, coinciding with massive losses of armoured brigades brought Allied troops to the point of despair, one could not help feeling that the absenteeism was from a sinking ship.

In highly mobile warfare and especially reconnaissance you get to know just about everyone because the frontline is in a state of flux. You also see the daily list of your own battalion casualties which are searched for friends, acquaintances and even relatives whom you visualise in their final anguish.

After the war, reading the various N.M.R., published lists of combatants, I was shocked that I could not recognise the majority of them despite my five years of active service in the regiment. So many mice nibbled at the war and overlooked their raison d'etre for volunteering to serve.

CHURCH PARADES

Divisional parades were usually washouts or hugely unpopular. Unless there was some famous figure taking the salute interest was at a low ebb. There was a good turnout when Churchill was promised and great disappointment when there was a substitute. Not even Smuts attracted interest anymore. Field Marshall though he was he could not yet have known about forthcoming allied secret weapons (like the atomic bomb) because he was now always full of doom and gloom.

Oom Jan's 'boys' had now grown into what some of the media called the "tall lean greyhounds of the desert" and were not going to put up with the old bullshit. Divisional church parades were even more greatly loathed than march-pasts. Not even bringing in the women's various services to the church parades had much positive effect. Summer temperatures and long waits for the various elements of the division to take up their places produced an unutterable tedium in the strictly uniformed congregation. I don't remember at which parade it was, but at the moment of greatest ennui and resentment, someone inflated a condom and patted it upwards to float above the bareheaded and now stunned soldiers. This dirigible had no will of its own and somehow avoided descent through the directed breath of some monsters in uniform.

The congregation was divided. Some in their embarrassment refused to see it. Others horrified or with the giggles, looked around to see if there were any more launchings. I looked at Derek and he glared back at me in case I drew a comparison. A very slight breeze wafted it to the periphery of the assembly narrowly missing a group of W.A.A.F.s and I heard one brute pun the episode with the comment "Great Stuff." Some how I kept my chortles to myself.

At the end of the day, a day in which the regiment had collectively let its hair down after having to keep it permanently waved until the Bishop of Cairo had said his piece, the gun salute to the Empire had done its job, and the march past rigmarole had smartly come to an end, the N.M.R. boys given three hours leave in the middle of the day filtered back to their waiting convoy of parked trucks which would take them back to Khatatba strictly on time.

Everyone was late, even the arse-creepers. Shorty Carneson and his cohort Ciggy Marais had arrived almost on time with their guitar as buskers. They had set up outside the main gate and were serenading everyone who entered the Car Park. Someone had put an inverted beret down in front of them as if they were true buskers. Fortunately the regimental badge was half hidden. The Colonel's car sailed past them without stopping. Shorty, number two on my Bren gun at Alamein for which he was mentioned in dispatches sang the regimental anthem:-

> *"The N.M.R. boys are happy*
> *And the N.M.R. boys are free,*
> *The N.M.R. boys are sober*
> *When they go on the spree..."*

Boogies arrived in the Car Park motherless and the ones on each side of him in support were not much better.

He didn't know whether he was in Cairo or Alex, and what was worse, he didn't care. His face was almost purple as if he had ended the day on the hubble bubble. Someone had pulled his shirt-tails out so that he looked like one of the Abyssinian irregulars which Col. Jenkins himself had commanded. And when Jenkins arrived he surveyed the scene with a baleful eye. No film director could have set it with such preciseness of intent. The mustering time in the Car Park had been fixed with a precision that was intended to fill the waiting trucks with soldiers in their Sunday best, orderly and respectfully passing by their lord and master, the Colonel, who just happened to be there to take a polite salute as his entourage entered the car park precincts. Nothing could have been further from the truth. Soldiers were arriving from all directions, some not even looking for a gate, climbing and falling over fences and barriers. Some soldiers were finishing off the dregs of their companion bottles and then consigning them directly to bricked barriers with loud crashes. Aga Kahn not being of the Christian faith, had spent the day elsewhere giving the flesh-pots a miss. Always the peacemaker, he went up to the stupified Colonel on some pretext and with salutes and other urbanities led him away, still with some majesty.

Instead of fifty trucks, all with their division signs immaculate, leaving in convoy with police precision, and with the Colonel's car leading of course, Aga packed the transports off as best he could in a ragged retreat to Khatatba. The next morning the battalion was paraded and thanked for the sober part of the day which included the church parade and march past and then scolded with a cold fury by the Colonel for their car park conduct.

Aga, in the background, took everything in and marched his company away understanding that men in hangover still had to have sympathy until recovered rather than bullying.

Chapter XX

Our squadron was sent on various technical courses to Abassia Barracks in Cairo, a dreadful place, full of bugs and the shocking vibrations of a hundred different genre of soldiers during the past 50 years. It stank of tobacco and various brands of hash.

Cairo central was however only a short distance away and short visits to get away from Abassia were frequent. Thus run my diary notes:

Monday, 7th May '43 – Abassia

Classes started at 6am and end now at 2pm. Tennis with C.J. (Ritson) and saw an excellent Tarzan film.

Tuesday, 8th May '43

Wrote out (class) notes and to see 'Bad Man' with Wallace Beery.

Thursday, 10th May '43

Phil (Bullimore), Joe (Rawlinson), Richard (Platt) and I played foursome at tennis in the afternoon and we all went to the Swimming Gala in the evening and enjoyed it thoroughly.

Saturday, 12th May '43

Paid in the afternoon. Wrote some letters and (class) notes. Went into town with Pooch and Richard. Did a pub crawl via Pole Nord, La Americane, and North's cabarets and sundry illicit drinking dens. Got really tight and sold one pub's glasses for another's drinks. Got half the price of a meal free – swiped half a packet of blades from a gypo. Separated a fight between Bully and Pooch. Sprained two fingers, was pick-pocketed but lost only an Abassia Course document. Bully lost his pay book. He and Joe fell off the tram. Pooch cleaned some Gypos up. Richard got lost and we all got home (Abassia) safely.

Every other night at Abassia was one in which we had to use a blow torch to burn out bugs in their hiding places in order to get a full night's sleep.

On the whole the range of courses offered at Abassia were purposeful and effective. In the morse code classes I reached (I believe) about 15 words a minute, above average. It was a procedure I valued for the rest of my days using it as an effective alternative to ordinary forms of communication. In practice it never had to be employed in our tank warfare.

Out of sheer boredom I had begun to write a novel which I concealed from prying eyes amongst my course notes. It concerned the Zululand events of the 19th century and a Zulu chief who resisted the ruthless tactics of Shaka and endeavoured to form an alliance with the British forces then weakly spread out in Natal.

From Abassia we returned in June to the Divisional Tank School at Katatba and went on with more courses there for 9 hours each day.

AUGUST IN EUROPE

Over in Europe at this summertime in 1943 Clark Gable had flown in a bombing raid over the Ruhr in Germany.

In Sicily, Messina fell to the Allies and landing on the Italian mainland was imminent. A secret peace agreement was also pending.

The Allies landed an amphibious operation at Salerno just South of Naples and Italy surrendered.

Mussolini was snatched at this time by German paratroopers.

Germany's largest battleship TIRPITZ crippled by British subs, Sept. 20th.

Away to the east in the waters around the Solomon Islands Lieutenant John F. Kennedy (future president of the U.S.A) had his boat sliced in two by a Japanese destroyer.

Les Enfants Terrible

Seen in better days at an air force rally. Hitler (right) is wearing a hat strap to retain his hat on a windy day. Mussolini, used to windy times, gives him a sly smile.

SECRET REPORT

Secret Report of the German SS SECRET SERVICE on internal affairs, dated 16th August, 1943:–

Present report from all parts of the Reich indicate that the German people at present feel their powers of emotional resistance are being strained to the breaking point...

The reports emphasize that the broad mass of the population are not convinced that we have in our hands all the requirements of victory. Instead they are on the defensive, trying to ward off overwhelming odds: we are unable to prevent local breaches in Fortress Europe: Italy will defect as soon as the other side makes her some definite concessions...the Balkans are under threat and with them our supply of oil! The huge material deployment and seemingly inexhaustible manpower reserves of the Soviet may lead to a new catastrophe in the East this Winter.

Those wearing Nazi Party insignia have frequently been addressed by other Germans, who say "What, are you still wearing that thing?" There have also been numerous reports of the following joke:

Anyone who recruits five new members into the Party gets to leave it himself. Anyone who recruits ten new members gets a certificate testifying that he was never in the Party

E.N.S.A. presented a few nights of entertainment for the troops in the Middle East but nothing as glittering and sophisticated as the night with Geraldo and his orchestra. Standing out in my memory was the rendering of Sleepy Lagoon written by one of his own musicians. It was great stuff and no sign of dirigible condoms floating above his audience.

I don't have a record of his other pieces but it was a very productive time for songs of romantic certainty now that the allies were dead certain to win the war.

'A Nightingale Sang in Berkley Square', 'Don't sit under the Apple Tree with Anyone else but Me' and 'In the Mood' seem to have been heard for the first time then by M.E. forces.

There were also shows on in Cairo and I remember going with Len Clark to see the 'Merry Widow' and from an American group we heard 'Accentuate the Positive.'

SOME COURSES AT ABASSIA AND KHATATBA

Morse Code and Wireless – Visual – Lamp Communication – Armoured Cars – Diesel Engines – Flag Signalling – Semaphore – Breaking and repairing tank tracks – 20mm, 50mm, 37 Mountain guns – Two-pounder anti-tank – D & M, driving and maintainance – Driving lessons on Grant Tank – Crusader Tank – Repeat Bren gun.

DESERT DREAMS

Some months after Alamein I had a dream of Jack Gray who had held the sangar with me at Gazala on June 7th 1942. In the dream, Jack was struggling through some scrubland on the veldt when a thorn on a kaffir-boom tree tore his hand. As it did, the tree burst into bloom with its brilliant red flowers, each cluster looking like a parrot's head, saying "Soon, very soon." A few months later Jack was dead, a mysterious infection had killed him on the way to Italy.

I had an ageing aunt who had clung on to life despite many heart attacks but she died a few days after I had seen her in a dream standing by a tall honeysuckle creeper ablaze in flower. It seemed that when people close to me were about to die I would have a dream of plants or shrubs near them which would come out in full bloom.

Through the never-ending war years I developed a strong belief that dreams can have a deeper significance and were, at the worst compensatory and at the best foretellers of better times. Whenever I see mention of the legend of Cassandra, memory returns of a dream I had when, in the South African forces, we were garrisoning the fortress of Mersa Matruh, heavily bombed as it was every night and often right through the night making a late sleep-in after the dawn stand-to, a necessity. These sleep-in episodes were charged with psychic energy and their dreams were vivid.

In one of them coming out of sleep I was aware of men in ancient armour everywhere busily making preparations for action. Out to sea was a fleet of ships with their sails painted like Vikings. Some had pulled up at the water's edge and men in armour had placed their round shields on the sides of the boats to act as wheels and the ships assaulted the fortress. As I looked hard at the distant ships, the waves they floated on turned to sand. Soon the armed men were beating at the walls of the fortress which were made of iron girders and barbed wire. They gave shrieks of triumph as the walls gave way and I awakened. That the fortress of my dream was Mersa Matruh I had no doubt. But I could not believe that its extensive defences could be overrun. Yet within the space of a single year Mersa Matruh had to be abandoned to German and Italian forces as the Allies fell back to Alamein. The conquerors were borne on those 'ships of the desert', the tanks of the panzer divisions.

From a letter home...

On Sunday we had a welcome break when ten chaps from each squadron were allowed to go and see S. Africa play New Zealand rugby in Cairo. I didn't click but took a chance and ducked in with the boys. First of all Len, Joss and I went and had a rip-snorting breakfast consisting of 6 eggs (fried), sausage, bacon and tomatoes and then went to a morning show called the "Gay Desperados". It was a good film but we were disappointed at not being able to see "Random Harvest" which was booked up. From there we went and had a few cool glasses of draft beer (I'm off spirits) at a favourite pub called the "Pickwick" where there is by the way an old girl about fifty who surprisingly is not a "tout" but comes in daily and chats with soldiers and sews their buttons on and mothers them generally. She is French and no doubt has a sad story behind her life.

At 2 p.m we arrived at the Alamein Club where the matches were being played and there was a crowd of nearly 10,000 soldiers but we managed to worm our way in to a front seat on the grass. The matches were thrilling and we cheered S. Africa to victory in both of them. But Anthony Eden*, later prime minister of the UK during the Suez crisis, stole the whole show when he arrived to see the matches and shook hands with the players, not very far from us. He still looks

fairly young – very well dressed – rather shy but still good looking. He was wildly cheered and we all wondered what he had heard from Stalin and felt sure he could tell us how long the war would last to within a few weeks – if he were allowed to. Incidentally, I gave rugby a go here in camp but found I was yellow when being tackled mainly because I instinctively felt I would get it in the back. So I am afraid I shall no longer be able to play the "King of Sports". Coming home in open railway carriages that night was a bit bloody as we foolishly took no coats with us but it was well worthwhile.

One night last week a "Jedeboah" (a desert rat with a large bushy tail) burrowed beneath my kit bag and bed. I wondered why I had slept so badly that night and next morning I found my bed full of stones from the cursed thing. It makes a burrow the size of a rabbit's. I had to pour a bucket of water down to chase it out.

As manager of the squadron's lending library, quite a few books passed through my hands and in times of chaos and uprooting at the front, I turned briefly to Buddhism. Sickened by successive analytical courses on weapons like the Boyes anti-tank rifle and Two-pounder, the Crusader and Grant tanks, all of whose equipment was hopeless against the Germans, I had no stomach left for even the scriptures, whatever the religion and, in revolt, addressed my gropings towards Buddhism's Mahayana school favouring zen, meditation and intuition.

Slipping into the former during long spells of monotony, I was surprised at the freshness it brought, and with it flashes of intuition which gave the meaninglessness of war a deeper significance arousing hope and enthusiasm, whilst companions had remained downcast. The matter of sovereignty over my consciousness was waking me up to all kinds of deeper meaning.

Praying only when you were being threatened by imminent death disturbed and humiliated me. I had resorted to prayer and the mouthing of Christian incantations during severe shelling when I was alone.

Momentarily I had felt, as shells burst close that the something in charge of my sanity and awareness was slipping away and I hoped that meditation would strengthen that sovereign lord of my consciousness which I had nearly lost altogether under bombardment in Libya.

AGA KAHN

The two big nobs in 'B' Squadron were the O.C. Major Meeser and the Sergeant Major, Aga Kahn. The former was a god incarnate whose word had to be obeyed without question because he probably knew more about mechanised forces and their tactics than anyone in the N.M.R. and he was known not to put men in jeopardy if he could help it. Aga Kahn was a nice man despite being a lawyer by profession. He was kind and fair and he knew how to assess his men accurately. If you were in trouble he would help. If you were about to get into trouble he would help doubly. There were those he trusted implicitly and there were skivers who would duck out of anything if they could. Aga never stopped prying into matters and gossiping about them. If you really wanted to know anything about 'B' Squadron, Aga would know!

Phil Bullimore's father was headmaster at the Durban Prep. School when I was a pupil there in the early 1930's. He had caned me for something ridiculous like pushing around the crowded corner of the school quadrangle on a wet day. He could hurt with the cane even though like his son Philip, he was tiny. To get a good register on your bent backside he had to get really hot under the collar and somehow managed to jump a little off the ground as he struck home.

All this was preceded by fierce looks that were not unlike those given off by one of the more exotic apes at Mitchell Park Zoo just up the road, exotic because the creatures' testicles were a decided blue whilst the fur was almost white. Headmaster Bullimore was therefore nicknamed "Blue Balls" and with the white suits he always wore, summer and winter, the comparison was fair.

My woodwork in the carpentry class was awful, and the head master on his rounds of the classrooms rapped my fingers with some skew objet d'art I produced. His son Phil Bullimore was one of the eight occupants in our tent at Katatba where conditions were a bit crowded. We had our idiosyncrasies and learned to live with them. We all joined in when there was a birthday party for one of the tent inhabitants and it was usually on a Saturday night following sports events during the afternoon. We then generally slept in on Sunday morning. Bully sometimes drank a little too much beer and tipsy would do a review of camp events and a tally of those who had offended his sense of propriety. Joe Rawlinson would chime in if the details became too lurid. On Phil's proscribed list, at the very last, came the base-wallahs and with the tautology of certainty he would end each criticism with his "Yes, yes the bastards!" etc., and we would all chortle. But he would go on and on long after we had all gone to sleep much as his pedantic father had at the school morning assembly. Only Joe Rawlinson would be left to receive the finales, which got less and less savoury as the night drew on. Bully would end with telling Joe he was the only gentleman in the tent because he was, as a listener kind and patient and they had been together through thick-and-thin and thin-and-thick, fought in the same battles, drank in the same pubs, played in the same hockey team. Rawlinson, exhausted listening to this endless panegyric would answer, "Yes, well don't go on Bully." But Phil would…"and slept in the same bed…and tended each other's desert sores" and someone else also irritated by the cathecism would grunt "and shat in the same shit house. For God's sake go to bed Bully." And eventually he would. But it would not even then be like Tom Pearce's grey mare, the end of the sorry affair, which would have its repercussions on Sunday morning at about dawn. Bully was normally the latest riser, especially on a Sunday. But occasionally he would be up at an ungodly hour and, low and behold, would have been to the kitchen and drawn breakfast for the whole tent. Whilst delighted with this subtle bribe, from repetition we all knew what it was about. Bully had drunk late into the night on his own, fallen asleep and wet the bed. As he would point out, over breakfast and only a little shamefacedly "I know you guys won't mind because you are all my good friends; well you know how things are. I had a bit too much and, well I've had another accident." To make matters even more difficult he would by now have dragged his sleeping bag outside, or half outside the tent and straddled it decorously over the nearby guy rope. We would all be enjoying a bacon and scrambled egg breakfast sandwich (as he had planned) and the matter was more or less settled. However, there was always a final apology and with the fiercest look he could drum up under such difficult circumstances, he would say "I'm sure I can be certain no one will hear about this from any of you." And the answers would be mutterings of commiserations. On one occasion I did joke about it saying "You can count on us Bully; I won't tell a soul about it except Aga." It brought the house down. Aga was the most diplomatic but biggest gas-bag in the Squadron. Bully purpled up, even though he knew I was joking and shouted "By Jesus Baker, if you dare to say a word…"

Phil's secret held, the sun would come up, and with his careful attention the sleeping bag would be dry by the time we all came off parade and Bully, after all, was still one of the bravest men in battle I ever knew.

After a mind mutilating shelling that could last as long as ten days or just ten minutes, personalities were often changed, sometimes fragmented. An outgoing talkative extrovert like Colin MacArthur became sombre, reflective and humble, looking for and valuing periods of peace and quiet, above all else and taking note of the principle joys of nature and everyday activities in compensation.

Mac's attitude to those who had shared his miseries in a dugout, an open turret-less Honey tank or in a pinned down position during a hellish action was always softened; something that binds a younger to an elder brother and vice versa occurred, or had been stirred, a shared bondage like between a communion of saints would emerge if a group was involved and shelled mercilessly.

With Colin MacArthur, my closest civvy street friend, each pounding by enemy guns was a degrading of his spirit which one day reached a situation he had later sobbed out to me "was the limit". "No, no more. I'm just not going to sit here like the others and be blown to bits", he had said to himself, got up and ran, and ran. His friends caught him some miles away, broken and bewildered. Colin was, of course, never the same after that. Like Pooch Marais he pulled invisible screens down to shut out the unbearable, but unlike Pooch he had not the repertoire of mental stamina and resilience that competitive even combative sport had won for Pooch in close encounters. Colin was invalided back and coming out of the army, quickly married and had a family around him in no time. We had corresponded and I healed where I could, but I was part of that terrible past that he never wanted to hear of or be reminded of in anyway, ever again, and I understood.

Tent mates at Katatba, survivors of Plattoon B9 who overran the enemy lines on the Miteirya Ridge at Alamein, Back row, left to right: Joss Deacon, The Author, Len Clark, Front Row, left to right: Phil Bullimore, Pooch Marais, Shorty Carneson.

Under protracted gunfire never take counsel from your own fears. If they are becoming vocalised then they must be prevented from intruding on your consciousness, your hold on it, your sovereignty. To shut them out, for me the way was to match their vociferousness with your own. I would use something rooted in me that can be drummed along, occupying the same anatomical and psychological processes as the voices of my worst fears such as the credo or times table.

One tent, not very far from our clique's own, had Ali Baba in it and we maintained a modicum of goodwill towards him because occasionally he had access to exam papers of the various courses and would be inveigled into revealing answers, especially if nights in Cairo had occupied our time instead of swatting. If you had bunked off to play tennis or hockey when you should have been at a course learning about epicyclic gears, you might need Ali Baba, but that was not often. We were close enough to hear comments coming from his tent after lights out. A group of "Tobruk Avengers" fresh up from South Africa had filled his tent and because he spoke with a northern English dialect they addressed him as 'mate.' It was after lights out that Ali was heard to give one of his cliché's in answer "'Ere chum, don't call me mate! Mates f**k, call me chum!" The avengers giggled and we, in our tent chuckled at the giggling.

Some soldiers, especially when drunk shared their jokes loudly, but if it went on too late Aga Kahn intervened.

CHAPTER XXI

It was in August of '43 that I met the two hunks. They were miners from the Witwatersrand, huge in frame and not much up the top. We were all on a course of explosive mines… the English, Italian, German mine, you name it. The common interest for the hunks was explosives and the way they handled the damn things made me shy away from them. But they interested me through their vigour and unconcern for army refinements. Oscar Birmingham never minded too much when I noted aloud that he was the size of an ox and half as smart. After knowing him for any length of time everyone agreed with this summation of Oscar's talents. But he had a smile like Wallace Beery from ear to ear and a heart of gold. He and his pal Basil Mower were like chalk and cheese. Oscar had a bull's neck and shoulders like the god Atlas; Basil was even taller, very blond and even elegant. Basil was an Afrikaner and a bit more uncertain about matters than bull-in-a-china-shop Oscar. They thought they could play bridge and I told them it was their one virtue. Oscar agreed so long as it was played for money. At that stage I took the hustle no further and gave Len Clark, my bridge partner a quick wink. Their handicap was that when they operated together, they were accident prone. Oh boy! No matter whether it was donning sandals or cocking guns, things would go wrong and then I would call them Gog and Magog. I don't think either had ever heard of the Old Testament and they didn't mind. Basil Mower's good looks came to an end in Italy when a car accident disfigured his face into that of a gargoyle. One accident that Oscar became involved in embarrassed even him. A group of us had been into a small Italian village one night in the Apennines and were walking home (our billets) in the dark. Oscar had lagged behind a little and we waited for him to do his business for which he always, being accident prone carried a supply of toilet paper. Suddenly, out of the dark came a terrified scream. We rushed back to him, some drawing pistols fearing an attack. Shame-faced, if that was possible in the dark Oscar, walking around without his trousers on, explained. He had got his trousers off and was crouching to do it when to his horror, a snake or some creature began to crawl up his back. The disaster had made him scream and it then became clear to him that he had, half-drunk, left his underpants on, and the snake was of his own making. We all rushed off leaving him to his misery.

Suddenly we were transferred to do courses in Alexandria where my brother was aboard a Royal Navy vessel waiting to sail to India or Italy. Things became a madhouse as my diaries recorded.

Monday, 16th August '43

Are in a heaven of a camp. Started classes at 9:30a.m. Have a mad mob in our tent. Have to march 1.5 miles to our tank school every morning. Into town and saw 'North-West Passage.' Back by 11p.m.

Tuesday, 17th August '43

Course is very interesting but the hours are very long from 7am to 4pm. Spent quiet evening writing letters and fixing up notes.

Wednesday, 18th August '43

Went out to Amoriya for a (tank) driving lesson which I thoroughly enjoyed and developed a healthy respect for a Crusader tank. Classes in the afternoon and on orderly corporal (duty) all night – a general stooge in fact.

Thursday, 19th August '43

Went for swim after classes (in the Mediterranean) and experienced a strong backwash getting back. Went into town with Len and met Des (brother) at the Springbok Club. Then we bought booze and went drinking at various bars and cabarets and had an excellent time. Got Des and selves home (Tank School) safely.

Saturday, 21st August '43

Went to Springbok Club for dinner. Bought some liquor and Len and I went to Top Hat (cabaret) and watched some fun.

Went back to Athenos and met Tom Mix (Sterzel), Oscar and Basil and from there made a mad round of the cabarets. Barged into Warrant Officers and Officers' Club. Nearly involved in a naval fracas – Out to Stanley Bay to Cabaret where we saw some hot dancing. Caught lifts back to camp and reached it at midnight.

<u>Saturday, 11th September '43 – Alexandria</u>

Went yachcting again outside the harbour and encountered some pretty stiff breezes but had a wonderful time. Went on the tear with Howard Foss & Co. and got tight and had a hectic, hilarious time.

<u>Monday, 13th September '43 – Alex.</u>

Went yachting again right out past the burning wrecks. Saw 'Rio Rita' in the evening and downed a bottle of Egg Nog between two of us before going to bed.

AUNT RECOMMENDED FOR GEORGE MEDAL

It was about this time that some family news broke. My Aunt Rose well into her 60's had been recommended for the George Medal. She was an ambulance attendant in Plymouth and had been driving night after night through the worst of the Blitz. We all knew that Plymouth had taken a severe pasting.

Rose was a great favourite with the family for her cheerfulness and stoicism. Subjected to the constant barrage of the city's anti-aircraft fire, Rose's eyes had reacted in such a way that she had almost a perpetual blink coinciding with the barrage explosions and this was to persist throughout her life.

With the photograph came a framed commendation for her brave conduct, signed by Winston Churchill. I remember on her visit to my dying mother in South Africa how she kissed all the Zulu babies and cuddled them in the face of great wonderment amongst the white population, if not actual disapproval.

(King George VI's order to this effect is in Appendix V)

Aunt Rose

While about it, I should record the contents of a letter from Rose's sister, my Aunt Lil, who was blitzed out of her house in North Finchley. Her letter told how for safety she would sit in her sandbagged loo, clutching Bruce (an Airdale) as the bombs came down. A brave soul who then moved from the ruins of her home to Mount Grace Road in Potters Bar and again to Brookman's Park.

Lil's husband, Ernie Paine, had a men's outfitters' shop at Tally Ho Corner in Finchley where the bombing was particularly heavy. He did not long survive the war; his nerves were shattered by events.

I always associated Buller Fenwick with one of the regimental families that had fought in the Boer War because Bulwer and Buller reminded me of the names that these old fossils left around in prominent places of Natal's Victorian culture... Bulwer Park in Durban, Bulwer Lytton, the Victorian author, General Bulwer and so on.

Buller Fenwick was very tall, angular and delicate, but on the hockey field he was a delight for sore eyes. His hockey stick flipped and poked, dare-devilled and ran amok in bullies. Accordingly, he was

By the KING'S Order the name of
Rosina, Mrs. Lloyd,
Ambulance Attendant,
A.R.P. Casualty Service, Plymouth.
was published in the London Gazette on
20 June, 1941.
as commended for brave conduct in
Civil Defence.
I am charged to record His Majesty's
high appreciation of the service rendered.

Winston S. Churchill

Prime Minister and First Lord
of the Treasury

squadron captain of a hockey team that was rarely beaten and everyone wanted and loved a game of hockey whereas rugby was a call-up game that had to be organised weeks in advance and most devotees were too crocked to play. Rugby was alright for players like Cecil Ritson who were good-natured and well-padded, but for others it only added, with its injuries, to their desert sores and other aches and pains. Whereas just to hear the shout 'Hockey' would bring out the doughtiest to grab their sticks and make for a field scratched out on the desert surface. Buller was the perfect captain, encouraging at the beginning of the game, thanking and congratulating at the end of it.

Many a time on the field he would pass the ball to someone when he could easily have scored himself. Everyone loved him and wanted him to be one of their Sherman crew, but alas it was not to be. Buller, always sharp and scintillating in conversation, drawing on old regimental historical analogies to illustrate a point, had a dark secret, one social grace amongst his many that sometimes went missing and it was sobriety. Companions covered up for him even through his 'spells' of recovery which could last 36 hours or more.

<u>Saturday, 23rd October '43 – Katatba</u>

Finished gunnery course with 2 pounder (anti tank). Went with Len and Breeze (Barrow) to C.T. H. Corporal's Mess and got drunk in celebration of this most important day (1st anniversary of the Battle of Alamein). Much scuffling and a scraped face. Bed at 1am. Whole camp drunk.

<u>Monday 29th November '43</u>

[still at Tank Instruction School]

Had the day off and therefore washed (my) clothes, sewed, packed for leave and read. Played bridge in the evening with Jock (Dickens) as partner against Len (Clark) and Joss (Deacon) and won by 26 points. Phil (Bullimore), Joe (Rawlinson) and Richard (Platt) back from leave and we go tomorrow.

<u>Tuesday, 30th November '43</u>

On one week's leave in Alexandria. Len (Clark) and I left camp on time and after the usual journey reached Alex. At 12:10 we were the first into town. Lunch at the 'Stella' (restaurant) living at the Imperial at 40 (piastas) a day with everything laid on. To a "horse" barber where we were treated like a couple of ladies because we asked for a scalp massage – most disconcerting. To see cinema in the evening but rather a lousy show. To bed early.

<u>Wednesday, 1st December '43</u>

Played squash in the morning and stiff (right) arm next day – magnificent meals at the Stella. Down to the Docks to contact (my brother) Des but frustrated by stupid South African officer at dock gate. Went on the tear in the evening via the Trianon and Diana and Regent (cabarets). At the latter we fought Gypos for possession of a table – neither side won because the table disintegrated. Very merry evening. Punched in the back by blonde cabaret girl dressed in black for being too inquisitive… then fate hit back after I had enraged six M.P.'s by sticking around sipping my drink slowly after the cabaret had been cleared. Des had called (at the Imperial) while I was away and left a note to say his ship was leaving (Alex) next day – very sorely shaken. Then Buller had a horrifying experience of falling 20 feet to the street below when he turned in for the night. The window was right next to our own and he was taken away unconscious. To bed about midnight.

<u>Thursday, 2nd December '43</u>

Went yachting with Basil Mower, Tiny Doidge, and Sterzel (Tom Mix) in a vain endeavour to contact Des (my brother) before he leaves (sails). He was working and couldn't see me even though we got right next to the ship. The wind dropped and we had to be towed and paddled back. In the afternoon we went round to the vegetable market and all the out-of-bounds areas to get a cheap primus (stove) but the cheapest was 170 p.t. – we didn't buy it. Bought silk pyjamas for Bill Askam's girl and arrived back home (Imperial) with them and a mug (for me), some radishes and a sharp knife. Saw good picture in evening – Gentlemen After Dark – Buller (in hospital) only just conscious – no bones broken but landed on his head evidently.

Friday, 3rd December '43

Played tennis doubles with an American, Gosselin included
…Buller much better but has five fractures…Out to the Bella
Vista for an amusing evening where we met a 'Helen of Troy' –
All four of us tight but couldn't get liquor to make us drunk.

In five years of active war service in my regiment I never
experienced or sensed any use of drugs let alone addiction. Alcohol
was a different matter. The average recruit simply used alcohol to
switch the war off and let himself go for the leave he was on or even
a rest period or break from the front. In that respect it was a morale
booster and acted on many to produce a catharsis, simply a letting out
of emotional detritus, a releasing of the repressions and resentments
that accumulate when free men submit voluntarily to military discipline.
There were alcoholics who had joined the regiment as such and
continued to be. Very, very rarely did the alcoholism of wartime induce
the chronic condition. Army life gave you the useful opportunity by
sheer repetition of discovering just how much you could drink without
making an arse of yourself.

There were some who never learnt this lesson and had always to
be wary. For others it was a useful device for shifting the blame
away from a fragile personality or to be used as an excuse. It was
helpful on bitterly cold nights or as Dutch courage. So long as you
used it, even as a medicine, it seemed to be safe. When it was misused
or established some sort of mastery over you, then it was a curse.
This is true in any profession, even amongst doctors and it was true
especially of officers because they had access to whisky and gin in
quantity which other ranks did not. Rabid teetotallers were rare. It
was hard for them to live in a tent or a troop and refuse a toast when
a birthday celebration occurred say after a helluva week at the front
and well…you know how one thing leads to another.

Mousie Bell was jealousy incarnate when it came down to schools
as we have seen. One only had to use a word in common conversation
that was unusual and picturesque and he would extract it for further
meticulous examination. Referring once to a tank commander's
performance on a simple reconnaissance I called him a "buccaroo,"
meaning a cowboy. The gentleman concerned happened to be a
Glenwood High School old boy and my remark was innocent of

innuendo, but Bell flew into a temper demanding to see the offending word in the dictionary. The worn-out old 'Collins' we had in the tank did not carry it and so the sour remarks, huff-and-puff etc., went on until it was found, not by me, in Ken Manicom's dictionary when we were all in harbour.

Ken was another of the many good guys in the regiment and no cowboy. I believe he had connections way back in the N.M.R. Glenwood regimental history. Then a quiet, introvert, strongly recommended on the pathway to promotion, he showed an interest in poetry, my own flair being for recent S.A. poets, especially Roy Campbell whose craft plucked typically at the strings of African wildness:-

"The wind with foetid muzzle
sniffed the evening air..."*

Roy, five years ahead of me at Durban High School, was in conflict with Langley the headmaster whose son Noel later wrote "Cage Me A Peacock" which was an event in my life. Manicom liked him too. I have a copy by Ken, still in my possession, of 'Poet's Walk' which he lent me at Helwan or Khatatba in 1943 with his name, rank and number in it – 6380 Lance Corporal Manicom.**

Two well-worn pages in Poet's Walk pay tribute to poems we both loved and would have recited to each other at times we could get away from the hurly-burly of camp life: "Ode to a Grecian Urn" by Keats and the sonnet "On Westminster Bridge."

It was Ken, more than any helped me set up the squadron library which was eventually carried around on the back of "Bechan", our Sherman which was commanded then by Howard Foss.

Whilst we were in Khatatba camp, Ken Manicom continued with his studies towards B.Com. He spent evenings pouring over papers etc., in the mess room. I think he sat and passed some subjects under special exam. arrangements there. When he "joined up" he had passed most of the subjects (over 2 years). This was a very stout effort, and he has to be admired in the circumstances.

---

* *African Moonrise* by Roy Campbell.
** At the time of writing a Major in the N.M.R regiment

Shorty Carneson never got past the most elementary fringes of the courses offered at Katatba, Abassia, Helwan or, for that matter, Timbuctoo. They were all vagaries that surfaced in between his chain smoking and 'sippies'. He collected the camp's bottles and before he sold them to some vagrant Arab or itinerant peddler, made sure they were empty, sometimes even before the soldiers had finished with them. A 'sippy' was a sippy no matter where it came from. By the end of the day a few hundred sippys had him ready for the guitar and by the time we got back removing the grease and dirt of the courses with a brisk shower, you could be sure to pass Shorty, his serenading intermingled with none too crisp side comments and piles of stompies. He would be just outside whatever tent he was using for accomodation.

I think he passed the maintenance part of his drivers and maintenance course but his feet and paws didn't reach the pedals in the Sherman and no one would let him drive if they were in their right minds. Usually he secured a majority vote for his ejection from the tents he managed to stay in for any length of time. Inexorably he came to our tent of eight when all else had failed. But none of the eight had ever smoked and the fags that Carneson lit up were of the lowest order and the strains of their aromas were mistrusted. There were some who suspected he had a hubble-bubble in his kit. Nevertheless Carneson had a brain and he had not been 'mentioned in dispatches' without some justification. He could count change and he knew his rights.

You became conscious that Shorty had spent the night in our tent when daylight came and you were aware of distant thunder. Then Carneson would be seen as a lump snoring at one end of the tent. Completely uninvited he would arrive night or day and secure his belongings under the flap at the entrance to the tent. He knew that smoking was unacceptable to all eight of us, and then the tent flap would come down putting him temporally outside and here he would smoke and drink and be happy for most of the night. However, if his security was threatened or the weather became inclement he could adjust the flap so he was inside, safe and dry. None of us would object so long as he obeyed the rules. Otherwise he had the most offensive habits with cigarettes lit and smoked under his blankets at night and 'dead marines' rolling around him by day. When Colonel's kit inspection loomed, he and his kit dissolved into the kitchen equipment where he had a secret lair. Aga thought he belonged to the Carbineer regiment nearby. The more acquaintances he made the bigger bum he became. Richard Platt, Len Clark and I were 'safe touches' in his estimation and suffered most.

PADDY GILL

On one of the Cairo or Naples furloughs I met up again with Paddy Gill, a very lean but never hungry trooper from one of the tanks in our squadron. He was the most emaciated guy I had ever met on active duty and there must have been something fishy about his being on the regimental roll at all. I vaguely remember a non-routine exception being made in his medical boarding because, after Alamein, I too had had to be specially boarded 'D' which meant 'Deferred' because my wounds had not yet healed when the regiment had left South Africa after home-leave, bound for Italy.

'Deferred' meant medically that I was becoming stronger with convalescence and could be boarded again at a later date (which I never was).

From Paddy I had gathered that his anxiety was to become separated from his close friends who made up the tank crews. He hardly touched the food at the cafes where we all ate. I asked him how he felt as wireless operator and loader of the Sherman's 75mm gun. Netting-in the individual tank wireless to the squadron's was sometimes a tricky business, but Paddy was brainy and had no trouble there. But loading the 75mm gun inside the cramped Sherman turrets was a helluva task. If you were slightly built you had more room, but the weight of the shells was not the only problem; you had to slam them into the gun's breech wearing a heavily-padded glove made of asbestos, and the guns sometimes became red hot in sustained action. You had to get the ejected shell case out of the way, and the next shell ammunition ready for loading. On top of it all you were expected to watch for hostile infantry by means of an adjustable periscope and fire at them with the turret's machine gun. Maintaining firepower in action created an unimaginable cacophony that reflected into your dreams for years ahead. Paddy was nonplussed and I noted a sparkle come into his eyes at any mention of battle.

Paddy Gill at El Yibo waterwells. He is standing in the top left hand corner of the picture watching operations.

Nevertheless he could not ever hide his fatigue, and avoiding meals did not help. Two decades later, at medical school, I realised that Paddy, that nice little guy was suffering from anorexia nervosa, a rare condition in men, which explained his symptoms of depression and semi-starvation. His fate was tragic, made more so because he need never have volunteered for military service and should anyhow have been getting therapy for his condition, which was suicidal, instead of struggling with soldiering. Every tank man knew that in a brew-up the loader had little chance of getting out of a Sherman turret alive.

Partly out of a good friendship and partly as a defence mechanism Len Clark and I kept up a screen of baffoonery. It was a defence duo against the humourless conditions of desert life, the spells of constant action, mutilating bombardments, strafing, mortaring, bombing and the monotony of military manoeuvres and training. We ragged the susceptible and were ragged ourselves sometimes mercilessly, but it did help pass the time.

Len was a quiet guy from a large Durban family, the eldest of three brothers and two older sisters, all practising Weslyans. He, himself deeply introverted lacked imagination which might explain his preparedness to accept the horrors of war when he could easily have backed off. I had been with him under the devastating mortar fire of 'sobbing sisters', the nightly bombing of the fortress at Mersa Matruh and in squadron reconnaissance against German dug-in positions where at every bend on mountainous roads between Cassino and Florence there lurked 88mm anti-tank guns. Despite the stress, he stuck mainly to his Christian principles...no booze, no birds and no smoking. When the sheer weight of camaraderie pressured him to have a drink with the boys he rarely gave way, but when he did, he could be so consumed by what he was consuming as to be almost satanically possessed.

SHERMAN IN BATTLE-STATIONS

Our year's training showed us that a *Sherman* crew consisted of 5 members – a driver and a co-driver, a radio-operator (at the left rear), a gunner at the right front, and the crew commander seated or standing behind the gunner and positioned so as to have his head protruding through the turret opening. The driver and co-driver were also able to elevate their positions, so that their heads protruded through their respective hatches. The radio-operator and gunner were equipped with peri-telescopes which enabled them to view the terrain over which the tank was travelling. These elongated *telescopes* could also be rotated so as to afford a view in any direction. They were also fitted to the drivers' hatches and were often put to good use when shelling necessitated the closing down of all hatches. Mounted in the turret was a 75mm gun, and co-axially mounted next to it was a .30 Browning machine gun, belt-fed.

My job on the Sherman was not clear-cut. Primarily I was trained as a radio operator because I had enough savvy to keep the tank's wireless netted into the Squadron Commander's tank. A tuning in was done each morning before operations began. As such you were also expected to be in contact with the crew commander by throat mike on an intercom. In battle you had to act as loader for the 75mm tank's gun whose breech opened 10 inches from your right hand when you were seated. The turret at its best was 6 feet in diameter and rotated automatically and you could observe the driver and co-driver through a grid if you wanted to know in what direction the tank was pointing. The 75mm shells were clipped in around the turret arse downwards and percussion caps up and stood about 30 inches high. You had to be clear of the breech when shells ejected and they could be damn red hot. You wore an asbestos glove to accomplish this loading. The noise and smoke in the turret was pandemonium during action. In addition, on the left side of the tank you had a periscope through which you were expected to watch for infantry, yours as well as enemy, and to engage the latter or support the former with a .30 Browning machine gun. On either side of the rotating turret were 120-gallon gasoline tanks which were vulnerable to any anti-tank gun that could pierce the 2" thick armour plating.

Whilst the driver and co-driver had escape hatches beneath their feet, and the gunner and crew commander could exit promptly via the turret hatch, there was no direct exit for the wireless operator loader. He had to get past the breech of the 75mm gun, scramble over the red hot shells and pray that the turret exit overhead was clear of crew commander and gunner. Even the slenderest of loaders, like

Sherman tank holed in two places by an 88mm German anti-tank gun and survived by its commander Corporal Dore of C Squadron of the N.M.R.

Paddy Gill would have had a ghastly job of fighting his way out of a brewing tank. A .50 Browning machine gun was mounted on the turret for anti-aircraft protection.

The maintenance of the gun and the vehicle, its refuelling and the replacement of spent shells was a task that could take hours, so that even if your tank leaguered at sunset it was midnight before you could lay your blanket roll out.

Most men can't cook but I could, and I pulled out the primus and turned out something hot by bedtime and again at sparrow-fart (dawn) when it was time to get operating again. Food maintained the crew's morale and the arrangement was that because of my earlier injuries, if I did the cooking and skiving I would, with a weakened right shoulder, be spared the maintenance.

We all knew even in training that the armour plating of the Sherman could not withstand the armour piercing shells of the German 88mm. What we were not told was the appropriate tactics and strategy to advance against them. Penetration of the tank was always a disaster, but especially so when it came from the sides. The armour piercing part of the German shell punched straight through the tank and its crew and out the other side. The hard metal core might ricochet around inside the Sherman mutilating or killing anyone in its path. With the hazardous countryside of the Italian Apennines adding to your dangers, even escaping clear of the tank only presented further obstacles so that the chances of survival were almost nil.

From an early age I had a hobby-horse that gave me much pleasure when I could get away from the hustle and bustle. It was the reading, drawing and study of maps, probably a throwback from my ancestor Sir Richard Grenville, an Elizabethan sea-dog. Suddenly operating wireless in a Sherman gave you time and seclusion to pursue such interests as cartology. Ancient maps of the Middle East in particular now drew my attention because of an extraordinary event that occurred in the tedious and routine procedures of our tank manoeuvres in the Eastern Desert. Our troop had laagered in the early afternoon and after a cramped morning in the Sherman the opportunity to stretch the legs was welcome. I wandered off towards a small escarpment which appeared from the distance to have cliff faces, wadis and caves that gave the landscape more of a Martian rather than a lunar appearance.

After walking along in front of the escarpment I was struck by the feeling again that the scenario displayed before me was really of a coastline rather than a desert feature. I entered one of the narrow clefts between two of the cliff buttresses more to seek shade from the mid-afternoon sun. Entering this gully and looking around in it for a place to sit, I was staggered by what I saw and had to go forward to touch the object to make sure it wasn't an illusion. In smaller clefts in the gully's rock face, now shaded, there were jammed, as it were huge sheets of mussel shells, coats of them just like they can still be seen today on the coastline rocks of Natal at low spring tides. Perfectly shaped, these shells, each about three or even four inches long, were petrified.

I had to look outside at the desert landscape to make sure I was still in a valley amongst the foothills, even mountains of Egypt's Eastern Desert. What on earth were sheets and sheets of specie lamellibranchia doing in the midst of the Eastern Desert, far above sea level? The shells were fossilised, still packed neatly by the hundred in what must have been once their natural habitat. But how long ago? Perhaps 10,000 years when the great glaciers had covered Europe and North America in the last ice age. Or had there been an incredible period of earthquakes which had thrown up mountains in the west and fashioned the Red Sea, east of them? Or had there been such a change in climate that this area had once been covered by fresh water lakes or even spillings of the Nile? Obviously this area had been deeply innundated by water at depth not too long ago.

Fresh from viewing Egypt's historic sights I had been left with an inner conviction that the marvels of ancient Egypt's civilisation, had a far, far more ancient origin than that mapped out for it by orthodox Egyptology. Who then, for instance, had started, even planted the civilisations at Luxor, the site of Thebes, so far inland?

Was the depression at Quattara which had saved Britain's bacon by causing a narrowing of the workable desert at Alamein part of a sea that had produced these palpable fossil shells? I heard shouts from outside. Sitting there pondering these enigmas my absence had become a cause of concern and I hurried out into the sunlight and at least knew that water, in vast quantities had once covered the land in North-eastern Egypt.

Training in Egypt had been concentrated on how to use our new equipment i.e. its guns, tanks, wireless sets, etc., but to our amazement there was nothing on tactics. As the reconnaissance unit for an armoured division, everyone in the regiment knew that our destination was going to be Italy or Southern France, or Greece and they all had hedges and houses and other obstructions. We were landed in Italy with lots of time to spare because Monte Cassino was part of the Gustav Line and no one could get by it. Our Colonel was in charge; he knew what we were in for, but once in Italy, we sat in a little shit hole called Altamura and were employed daily in the same old nonsense of marches, squad drill and parading for six precious weeks. All that training in Egypt had been on equipment that was mainly out of date or inferior to that used by the Nazis who were waiting for us, in our benighted ignorance to attack. If the officers had been trained in the appropriate tactics they didn't show it and had to triumph, like their men, by sheer valour, often with 'blood and guts.' Through the use of sand tables and models which anyone could have constructed, opposition could have been anticipated, tactics worked out, and appropriate manoeuvres practised in the field. No, nothing! There was woolly thinking in high places and we were some of the lambs. It is no consolation to know that the same occurred elsewhere.

At the battle of Goodwood in France six weeks after the D-Day landings a few German 88mm guns (perhaps thirty?) wiped out 400 Sherman tanks before they could line up on their targets.

Our Colonel in Italy at the time, had come from a regiment of armoured cars and knew quite well that the Shermans we had trained in were out-ranged by many hundreds of yards and similarly in penetration power by the 88mm German gun. Devastating though our own losses were, at least we were in reconnaissance and did not have to remove the obstacles but only locate them.

Any mutton-head could have thought up a system of training to meet our needs in Italy.

JAN/MARCH '44 - HELWAN, EGYPT

My 21st birthday at Helwan on the 31st of December '43, heralded a New Year that was going to mark me for life. It began with intensive training in tank manoeuvres, live gunnery and wireless procedures which occupied us almost unsparingly until we embarked for the battle front in Italy. My diary entries show how relief from the tedium of these operations was obtained:

Saturday, 22nd January '44 – Helwan.

Scheduled to start (manoeuvres) at 8a.m. but the Colonel overslept and we were late in getting away. Passed through very hilly country strewn with lava and oyster shells millions of years old and fossilised sea fish. There were also many Arab wells surrounded by the nomads and their herds. We crossed very high hills and luggers corroded by many floods. Tore through Helwan streets and (the tanks) tore up part of the road. Had slight trouble with Bechan's* petrol filters. Reached new camp and slept the night next to the tank. Letter from Des.

[As I recall it, the tank crew at the time was Howard Foss (Crew Commander), Charlie Mellon (Driver), Rod Purdy (Co-driver), Cecil 'Boogies' Boik (gunner) and Self (Wireless Operator, loader.)]

Tuesday, 25th January '44 – Helwan.

Worked on tanks till 11a.m. Then Jock (Dickens) and I dressed and hiked to Helwan station in a staff car. Were in Cairo by train at 1:30. Had a good meal of fillet of fish and strawberries and cream. Then visited Buller (Fenwick) at No.5 (General Hospital). He has made a remarkable recovery. Had plenty of beer and a haircut. Saw Dr. Jekyll & Mr. Hyde and had a cold time getting home.

Caught the last train as it was steaming out of the station. Followed Captain Meeser into a truck and got back to camp safely at 1a.m.

Saturday, 5th February '44 – Helwan.

Washed clothes early and then Cousin Ken arrived and then we went into Cairo and tore things up. I wore a crown and went with him to the Warrant Officers and Sergeant's cabarets. Had a bath and two good meals (at Ken's) – saw Bello (Theunessen). Got very tight and had a helluva time getting home – met Oscar on guard at the (camp) gate at 1a.m.

Between Khatatba and the base at Helwan, just south of Cairo, these two shared a saving grace. It was where all kinds of mysteries concerning the regiment were solved. Men who had faded out of prominence suddenly re-appeared, non-the worse for wear. If anything they were wearing Sam Browns or pips on their shoulders. My old acquaintance, Roger Ellis who had disappeared at Gazala, had becomean officer somewhere in the Imperial Army, had been smashed up in a heroic encounter and now bore the scar of a nasty gash on the head which somehow did not disfigure the body beautiful. Shortly he would return to his wife Mildred in South Africa with all our good wishes, immaculate and suave, a really nice guy.

Equally surprising, Nigel Downes, brother of our troop's heart-throb Honor, appeared in the tent for a visit one night, with a pip on his shoulder. The heroic work he did almost solely, giantly conspicuous in the ambush at Gazala with his mortar barrel, was now rewarded. Quite unaffected by his elevation and with his usual innocence, he spent some hours with us in reminiscing during which we realised that our back gardens in Durban had both abutted that of the Wishart family and we had both taken their daughter out, the sweet girl called Nel whose name figures amongst the addresses in my war diary of the time. Nigel survived the war in another South African regiment. And there were others of course, too numerous to mention who surfaced at this time in Khatatba.

AGA AND MEESER

At this time I came under the attention of Sergeant Major 'Aga' Kahn whom I found appealing in his fairness and foresight. He even bothered to relate some of his civilian law cases which had me in fits of laughter. The ulterior motive never then became quite clear. Several of us had been made infantry corporals at Gazala and with new brooms

---

*Our tank named 'Bechan', the Zulu name for rhinoceros.

sweeping Meeser had his own men from 3rd Recce and elsewhere to promote and asked us to surrender our stripes. As I recall, Pooch Marais and I accepted demotion and Aga was called in to clean up the mess. Meanwhile I had been giving instruction at the Wireless School, had run the squadron mobile library and sat in on some sort of section purchasing green vegetables etc., etc. By the time he had finished with me I didn't know whether I was being thanked for my volunteered demotion, recommended for an Officer's Training Course, for re-boarding, for the Victoria Cross or Nobel Prize. In actual fact I had merely lost my stripe.

Tuesday/Wednesday, 21st/22nd March '44 – Helwan

Up at 4 a.m. on a (tank) scheme till 8 a.m. Had a terrific breakfast and watched Len (Clark) fire the Piat gun and fired one round myself. Took a long time getting back to camp because of petrol feed trouble. Got back to camp about 4:30 p.m. – too late for a shower. Spoofed all evening with Aga (Kahn) and Len's pal Doug Alexander (N.C.)

Worked on tanks all (Wednesday) morning. Walked over to Helwan for a shower, to the laundry and some coffee. Played crib. Had a lecture on tank tactics by (troop commander) Bunny (Evans). Read a little and went to bed early.

EMBARKATION FOR ITALY

Allied infantry were having a helluva time in South Italy and now converging on Monte Cassino which was expected to fall any day. The time had come to embark for Taranto in what became a logistical nightmare. Egypt was not Britain and its railways had to start from scratch learning to take on Sherman tanks for shipping to Italy via Alexandria. The honey tanks had gone ahead of us with their crews and were safely embarked. The heavier Shermans went aboard last, and what with their crews temporarily in attendance, the operation was abstruse. The tanks were destined for Bari on the Adriatic coast and the personnel were for Taranto. For the latter there would be more training before picking up their tanks at Bari and entraining them for the front.

Monday, 27th March '44 – Helwan

Dust started blowing earlier and was worse than ever but this time it was a cold wind. It persisted and dampened all our spirits and we couldn't write or read much. Packed up the [squadron] library, which took up most of the afternoon. Wanted to get drunk but we had no hooch. Bully and Joe to Carbineers to get some. Dust blew all night. Bully drunk and aggressive. Corporal Dore his adversary this time.

Tuesday, 28th March '44

Honeys with Pooch left for embarkation. Dust still blowing – No water for showers. Wrote letters and read. Played poker in the evening and won 12 shillings. Made coffee and to bed. Melly (Ratcliffe) and Angus in drunken brawl.

Wednesday, 29th March '44

Exit Joss (Deacon) with the heavies (Shermans) for embarkation. Dust continues to blow inexorably – Played Len a game of chess and of course lost but feel I'm improving. Over to Helwan for shower and cup of coffee. Thence to Carbineers to see Joe (Cowley) and Doug Alexander. We had some brandy etc. and a bit of fun. Back to camp and knocked back two more bottles of wine. Played another drunken game of crib and wrestled and cracked jokes with Len.

Sunday, 9th April '44

Slept in. Bully fetched breakfast. Went to service by new padre. It was outstanding especially the sermon. Received two letters. Were paid at 2pm. Drew £5.00. Went over for a swim with Len and went to another service with the same padre and the I.L.H. band playing. Very witty and good sermon. To bed after a game of chess and crib.

Monday, 10th April '44

Route march again and developed a blister. Over to Helwan for a swim. Watched boxing in the afternoon when reserves beat us in every contest. Saw Serzel flattened again and a couple of other K.O.'s. We then had a cold drink and returned. Wrote three letters in the evening and to bed early.

Tuesday, 11th April '44

Arose and started packing and this continued thru the day which was very hot. Played chess and won one game. Showered and put kit on to trucks. Travelled by truck to Giza passing base – wallahs and saw 'Bello' (Theunissen). Had an amusing fracas with Gypos. After nearly 4 hours we got to the train – 25 of us were put into each cattletruck. On our floor was cow dung. The officers of course were in clover! Train pulled out about midnight.

Saturday, 15th April '44 – Alexandria

Arose early and completed packing. Had breakfast and travelled by truck to the wharf where we embarked to perfection…congrats to the adjutant. Are fairly comfortably ensconced on F deck which is three down. Rather crowded. Ship, I should say is about 12,000 tons. Played bridge and had our usual foul luck. Went to sleep on the deck and found it a bit nippy. Food is good.

Sunday, 16th April '44

Set sail about 8am. Convoy is well guarded by about 5 destroyers. A high wind caused a choppy sea and fellows were sick all around us. It was bitterly cold in the morning. Food was plentiful, more so because the pork put most chaps off. Finished 'A Man's Man'. Played some more bridge. To bed early and slept well, it being a mild night and fairly warm.

Monday, 17th April '44 – (off coast of Libya)

Len, Joe (Rawlinson) and I on kitchen fatigue. Had to draw food for our table of 18 men and wash the plates and dishes and tidy the area up. Played chess and contract to pass the time. Sailing off the coast of Libya. Water calmer and weather milder. Slept near some Tommies whose feet were pretty ripe. Had a glorious hot shower bath. Started Darwin's "Origin of Species".

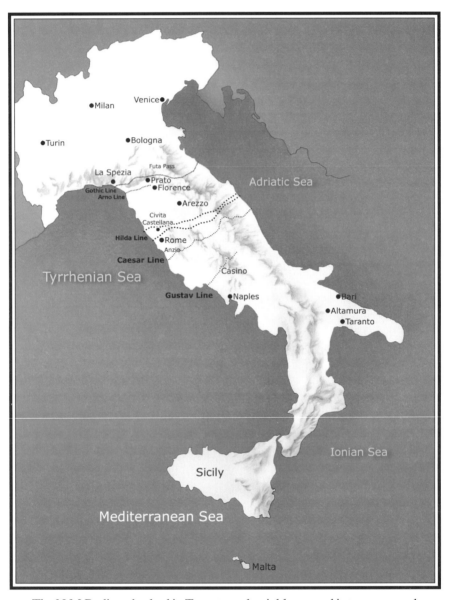

The N.M.R. disembarked in Taranto and quickly moved into a prepared camp at Altamura a few miles north east. The map shows a series of previously prepared German lines, all of which the regiment was destined to breach.

Thursday, 20th April '44

Convoy reached Taranto 8am and the day was spent packing and waiting for disembarkation. I read "Beany Eye" and started "Quo Vardis"!

Left the ship about 3pm. I was in trouble having to walk half a mile with all my kit. We then unloaded (the kit) and then marched six miles through Taranto to a transit camp. Taranto is rather decayed. There is little else in the shops but wine, scent and art. The people have an air of defeat about them and poverty is rife. Mentally, physically and morally they seem to have degenerated.

Read "Origin of species" Charles Darwin.

Some pretty children and a few beautiful girls – Transport is made up of motorbikes, cars, carts, and bicycles. Town was full of troops – mainly Italian sailors. Had a good meal and slipped into bed. Shoulder very stiff and sore after the carrying. It is the anniversary of our leaving Durban for the second time.

Saturday, 29th April '44 – Altamura

Rehearsed during the day. The sketch is on "SANDY THE BURGLAR". Had a frightful shower in the afternoon. It is bitingly cold. Had some wine and went up to the concert which was a great success. Len's voice was hoarse through practising for the sketch and he didn't sing so well. Our sketch went off without a hitch and Bill Janks* as Martha, brought the house down R.S.M. invited us to the sergeants' mess where we had a terrific drink-up on whisky, wine and gin. Aga on tops. Len helped me to bed, pushed me into some mud and sang me lullabies.

Sunday, 30th April '44

Had a bit of a hangover but was shaken when I was put on an all-day hygiene fatigue. One of the worst I have ever done – certainly the filthiest, mainly by hand and shovel. Bitterly cold with hail and sleet now and again. Went to Y.M. for tea and cake and listened to the Italian band. Came back and had my back

---

*Mentioned in despatches, June 7th '42 at Gazala.

massaged (Bill Janks, R.A.M.C.) and his cocoa before bed. Played game of chess with Len.

Monday and Tuesday, 1st & 2nd May '44

Had a bout of squad drill. Then a lecture on armour-plating by Bunny (Evans) before lunch. Terribly cold day. Lecture on 'section leading' in afternoon. Went to Naafi in evening and heard the Italian band and the voice of an exceptionally gifted bambino. Wrote 2 letters home. Went on a useless and beastly map-reading tour over 12 miles of rough country. Raced back before lunch. I got the needle. Played a hectic game of football in the afternoon which was pretty nippy. Had a shower and caught a cold. Washed some clothes, went to Italian lessons and then to Naafi.

Wednesday, 3rd May '44

Went map reading as a squadron by truck and had quite an enjoyable and enlightening day in amongst the green fields and grey walls. Went through Altamura, Cassana, Aquaviva and Santarana and saw a bit of local colour. Got back to camp and went on guard for 24 hours. Went on first beat with Joe and wore mosquito veils. Finished "The Fatal Years".

Saturday, May 6th '44 – Altamura

Did very little (work) this morning. Had a lecture first by Vic Paul on "Mines and Mules," then a lecture after it on this province of the Apennines. After lunch (M.O.) Nelson Eddy took over with first aid. Read and wrote a little. Listened to the Italian band and went to a lecture given by the Padre on 'Psychological Interpretation of Dreams.'

After the last talk I stood up and asked the Padre whether he had heard about the Duke of Hamilton's dream at the beginning of the war. He encouraged me to tell it. The Duke had dreamt that Hitler had visited him in search of peace. The next day, Rudolf Hess landed by parachute from a plane he had hijacked in Germany bearing a peace offer and flown to Scotland.

<u>Wednesday, 10th May '44 – Altamura</u>

Our duty (day) and not having anything on I went up to the Recce tent and completed (writing) Chapter II after making several alterations and half of III. Had tea at the NAAFI with Len and washed some clothes before lunch. Went on to Altamura but did not enjoy it much. Town was not impressive but the cathedral was lovely. Beautiful gold leaf decorations inside and many altars and old oils on the walls. Went up to the Belfry and obtained a wonderful view. Visited Padre's library and had tea there and took two good books. Had some ice cream and half a bottle of vermouth. Went to NAAFI for sandwiches and listened to their excellent band. Saw Ros. Russell in "My Sister Eileen." There was no transport to take us back, but I was fortunate in getting a lift back to camp in a jeep. Bought two bottles of wine and lent Shorty a pound.

<u>Friday, 12th May '44 – Altamura</u>

Push started (overnight) 11 p.m. On another route march but a more pleasant one. Thought up a new sub-plot for 'Traitor's Hill' while marching. [Episode of Horse Brompton smacking Bunny Evans on the behind]. C-in-C Alexander and Lees order of the day read to us. Went on driving instruction in Pooch's tank. Cleaned guns in afternoon and prepared for guard mounting. Had some sweet wine before dinner which was Roast Pork. Lucky to get first beat which passed quickly as did the dog-watch from 1 a.m. to 3., which I spent telling Len of the plot of 'Traitor's Hill.'

The routine of guards, route marches and inspections reared its head again and tempers were near to breaking. Bullimore's proscribed list of defaulters had grown beyond restraint even into Sundays.

<u>Sunday, 14th May '44, Altamura.</u>

Up later than usual. Had a whopping breakfast and cleaned the Bren guns and fed the library. Had a smashing game (hockey) with No.1 troop (ours) against the rest of the Squadron. Drew 4-4 but they scored two crooked goals. Had a deal of wine in the evening and got tight with Bullimore and Len (Clark). We stopped fights when they got obstreperous. Bumped the cooks, the Officers' mess, the sergeants' mess and put Bully to bed. I carried him like a baby as he was paralytic. Len kicked the back door down on top of Inky. Had some more wine. We had a bit of a tiff – not serious and then to bed.

Access to your own Sherman tank in training was like entering a different world. Everything was new and it brought with it that sensation that comes with acquiring something personal and enthralling like a new automobile.

Then, to find progressively that everything worked to your command and gave you power, helped you to understand how those frightful usurpers, the Nazi, could assume the role of dominators and mechanised transgressors in a world they were fast reducing to misery and barbarism. I had thought my patriotism was only skin-deep and wiped off with every dust storm and setback. This brand new, unexercised monster was here and now, ready for the taking as was also that something being thrown off by other members of the crew sharing her with you, a kind of fellowship that had been eulogised and even deified by the Napoleonics and bombast of militarism down through the ages, a numen, fairy godmother, community of spirit, fellowship.

The 'dulce et decorum' that had been threatened, almost quenched by three years of defeat and re-lit by Alamein and all that, now began to brighten once more. Our Sherman, hardly out of its wrappers became a fairy godmother, a sacred place in which separately and together we were touched by her wand. Blessed now with new opportunities, privately we could write home, pray to a neglected god, eat a surreptitious bar of chocolate, test out for ourselves private realms of equipment and collectively share on manoeuvres the coordinated potential of this mobile steel fortress.

In those early months of blissful naiveté we walked with a spring in our feet and looked more kindly at instructors who had little more knowledge of our equipment than we did, but never once were able to impart the kind of experience that would prevent these personalised fortresses becoming our iron coffins. The Sherman was the finest armoured product the Americans had come up with after only two years since Pearl Harbour. On their first entrée their crews thought she was marvellous and that she was brilliant in manoeuvrability, all had agreed. That is until the D-Day landings in Normandy which coincided almost exactly in dates with the 6th South African Division's first encounters with the Tiger tanks in Italy. These were what turned Shermans into mobile coffins as well as by sheer numbers made them winners of World War II. The Tiger a frightening, mind-searing product of organised vandalism, affectionately known to the vandals themselves as a "Tommy Cooker" was presented initially complete to Hitler on his 51st birthday in 1942. It was by his orders to be the biggest and heaviest tank on earth with a firepower beyond anything envisaged by the Allies. It was like pitting the Boers against the might of the British Army one hundred and fifty years earlier. The Tiger became a morale smasher so that you envisaged it behind every derelict wall or leafy hedge. It didn't need to appear in formation. Once, on its own, well camouflaged it did its deadly work and backed off almost at leisure. The Tiger's armour plating could be 4 inches thick in front and sometimes a slab of concrete was added to it there or it stuck itself behind a hillock or garden wall with its turret just visible.

Even more deterring was the Tiger's 88mm gun that could outdistance in range the Sherman's 75mm gun by hundreds of yards. If you just sighted an 88mm gun from your tank you could be pretty certain that you were going to be knocked out. Even hearing over the Squadron wireless net-in that one of your troop tanks was engaged by a Tiger suggested their impending death by incineration.

Somehow the 88mm gun fired almost without a flash and it was easy to camouflage in Italy's leafy landscape. Most likely a friendly tank actually going up in smoke gave you the best whereabouts of an 88mm. It was not surprising that this invincibility coloured the thinking of 8th Army tank crews.

By the time the drive up the spine of Italy from Cassino to Florence began, the Sherman tank had earned two, far from affectionate terms. The Germans called them "Grave diggers" and the Yanks themselves said of the Sherman "It's a good Ronson; it lights up first time!" and by that they meant the most ominous.

They say that "all roads lead to Rome" and it was certainly true in the early days of June as the N.M.R. began its operations, which were initially in support of the British Guards Brigade. The infantry of the American 5th Army, recently breaking out from the Anzio bridgehead was hot-footing it to Rome with forced route marches, as well as on top of anything that moved.

Free French, Tommies and the South African 6th Armoured Division also had their sights fixed on a bridge in Rome that crossed the Tiber. That was us, the N.M.R., and low and behold Aga and Meeser of 'B' Squadron were in the thick of the roads which in places were jammed three vehicles abreast.*

<u>Monday, 15th May '44</u>

Move at 6am cancelled because the battalion stands by to move up to the line. Slept during the morning but worked like a Trojan loading ammo in the afternoon. Leaving for Naples tomorrow to fetch trucks. Wrote letters home in the evening.

<u>Tuesday, 16th May '44</u>

Left at 6:30am and travelled all day. Had a bit of brake trouble. Saw the most beautiful scenery ever. The roads are stupendous and weave up and down the mountains. Messed around at Salerno and then on past Vesuvius to Portici where we stayed the night at a transit camp. Vesuvius a bit disappointing. Salerno the most beautiful town but like many others badly mauled. Covered 160 miles.

<u>Wednesday, 17th May '44</u>

Slept well and were pleased to hear that 7 of us were not required to drive cars and were sent back to camp. Missed Naples except for suburbs and did not see Pompeii ruins except from the distance. The trip back was fast and fatiguing. Saw a lot of equipment moving up to the front. Witnessed two Tommies with Italian women in their truck. Very amusing. Gave lift to pregnant woman and a couple of intriguing sailors making for

---

*Numerous reports later suggested the 8th Army had been held back from Rome as a political move to allow the American 5th Army to enter Rome first. It was a political decision.

Bari having jumped their ship at Naples. Reached camp after stopping at Potenza at 7 pm. Very tired after having covered 320 miles in 36 hours. Went to bed early.

Saturday, 20th May '44

Had Colonel's inspection. Parked kit and left to Bari to join our tanks. Reach Bari at lunchtime after an uneventful trip – an impressive town. Taking Mousie's place temporally as he is now a Sergeant. Suspect dirty weather at the crossroads soon – C'est la gueure. Spent the afternoon loading the tank with ammo. Slept badly with the weather playing up at last.

Sunday, 21st May '44 – Bari

Worked all morning and finished stacking kit, ammo and rations. Bought cherries and ice cream. Eating well again as the tank is now loaded with provisions. Mounted tanks on to Portés in afternoon (see picture No 22). Rigged up Meeser's wireless set and awaited departure for the front. Left at midnight.

Monday, 22nd May '44

Slept rather coldly on the back of the tank as the train hustled at about 60 m.p.h. along the line. Lost my pillow. We went on to the Electric Line before dawn. Many tunnels and beautiful scenery. Jack (Ayers), Alan (Day) and I traded bully beef and lira for 4 bottles of champagne and a bottle of vermouth, which we knocked back quickly. Went through Benevento to our destination which we reached about 1 pm. Had lunch and travelled to the camping area where we bathed and bedded. Slept well. A 3-squadron chap was electrocuted during the trip.

Saturday, 27th May '44 – Nr Cassino

Arose late and had fresh meat and porridge for breakfast. Tank tracks had to be tightened and it was an all-day sweat job. I bathed in the river down in the valley about ten. Stewed some cherries and gave Bokkies (gunner) fire orders for practice. Refuelled tank and after dinner went for a stroll alone through the poppy strewn valley. Am once again in the depths of despair and morbidity.

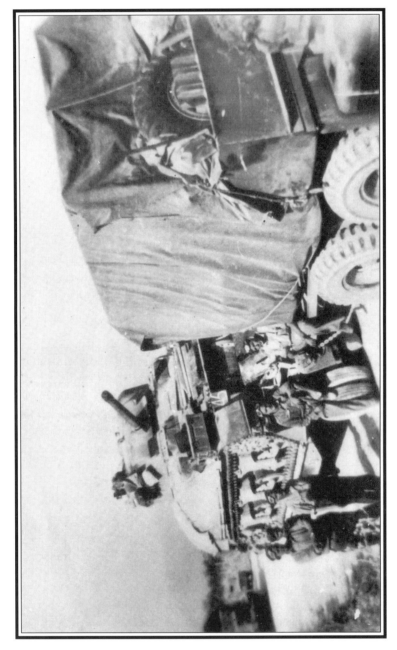

N.M.R. Shermans loaded onto portees in preparation for the journey by train up to the Cassino front.

<u>Monday, 29th May '44</u>

Adjusted sights in the tank turret and gave Bokkies more practice. Went for bath with Len down in valley. Opened up (Squadron) library for afternoon otherwise lazed around reading. Len around in the evening and we played crib, talked and had coffee. Fixed up my will finally with Len as executor.

<u>Wednesday, 31st May – Liri Valey</u>

Painted in the morning and read. Went for a lovely swim with Len and met (Brian) Barrow (who later lost an ear in his blazing tank). Packed up and travelled 28 miles to the intersection of Melfa and Liri rivers. Saw some beautiful country, the shattered Monastery, destroyed bridges, pottered around and smelt the nauseating stink of dead bodies again. Pontecorvo and every village were absolutely shattered and smashed flat. Saw dozens of Churchills and Shermans bashed out on the Hitler Line. Went over a Churchill. Carried out maintenance – heard some dope and went to bed to die.

<u>Thursday, 1st June '44 – Nr Cassino</u>

Had a real humid snorter of a day. Went down to Melfa River to bathe. Len and I fired my Tommy gun. Slept in early afternoon and read. Had bad meat and dehydrated vegetables for dinner. Swam in the Liri in afternoon. Went to bed in clothes and were pulled out to move up 24 miles to Ceccano which took us all night no sleep. Finished Cakes and Ale (book). Many vehicles and tanks crashed off the roadside. Cecil Ritson's (tank) into the river.

THE GOTHIC LINE

The Gothic Line was a series of mountain fortresses which occupied Allied attention from August '44 until April '45. It had been possible for the Germans to establish the line in time as the result of Mark Clark's obsession with occupying Rome instead of securing the surrender of the German 10th Army trapped at Anzio.

Unaware of what lay ahead I had continued in the army after my severe injuries at El Alamein believing I could manage in tanks but would not be much use as an infantryman.

General Mark Clark talks to a priest outside
St. Peter's on his arrival in Rome

Chapter XXII

General Mark Clark was hell-bent to be the first to enter Rome. Having been successful at the Anzio beach landings with the German 10th Army virtually trapped, he pulled soldiers out in order to occupy Rome. It was a prize that he could not keep his eyes off. The German 10th consequently escaped northwards and the British 8th Army (including ourselves) had to fight them later.

It was this kind of disarray at high levels that had produced so many absurdities. In our own instance, successful as infantry in the desert at Alamein and mountainous Abysinnia, we had been retrained for a whole year to fight in heavy and light tanks only to be dismounted before the Gothic Line and used again as infantry and this oscillation continued till the end of the war. The Italian front was never going to reach Vienna before the Russians which had been the hope held at the highest levels which had included Churchill and Alanbrooke.

Approaching Rome confusion reigned everywhere. Sergeant Major 'Aga 'Kahn, nobody doubted, had the gift of the gab but there was one occasion on which Aga met his Waterloo.

In his own words this is what happened:

On the eve of D-Day, we were leaguered at Ceccano, when we received orders to move with all speed towards Rome to capture a bridge over the Tiber on the east of the City. The American 5th Army had broken out of Anzio and were also moving towards Rome. We sped through the night towards the objective and were mixed up, at times, with the Free French who were milling around the road.

The 5th United States Army at the ceremony before the Victor Emanuel WW1 Monument as part of their occupation of Rome.

Early next morning we approached the bridge by means of a sunken road. The tanks were virtually nose to tail and the area was alive with American infantry, almost dead on their feet with weariness as they had walked all the way from Anzio, which was approximately 30 miles away.

The Jerries on the opposite bank of the river were enlivening the proceedings, sending over salvoes of mortars from Nebelwerfers.

I was sitting in my half-truck half dozing, when my siesta was shattered by a raucous American voice enquiring: *Who's in charge here.*

The owner of the voice was directed to my vehicle, I beheld a fierce looking General with a large hooked nose, whose shirt was adorned with more *fruit salad* than I had ever seen before. I recognised him before he informed me that he was General Mark Clark of the American 5th Army and demanded: *What the hell are you doing here?*

With the utmost politeness but with considerable trepidation I pointed out that I was only the Sergeant-Major and that my C.O. Major R. D. Meeser, M.C., was in sole charge and was to be found at the head of the column.

The General then demanded: *"Send for him."*

Major Meeser's code name was *Sunray* 1 and I was *Sunray* 6. My message was as follows:

Sunray 6 *calling Sunray* 1. *I have a message for you,* which he acknowledged and in order to observe the utmost security in view of the presence of my exalted guest I said: *I have the greatest gumchewing Sunray of them all here who demands your immediate presence.*

Within a few minutes Major Meeser arrived and before he had completed his salute, the General demanded in a stentorian voice. *What the hell are you doing here?*

The Major promptly informed him that we had orders to capture the bridge across the Tiber: whereupon he was brusquely informed that he could tell his General – the 8th Army Commander – that the American 5th Army neither desired or required the assistance of the 8th Army and / or the South Africans to take the bridge. His words were more or less to the effect: *Get the hell out of it – your tanks are cluttering up the place.*

Orders were then given for us to move and on our way back General Clark passed us, stopped and having somewhat relented told us to *stick around, I might have a job for you after all.*

Rome was declared an open city so neither of the two Armies had the honour of its capture, but by a strange coincidence a few weeks later we fell under the command of the American 5th Army and vied with our South Africans, some of whom were still under the command of the 8th Army for the capture of Florence. In fact, our squadron, for a short while, were the first and only troops on the south bank of the Arno, the Bailey bridge erected over the river having collapsed after our crossing it.

The tanks were dispersed in a field close by and we started *brewing up* but became the target of a few Messerschmitts in the vicinity. At this juncture our O.C. wisely contacted our H.Q. and obtained permission to withdraw to join our forces.

I don't think anyone succeeded in claiming to be first into Rome. Being on the extreme left flank of the 8th Army meant we were always going to be brushing with the Americans and they certainly kept treading on our tits anyway.

ENTRY TO ROME

The distant background to the 'march on Rome' was of course the second front launched on the coast of Normandy. Added to this was a series of delays relating to Sherman Bechan's engine, a thrown track and trouble with the traverse. This was exasperating because of news continuously filtering through of our Squadrons now being engaged by Tigers and the reporting of casualties as our tanks were successively brewed up. Being constantly in touch by wireless with those different scenarios added to the excitement and tension.

<u>Wednesday/Thursday, 7th/8th June '44 – south of Rome.</u>

Awakened at 1 a.m. to move at four. Had coffee and made good time. Travelling on highway six up to K(ilometre) 30 where we stopped.

Another maddening delay for our squadron, tuned in, after a lot of difficutly, they are operating against the enemy N.E. of Rome. Thank the Pope that our troop is not apparently doing anything but reserve work. Completed (reading) Nana and I roamed around doing nothing until we pulled out about 8:30 p.m.

– Heard Dream Sanders calling from his tank that one of his tanks was hit and burnt out – No news of Bob Smith and rest of his crew (Paddy Gill, Bobby Gibson, Jan Calpin and Eddie Salmons). Melly (Ratcliffe's) tank (Sterzel as gunner) hit through the sprocket. Five missing today.

Thursday, 8th June '44

Travelled right through the night – through Rome and out to 40km (N.E.). Had little sleep – more stenches and raids on Rome during the night – very struck with the city but had little chance of gaining impressions. We went through by moonlight. We had early morning coffee and walked into a shop for haircut and shave – long chat with the Ito's. Raced along up to our Squadron and got permission for our tank to return to the line immediately.

While there our squadron was shelled and Meeser, Doidge and Dalgano were wounded and (Andy) Schou killed. Ammo truck destroyed. Travelled back to our tank by despatch rider to tell Mousie who didn't pitch up with the tank till later. Sorted out troop rations and went to bed late only to do a guard. Gordon Swales and another (Rigby) killed in 'B' Squadron. Echlon shelled again and another wounded.

3 wounded, 1 killed.

The centurions of Ancient Rome were wary of moonlight when they were on active service. The soldiers going to sleep under a bright moon covered themselves in a white sheet in order to offset the malefic influences of the moon at a time when the lunar rays were believed to produce lunacy in the unwary or mentally unstable.

The advance through Rome had been monumental, for almost everyone had contended they were the first in and the delusion was heightened by the presence of moonlight which gives objects in white marble still life and fake movement. It seemed for a long time, at top speed we cruised towards the massive Victor Emanuel marble monument to the dead of World War I in the centre of Rome. By the light of the Full Moon (in Sagittarius) with its two white wings widely extended, a ghostly engulfing death was being proffered. To some, who were never to witness the giant edifice again, it could have been the symbol of death enlivened once more. To me it was both the W.W.I. mausoleum and the W.W.II. optimistic embracement of the white cliffs of Dover, symbol of peace. In less than a month I was to walk hand-in-hand with both.

As we pulled out of Rome and hastened northwards into death and destruction the cats of Rome raced us on the sidewalks in their terror at the commotion.

Almost immediately, our squadron ran into trouble, ambushed on the distal side of Civita Castellana, two years to the day after the debacle at Gazala.

Account of events by survivor
Corporal Cecil Ritson of 'B' Squadron.

On entering Civita Castellana on 7th June, our troop was ordered to proceed on a lateral tarmac road to try and establish contact with the Free French Division which was operating on our Division's left flank.

Along the road we captured two stray German soldiers. I placed them on the front of my turretless Honey tank and we continued with our journey. Further on, where the road was straight, we entered an area of trees. Suddenly an anti-tank gun fired on us. The shell, fortunately, whizzed past our three tanks. We hurriedly reversed into a slight dip in the road and out of sight of the German gunners. Lieutenant 'Dream' Sanders and I pulled our respective tanks off to the right of the road, whilst Sergeant Bob Smith took his tank to the left facing the enemy.

We were afforded protection on the right by a line of trees, whereas Bob Smith had apparently gone into open ground. Our crews on the right could hear the noises of battle on the left, but could not see what was taking place. Also, we had lost radio contact with Bob. 'Dream' asked me to accompany him and we crept up past the foliage on the roadside. There, across the road in an open area, we saw the Sergeant's Sherman on fire, and Bob and two of his crew being escorted by several German soldiers.

There must have been well-placed 88mm anti-tank guns covering the open area on that side.

Our position was hopeless, and we returned to our tanks. Then the artillery and mortars started ranging on our two tanks. The prisoners were becoming very agitated in their exposed position. We then pulled back and returned to Civita Castellana and handed over our prisoners for interrogation.

This exercise was not intended to be a normal reconnaissance, where the point troop is backed up by other tanks and infantry. Our lone troop of three tanks' task was to liase with the French forces.

Paddy Gill and Bobby Gibson who were killed in this action, were colleagues of mine at Glenwood High School, Durban. Bob Smith suffered facial and hand burns and Ian Culpin received a bullet wound in the thigh.

According to Altmeyer two Germans were killed by the second shell fired by the Sherman tank. *Cecil Ritson – (2003)*

[We are grateful to Altmeyer for the photographs of the action that follow...]

Sergeant Bob Smith's tank is sighted (top right). Note the conspiratorial motions of the German anti-tank crew in the foreground.

The N.M.R. tank scores a near hit on the anti-tank position.

The 88mm anti-tank gun returns the fire and scores a direct hit on the Sherman on the skyline far right.

The N.M.R. tank brews up and survivors begin to vacate. Three of the crew scramble out of the Sherman but Paddy Gill and Bobby Gibson are killed. The three survivors were machine gunned but lived to tell the story as POW's.

Chapter **XXIII**

Friday, June 9th '44, Viterbo - Soriano

Moved out of camp early and immediately went into operation. Len and Co's (tank) engine gave trouble and are not in (action) today. Our squadron headed the column, which entered Viterbo. Then our troop was detached and sent on a sticky task up the road to Soriano, up which the German armour had escaped. The road was interspersed with burnt out Tiger tanks. We would have had no chance against…

… the Tigers because the road was all bends around a hill heavily wooded. Contacted 3 Squadron (C) the other end. The population of Soriano turned out (to greet us).

It has been a nerve-wracking day almost constantly under mortar and machine-gun fire. Breaking through the undergrowth and finding the best way through had necessitated using Zulu to keep in contact with each other. Leadership under Major Haupt that awful day was outstanding. He won the Military Cross.

Citation from *N.M.R. History* - by Eric Goetzsche:

MILITARY CROSS
W/S CAPTAIN (T/MAJOR) JOHANNES SECUNDUS HAUPT
N.M.R./S.A.A.F., 6 S.A. Armoured Division.

On 9 June 1944, Major Haupt was in command of a Squadron of Tanks operating along the Vignanello-Soriano Road. The Squadron was repeatedly held up by deviations and reconnaissance was difficult due to wooded country and enemy Machine gun and Mortar fire. Major Haupt personally led the forward reconnaissance on foot and although under heavy fire

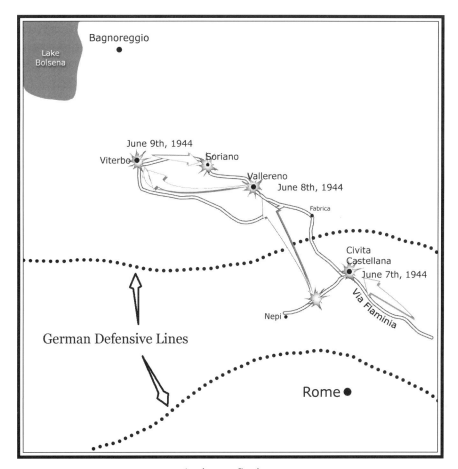

Action at Soriano

succeeded in finding deviations through difficult country. Due to his courage, devotion to duty, and outstanding leadership, the speed of the advance was maintained throughout the operation.

After the occupation of Rome the 8th Army was instructed to chase the Germans all the way to Florence and even beyond hoping to prevent, through a rapid advance, development of enemy positions in the mountains south of Bologna. The advance was reconnoitred by the N.M.R. It's rapidity even surprised O.C. General Alexander and Whitehall itself where C.I.G.S. Lord Alanbrooke commented:

"News from Alexander continues to be excellent. He is all for dashing off to the Pisa-Rimini Line. And I have been trying to enduce him to send something to Ancona as he moves up."

On the morning of the 8th shells plastered our Company area and Andy Schou, who looked like a tall, wild Anglo-Saxon chieftain was killed and my friend Tiny Doidge was wounded. The latter survives still living healthily in Natal. For all our gains it did not seem likely that the 8th Army's advance up the Apennines was going to be a piece of cake and resistance was stiffening with the 6th South African Armoured Division spearheading the operation.

It was now at a time that the regiment's new heroes began to come to the fore and when a number of them, often distinguished already in sport, were to pay the ultimate price. Central to all of them was Lieutenant Howard Butcher. His daring and his dash had already been noticed in the western desert and in East Africa. Howard was never in my Squadron but we had all been thrilled by his sportsmanship. He was superbly built, surprisingly handsome and greatly admired. He died, as he had lived, heroic in devotion and action in the name of duty.

It was on June 10th that a serious engagement took place at Bagnoregio where two Shermans were lost early in the day, one of them under the command of Howard Butcher. Both tanks had got amongst a nest of the enemy hiding in rough country. Though they had been put out of action, such were the efforts of Butcher and his men, the advance was able to continue, the Squadron now getting the support of the F.F.B. in strength and the fighting continued throughout the day. Howard Butcher's part on that day was written up by a trooper in his squadron at the time, reproduced in the regimental history.

A survivor of the encounter, Trooper A.P. Goodwill wrote:–

I can recall quite clearly that June morning when Lieutenant Howard Butcher spoke to me; it was quite evident that he also felt the strain… He appeared so tired… Our engines just would not start that morning and I overheard him arranging with our crew commander, Bob Clark, to call the mechanic, and suggest that he (Bob Clark) follow once the trouble had been rectified. We stood there watching our officer's tank and Dudley Pringle's

Howard Butcher, N.M.R. hero who fearlessly fought the Nazis Panzers at Bir Elweit Tamar before Tobruk and again in Shermans later in Italy being killed in action when his tank "brewed' under heavy attack.

move off for another day of reconnaissance towards a town named Bagnoregio, not realising what that day would bring.

As soon as the mechanic had found the fault and the engines roared into life, we were on our way to join the rest of the Troop, accompanied by the Honey at the rear. We were on the move for some considerable time when Bob instructed our driver to halt just before a bend in the road and before the summit of an incline. He stated that he was not very happy and had a feeling that something was wrong. He instructed us to remain where we were, and he set off on foot, not on the road but off into the fields on the right. He had hardly left us when we were bombarded by the enemy with heavy artillery. We were down below the skyline, but our whereabouts was apparently known, judging by the heavy shelling all around us. Bob had been right in his premonition and we were worried as to where he had got to and also whether he was safe.

It was apparent, however, that there was trouble ahead as there were frantic calls on the radio. I then stuck my head up out of the turret and looked behind. There along the road and spread out across the fields to the right were many Sherman tanks coming up behind us. It was a memorable sight. It was then that I received a call on the air requesting us to give Headquarters the position of our *friends*. Then we knew – Howard Butcher and Dudley Pringle were in trouble and had called for assistance. Our *friends* happened to be the S.S.B. coming up fast, and I replied to our Headquarters giving them their position.

A short while later Bob returned in the midst of heavy shelling and immediately contacted headquarters and, in a hesitating voice advised them that our two *cows* (tanks) had been *brewed up*. Howard Butcher, van Rosenveldt and Jack Gardner were dead, but he could not find the other two members of the crew, one of whom was Neil Dore. Corporal Pringle and his crew had also disappeared. In the meantime one of the F.F.B. had gone forward and, just as we expected, came to grief on reaching the curve of the bend. The tank was hit and burning furiously and we could hear as well as see the rounds going off inside. Fortunately the crew had managed to bail out and take cover, and were making their way back to the safety of their lines. In the meantime a second Sherman had come up alongside the *brewed up cow* and was inching its way alongside, very, very slowly; it was clear that the crew commander was looking for the tell-tale sign of smoke issuing from the muzzle of the 88mm as she fired. At that moment the whole squadron of tanks, line abreast, were appearing on the skyline and, although one or two were *brewed up*, the rest spotted the enemy gun and it was only a matter of seconds before it received the full onslaught of high explosive from about fifteen 75mm guns.

We then continued the advance and drove the enemy in full retreat from the district of Bagnoregio. Special mention must be made of the bravery of the crews of the F.F.B. and also of the outstanding courage of the truck drivers who brought their open trucks right up into the thick of battle, to refuel and replenish the tanks with ammunition. This was executed probably in full view of the enemy's observation posts, who were directing their fire on all of us. Two truck drivers were decorated with the Military Medal and how well they deserved them! Lieutenant-Colonel (*Papa*) Brits, who commanded the S.S.B was awarded the D.S.O.

We were fortunate in that we only suffered a few glancing hits from a 40mm gun and therefore survived to fight another day.

The loss of Howard Butcher and two of his crew was felt keenly by the Squadron, not to mention the loss of two valuable Shermans, and when we returned to our harbour area, Major Haupt was there to meet us, and it was clear to one and all that he was very upset...

The next day we pulled out for a well deserved rest, and it was then that we discovered that Dudley Pringle's crew and the rest of Howard Butcher's crew had sought shelter in a cave, which faced our lines. It was while they were sheltering there that one of our Shermans coming over the rise, spotted the cave and trained its guns on it. They mentioned that they prayed as they had never prayed before and thanked the Lord when the tank commander decided not to fire. They (those rescued from the cave) were all suffering from shock, but after a rest were back at work again. We were also informed that Howard and Dudley had given a very good account of themselves before being knocked-out, as a considerable number of German bodies and equipment bore testimony to the fact that they were engaged in a pitched battle. If only they had observed the anti-tank gun in time, what a different story would have been written!

Bob explained to us that although Howard Butcher had had his leg shattered by one of the two projectiles, which penetrated the side of the tank, he had assisted the crew from the tank, and *only then* did he attempt to crawl away. Jack Gardner and van Rosenveldt were machine-gunned and killed as they ran, but Howard died from shock and loss of blood. Bob found him before he died and he requested Bob to convey his love to his wife Peggy and to the rest of the boys...

He was no ordinary officer and even wrote to the next-of-kin of each and every member of his troop. He would also never settle down until he was sure that all his men had been attended to.

Thus died Howard Butcher, a true Desert Rat who, through many acts of service to his regiment, and acts of valour should have been decorated many times.

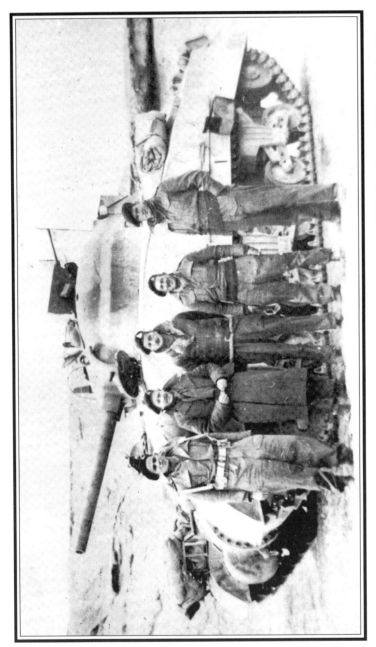

Training for tank warfare the N.M.R. found winter in 1943/44 very cold in the desert. Right to left: Lieut. Howard Butcher, Tpr. J. Gardiner, N. Dore, Cpl. D. Pringle and Tpr. Max Harris. Butcher, Dore, and Cpl. Pringle all had their tanks destroyed by 88mm guns in Italy.

Nebel Werfer

The Germans had grouped a bunch of mortar barrels together and called them the Nebel Werfer and their bombs came over one after the other creating a sobbing sound so that they were termed "Sobbing Sisters."

If you were closed in and battened down in a Sherman they were no problem but if you were caught out in the open by them or by the observation post directing them, then you would be lucky to escape with the fright of your life. Even seated or crouching in a turret-less tank like a Stewart, there was a risk that one of the group of mortars that had positioned you might land in the open well and blow you all to smithereens.

Sitting with Len Clark one wet afternoon in such an open-turreted tank we must have been spotted by a nebel werfer crew and the sisters came down all around us. If our tank was the actual target then the grouping was stunningly accurate. I think we were killing time playing crib and I pegged them on the crib board. Number eight was the most accurate and I grunted "infinity." There must have been several of these clusters before the mortar men were off and away.

SALERNO

The allied landings at Salerno (south of Naples) and at Anzio, south of Rome were tactical errors. Whatever happened in southern Italy, the main impediment to advancing up the Italian Peninsular was going to be in mountainous country where tanks would be useless. Anzio and Salerno did not affect this main issue. The newly-equipped and trained 6th South African Armoured Division rolled up the Germans as far as Florence and then were dismounted and retrained again as infantry to dislodge the Germans finally from the Apennines.

THE ITALIAN CAMPAIGN

The Italian campaign was made more difficult for many reasons. The Anzio landings were poorly led even if mightily conceived in an atmosphere of hopes and wishes. The landings were a complete surprise which pleased the high command, but not the fiasco and withdrawal that followed.

Amphibious attacks were planned as main events and both Salerno and Anzio failed to the extent that mountain warfare in the Appenines had to replace them.

The line anchored on Cassino alone held up operations in Italy for months because armour could not operate in a major part of the mountainous countryside. With tongue in cheek the current film 'Where Eagles Dare' suggests means that would have been more appropriate for the Italian campaign. As it was, South Africans, experienced infantry in desert warfare had been retrained as cavalry and reconnaissance for Italy and then had to be reconverted to infantry against Germans dug-in in the mountains in the mid-winter of 1944/ 45.

As tank men, expert in the use of Shermans, we were forced to act as front line infantry to maintain the advance up the spine of Italy. I should know as one of the hundreds of tank men maimed or killed leading our own tanks up or down the mountain roads, until shot doing reconnaissance more suited to mountain troops than in Shermans.

Higher command, in planning the Italian campaign well knew that the enemy would be in defence and that attacking forces required strong superiority. The landings drew off such hope of superiority, leaving an undermanned army to attack Germans entrenched in the Gustav line, the Gothic line etc., straddling the Appenines.

The Germans were so confident they could hold their Gustav line in the mountains, that they were able to send a division to reinforce their defenders in Anzio.

"We hoped to land a wild cat that would tear out the bowels of the Bosche. Instead we have landed a vast whale with its tail flopping about in the water."

– Churchill.

The whale flopping its tail on the Anzio beachhead sent strong currents across the Mediterranean soliciting help for the stalled Italian campaign especially at Cassino, from the Eighth Army in Africa.

Even as late as April, 1944 with endless infantry assaults failing to take Cassino Mountain, the C.O.G. (A.B.) was only then discussing mountain troops for Italy, something that should have been envisaged when Wavell was carving chunks out of the Italian Army on the Egyptian frontier in 1940, and when the Italian fleet was almost mortally wounded in Taranto in 1941.

The Yanks wanted to get rid of Victor Emanuel and the aged General Badoglio, but Winston passed on to them his comment which was why break the teapot handle at this stage while holding the pot might burn your fingers. Why not get to Rome and let it cool down first?

Fifty years later in the Gulf War, the USA president, George Bush Snr., had the same opportunity with the regime in Baghdad and balked the issue. His son corrected the mistake. The Italian pot did not cool down and Monte Cassino kept it boiling because it was an almost invincible mountain stronghold. Hitler's underbelly, which was Italy, never became a threat to him again, nor did Victor Emanuel or any of his generals hold power. It was Mussolini who was the threat and Hitler rescued him from his mountain exile.

The countryside which the N.M.R. was to reconnoitre in tanks was totally different from the deserts it had gained its infantry experience in. We were now in terrain that was almost impossible for armoured forces. It was close country with demolitions just about everywhere in amongst hedgerows, ditches, ravines, gullies and dykes. Most important of all was the lack of visual distance which tanks must have especially when battened down for action and, horror of horrors we came to realise almost immediately that much of our reconnoitring would have to be done on foot ahead of our tanks in perilously close situations.

RATS & MICE

There were different grades of participation in the conflict at all levels in the army. There were troopers shot out of four different tanks and others who never saw an enemy tank in anger. In the infantry some soldiers were wounded on several occasions and others who made sure they never came under fire twice. Many heroes were never mentioned either in despatches or even in regimental annals. Many were not cited for their acts of extreme bravery or medals because they lay in hospital recovering from their wounds. Some old soldiers were never compensated or pensioned for injuries that crippled them for the rest of their lives.

Real acts of valour and momentous incidents were often masked by showmanship. Time and again you could see men who never got further than a base camp posing for camera shots in front of a burnt out German tank, holding a pistol or Tommy-gun at the ready... photos of mock bravery to send home to their families.

Just as there were Desert Rats, true and brave, there were also desert mice unworthy of any honour and crafty in hiding their cowardice. Unfortunately it was often only in a crisis that the mice showed their true worth.

NEUROSIS AND THERAPY

The rowdyism in periods of leave and the accompanying imbibing of the local wine in bars and cabarets were partly indicative of the underlying neurosis of men isolated under their pressures in and out of battle conditions, but it was also therapy emphasised, when relaxed and in the safe company of buddies, even groups.

It was tough on the civilians especially where the rowdyism extended into the opera houses (of Rome, Naples and Bari) and other sacred cows, but it did help somehow to relieve tensions because these episodes were talking points other than daily matters of killing and being killed, the stench of death and destruction wherever the moving front lingered.

On a Union Castle boat making for England in May 1959, I met Doc (Nelson) Eddy who had featured in the cruel times of the Italian Campaign. We spent many hours promenading or sitting on deck chatting. I was studying Medicine at the time and we reviewed the Patton 'yellow health' and subsequent reactions of men we mutually remembered in our regiment and Eddy told me how widespread neurosis became because of the increasing battle fatigue. He was especially interested in the ways of dealing with this condition, which troopers wished to keep secret at all costs and never asking to be withdrawn from the affray. Sometimes men had to be ordered by him or through their squadron commander back for rest and recoupment. Men like Dennis May, still a youth who won the M.M. for gallantry was one such, shot out of his tanks four times. Others, less resilient, simply broke down; Sterzel was only one of these. Colin MacArthur was another. They were both friends of mine and had done their best and shown their worth up to the point where their sovereign consciousness became uncrowned.

Doc Eddy and I also exchanged ideas about the role of hypnosis in the treatment of shock and battle fatigue. There had been the General Patton controversy with whom he had some sympathy. What are you to do when a desperate soldier tells you he is at the end of his tether? Do you let him stay put and return him to his private hells ensconced in an iron coffin or, at his best, a poor example to others?

The circumstances of Patton's attack on shell-shock patients are worth noting from a news report of the time.

Santa Agatha, Sicily, 10th August 1943

Doctors and nurses at a U.S. military hospital looked on in amazement today as a general slapped two soldiers, threatening to shoot one of them. Lieutenant-General George S. Patton Junior, the volatile commander of the 7th Army was making an unscheduled visit to the 93rd Evacuation Hospital when he saw the soldiers. The first had malaria. Patton slapped him three times. When Patton asked the second man what the trouble was he replied: "It's my nerves. I can't stand the shelling anymore." Patton slapped the man shouting "Shut-up that God-damned crying. I won't have brave men here who have been shot see a yellow bastard crying." He struck the soldier again and asked the medical officer not to admit him.

Patton turned to the man and said: "You're going back to the front lines and you may get shot and killed, but you're going to fight. If you don't I'll stand you up against a wall and have a firing squad kill you on purpose." The general reached for his pistol. "I ought to shoot you myself, you Goddamned whimpering coward," he yelled. This was the second such incident in a week and will anger General Eisenhower.

I had come back to some sort of advanced M.A.P. for treatment of a minor wound and heard that Melly Ratcliffe's tank had brewed up and that Sterzel, our Tom Mix, was missing and then located him half-crazed in a state of shock. Taken into the same M.A.P., he was sitting alone in a tent and wouldn't talk to anyone. I sat down in front of him. He appeared demented with his eyes out of focus and I recalled the same look when he had taken that final pummelling in the boxing ring in Khatatba. His hands were tightly clenched on the table and I put forward mine to comfort him. He recognised me with a faint, forced smile and unclenching of his teeth but couldn't speak. I left him and went out to ask what had happened. Their tank had come under incessant fire and Sterzel's nerve had given way. Ratcliffe, the tank commander had been directing Sterzel, the gunner, on to the offending Tiger but the sight of it was the final straw and Sterzel shot up out of the tank's turret and ran for cover.

Later, Melly somewhat inebriated, had commented "Sterzel shot past me like a champagne cork." Returning to Sterzel I tried to comfort him but he kept shaking his head as if he didn't want to hear. I told him I was scared stiff too and couldn't take much more but it would all be over soon and we could go sailing again, perhaps on Lake Como and get drunk. Then he turned to me; his eyes had become momentarily unclouded and an element of will came over him and he shouted hysterically "Doug, I don't want to see any of it again – no more tanks, nothing," and with this he pounded the table with his fists.

I left him as he sank back into the same stupor and returned to my Sherman just as the crew finished pouring the last of 120 gallons of high-octane fuel into each of its tanks. Sterzel disappeared from the regiment for some time and I never ever found any mention of him in its War History book of records. He sent himself to Coventry and like others in deep shock just withdrew his connections with a life he found too much for him.

It was not until I was in convalescent camp later, that he surfaced briefly and I tried to help him.

CHAPTER XXIV

Some of the most intensive action that was encountered by the N.M.R. in Italy, occurred on the 11th June when Dream Sanders and Cecil Ritson should have won citations for their brave actions. On that day, the author's own troop was only out on the flank of the main action but he was netted in on radio to the events. Cecil Ritson gives his own more intimate account of events:–

ADVANCE IN THE MIST – NEAR BAGNOREGIO

On June 11th, it was our troop's turn to lead the reconnaissance. The day dawned with a heavy mist. Because of greatly reduced visibility, our troop commander, Lt. "Dream" Sanders decided he would ride in my Honey tank, as he anticipated that the reconnoitre would be on foot for much of the time, and it was more convenient to operate from my tank which had the turret removed. Going ahead of the tanks on foot, 'Dream' asked me to accompany him. He carried a Tommy gun and I a Sten gun.

After a while, we reached a dip in the road and came to a small bridge. There was the noise of a vehicle approaching from the other direction. Out of the mist there loomed a half-tracked truck with a driver and passenger seated in front. We fired on the windscreen and the vehicle veered off and hit the sidewall of the bridge. The next moment there was an almighty noise, as the truck's load of ammunition started exploding, possibly mortar bombs and/or landmines. We rushed back to the Honey tank and quickly led the troop across the narrow bridge. We had a very anxious moment as we had to pass close to this inferno of exploding missiles and intense heat, with our turretless tank.

The driver of the third Sherman tank coming along the bridge, apparently blinded by the flash of an exploding shell involuntarily drew back and, in so doing, pulled on one tiller, with the result that the tank plunged into the stream below. On the radio link, we heard that the crew were not injured. They evacuated from the tank, but were then caught in a mortar attack on the area, and Cpl. George Fox and Trooper Domoney were fatally wounded. The enemy must have had pre-determined fixed lines of fire on the bridge, because the mist restricted visibility to about 50 yards.

Our troop of one Honey and two Sherman tanks continued up the road. We saw landmines placed on the surface of the road ahead, obviously put there in a hurry. We got past the obstacles without mishap. We approached a forest area on the right and could make out vehicles with camouflage parked on the edge of the trees. My first thought was that they were tanks. It turned out that they were half-tracked lorries, and our Shermans pumped 75mm shells into them as we advanced. After this action, one of the gunners, Harry Swales, earned the nickname of 'Half-track Harry.'

Rounding a bend we found that we had run onto a line of infantry straddling the road. They were dug in slit trenches. The soldiers lay doggo and were not prepared to tackle us. We called for our platoon of supporting infantry to come. Someone on the forest verge started firing single shots at the Honey tank. Fortunately, the first shot missed, and we had to keep our heads below the rim of the tank.

Corporal Bill Meek in the Sherman tank on the left noticed a hut on the edge of the forest. His gunner fired on the hut, but the shell hit a tree alongside the hut. A person fell out of the tree. It turned out that this was the commander of the German Company. He was very shaken and he immediately surrendered. Our infantry arrived and rounded up the Company.

A decision was made to bring up a Battalion of the 24th Guards Brigade. The Guards made an extended line and, together with our tanks on the road, we made a sweep through the forest. We encountered no enemy, but there were signs that the forest had been used as a huge sheltered camp. The Germans, in their haste to leave the forest, had abandoned hundreds of items of ordnance – camping equipment, mobile kitchens, stores of materials, guns, etc. Later it was advised in a Divisional Report, that 360 items of ordnance were captured.

Coming out of the forest the mist started to lift, and in bright afternoon sunshine, it was apparent that the enemy were making signs of a stand. Our troop commander, at this point, asked to be relieved of the front position, as the weapons were clogged-up. We moved back, only to find that we were mixed up with a shelling duel between a battery of our guns and the enemy's. It was time to move further back and take a well-earned rest.

For this action on June 11th, both 'dream' Sanders and Bill Meek were mentioned in despatches.

The author's own memory of events of that day were from the side line but may help to convey the helplessness of those close by but too distant to participate:

On the morning of June 11th the squadron wireless gunners, myself included, became increasingly aware of tank terror and panic as a troop under the pressure of probing the enemy line made contact with an 88mm and its supporting infantry. On this day the going had been slowed by a heavy mist which put paid to the enemy's hope of getting our tanks into their anti-tank sights. Our squadron was supposed to be in support of 24th Guards Brigade but visibility had dropped to 50 yards. The countryside was densely wooded with great ravines making tank driving hazardous and one tank in particular began to give out alarm signals. It had come under sustained mortar attack and with yawning gullies and slippery ridges on both sides the crew sounded over the radio to have lost its nerve.

Listening in to their appalling situation we realised that it was a tank crew with a driver called Dos Santos of Portuguese origin who unfeelingly was given that day the sobriquet of "the screaming Diego." The Sherman's crew in such terrain was doomed when it was attempting to cross a narrow bridge over a yawning donga. A mortar bomb exploded immediately in front of the tank. Dos Santos, with his head out of the driver's hatch was wounded. Blinded by the flash of the explosion, he drew back and in doing so pulled on the left tiller with the result that the Sherman plunged into the donga. The crew then evacuated their tank but came under terrible mortar fire once more during which two of the crew, Fox and Domoney were fatally

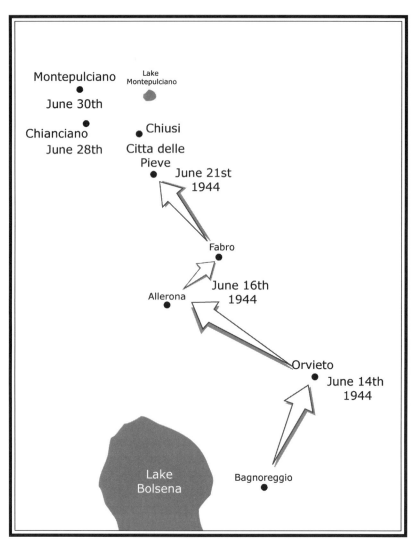

Rapid advances on the road to Florence.

wounded. Dos Santos the driver was badly shaken. Wounded and filled with remorse for his error of judgement he was rescued and evacuated.

Meanwhile, up on the flat, the mist had cleared enabling us to penetrate the enemy position, destroying many vehicles and weapons and inflicting heavy casualties. With the help of our squadron, the guards had dispatched Nazi defenders and driven them northwards. The hamlet of Cellerio fell to the South Africans indicating that other squadrons that day had been successful on the side roads.

Extracts from letters home –

12th June 1944

The population is far friendlier now and we have been given presents of eggs, veal, fresh milk, bacon, cherries and wine. The Germans have been absolutely brutal in their hold on the land. Everywhere they leave their equipment, burnt or mangled yet fight on stubbornly through the hills, valleys and across rivers and plains though they must realise all is lost and they fight with devilish cunning and fiendish sadism. I get a lot of practice with my Italian and am coming on with it.

17th June 1944

Len and I are going to see if we can get a couple (of fowl) this afternoon at the nearby villa. I shall take my Tommy gun in case we meet a few stray ones before we get there. Yesterday afternoon we visited the nearby vegetable fields with shovels and brought back a back-breaking load of new potatoes, beetroots, onions, lettuce and beans. We had a variety of salads. I was forced to make mayonnaise out of a teaspoon of curry, pepper, egg powder, milk and sour wine, as we have no mustard, salad oil or vinegar. It was quite a success. Weeks ago, I saw the remains of Cassino and we have seen almost as bad in many places since then. Just outside Cassino there was a little village on the mountainside of a huge valley. The Germans decided to hold it with its three or four hundred odd houses. We bombed. Do you know that there is not one house that wasn't shattered, almost flattened. What the casualties must have been I hate to think.

From a distance I thought it looked so beautiful that when I had a spare moment I went closer to paint it and I was shocked to see the devastation.

If the Germans wanted fresh meat and as usual hadn't the vehicles to carry much food, they'd kill a cow and eat what they wanted and leave the rest to rot.

It was rather amusing to watch the various entries made into the ravished town – quite often the first entry, when everything appears like one of the old Roman "Triumphs" in Caesar's time with rose petals thrown and gifts made by inhabitants. In the end two-gallon tins were kept handy on the front of the tanks so that gifts of wine could be received without delay or trouble. The quality varied.

Strategies had to be used against the Tiger or 88mm guns. When a troop of four tanks attacked, the front one was used as a decoy to attract fire and was knocked out. The next in the troop located the position of the gun and was knocked out. The third engaged the located 88 and was knocked out while the fourth was meant to creep round and attack the tiger in its rear where armour plating was weakest. Sherman high explosive shells were required to shoot at 88mm gun emplacements: armour piercing at closest range against the tank itself. Brewed-up Shermans showed punched holes clearly in their armour plating but Tiger tanks, eventually destroyed, had in excess of a dozen or more marks showing where they had received Sherman shells without any penetration. (See Photo Neil Dore's tank, page 351).

Inevitably an occasional romance sprang up when the line was held up and troops rested as best they could during reconnaissance with armour and more so when working as infantry once again in the Appennine mountains south of Bologna. A protracted leave, convalescence after being wounded and sometimes when A.W.O.L. would turn a soldier's attention to the neural urge below his belt. The war in Italy had afflicted the nation already sacrificing its luxuries for the sake of building up armaments for fascist political schemes. Food was especially short and families were bordering on starvation. Mothers fought each other over the contents of army trash bins, for the sake of their children. Whereas the army was replete in its food supplies, no less supplemented now that the U.S. Fifth Army formed part of the allied line, the civilian population was in desperate circumstances. We were ordered not to fraternise with it and a compromise arose whereby army units would hold dances in their areas to which the women of the district were invited and hopefully their daughters would come as well. The inducement was the refreshment break at the dance where meat, cheese and tuna sandwiches would be offered as well as generous portions of cake. The dance itself began as a timorous affair, taking some time for the soldiers to win over the confidence of the ladies. But no matter how well organised the music and other entertainment, the refreshment was the climax of the evening. Until they got used to it the soldiers were shocked at the brawls that then occurred. Suddenly the ladies at the dance assaulted the refreshment tables often drawing out knapsacks to hide what they could pilfer. It was a pitiful reminder to the soldiers that there were more important drives than those for sexual response. No one would have minded if the good ladies walloped down the refreshments themselves. They made no bones about it. Their bambinos were starving and they cleared all the food from the tables.

Inescapably you hid bully beef, tinned milk, canned fruit, baked beans, even bread when you walked into town or sought out your accommodation when going into Rome and Naples on furlough and of course your hosts were grateful. Mamas even encouraged their daughters or their sisters or even themselves to repay such hospitality. That was the way it was. With their men away in the army or taking refuge in the hills, people shut their eyes and men, being men, took advantage of the situation adapting their biological needs to what was on offer. There were ways of thanking a sincere young man without necessarily breaking the ten commandments or marital vows.

A young signalman I knew found his own way of being rewarded, but was made to sit on his hands while he was given oral sex. Others fell genuinely in love and met clandestinely whenever they could. The army warning was clear enough on posters up in all sensitive areas. It famously read: Vino, Venus, V.D. and the signalman pointed out that his method averted such a disaster.

Occasionally a woman would come back to the billets with a soldier and spend the afternoon alone with him. The event might only last an hour for him to be surfeited and then, men being men, and soldiers being what they are, his friends would be invited to keep the kettle boiling and she would be willing to continue because more food and luxury items would be forthcoming and so on. There was never any question as to whether the girl could manage another and another. If she didn't want it she could leave. No one would stop it and the capacity for series sex was well known from the army brothels in Egypt. Those who were not involved in such an event mainly didn't want it, were married and revolted by it or were too highly principled. It was never a matter of rape. Girls with vast experience and not necessarily prostitutes said men came into them roaring like lions and left like lambs. It is through lack of understanding that a community of men might be excused of gang rape because of interpretations of the law and its attitudes to such matters. I knew of no associations being brought up for court martial. Of course there were violent and unforgivable rapes which were quite rightly dealt with.

The countryside now became ferociously difficult and although the pace of advance was slowed there was tenacious fighting. Our 'A' Squadron moved forward to a position 2,000 yards south of Bagnoregio and inflicted severe casualties on the enemy there. Two of our best men were killed. 'B' Squadron meanwhile leapt forward to join 'A' Company in Orvieto. At Orvieto there was a tiny airport from which, two weeks later, dangerously wounded I would be flown back to the 92nd General Hospital in Naples.

Meanwhile moving north from Orvieto which was occupied on the 14th June we came under continuous fire of the retreating Germans who were now fighting a stubborn rearguard action from the rough countryside where they were in numerous diggings enabling us to be shelled and mortared continuously. German stragglers remained behind to become snipers and one needed to be almost continuously battened down in the tank merely to survive, let alone advance. Sergeant Norrey was killed and five other ranks were wounded in this resistance.

Rainy weather produced sloshy roads and banks often too weak to support Shermans. The Germans too, with their heavy Tigers were finding that they had to keep to the main roads. This meant that to outflank the enemy and to maintain the impetus of the 8th Army we would have to take to the small, twisting, 'lateral', country roads and these often gave way under the weight of our tank squadrons. Despite the urges of a screaming colonel we still had days of rest resulting from these poor conditions. With time to pause and ponder, our futures were often examined. That the going would worsen as the Germans shortened their lines and employed fanatics straight out of their homeland to defend them was inevitable. We all felt the immediate future to be precarious, some more than others. None of us wanted to go into it without making our peace with those around us. I began to develop a sense of foreboding that was not dispelled by well-wishers who would say comfortingly to me "You'll be all right. You've been bashed once. They won't get you again." I was scared of course, like everyone else but I wanted to get on with it, not to side-step it like Mousie Bell with his endless tank breakdowns. Richard Platt and I would always close ranks in times of pressure and feed each other encouragement. It would be mutually ongoing for the next sixty odd years and we would not allow differences to develop seriously between us. We both thought each other took far too many unnecessary risks and discouraged them to the point that it could be contentious.

Shorty Carneson had earned the reputation of being something of a Cassandra during his most serious binges and had recently been spouting some of his omens. I was again at the centre of them as I had been just before Alamein. Richard had told him to shut his trap but I had been forced to review my future as everyone did and the predictions of Marcia after Alamein had not gone unheeded. During a rest period laagered in a vineyard we had a long discussion about what the future offered. He dismissed Shorty's forebodings but said if I had any doubts, I should remember the scars I already carried and should withdraw now from the army with honour. We finally agreed that Shorty was a bum and his premonitions just beer talk.

Saturday 17th June '44 – Nr. Allerona

Had several alarms before pulling out for our new rendezvous. Shortly after lunch was on air (wireless net) for our troop. Finished letter home and drew some kit. Made lunch and dinner (for the crew). Travelled for almost 2 hours (by tank) over very mountainous country and passed through Allerona. Camped in another vineyard and we had a terrific storm with hail. There is also a nip in the air here. Crashed a bottle of champagne with Richard Platt before retiring.

GERMAN TACTICS IN ITALY'S DEFENCE

The German defenders never seemed to be to deterred by military setbacks. They appeared to have perfected an ongoing system of slinging a line across a new series of strong points ad nauseum. When our reconnaissance reached the precincts of Lake Trasimeno a new German line used this feature as a consolidating point with Chuisi and Sarteano extending the line westwards towards the sea. Only two weeks earlier their line had used the area of Civita Castellani as a strong point which had been probed by N.M.R. squadrons and overcome. The enemy line now ran from the southern shores of Lake Trasimeno through Chuisi westward to Sarteano, with southward bulges to include strategic features and road junctions here and there. It transpired that the Germans had been ordered to hold on there for three days at all costs.

Chuisi was cleared on 26th June. The Guards Brigade, in the meantime had orders to strike at Sarteano, west of Chuisi 'B' Squadron had been sent on the 24th to support the Brigade. The enemy put up a determined resistance with their TIGER tanks, mines and booby traps and our progress was slow. But the 8th Army advance accelerated again through the sheer momentum of its armour. Montepulciano, Statzione Chianciano, were cleared on the 30th June. Opposing our forces in the breaking of this line were the Herman Goering Division and the 1st and 4th Paratroop Divisions.

The advance became more precarious and the weather worsened. The slippery roads themselves became obstacles as the going shifted into the Chianti Hills and the areas south of Florence which Hitler had now declared an open city. New uses of mines and their booby trapping were encountered. Quite frankly this was not tank country and sooner or later the mountainous region north of Florence would force the employment of infantry almost entirely. So diminished became the

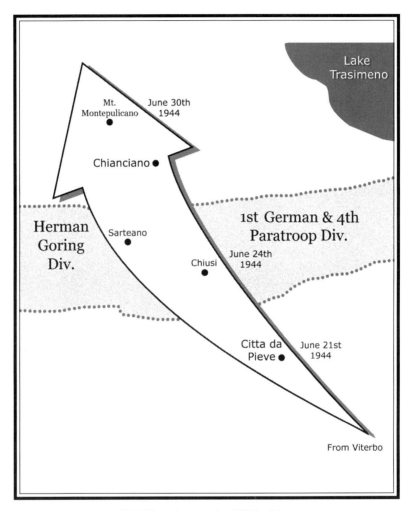

N.M.R. pierces the Hilda Line

main roads and with them the competency to support tanks, it was inevitable that squadrons of the N.M.R. had to operate in smaller units. Each of the numerous tiny roads had to be cleared, villages to be passed through and demolitions and pockets of resistance to be overcome. Tank after tank lost its tracks. In the absence of competent engineers, mined roads and villages were freed from diabolically laid, booby-trapped teller type mines in wells, trees etc. A period of rest became possible as British Guards regiments of infantry took over who were, nevertheless able to call on us for support. The temptation now was to live off the land and where it was possible to lure a chicken into a pot roast with baked potatoes and fresh vegetables. But obtaining fresh local produce bore the risk of enteritis and we all had tummy trouble which however never kept us off active duty.

Saturday, 24th June, '44 - Nr. Sarteano

Very troublesome tummy all day. Len (Clark) & Co's (tank and crew) back to rear H.Q. to change tracks. We went on a few more miles to just outside Sarteano in pouring rain. On guard during the night. Heavily shelled in the area by mortars and early in the morning by enemy tank. Caught a fowl and roasted it.

Sunday, 25th June, '44 - Nr. Sarteano

More rain during the day but kept fairly dry. Had a bath in the stream and washed some clothes. Wrote in the morning and began (book) "Enter Three Witches" and rain cleared today.

Howard Foss, who played cricket for Natal (now Kwazulu) became my crew commander which was a relief after Corporal Bell. Foss was one of the sweetest guys you could meet under such harsh circumstances and joyfully played big brother to me.

Fate struck both of us down individually in the same July week of 1944 with death-dealing intensity that killed him, but allowed me to survive.

The same mortar that killed Howard Foss badly injured Dream Sanders who was apparently in discussion with Howard when the mortar landed next to them. This occurred on the 27th June and Howard died on the 28th June.

Such frequent events in the lives of crews in our squadrons were bound to raise, on every disastrous encounter with the German 88mm guns the question of our individual and collective survival.

Some intellectual in the regiment had read bits out of the Secret Doctrine, a work by a Russian savant Madame Blavatsky, and had introduced us to the word 'karma' in the place of 'fate'. Others recalling experiences in Muslim Somaliland and Egypt were using the word 'kismet'.* As for Christianity, interest in its vagaries like resurrection, transubstantiation and its non-support of metempsychosis had been undermined as the war lengthened and the chances of survival had lessened. The ghastly death of the regimental padre Napoleon Wheeler ** who had promised us the reward of eternal life at many services and then been blown to bits at El Alamein had not furthered Christianity's cause to my mind. Death was a horrid reality all around us daily, and we demanded justice from God, even if survival could not be guaranteed. Justice, a law of compensation for good services rendered, seemed to be embodied in karma and we liked to believe it and that our decimation had some kind of logic in it.

We had become guruless, and Somerset Maugham's 'Razor's Edge' read avidly by everyone in the squadron had posited that if God was all-good and all-powerful he would stop the war, and if he wouldn't or couldn't, then he was not all-good and not all-powerful.

Many of us had become disenchanted with religion and were turning our eyes increasingly to what seemed our only hope, the Red Army and its Joseph Stalin to end the war. Bushy had been even more disillusioned and upon my questioning he expressed his atheism with…

"If there was a God, he wouldn't have permitted war in the first place.…"

…and his taunts were ever stronger with … "Don't forget the communists are taught that religion is the opiate of the masses and they are damned successful at the moment."

---

* The Will of Allah (Islam) Fate or Destiny.
** Napoleon Wheeler had not long survived the loss of both legs in a shell burst. He was a minister at St. Paul's Cathedral in Durban, where I had prayed before the war

When a shell aimed at our Sherman, Bechan (the rhino*) burst close by, the crew was outside the tank and a piece of shrapnel penetrated our crew commander's skull and spilled out part of Howard's brain. I had read with awe, while at high school, the classic 'Last of the Mohicans' and was of course, now reminded of its horrifying detail. Almost with unconcern Howard went back for treatment unaware that his head wound was lethal under such conditions, even though he had eventually reached an advanced casualty station where there was first aid and morphia.

He had always held the comforting belief that the 'Inkos pezulu**' was guarding us all from harm, whereas, I had argued with him that 'Nkulunkulu'^ was a more august word for God, and especially because I had read that name in John Buchan's Prester John, one of our set books at D.H.S and had jokingly suggested I was more likely therefore, with such deference to survive the war than he.

Howard Foss, a family figure himself in civilian life was kind and fatherly to the youngsters in his crews. Often at expenditure of his own precious time and resources he would encourage you to take a break, have some fun when occasions would permit and throw himself in as first reserve when emergencies imposed on you were fatiguing, stressful or demeaning. Even if he could not himself join in extra-mural adventures he would love to sit you down and hear about them. Always encouraging I remember him as an example of cricketing literature:

> And his captain's hand
> on his shoulder smote
> "Play up, play up and play the game"

Monday, 26th June '44 - Sarteano

Had a very easy day. Spot more rain. Were shelled very heavily by Tiger tanks and mortars. Wrote home and read.

Tuesday, 27th June '44

Arose fairly early and were then called out on a sticky job delivering a left hook up to Chianciano. Climbed up out of

---

* *Zulu for rhinoceros – Ubkejane*
** Zulu endearing name for 'my father above'.
^ Zulu for 'God'…the ancestral spirit for all mankind.

Sarteano and made a surprise thrust across almost impassable country and got through to La Foce and began operations. Went down a road to Chianciano and were mortared as we by-passed a tremendous demolition. Bashed a house said to be an O.P (observation post) with our 75mm and then bumped a Tiger with two self-propelled (tracks) guns. Withdrew safely with mortars raining down in a narrow defile. Got to bed at midnight. Dream Sanders and Howard Foss badly wounded by mortars.

Wednesday, 28th June '44 - Chianciano

Went up the road again to Chianciano in an endeavour to locate Tiger tank and self-propelled guns. Had no luck - or all the luck and stayed under shade and cover all day. Located a house - procuring cooking utensils, an umbrella and some pure linen sheets. Rained quite a bit. Slept and read (in the tank). Howard Foss died today!!!

I had been taken over to Mousey Bell's tank when Howard was wounded because with so many casualties those equipped in specialised work (mine was with wireless communication) we were at a premium. In Howard I had lost a father figure who was always greatly supportive of his crew.

Thursday, 29th June '44 - Montecielo

Went out on a mild job through Piensa to take the town of Montecielo which our troop did without mishap. Roads heavily mined and booby-trapped. Got pickled on gifts of wine and fortunately returned to harbour safely. Gave some of our tank's first aid equipment to an Ito woman with pelvic fracture (caused) by German demolition. Len & Co., back again during the day. Pleased to see them. Drew rations and to bed late.

Friday 30th June '44 - Piensa

Arose early and started on our sticky task. Have all four tanks now in the troop and we led the advance past Piensa. Advanced well but were delayed by demolitions, mines etc. Inhabitants gave us helpful information and some wine. Progressed well. Were at one stage at least five kilos ahead of the rest of the division.

Struck some heavy opposition in the afternoon. We pelted a wood and then Spandaus and mortars opened up the other side of a demolition – got out safely bringing our infantry with us and wounded Guardsmen. Harboured some miles back. Personally pinpointed a battery of guns. Happy John in a tank which went up on a mine and brewed up and he and one other wounded.. (Happy John, was Captain John Reynard, a greatly loved figure who survived the war but was never decorated for his many acts of valour).

Chapter XXV

With the death of Howard Foss I now drew closer to another father figure, sergeant of our troop Ken Frank, elder brother of Geoffrey Frank killed at Gazala, cousin of Marcus Frank killed at Alamein, all from the same Frank family and in the same regiment. Ken had formed a close companionship with John Jeffries who was more my age and with Len Clark we played a foursome at Contract Bridge whenever our appalling circumstances would allow it. Ken had by then overcome the natural psychological barriers that separate elder brothers from their younger brother's friends. He now remembered hearing Geoffrey sing some of the songs he and I had learned at Dora Jackson's singing classes like "Hark, Hark the Lark", "Ye Banks & Braes" and "Early One Morning".

And as we died, singly or together it was like being in a dark room with no windows and many doors. The doors closed one after another, sometimes silently, sometimes with a loud clang depending how this guy or that left you. Sometimes you sat alone for a long time despairingly in this room, the darkest, spare room of the mind. When Geoffrey Frank's door closed I thought I once again heard his shrill voice singing Danny Boy at Dora Jackson's before tea…

"And I am dead.

As dead I well may be"

…always a trigger point for the preps. high school class of 1934 as it had been when I met Geoffrey's father on home leave in '43 and wept a little with him as I had with Percy Baker, Dennis' father too.

Ken Frank and I also had a bond through Richard Platt who we both thought of as a hero figure but was no card player. Ken was popular because he would not suck up for the promotion which the regiment was anxious to give him and certainly not if it was at the price of needlessly endangering men under his command. Colonel Jenkins could have learnt a lot from him in this respect. Playing bridge with Ken and Jeffrey arose as a matter of convenience because usually the sergeant of the troop was nearby whether on active days in close contact with the enemy or on rest days when the squadron was at rest but always on call near the front line. It was also becoming, for me, a welcome break from the brooding presence of the crew commander Bell, who needed the solace of the turret for his soul-searching as much as I did. To have had him in the bridge party as a fourth, whoever he partnered, for me would have been intolerable.

Saturday, 1st July '44 - Rest Break.

Had much needed day of rest. Slept until 6a.m. Played bridge with Len (Clark), Ken (Frank) and John (Jeffries) Had some baksheesh white wine and the four of us played an erratic game! Made lunch and chatted in the afternoon. Made evening meal and bathed and washed clothes at the well of a nearby villa.

Sunday, 2nd July '44 - S.E. of Siena

Pulled out at 5.30a.m. on a very sticky job. Advanced some ten miles and then bumped some heavy opposition from Tigers and self-propelled guns, infantry, mortars and anti-tank guns. Our troop tried to outflank (them) but was unable to. One of our squadron tanks was knocked out, inmates unhurt…pulled into a wood to observe but were heavily shelled most of the day. Sat with Len in his tank (Honey). Three more wounded. Chatted while the 'stonk' went on. Bill Janks escaped near miss in ambulance not 40 yards from us. Put on insane job* after sunset but were so heavily shelled we had to pull out of it. Bully & Co., in a Sherman over the bank. 3 wounded.

Monday, 3rd July '44 - En route to Siena

Drew rations and canteen stuff then bathed before starting operations. Advanced about 10 kilos. Stooged in reserve of (troop) four who were held up by demolitions on the road most

---

*The pullout from the "insane" job was certainly because of Ken Frank's objection to it.

of the day. Dug up (wayside) potatoes and made chips for dinner. Harboured in twilight and were in bed by eleven and slept well.

Tuesday, 4th July '44 - En route to Siena

Awoke at a respectable hour. The whole squadron (4 troops = 16 tanks) moved up towards Siena. A terrific hail storm came down the size of pigeon eggs. Roads turned white with it. Rain poured in through the turret and shorted the wireless set [turret kept open for observing enemy, which was at close quarters]. Had to go on a diversion to make our objective. Had a good meal, cleaned the guns and went to bed. Awoke to do a guard and make coffee for myself and Len Clark who followed me (on guard).

JULY IN ITALY

July 1944 began a month of the most ferocious fighting. The Supreme Commander of the Armies in Italy, General Alexander sent this message out to our troops in Italy:

"The eyes of the world and the hopes of all at home are upon us – we shall not disappoint them…"

And on the 3rd of July our Corps Commander:

"In the last two months, 13 Corps has not only broken through the fortress position of Cassino, but has advanced some 250 miles, inflicting great losses on the enemy…"

It soon became evident that our tactics had to be changed profoundly and that infantry were required to work very closely with our reconnaissance squadrons. The cause of this was that the foliage on the sides of the roads during an advance gave the enemy excellent cover. They deployed so-called 'suicide squads' armed with anti-tank guns.

AMBUSH

July 5th dawned brightly enough and cheering crowds on the roadside added to the proceedings. Then we hit a large demolition North-east of Siena whose red-tiled rooftops I first caught a glimpse of. A

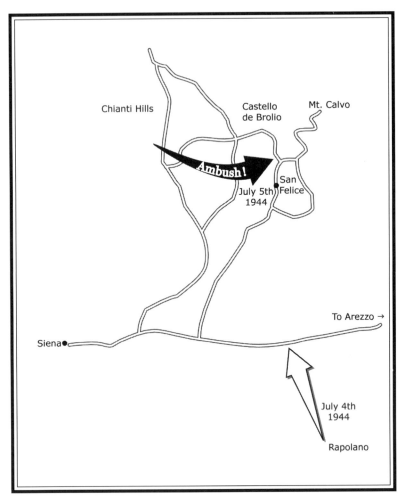

Ambush and Disaster at San Felice

demolition was always bad news because the Germans would have it marked on their maps. Usually they left someone behind to wireless their artillery the moment Allied reconnaissance units reached the demolition. Today was true to form and the shells came down and the next procedure was ordered. This was to take an alternative route, usually on a lesser by-way. By midday a heavy mist had enshrouded the Chianti Hills around us. Our road climbed one of these hills towards a village marked down on the map as San Felice. It was more of a hamlet with mud brick houses built into a field of long dry, yellowing grass. With mist it became dangerous and infantry came up to clear it. We had to shell some distant houses and eventually manouvered ourselves into the main street.

Orders came through to speed things up but San Felice, on discovery, had a main thoroughfare too narrow for the Shermans. Accordingly, we had to force the tanks through the narrowings and this meant taking the front of the houses with us, by which time the tiny outraged population was in no mood to co-operate. Beyond the village was a more prominent dirt road, which meant trouble. The road itself hugged the steep hillside as it descended with a nasty drop at its edges. The way ahead was fringed with trees and scrub, boulders and a gully between road and mountainside. Tank wise it was a nasty piece of work with the odds of an 88mm gun somewhere on its course a good two-to-one on. Lieutenant Bunny Evans had viewed conditions with some alarm and sought for a companion to 'walk the plank' with him and looked at Mousie Bell who became unresponsive.

Taking out a Sherman's wireless operator gunner was virtually to render the tank incommunicado. However there were no other volunteers to go ahead of the tanks with Bunny and so I was dogs-body, but the mist had now evaporated and we would have infantry to help. They, the infantry, were going to move ahead under cover of the trees and brush. Accordingly, a young Afrikaner signalman was assigned to me. He gave me a handheld microphone of a 38 set and showed me how to work it and stuck it in an open pocket in my khaki shirt. I can only recall his surname, which was 'Van Niekerk.'

The arrangement was that he would call me regularly and I could call him back anytime we struck trouble necessitating infantry.

It was a suicide mission and Van Niekerk knew it. But he had come from a family that had fought the British to a standstill somewhere in the Transvaal in the Boer War and I knew he would be reliable.

We set off in slow and wary procession down the road into Chianti country, a no-man's-land of retreating Germans now defending the fatherland, four tanks hugging a dirt road on a precipitous mountainside anticipating ambush. The most disconcerting factor, I thought, was that there was no room to turn a tank anywhere. A brewed-up rear tank would cut off the rest of the troop. Reversing on the road with the driver steering blind, the crew commander directing the gun, a precipice yawning on one flank and a gully on the other was not a good scenario for tank men.

One of the most important factors of living out a sustained period of tank warfare was that of relationships with who was in your own tank crew, in your troop and then who was in your squadron. Crews changed from time to time for both predictable reasons and unpredictable. Troop commanders in the N.M.R. were officers in about one in four instances. The same ratio functioned in regard to sergeants. The remaining 50% were usually corporals suddenly promoted from anywhere in the regiment when there had been tanks knocked out. Another factor that varied tank crews was the standards maintained in wireless operating. The heart and soul of a tank reconnaissance unit was the information it was able to send back. Jules Ryder had been in the decidedly difficult position of the Squadron Leader's operator with perhaps two score or more tanks netted into his wireless set at the beginning of a day's operations. He counted on one or two reliable operators in each troop to keep the squadron working especially so when tanks in the squadron were engaged by the enemy and intercom between tanks and between tank crews had to function additionally. Squadron wireless co-ordinators like Jules Ryder and Major Meeser, therefore, did not like to have poor wireless operators in troops of tanks on selected tasks and shunted operators around according to their efficiency.

It was a great help to be located in a troop and tank crew you knew well or who were perhaps close friends and even confidants. The occupants of our tent in Katatbah, being old friends tried and tested, made welcome crew members. For various reasons I had been committed to a tank which had no Katatbah components of old and most unpleasantly of all the crew commander was Corporal Bell, someone with whom I had difficulties in the past, a man filled with vagaries, notions and fears.

We two did not take to each other from the start. His appearance was weird, six-foot-two and a half, thin, angular with tendencies to flush, not so much from embarrassment as from causes unknown. He did not like me; he did not like my bridge playing. I suppose he did not like the general atmosphere of intellectuality that I tried to disseminate in my youthful immaturity, a red rag to his own. He would pounce whenever he could on whatever bridge call I made. He would be scurrilous in his descriptions of famous school rugby matches between Glenwood and Durban High. But I put up with him and he put up with me. He reckoned he was a student of architecture and when we had reached Mersa Matruh there were architectural problems galore. He had tried to build bombproof dugouts in sand dunes. He assumed superior architectural knowledge as to how to do this. He never really succeeded. The rest of us had to be content with very crude trenchlets made up of sandbags pulled together. It was as if there was karma existing between us. I could do nothing right in his eyes and it was mutual. As fate would have it we were thrown together again when the regiment became converted to tanks in 1944. Mousie Bell and I ended up in the same tank group. By then he had become the Tank Commander and I was wireless operator/gunner. The mutual hostility never really dissipated in spite of the necessity to rely on each other. The remainder of the crew were good companions and shared the work. We all slept together under one canvas through the worst fighting before and beyond Monte Cassino. I made it a point to be scrupulously fair in my dealings with him. But there was always a faint hostility present. My misgivings with regard to Mousie Bell continued on the road from Rome, northwards, two days before D-Day, The tank threw a track on a difficult piece of road and Bell had it driven into a field nearby where repairs could be made. I myself was furious at the delay in reaching our regiment, which was by now heavily engaged against the retreating German tanks. I began to notice that every possibility of delaying the repair of the tank seemed to be engineered by our crew commander.

It seemed that by one means after another he would impede the progress we were struggling to make returning to our troop in the Line. Added to this was the background of the D-Day landings in Normandy. The atmosphere everywhere was electrifying.

News began to filter through of many casualties, many friends being lost, many tanks burnt out. When I persistently urged Bell to try various methods to obtain the necessary spare parts he turned to me and said, "What's the matter with you? Do you want to get yourself killed?". I suddenly began to smell the scent of cowardice. It wasn't very pleasant to have it among your own crew. Eventually, we reached the front and again for several weeks were engaged in tank warfare of vicious intensity.

On July 5th 1944, as a reconnaissance group we were in close contact with Germans retreating down side roads. It was the day of my own grievous calamity. Our troop of four tanks was creeping down a road along a very steep mountainside and we knew that somewhere ahead a German 88mm would be hiding waiting for us to reach a position, which the enemy would, in retreat, have noted down accurately in terms of its range. To make our survival more likely, I had volunteered to accompany the troop officer, Lieutenant Bunny Evans walking ahead of the tanks to draw fire. It was clearly understood in the regiment, an unwritten regimental law, that whilst one member of the tank crew was outside the tank, the hatches in the turret would never be closed. This would allow anyone trapped outside by gunfire to take cover in his own tank. The officer and myself both outside our tanks reached a position, which was obviously in range of the enemy, and shells began to land all around it. We were creeping forward with our tanks about thirty yards behind us. We reached a point where the Germans had the range accurately. Their machine guns began to rattle and bullets snaked into the rocky hillside next to us. The officer shouted to me to get into my tank and jumped into his Honey, which was the closest. I started to run for the next tank, my one, a Sherman and the German machine gun followed me tearing up the dirt road. Hard smacks on my right leg told me I had been hit. Reaching the Sherman I struggled up on to its left side. At that very moment, three feet away, a high explosive shell hit the rations box on the rear of the turret and it splayed open. I took the blast and shrapnel of the shell in the upper half of my body. I reached for the turret opening and to my horror found the hatch down, closed. I pounded on the closed hatch and became aware that there was a large hole in my chest that was pouring blood and a ghastly sucking noise as air rushed directly into its cavity. Machine gun fire and mortars lambasted the turret. With my remaining strength I kept pounding the top of the hatch. Bell had done the unforgivable. His cowardice had caught up with me. In fear of his life and of shells dropping on the troop and against the strictest regimental rules he had battened down with me outside on the superstructure unprotected. By then the tanks were reversing out of the ambush and the hatch opened. Whether he had heard my despairing poundings or was opening to guide driver Jack Ayles' reversing I never knew. He withdrew into the turret interior and with my last fragments of consciousness I was able to pull myself into the turret gangway and fall down on to the floor of the tank.

The whole troop was being raked by shell fire which was terrifying enough for our own tank crew, but my sudden appearance, ashen and bloodied, gasping for air through a gaping wound in the chest and a rattling noise stemming from my windpipe scared the living daylights out of them. Added to this was the phenomenon of the rotating turret as the tank began to back out of the ambush and my shocking personification of Armageddon framed on-and-off in the window of the rotating turret grid. The crew told me later that I lay there with eyes closed speaking incoherently to them. That was not quite my experience. Lying there, I felt this strange force take me over and still enabled me to see with eyes shut. I was fascinated by the eyes of each of the crew, which were goggling almost out of their sockets at me as the turret rotated. Despite the pain, I felt an overwhelming compassion for them, for their fear of death. Yet never once did I believe I was about to die.

It was a long, slow haul backing the tanks out. Fear replaced the compassion. Now I was afraid of the hurt that would come to me pulling me out of the turret for transport down the line. So far forward, there were no ambulances and a Dingo armoured car had been wirelessed for. It reached me at the top of the hill and I was wedged in on its rear deck above the engine. Len Clark insisted on accompanying me. By that time I had completely lost consciousness.

It must have been a couple of hours of driving at speed before the fresh evening air suddenly revived me. My head was on Len's lap. He was distressed but I comforted him by insisting "I'm going to survive this Len," and he answered "And may God help you Doug." I had vague recollections of passing through a casualty clearing station, bandaging, injections and asking for the bottle.

It was not till much later I learnt that our infantry had closed in on the enemy attacking us. Alas, Van Niekerk had been killed in the action. Because he was not in the N.M.R. I was unable to find his home address or I would have written his parents as soon as I was capable.

The casualty station had stuck a D.I.L. label on me and rushed me to a large casualty unit vacated by a German ambulance corps a few days earlier. Arriving very late at night I was shocked at the shambles that prevailed. Germans were usually very humane when evacuating casualty and hospital units leaving them more or less intact. The chaos that existed here now not only indicated the rapidity of our advance, but also our heavy casualties. The building, which I visited in later years was four floors and very old. The ground floor and a basement were almost packed to the ceiling with wounded. They were in stretchers on the concrete floor; all beds were taken and there was barely room for orderlies, doctors and nurses to reach every patient. The two top floors acted as staff quarters and kitchens. There was no room at the inn for me and I had to be taken down to the basement which was dimly lit and gave the appearance of being an old church crypt.

What I was seeing was only part of the problem. There was a small airstrip only minutes away and a plane from Naples came to take walking wounded, once every morning, back to the large British General Hospitals based in Naples itself. The majority of patients here, again mainly Tommies, were too ill to walk to the plane or were having emergency surgery. There was, for all the background disinfectants, the telltale stench of battle still there, the anxious faces, faces in coma or anaesthesia; nurses jogging around with trays of bandages and orderlies with their bedpans. It was the R.A.M.C. at its best in conditions at their worst. I had long lost my beret and the splinters of the shell that had peppered my scalp made me appear as if someone had broken a bottle over my head, and tiny outpourings of blood leaked downwards in thin lines making me appear half-crazed. My stretcher was jammed in between two beds waiting to be found a place somewhere. In the end there was only space in the crypt. My left eye had a splinter in the surface and it made movement of the eyeball difficult and painful, but through it all I could see an army surgeon working his way through a line of new casualties towards me. At a distance he seemed vaguely familiar.

He would check over each casualty, refer to their medical notes and add his own instructions to them and then struggle to the next soldier.

As the surgeon got closer I recognised whom it was. It was 'Hoddy', Captain Hodson from the 101st and 92nd General Hospitals in Egypt, whose team had sewn my back up after Alamein! Hoddy was shocked at my appearance but recognised me immediately with "You again". He glanced at my notes and said, "I told you to go home. Now look at what you have done." Hodson asked a few questions and said "You had that big scar on your back. Did it hold?" The orderly had sat me up for him and Hoddy drew me gently forward and ran his fingers down the centre of the scar on my right scapula, muttering "Excellent! We thought it might break down." He took up the notes, such as they were and he wrote on them, saying to me comfortingly "When you get to Naples they'll know what to do. You'll be alright." Then he squeezed my shoulder and moved on. In all that chaos of hundreds of casualties stretched across the whole peninsula so late at night, I had miraculously encountered the very one military surgeon who knew my history, having tended me two years previously amongst the masses of casualties pouring into the hospital based at the Suez Canal after Alamein.

Another injection put me to sleep again.

About 3a.m. I heard two loud crashes which seemed to me, lying in the darkened crypt half awake, to sound like mortars exploding on the roof. A moment later, it was as if a powerful electric shock had entered me through the crown of my head, which was now bandaged anyway. A torrent of energy began to pour through me. It was as if I was wedged between two great electrodes, one applied to the vertex of my skull and the second to the soles of my feet, and their current traveled through me. It was more like a force that lit me up similar to a luminous bulb and persisted for two to three minutes. It did not frighten me; far from it, because the luminescence was accompanied by exhilaration. I felt the exhaustion driven from me and a mounting of the force led on to an ecstasy I had never known before.

The phenomenon now settled into a sensation of fire, a subjective fire certainly, but incandescent nevertheless...a fire that warmed, energised and refreshed me. And then it left me and the darkness of the crypt closed in. The occurrence was not at that point revelatory and at the time I read nothing into it.

Almost immediately a clamour then arose at the main entrance to the ward and orderlies hastened in with lamps shouting urgently "Walking wounded! The plane is here to take walking wounded! Walking wounded only."

Suddenly I remembered something Dr. Hodson had said to his medical orderly, "You must get him back to the 92nd as quickly as possible." I remembered the two bullet wounds in my legs were flesh wounds and I could probably walk. The energy phenomenon of fire passing through me had restored my vigour and I decided the whole episode had been preparing me to get to Naples post haste. I sat up. The orderlies had just bypassed me. I swung my legs out of the stretcher, slid out of it and moved down the narrow corridors between the beds to the door of the ward where other orderlies had assembled to aid the walking wounded out of the casualty station to the waiting ambulance.

I staggered up to the ward exit dragging some of the bandages that had become loosened behind me and covered my D.I.L. label. Reaching the steep steps into the courtyard an orderly stepped forward to help me.

Wednesday, 5th July '44 – San Felice

Netted in and pulled out at eight on operations. Made excellent progress and passed through towns where wine and flowers and eggs were showered on us. Then we struck a bit of trouble. Jerry began shelling the demolition but we were OK until someone let him know where we were. We suspected some houses as 'O pips' and plastered them. Then we got the order to advance. I volunteered to act as link on the 38 set (walkie-talkie) with the infantry. The 88mm shells came down and mowed us. One hit the tank just as I was climbing it. Didn't damage the tank but I'm in a mess. After a nightmare of a ride the guys got me back to a C.C.S. Len with me all the way. Was dosed up with morphia and operated on before midnight.

A further criticism of Corporal Bell was that during the action while I was out of the tank he had not placed the co-driver in the wireless operator loader's vacated position which meant that his tank could not use its 75mm gun. Thus practically half the firepower of the troop had been lost for most of the period of our ambush. This alone would have been an offence warranting a court marshall. In fact no action was taken and a very bad example had been set by Bell's cowardly action.

Chapter XXVI

Because of heavy sedation and pain-killers the following diary notations, being very sketchy and interspersed with varying periods of sleep, breathlessness and exhaustion have bracketed areas where I have added comments to keep events coherent: –

Friday, July 7th '44 – Orvieto, 3:00am

Left Orvieto by ambulance for the airport and had a gruelling journey [through a small battered town in which there were demolitions and diversions.]

Felt very ill with breathing and so on [I had hardly had time to take stock of myself but was aware that the sucking noise through the hole in my right chest had stopped, probably because of the dressing. The rib cage on the right was not moving at all but thankfully my left lung seemed to be inflating normally, despite several tears in the muscle overlying the heart.] Air trip very uneventful. [We had taken off just as daylight was breaking and from a tiny airstrip. The plane itself was only able to hold about twenty sitting patients. I was sorry that the blood I was coughing up scared them. No one had parachutes and that may have been a factor. The orderlies had an oxygen cylinder and would have given me a mask but the altitude didn't seem to warrant it.] Comfortably settled in the old 92nd [General Hospital] again. Can't think about much except sleep these days [I slipped into and out of consciousness. Nurses just came and went.] Slept well. [I was aware of increasing restriction to my breathing. The nurses noted it too and said I was bleeding into my right chest and they would have to take the blood out with a syringe.]

Saturday, 8th July – Naples

Doctor in to see me. [He read my medical notes and seemed to follow them when examining me and said he knew Hoddy, the surgeon who had tended me after Alamein and had seen me the night of the 5th July when I was admitted into the crypt at Orvieto.] Will rest for a couple of days before they sew. Am making good headway.

[The main reason for feeling much better was because a nurse had drawn 800cc of blood from my right lung cavity and this had relieved my breathing. The puncture between the ribs added another lesion to the long list.] Still in a lot of pain. [Which served me right for refusing the bedpan.] Wrote home and read a little. Slept mostly. Ward full of Tommies [guardsmen mainly who we had been supporting up in the line on reconnaissance. I found them a tonic for morale]…decent chap in the bed next to me [and not too sick to ogle the Italian woman cleaner who came on duty].

Later at 92nd

Daily events began to change. There were realignments of intent and my aspirations were reborn. Every day brought news back from the regiment either through casualties from our squadrons closely engaged with the fleeing enemy, by mail from comrades in the rapidly advancing line and from the B.B.C. In addition many guys on leave to Naples or Rome visited. The ward sisters became frosty as I "turned the ward into a Charing Cross station!" It was a repeat performance of November '42 after Alamein. I was not yet robust but getting fitter by the day. The terrible carnage of tank warfare in close country began to nibble at my conscience. This was beginning to show up in nightmares as I struggled to reach stricken comrades, and sometimes relatives caught up in the miseries and dramas of the fifth year of the war.

ITALIAN WOUNDS

My left arm hurt, often with the slightest movement and sometimes through the night when held, because of the chest wounds, in a cramped position. It was plain that I had lost most of the deltoid and triceps muscles because the guy in the next bed watching at dressing time said he could hide his fist in it. But I was determined not to be 'winged', a Tommy expression for someone rendered armless, and made every effort to get it properly managed too instead of the hole in the chest, fast closing, stealing all the limelight. I could at first using the grasp of my right hand, between forefinger and thumb almost encircle the site but for one inch, then but for two until suturing pulled the whole thing together and out of danger.

Sunday 9th July '44 – 92nd General

Didn't sleep too well last night – am refusing drugs [The need to send letters home to anxious friends and relatives required a clear head and in any case the boy in the next bed was stealing marches on me in relation to the Italian girl.] Read THIRTY-NINE STEPS, very weak I thought. Wrote to Len [Clark]. Am eating well. Got Maria [the cleaner] to buy me 100 lira of fruit. Will be sewn tomorrow. [Two main suturings would have to be done. Most of the triceps muscle on the back of the left upper arm had been removed by shrapnel and the large penetrating wound of the chest had cut across the pectoral muscles leaving a gaping deep wound through which you could see the layers of yellow fat and muscle down to the bone.] Eyes inspected and a minute shell splinter to be removed. Very much cooler today. [A very sweet English nurse sponged me down.]

Monday, 10th July – 92nd General

Skipped breakfast and went to the theatre early. Had a chat to the surgeon who thinks I have had enough. [He was part of the team who had sewn my back and head up after Alamein. Hoddy had been in the team too and he read Hoddy's note.] No trouble at all. Had chest sewn and [bits of] shrapnel taken out of head [chest] and eye. Woke early in afternoon and had some lunch. Read and slept. Had a bad night. [The Germans were still bombing Naples then and I think this was one of those nights. I noted that the left arm had not been sewn yet.]

Tuesday, 11th July – 92nd General

Wrote to Des during a very monotonous day. [My brother in the Royal Navy.] Food is very good. In fact everything is fine but I can't stick being in bed. [I began to take further stock of myself. Two bullet holes in my right calf had not yet been investigated and a nurse probed them for foreign objects in vain and then dressed them. It was then I heard from her that I was getting a new wonder drug called 'Penicillin'.] Started reading FLAMINGO. Feeling anxious about Len [and the other guys up north in the line.] Visit from Ted Borchard's brother. Received beer…½ pint per man. Had air raid – no bombs near here, but some gunfire. [The hospital was high on the hill overlooking the Bay of Naples. The Nazi planes were probably after the ships in the harbour.]

Wednesday 12th July – 92nd General

Had a bad night and dreamt about Des and Len and Mum. Lot of pain from my ribs. [A lump and redness had appeared in the ribs below my right scapula and having to lie on my back aggravated matters.] Have arguments with the Tommies about the army. [The topic was mainly about poor pay and the failure of British armour to match the Germans in the desert.]

Are very interested in South Africa [and I used to send them into fits of laughter about Zulu practices.] Wrote airographs to England [and the Tommies wrote kisses on them for my Aunt Lil who lived in Finchley near Tally Ho Corner which some knew.]

Thursday, 13th July – 92nd General

Felt very well during the day having had a fair night's sleep. Visit from same old S. African nurse that came [to see me] at the 92nd in November 1942. She considered Natal men to have airs and graces. [She took me downstairs and outside where the frigidaires housed my penicillin and showed me what it was all about. She said only three of us in the whole hospital were getting it. It was then that I realised specifically what Dr. Hoddy meant when he had written something on my medical notes in the crypt at Orvieto and had smiled at me saying, "No you'll be alright!"] Wrote a longish letter home after dinner. A lot of South Africans from here going to Bari [where there was a South African Hospital.]

<u>Friday 14th July – 92nd General</u>

Slightly hotter today. Had all the bandages off. Doctor satisfied. More sewing, aspirating (blood taken out of right lung cavity) and shrapnel removing to be done. [It turned out that the piece of shrapnel that had penetrated the chest had gone right through me and wedged itself between the ribs in my back below the scapula. It had caused the severe back pain that kept me awake at night.] Read a fair amount of FLAMINGO which is a queer book. Grub a bit short. Had a nice hot bath [Maria ran it for me and helped me in and out and the boy in the bed next door got hot under the collar] and slept well.

<u>Saturday 15th July – 92nd General</u>

Waited for the knife all day. Went without lunch and tea and was famished. Down to theatre at 6pm. Came to shouting and in a filthy temper. I put it down to the fact they gave ether late in the operation after an injection first. Ether makes me mad. Felt very sore and slept fitfully.

<u>Sunday, 16th July – 92nd General</u>

Felt lousy all-day and very short-winded. In addition have picked up a cough. Received first letter from S.L. (Springbok Legion) which is a good sign. Wish I could get some kit. [My own khaki clothing had all been cut off me when I was wounded. I was itching to have fresh kit so that I could walk out in the street. The hot wards and flies were killing me.] Slept most of the day. Flies very bad. Wrote to S.L.

PRIVATE ELLIS

The 92nd British Hospital was like any other in W.W.II., subject to crowding when there were big pushes up at the front. Then when alarm signals would go, nursing staff would rush around preparing beds and linen for sudden arrivals. Casualties in this Naples hospital sometimes came by bumpy plane journeys from tiny airstrips close to casualty stations, a few miles behind the rapidly advancing front. These were the walking wounded; anyone capable of getting up from his bed or stretcher and walking to the troop carrier that bore them to the waiting plane usually in the very early morning for rapid transport to Naples and the 92nd. They were strictly war casualties, sometimes sailors from convoys trying unsuccessfully to reach Malta, or from other sinkings off the coast of Greece, Crete or Dalmatia. Some came in long or short convoys of ambulances especially when there were infantry attacks at bastions and bridges like Monte Cassino and the Rapido River.

Casualties were often bloodied and exhausted and immediately checked out for urgent surgery and X-ray. These, sometimes macabre incursions could last a few hours or even days, more especially, if a hospital ship was disgorging wounded from some battle front. There was occasional hysteria among young nurses freshly out from England or only semi-trained. Ambulance men would bring in the seriously or dangerously ill; theirs' were the acts of unspectacular heroism which only the critically wounded would be aware of, gentleness and devotion to their patients, without panic amidst appalling chaos and tragedy.

It was during a lull between such turbulent episodes that I first became aware of some loud, defiant and despairing shouts from a patient several beds away. The patient was Ellis, a guardsman if I remember rightly, with most of his left shoulder and some ribs blown away, leaving a hole that you could put your fist into. He had survived a long time, and you could look into the pleural cavity where several lobes of the lung had collapsed and the rest bubbled and frothed as he breathed. Ellis was a long time dying having been admitted to the 92nd several weeks before me. He had become not just terminal, but had assumed the behaviour one associates with the chronicity of a disease.

Ellis swore at nurses when they got him ready for dressing his wound, was tickled pink when the young ones showed resentment at his language and hee-hawed with laughter when his private parts were laundered or if he farted with protracted exuberance when mobile patients, encouraged to assist in the management of such dangerously ill or incapacitated sick, handled him. Being eventually mobile myself and Ellis still defying death, I approached him offering to write letters for him home. He told me none too politely to fuck off. I persisted and instead asked him if I could tell him stories about savage, historical places like Zululand. He relented and I managed to get a smile, even a question or two out of him when he was lucid. Later I was told he had chortled and ragged the staff-nurse when I absconded from the hospital and went back to the front in bandages and he had missed my visits to his bedside.

HODDY IN NAPLES

Around this time I had a surprise visit from Hoddy. Passing through on his way to another battle zone he stopped at my bed and examined me. He was pleased with my general condition but felt more X-rays were required. We talked rugby and about which sports might modestly be possible for me when I recovered. "You should be invalided back to South Africa but such matters are never in our hands here", Hoddy said. He had almost lovingly examined the huge scar over my right scapula which his team had so competently put together in Nov. '42. He concluded it now would not break down. Hoddy ran his fingers over the spines of the half-dozen odd books I had borrowed and read from the library. We agreed we would meet after the war, perhaps in South Africa as he intended to buy a small yacht and I of course was already a keen sailor. He impressed me greatly and I suppose it was then that the first urges to become a doctor myself were planted. But he warned me "You are not recovered yet. Be patient and let nature do her work."

SURGERY AGAIN

The operating theatres were busy, sometimes night and day. New pieces of shrapnel had been located in my neck, chest and ribs and a piece in the abdomen which meant further surgery. I cursed it because it meant further set backs to full recovery.

Friday, 28th July '44 – 92nd General

Awaited the knife all day but the theatre was too busy and its happening tomorrow. Finished [reading] MY SISTER EILEEN. Went down to the library and I'm going to give Thackeray a workout. Wrote to Pooch, [Marais.] Kay and Margaret, 26 pages in all. Am browned off with the hospital.

CHAPTER XXVII

Saturday, 29th July – 92nd General

Had cup of tea for breakfast. [Lay in the corridor and] watched the girls [theatre nurses] go by until they fetched me for the theatre. Came-to about 4pm. [The extended time was because they were searching for the many shrapnel pieces and having to decide which to take out and which (those near the heart) to leave in. I got up for a walk. Felt a bit groggy and rather sore [from the probes.] Fair size piece of shrapnel I found [tied to my wrist in a bandage as a keepsake – size of a thumbnail.]

Each day, visiting the library I checked the hospital register to see if anyone I knew from the regiment had been admitted. Suddenly events occurred that were to change my whole attitude.

Tuesday, 1st August – 92nd General

Had frightful news of the regiment this morning when I met one of our wounded [admitted as a casualty.] Worried out of my wits. Nearly every chap I know in 'A' squadron has been wounded and many in 'C' squadron. Already contemplating returning to the regiment. Received bunch of 6 letters

Wednesday, 2nd August – 92nd General

Bathed before breakfast. Doctor around early and pleased with my X-ray. Allowed to move [again] on to the corridor [which was always more interesting and lively.]

 Wrote to Valerie and finished the book MYSTERIA WAYE. Down to the library and drew more books. Mused over hotel possibilities. [?] Coffee given us by night sister. [Made my decision to return to the regiment.]

It was now exactly a month since I had taken the full blast of a shell on the Bechan's turret and had some how survived. More than that, I was off all the warning lists – no longer D.I.L. (Dangerously ill), S.I.L. (Seriously ill) and no one came to watch the fun at the dressing of wounds time. There was just a little physio-therapy and an ever expanding interest once more in life and its opportunities such as how to hide a pack of tinned beer behind the penicillin in the outside fridge or to hang it from the framework under my bed without the Tommies or the cleaners spotting it. The weather was warm, Naples was teeming with life and the operas full. Decision-making was the only cloud on the horizon and I was now formulating some positive plans.

Saturday, 5th August – 92nd General, Naples

A letter from Derek [at the front] – got into blues [hospital clothing] and spent the morning eluding small jobs – had breathing exercises [when I suffered my first sneeze it was as if a 10lb sledge hammer had socked me in the middle of the back.] After lunch I slipped into Naples and got a lift there and back. Saw only the centre of the town. Got rid of the oliograph [I had picked it up in one of the woods during our advance] and obtained some beautiful watercolour prints. [They were of Naples, Vesuvius in eruption, Pompeii.] Saw one act of Tosca at the beautiful San Carlo Theatre. Had tea at N.A.A.F.I. which is situated in a palace over-looking the Bay of Naples. Returned to the hospital at 5:30pm and was not caught. Felt very tired. Met the old nurse [aged + – 40] from Kantara [Nov.'42] days. Received coffee grains from the kitchen and made some with it in the evening.

I now needed to do some deep soul-searching about my immediate future and looked back through the last four years on active service.

My recall of the desert days was that we, in the main, had been 'lions led by donkeys'. In Italy the lions were encased in iron coffins and the donkeys led them deliberately into ambush. I, myself, had played the role of lion and donkey. Did I want more of that? What I did know was that under no circumstances would I accept a base job. Well enough, I would fight. Crippled, I would go back to civilian life – no compromise.

That resolved, I sought the wherewithal for my return to the N.M.R. My plan was simple. First of all I needed a uniform. In Naples I had picked up a snazzy khaki shirt for a song. I still needed further kit to wear. Manna from heaven came when a huge batch of casualties swamped the wards and I, as usual, helped the worst of them to settle in. One, just about my size, surrendered his battered uniform to my scissoring. His khaki trousers fitted me exactly, even the belt. I gave him two packets of Woodbine for them and I was set up for the road.

Friday, 11th August – 92nd General, Naples

Arose and bathed. Read during the morning. After lunch completed Len's letter [telling the guys in the troop I was coming back] and thrashed out my own problems. Wrote [to my sisters] Margaret and Kathleen to pacify them over my decision [to return to the front.] Read SPRINGBOK [magazine] and swiped some kit and went to bed. Theatre sister mowed my [left] arm with silver nitrate pencil. [The removal of exuberant flesh from a newly sutured wound was inevitable and would have to be done for at least another ten days. I helped the nurse clear up and pocketed the pencil.]

Saturday, 12th August – 92nd General

A very sultry day. Another showdown with Flossie [a ward nurse who reported me for anything and everything.]

Did some strenuous exercises [despite the fact that I still had stitches in my chest and left arm.] Started another Zola book. Visited Eddy Hogg [in another ward] who has lost an eye.

[Eddy gave me an important message from my squadron buddies who would take me back to the front with them, the next time they were on leave.] Visit from [our M.D. Doctor] Nelson Eddy. Grand seeing the old boy again. Gave us all the dope. Freddy Flowers is dead. Put in leave passes. Up for parade and ward masters tomorrow – presuming for transfer [to a South African hospital.] My chance for escaping [from the 92nd] Wrote in the evening. Saw a Mickey Rooney film in afternoon.

[Stop Press] Have decided to do a bunk.

<u>Sunday, 13th August – 92nd General</u>

Bathed and attended parade which was late. Rushed down and drew my kit [personal effects] and packed and debunked leaving a letter for Sister Clemence. [The official designation for this was 'abscondment'.] Caught a series of lifts [on to the Naples–Rome coastal route] and there a final one which took me from Capua to Rome. [This was an American Army truck driven by a nice homely guy. It took about two hours. He thought I was a deserter. I told him my story and showed him my bandaged chest and arm to prove it.] In fair time and blazing heat, got into Rome and the Springbok Club about 5:30pm and met Jock [Dickens], Haddow and Bill Askham. Everyone thought I was my own ghost and registered both amazement and pleasure. Had a wash and plenty of wine ending up at Jock's digs where I slept the night. Saw Dennis and Stevie in room above and had enjoyable time. Jock and Wokkie [?] in clover. Haddow and I sleepless.

Rejoining the regiment was not going to be easy. The responsibility of accepting a soldier back under your command who was a ghost of his former self and still in bandages was not accepted easily whatever the rank and S.M. Aga Kahn was the first to take fright.

Marcia was in Naples. Her daughter, my ex-heart throb, had married a Sicilian and they had settled somewhere modestly in Calabria. Marcia wondered if she might see me before she returned to Cairo. She had my letter written in the 92nd General and thought to visit me there but had been refused permission. By the time she could contact me I was already at the convalescent camp on the Volturno. But from there we got leave easily to visit Naples. Derek had insisted on coming to meet again his old acquaintance. She was just the same with the deep-set panda eyes of the Lebanese, always penetrating, always wondering and sometimes asking. She hailed Derek brusquely asking him how he faired and he answered with one of his self-denying observations "Oh, you know my problem Marcia, fast women and slow horses!" Marcia sniggered with one of her polite laughs and got down to business with me pulling out some horoscopes and laying them flat on the coffee table. Derek wandered off to get Grand

Marnier. Poor Naples, the war had hardly touch there but it still looked so battered about. I had told Marcia in my letter about the demise of Dennis Baker and she had his natal chart spread out next to mine. "Dennis was born 10 hours before you and he met his death 10 months before you. You should have died at Alamein!" and she scolded me for not heeding her warnings. "And now you are in Italy. You have Uranus conjunct to Mars and you are again under threat. Why have you come here?"

I answered politely "Well they do say the girls are more beautiful here." Marcia threw up here arms in frustration. Derek arrived back with a bottle of Marnier and glasses. Naples began to look more picturesque and if you walked to the edge of the terrace you could see Vesuvius smoking away. Marcia, mollified continued. "You have one more difficult month ahead. November, the day for fireworks." She had learned to like Grand Marnier since our Cairo days and became more familiar. I was glad I had Derek as my chaperone. She turned once more to me and said, "I'm going back to Syria and won't be seeing you again. Your horoscopes, both of them say that you and your natal brother Dennis will meet again." And then she was gone. I walked over to stare at Vesuvius. "What did she mean?" but Vesuvius just grumbled on.

<u>Monday, 14th August '44 – Rome</u>

Met more fellows at club where I returned to catch Aga's truck back to camp. Aga in big flap at sight of me [He didn't have me on his roll, didn't know where I had come from or why I was there.] Spent the whole day travelling till we reached the regiment right past Siena. Had a burst tyre on the way. Pooch [Marais] also on the truck. [He gave me his rickshaw look and shook his head.] Felt very tired when we reached [regimental] camp where my arrival caused consternation and further amazement. I felt like a ghost returning from the dead. I had in fact been reported 'died of wounds'. It was wonderful to be back and see all the fellows; Len couldn't believe his eyes. Had a good meal, the first for 36 hours, and some wine and slept at Pooch and Len's tank – slept badly [always ominous!]

Tuesday, 15th August, '44, North of Siena

Reported in and there is trouble in the air. Bathed in the river, chatted to various fellows and awaited decision from above as to whether I could stay. [Aga had come out of the orderly room several times smoking furiously like the lawyer he was, waiting for the jury verdict.]

Everything rests with the doctor. Boiled some mealies – drew some kit – talking to Len and Pooch all the time. Mousie [Bell] very sheepish probably because of the poor show he put up the day I was hit. Over to the Y.M. truck to buy tinned food with Len and Joss. High altitude playing up with my chest [Doctor] Eddy back and insisted I be sent down [the line] for a rest. Wrestled and pleaded with him to let me stay and succeeded until Aga went and messed everything up when 'trying to do his best' for me.

The upshot of the debate over me was that I had to go back and stay at a convalescent camp for a rest period but, in compensation, I could take five days leave in Rome en route. It was something of a disappointment but the regiment was out of the line itself resting anyway and I would be with friends. There had been little time to ponder the set-up in Rome where our crowd from the line had established a good relationship with a family who could accommodate two or three for short periods. The drill was that you arrived laden with FOOD of any description and handed it over and the Madame of the establishment served you with a meal whenever you asked which was pretty frequent and at all hours. The girls were the main attraction. There were two sisters. Juliette was a blonde beauty whose fiancée was a German soldier named Franz who had left town when Rome was evacuated back in May. The elder sister was plain and down to earth. She had domestic problems and was accommodating in the other sense of the word. Warm and friendly, she would get the meal together, sip wine with you to all hours and be convivial to your friends. We called her Maria because she had an otherwise unprouncible name. The 'mama' was a frightened old lady who spoke no English and did all the hard work in the background. I teased all three of them in my five days and had to use my bits of school French to keep in touch with the old lady. I made it clear from the beginning that I was neither interested nor capable at the moment of the ultimate frivolities and they were more relaxed with me.

Evenings usually ended up with a typical Italian meal – antipasta, pasta (which we, the soldiers went for) and then thinly disguised with tomato, peppers and aubergines the 'meat and vegetable' out of the horde of tins we deposited with them on arrival. Cheese dishes, olives and figs made up a fair meal and everyone would be happy and hearty by the end of the evening. In my state I was essentially polite and gentlemanly and Juliette would say frequently "Diglees, vous êtres tres gentile" or some such. But she would attempt to make me jealous with stories about her "Franz" who was so vigorous and handsome. I would go along with it calling him (in his absence) cochon, German swine and so on. But Juliette had a gorgeous voice and would trot out songs at appropriate moments – not just the stream of Italian lyrics which the English still loved to call for but borderline ones much Americanised like Amapola, South of the Border and Isle of Capri. If Len was with us, he would add a few. We, the soldiers, were tired of the bawdy army versions and were delighted with her freshness and spontaneity. Jealous of its link with this household the group we were with forbade any reference to them at camp least the uninvited and the boorish present themselves there. It was on-going because it was Rome and Rome, after all was the eternal city.

<u>Thursday, 17th August '44 – Siena/Rome</u>

Left on the 9am leave truck and felt rather down. Had an uneventful and fast trip down to Rome. Sitting next to 'Rosie' [Rosettenstein] with whom I spoofed. [A good humoured but effeminate Jewish boy who worked in the H.Q. orderly room. I thought I could get some info out of him.] Reached the [Springbok] Club at 5pm and booked in at the same lodging as before. Had some grub and visited Bill King and Ruth upstairs and had a merry evening. Juliette got crying drunk and so on. Saw Joe Cowley and his brother. [Joe shot through the neck at Alamein had made a remarkable recovery. He thereafter joined the Royal Natal Carbineers. His brother, a fellow pupil in the class of Charlie Evans at D.H.S. was with him in pilot's uniform!]

JULIETTE

Predictably Rome had become a sightseeing target for every military group in the country including the air force and navy. The Cowley brothers were also sight-seeing but I knew Joe was searching for something else, not so much for him as for his little brother with whom I reminisced covering school casualties like Geoffrey Frank, Joe Hoffenberg, Aubrey Hampson, etc. He was as shy as ever and didn't know how to handle rank or even what brother Joe was searching for. Somehow the fact that his old cronies in the N.M.R. had an exceptionally useful connection in Rome had reached Joe, now a carbineer, and with his legal expertise he grilled me but I was as tight as a clam and the two sisters were kept in the snug circle of our group. I had got a few giggles out of the brothers with my stories of Sloppy Alexander, a D.H.S. teacher quite hopeless at class discipline, which they had forgotten.

Alas, on this occasion there was no room at the inn and we could not be accommodated with Juliette and her sister and found more precarious accommodation elsewhere. The problem was bugs and in high summer, Rome was swarming with them.

Saturday, 19th August '42 – Rome

Up early and had a hot bath and shave at the public baths. Then bought vegetables and had a good lunch. Staged another run-out on our landlady [because we had had a hectic night with bugs and very little sleep.] Then bought vegetables and had a very good lunch and went to stay with Juliette's people. Len and I to see SERGENT YORK. Then bought usual four wines and had dinner and Len and Juliette sang all night accompanied by us. To bed very tight and slept well.

Sunday, 20th August '44 – Rome

Started on tour of Rome very early but a flat tyre brought it to an early close. Then Len and I went down town and met Doug. Alexander and his pal/ saw a beautiful blond with them. Went on an excellent tour in the afternoon. Visited Coliseum, Arch of Constantine, Roman Forum, Pantheon, Piazza Venezia, St. Peters, St. John, Piazza del Papoloa and the Holy Steps. Found Pantheon the most beautiful – St. Peters being on its own. Religious fervour? I cannot appreciate such as going up the Holy Stairs on the knees. Bought more wine and met Doug Alexander and took them to the lodgings and spent a very pleasant evening loaded with bullshit. To bed again very drunk.

It must become clear to anyone who has studied the psychology of men at war that alcohol plays an important role in helping soldiers fit into the whole picture of this essentially human and sometimes revolting process of killing. At its best alcohol smothers out and makes acceptable the inequalities of rank and authority, the atrociousness of human conduct, the challenges to courage, the grief of bereavement, the imposition of chastity, and the tolerance of boredom and exhaustion.

At its worst alcohol aggravates all these with a debasement of personality that constitutes outrage even to the ego.

Few soldiers survive a war without resorting to alcohol. The happiest are those who can use it effectively to make life at its most appalling acceptable with some degree of reason. Each man must find his own way but the soldier at war, real war, is a man at bay and can be forgiven if he takes a medicine for his circumstances. Many perform acts of valour free of alcohol and should be praised for it. But when you have the ongoing interminable demands laid on you by a cruel war that goes on day after day for five or more years, most of them in retreat then surely, in the absence of a convincing religion, some sort of relief is permissible. It seems that, in the main, those who endured, thought so.

On reaching the Reserves Camp that was an N.M.R. appendage I was totally unprepared for the new conditions it offered. The purpose of my abscondment from the 92nd General Hospital was to avoid being drafted semi-fit to work in a base camp somewhere. The other reason was to rejoin the comrades I had fought with for the last five years because I believed them to be sorely pressed up at the front. The first person I met on reaching the Reserves area was Lieutenant Dudley Morning who knew me well both in the army and out of it where he worked for the Royal Insurance Company in Durban. Dudley was an excellent officer respected by all of us but he had been side-lined during the ridiculous process of amalgamating, merging and joining regiments to the original N.M.R. that had been mobilised in 1940.

The Reserve Camp arose because the task of supplying the N.M.R. in tanks (along with all the other regiments) had become so massive that it was easier to retain all unnecessary personnel in the rear where logistics were not quite such a nightmare. The Reserve was therefore sited on the banks of the Volturno River 30 miles N.E. of Naples at Alife where it could be easily supplied and administered. It contained therefore not only new recruits straight from South Africa but men for training, wounded and sick returning to the line for duty, the shell-shocked and any misfits from officers down to simple privates. Quite correctly only experienced and fit men were permitted at the front. I was therefore an 'enfant terrible', a misfit until I could resume the duties of a tank man.

Dudley Morning introduced me to Captain Schwart who ran the camp and to S.M. Purves who was in charge of training. Dudley also pointed out that the use of tanks in northern Italy was coming to an end as the giant obstruction of the Appenines began to loom. What would really be needed were men trained to fight in winter conditions. Dr. Hodson, sainted surgeon who had rescued me after Alamein and Orvieto, had warned me that my right lung was practically collapsed and non-functional and there were two conditions I should avoid. One was altitudes and the other was extreme cold. In both conditions functioning on one lung was hazardous as both reduced oxygen availability. Dudley Morning had said the regiment would eventually have to discard its tanks and fight again as infantry. I now realised that only two or three months of service in tanks would be possible for me. To become an infantryman again was just not on. I therefore agitated to be sent back to the regiment as quickly as possible. Major Meeser had promised this but he had other ideas in mind for me.

Tuesday, 22nd August – Volturno

After sleeping well was shaken up to have breakfast at six. Saw Dudley Morning and then Captain Swart and found that Major

Meeser had double-crossed me in his letter hoping that I would be kept here as a wireless instructor. I was mad about it. Then went down to the doctor who assumed I was swinging the lead being based on my crashing out of hospital. Took his recommendation for boarding to Swart who is putting things right [in my favour.] Went for swim in the afternoon. Very hot here. Sent letter back to Meeser via Eric Dyson and had a spot after dinner.

Wednesday, 23rd August – Volturno

Had a talk with the S.M. [Bill Purves] who told me to take things easy and not to worry about P.T. that has been prescribed. Took his word for it and sat around. Watched hockey. [Bill Purves], a massive man with a harsh reputation, was kindness itself. He says my difficulty is to appear fit for boarding A1 when in truth I needed rest.

In fact the climate was ideal for me and I set up a small camp on the banks of the Volturno and fed off the tomatoes that hung on the vines all around me. I read and swam, slept and sunbathed for hours on end. And in the midst of it shell-shocked Sterzel came to see me.

Thursday, 24th August – Volturno

Sterzel around after breakker and we went to a vineyard to get grapes and figs. Thoroughly enjoyed the walk [and Sterzel I knew enjoyed my counselling such as it was.] Bathed in the stream on the way back. Got badly stung by a bee. [Killed two birds with one stone and had the two wounds on my calf and the bee sting dressed together. The medical orderly looked at me strangely because, in the heat I was stripped to the waist…and now a bee sting on top of everything else. Even Sterzel had to laugh.] Went down to the river and slept in the shade and finished letters home. A few more drinks and then coffee before bed.

Living alone on the banks of the Volturno taught me the therapeutic value of resting in the sound of nature's running water and the seeking of retreat.

CHAPTER XXVIII

My many brushes with death had earned me something of a reputation. Sterzel of course saw me several times before going back as an infantryman into the line. I just told others who came to see me that I believed in immortality and, like Shakespeare in his sonnets, we live on in the people who read them.

Friday, 25th August '44 –Volturno

After parade went to the vineyard again and gave Sterzel what advice I could on his returning to the regiment and his nerves. Washed clothes after tea and saw Bill Askham who has returned as wireless instructor. Down to the river to write but I only slept and read. To the mess and drank vermouth till ten and then to bed.

Tuesday, 29th August '44 –Volturno

Went thru hell on the morning exercises and performed all sorts of diabolical antics. [The main exercise being with two groups tossing a ten foot telegraph pole horizontally into each others arms.] Had some good fun all the same and then swam in the river. Jules Ryder's birthday. We had vermouth before lunch. In the afternoon went to see the doctor again and after a long chat managed to get a discharge from P.T. to teach at the school here until I'm called for by the regiment. Discussed wireless course with Jules and Bill Askham and had some more to drink after dinner.

Thursday, 31st August '44 – Volturno

Spent the morning typing the programme for the wireless course. Completed letters to K & M [sisters]. Des Henwood arrived back from South Africa. Three of us down to river for a cool afternoon and had some more vermouth. [The secret was to hide the bottles in amongst the reeds to cool overnight.] Washed some trousers and swam generously. Packed our clothes and Jules and I are ready for 6 day leave in Rome via Naples.

Friday, 1st September '44 – Naples and Rome

Had a series of fast lifts and made Naples in good time. Drew our pay and met Basil Mower. His whole face has been horribly disfigured. [Basil had been involved in a car accident and he looked like Notre Dame!*]

Had something to eat then made for Rome. Had a spot of bad luck at first but were given a lift by some nice rats [base – wallahs] who are radio observers that wear uniforms. Made fast time along the coast road and made Rome in time to have dinner [Juliette's home] saw the damage and destruction on this route and the Pontine marches. Saw also remnants of the Appian Way.

Saturday, 2nd September '44 – Rome

Slept solidly until 8am and then met up with Joss Deacon and Richard Platt at the Springbok Club. Went on pub crawl to N.A.A.F.I. and got a bit shot there. Jules and I visited Bello Theunissen at Admin. H.Q. He fixed us up with rations [books.] and slung much bullshit across. [He talked about security and fifth columnists and pulled out a Luga and waved it around.] Met Joss and took him to dinner at the hotel where we are welcome anytime. Three of us got very tight. Managed to get back to the flat and while the others got drunk I made violent love to Juliette in the moonlight. Met up with Melly [Ratcliffe, Sterzel's tank commander and asked him to take Sterz back. He refused and suggested I get him sent home.]

Sunday, 3rd September '44 – Rome

[5 years exactly since we went to war.] Saw Joss and Richard Platt off after giving them some of our breakfast. I bathed and

---

*We had been taught to hug and kiss both cheeks by the Italians and I took Basil into my arms with a bear hug and kissed both cheeks to show him his disfigurement made no difference to our camaraderie.

shaved then we took our stuff up to No. 6. Had a nap after dining on chillies and tomatoes and then went to see "LAST DAYS OF POMPEII" which I had already seen before. Enjoyed it. Booked seats for the opera on Tuesday night. Strolled through the town and had some more to drink and then dined well at the hotel. Returned and had interesting discussion with the Italians here. Got some dope for TRAITOR'S HILL [the novel I was writing.] Jules took the count [went blotto] I stayed up to talk with the Ballila boys [Fascist Youth movement, a relic of the thirties] till after midnight.

Thursday, 7th September '44 – Reserves

The usual early parade. Helped mark out and clear the hockey field and had a few smacks before lunch [hockey practice]. Had another lecture on NATIVE AFFAIRS [Xosa]. Played hockey at 4pm and thoroughly enjoyed the game but felt very unfit. Much scrambling and I got a crack on the ankle. Bathed in the Volturno and made coffee after dinner. [Coffee drinking was a habit I picked up in the Acroma Box and I had a small coffee gathering in the middle of the long summer evenings when we joked and gossiped.] Slept well. Received a letter from Irene.

Sunday, 10th September '44 – Reserves

Into Naples for the day. Went with Des Henwood to Pompeii. Enjoyed visit to the ruins. Consider them excellent but the restorations overdone in places. Have pretty good idea of the Roman way of life now. Des lost his paybook.* Out to 92nd General Hospital and drew my kit [the remainder of my personal possessions from the day I was wounded (July 5th). I expected a frosty reception in view of my absconscion but staff there had either moved on or had totally forgotten me:

---

*A genuine loss of paybook meant delays in payouts from the paymaster until you received a new paybook. But there were many variations on this theme. Paybooks could be genuinely lost or fraudulently sold and soon replaced. The best story I heard was when Buller F. buried his paybook and later resurrected it to live (effectively) another day.

Time like an every-rolling stream
Bears all her sons away
They fly forgotten as a dream
Dies at the opening day

[– O God our help in Ages Past.]

Saw FOR ME AND MY GIRL and had tea at the N.A.A.F.I. Palace. Returned in twilight and found post waiting for me.

Monday, 11th September '44 – Reserves

Started wireless instruction and continued throughout the morning. Met very few hitches and quite enjoyed it. Arranged hockey matches and managed to get two games in before dinner. Drew with 'B' group but I played a rotten game. Went up and wrote to Des [brother] in the writing room and then had a drink and made coffee.

Thursday, 14th September '44 – Reserves

Wireless as usual – progress with some pupils good. With others hopeless. News received of death of Horse Brompton, Rex Lane and others in the regiment – others wounded – very worried. Wrote to Aga in despair.

We were all saddened to hear of the death of Horse Brompton who with 'B' Squadron had entered the village of Galciana where the inhabitants were very un-cooperative and sullen. They obviously knew something related to the enemy and were fearful. The Germans had rigged up a booby-trap to a bunch of teller-mines and a trio of our troopers fell foul of them. They exploded killing all three of them, one being Horse Brompton, who was so dearly loved by his comrades.

Friday, 15th September '44 – Reserves

Had a fairly successful wireless net – and classes showed great improvement. Wrote Valerie. Had hockey practice and went for bathe with the kid. [The kid is a new acquisition to our coterie. Befriended by Dennis May he had the audacity and the innocence to address me as 'Pop' in class (for the record I am 21). His name is Schick. He is one of the green new recruits up from South Africa.] Wrote to Len and Joss and sent it up the line.

Saturday, 16th September '44 – Reserves

Class finished early today. Arranged hockey for the afternoon
and the tournament tomorrow. Haddow and Basil – arrived
from hospital. Washed some clothes. Got tight with Dennis May,
Bill Askham, Jules Ryder and Schick. Had a few songs. Bullshitted
some of the officers. I tripped over the goal posts and bashed
my shins. Adjourned to the tent and had something to eat. Dennis
took the count [OUT] and I helped him and Schick to bed.

MILITARY MEDAL
Trooper Dennis Walter May
(See photo – page 449)

"On 30th June, 1944, at 0815 hours, No 1 Troop of the Squadron was
in contact with the enemy just north of Acquaviva and Trooper May's
tank was brewed up by a 75mm anti-tank gun. The crew baled out,
the co-driver being severely wounded in the foot. Snipers had the
tank covered from all sides and four enemy MGs opened fire on the
crew. Trooper May and Sergeant Vice formed a chain with their
hands and carried the co-driver, Trooper Trichardt for a hundred yards
approximately under this murderous fire. By a series of short dashes
they managed to succeed in their task and this saved the life of Trooper
Trichardt who was unable to follow them. Trooper May's action was
cool and deliberate and in the circumstances showed the highest degree
of courage and bravery."

Four days of heavy rain turned the Volturno into a raging torrent
and made life under canvas difficult. Tempers had to be held in leash
and wireless classes were not easy and sport almost impossible.

Thursday, 21st September '44 – Reserves

Had a very shaky wireless scheme today. Got some planks and
made myself a bed [As I got back to full fitness I became aware
that in order to breathe easily at night I could only sleep for any
length of time on my right side where I had the collapsed
uninflatable lung. This left my left lung free to inflate and to
grow into the right thorax as Dr. Hodson said it would. The bed
was deliberately built cock-eyed to accommodate these
idiosyncrasies.]

Our league hockey match cancelled. Had a party in the evening with Dennis May, Jules Ryder, Bill Askham. Got very tight and had a good time. Fanny Ward came in [Hygiene Corp.] and made an ass of himself [we ragged him a bit.] But apologised in the morning. [Despite the new bed] I got to bed under my own steam.

Saturday, 23rd September '44 – Reserves

Had a very successful wireless net during the morning and all fellows on the course greatly improved. Went with Dennis May in the water truck and got some kit altered by the tailor. Arranged for hockey match after lunch and we beat 'B' Group one nil. Watched football and then went for a bathe. Wrote up wireless reports after dinner [Dennis, himself from a sporting family, was invaluable in organising the hockey and the wireless classes.] Had a drink with Bill Askham, made coffee and went to bed.

As the end of September approached I heard on the vine that it was to be my last week at Reserve camp. I did not know whether string pulling had worked the oracle via my lettes to Aga or Jules having access, as top wireless operator, to Meeser's ear or my turning out two classes of wireless operators did it but I was to be on the next draft back to the line with Dennis. We celebrated accordingly.

Saturday, 30th September '44 – Reserves

Arranged hockey [for the weekend] in the morning. Gave a lecture before lunch. Played hockey and had a hot bath. Fooled around with Dennis making the coffee with wet wood. [We took some smoking charred pieces and secretly slid them into the occupied tents where guys were sleeping and in a few moments the camp was in pandemonium.] Turned in [innocently] for the night.

Sunday, 1st October '44 – Reserves

Had a smashing day in Naples: Rather rainy at times. Journey took 3 hours. Went to the barber and then got tight at N.A.A.F.I.S. [It was hard not to get tight in such a crowd. Hundreds of service men would be there and all the time fellows you knew somehow, from somewhere, in your five years of battle would

come up and slap you on the back demanding you have a drink.]
Into the opera and had a general scramble of drunks in the box.
It was really quite a disgraceful scenario with about 20 soldiers
trying to seat themselves on 2 highly gilded Louis Quatorze
couches. Somebody had put up OFFICERS ONLY notice on
the box entrance. The two Quatorze's gave up the ghost and
disintegrated with the sofa bits being dropped down on to the
American servicemen seating in the classy seats below. Quite
disgraceful! Left opera first act and got nicely tight and went on
the spree. Bought some vermouth for the ride back which was
rather bloody. Got back about 10:30pm

Thursday, 5th October '44 – Rome/Florence

Started out on the way up to the line, but bridge washaway held
us up for four hours. Saw a lorry of Italians turn over. Travelled
until about 8pm then stopped on the side of the road and had
dinner. Slept on the back of the truck with Ronnie Wittstock and
Berney. A little rain during the night.

Friday, 6th October '44 – Rome/Florence

Made fast journey into Rome and spent a couple of hours there.
Had a shampoo and brush up. Took Ronnie and Berney to see
'Mama'. The family gave us a very hearty welcome and a heart-
breaking farewell. Made a fast journey up to farmhouse near
Siena where we slept the night in pouring rain. I slept on the
back of a cart instead of in the stable. Made a good meal before
retiring.

Three consistent factors emerged on this crazy draft back to the
front. It never stopped raining. It had already poured for a week at
Reserves and the further north, the more it pelted. Secondly, my two
companions never stopped their 'cher chez la femme'. Our rations,
meagre as they were shrank every time they went out to hunt. It
wasn't just that but the hair-raising stories they would come back
with from cuckoldry to undisguised rape. And thirdly we hadn't the
faintist idea of what our real destination was. Our instruction was to
make for the F.T.D.S Prato which could have meant anything.

The Author and Dennis May on holiday at Scottsburgh, Natal South Coast, 1946.

Our mission was virtually a carte blanche to do what we liked as long as we reported to F.T.D.S. whoever the hell they were.

Saturday, 7th October '44 – nr. Siena

Up early, made coffee and shaved. Went through Siena early and reached Florence about 10:30am – didn't see much of it. Went on to Prato and then the bullshit started well and truly. Spent the rest of the day looking for F.T.D.S. Poured with rain most of the time. Ended up sleeping at a rations dump – very comfortably. Went into town [with half the ration dump] and had a hot bath and a few drinks, then to bed early.

Perhaps I should explain the army attitude to sexuality. Whatever it was it had scared the living daylights out of new recruits with its Veno, Venus, V.D. The conclusion was 'Don't do it', but if you do there was a safe remedy (which wasn't true anyway.) The army generously offered you a small bundle. Before you did it.

You squirted a measure of penicillin up your urethra from a tube supplied with a nozzle. You then capped it with a soft bandage and finally hung it in a jock strap made of bandages. You were then expected to wear all this as a preliminary to operations. Some wore it, some didn't and some wished they hadn't! There was still another category who would have none of any of this and preferred oral sex for safety. Berney was one of these.

GOTHIC LINE AND APENNINES

Those who have never seen the Apennines in Italy cannot hope to appreciate the formidable obstacle they present to any force advancing from the south. This great range of mountains rising to nearly 7,000 feet stretches across the peninsula from the Mediterranean to the Adriatic. To the south of the great barrier the mountains tumble into foothills as far as the River Arno…

For over a year labour organisations had been working for Hitler on the construction of a line – the Gothic Line – a highly developed series of strong points stretching for about 200 miles across the peninsula from Spezia, on the Ligurian Sea to Pisaro south of Rimini on the Adriatic. The line blocked every route North.

Reaching the River Arno, the 6th South African Armoured Division discarded its cloak of armour and became once more an infantry division ready to assault the Gothic Line which straddled the Apennines. Our division now infantry again was placed under the command of the American 5th Army until the end of the war. Its aim was to seize the highest point of the Apennines which was the Futa Pass with its road crossing the mountain range into the Valley of the Po. The terrain was bristling with difficult points; the enemy, now fighting for its very existence was brave and stubborn and we had no trained mountaineers for a winter campaign. At this stage I was still in the 92nd General Hospital in Naples recovering from the shrapnel wounds incurred on July 5th at the ambushing of our troop in the area of San Felice.

Sunday, 8th October '44 – Prato

Left early on truck in search of F.T.D.S. but had no luck (or lots of it) and ended up at another ration dump, where we slept well despite pouring rain and dined royally. Reading QUEEN ANNE'S LACE. Swiped some rations during the night.

[Ronnie and Berney reappeared around dawn weak at the knees.]

Monday, 9th October'44 – Prato

Left at 9am and went to F.T.D.S. in an unfinished hospital where we settled comfortably in a draughty, cold corridor [but at least it was out of the rain.] Having good food here and plenty of sleep. Went to cinema in afternoon but walked out because it was a bang-bang* picture. Had another bath and went to bed at 6pm. Went to sleep immediately.

Things began to clarify. To this day I don't know what F.T.D.S. meant but assume it was Forward Transit Depot S____? In charge of it was Sergeant Vice and amazingly in my pocket I carried a message for him from Dennis May who had been in his tank crew when the Sherman was knocked out during an attack. Both Sgt. Vice and Dennis May had won the M.M. in that action. As a friend of Dennis I was given a warm welcome and special treatment.

---

*bang, bang and two more bit the dust…cowboy nonsense

SECTION ON CITATION OF SGT. VICE FOR M.M.
MILITARY MEDAL
T/SERGEANT DONALD BERNARD VICE

On 30th June, 1944, at 0815 hours, No 1 Troop of the Squadron was in contact with the enemy just north of Acquaviva and Sergeant Vice's tank was brewed up by a 75mm anti-tank gun. The crew baled out, the co-driver being severely wounded in the foot. Snipers had the tank covered from all sides and four enemy MGs opened fire on the crew. Sergeant Vice and Trooper May formed a chain with their hands and carried the co-driver, Trooper Trichardt for a hundred yards approximately under this murderous fire. By a series of short dashes they managed to succeed in their task and this saved the life of Trooper Trichardt who was unable to follow them. Sergeant Vice's action was cool and deliberate and in the circumstances showed the highest degree of courage and bravery.

CHAPTER XXIX

<u>Wednesday, 11th October – Prato</u>

Up and on beat from 6 until 7am. Returned during the night. Moved with the rest of the F.T.D.S. to another part of town and Don Vice secured us a room and we are very comfortably quartered in a snug room. Went to cinema and saw a fairly good film and bathed.

We began to look on Sergeant Don Vice as 'big brother', a kind of high school prefect. He saw us as three kids, full of the joys of spring. We acted up accordingly and fed him with ribald accounts of our escapades and carried on conversations in front of him that at least stirred him from his very boring job.

We would set it up in front of Don Vice like this, Berney to Ron:

"I nearly had a fight over you last night Ronnie."

"Oh, how come?"

"Somebody said you weren't fit to live in a shit house and I said you were!"

Then Berney makes a quick exit chased by Ron.

Then after a visit by some Benedictine monks to look at their hospital, self to Don:

"Sergeant Vice may I ask a question?"

"Yep! Go ahead."

"What vice does a monk have?"

"How the hell would I know that?

453

"All right, what vice does a monk have?"

"None!"

"Cheeky young sod!"

Sat up late talking to Ronnie. He is a very wiry character and built for hockey. I detected insecurity in his early life which had left its mark. Coming from a large working class family he seemed to have missed out on education. At only nineteen he had an extraordinary gift of the gab but it was one crowded with confidentialities and feintly conspiratorial. He spoke with such a sincerity about the tiniest matters that I found it disconcerting. Ronnie had an elder married brother at home in Durban who had sheltered him and to whom he turned when under the whip. In the army he was hopeless at filling in forms.

Ron seldom wrote home and didn't expect parcels. He turned to me if there were forms or complicated matters. He had made a poor wireless operator, was put in my class for a refresher course and I didn't find him too bright. He had sisters at home and perhaps this gave him a predilection for younger women, even girls. Ron was caring and sensed where I needed help because of my recent vicissitudes. He had good judgement as to who were charismatic and who were too macho for him. Ron would nag hell out of the former (such as Berney) but wisely left the latter very much alone. I gathered he had endured his time in the regiment up at the front heroically despite his youth and great psychological fragility.

Thursday, 12th October '44 – Prato

Left with Ronnie and Berney with the intention of visiting the squadron. Went up to the top of the Apennines and saw Bully, Joe and Jock and some others but not the tanks. Established the fact that all is being done to get me back. Then returned (to Prato) in the rain after lunch. Had some ghastly experiences hell driving by Yanks. Had a long chat with Ron and then to bed early.

Ron was even more confiding about his home life which he had moved out of. He had no specific skills or training and had occasionally learnt to live by his wits. Berney was out chasing an Italian bint in town and Ron confided that he had had brushes with the police and with it there were a few tears. He was what the English call a whittler and could worry himself into near panic, even stomach ulcers. Now he turned morbid and full of foreboding. I had to tell him I was not his elder brother and to keep off! We were to meet again after the war in strange circumstances.

STOOL PIGEONS

<u>Friday, 20th October'44 – Prato</u>

Went on a filthy wood fatigue in the morning. Showered before lunch and saw part of an amazing show in the afternoon. Got wind of a draft coming off and went out to the squadron to pull strings. Had a wonderful welcome and saw all the mob. Major Meeser sending for me. Chatted with Len and Pooch! Caught a truck and got back by 9pm and was put on guard from 11pm to 3!! Did it sleeping fitfully in a truck.

<u>Sunday 22nd October '44 – Prato</u>

Awoke early and read before breakfast. An extremely cold day – soaked a jersey and ruminated over chess problems till lunch. To bed after lunch because of a cold. Expected Len but he didn't pitch up. Went for walk after dinner with Ronnie to the club and saw many 3 squadron chaps there.

Despite fine spells the weather was worsening by the day with constant rain turning to sleet. The painful fact dawned on me. There would be no more tank warfare this side of spring. The winter was closing in and the regiment was back again as infantry. The consolation was the issue of an extra winter shirt. Close now to the shooting we were about to replace a guards regiment which was being posted day and night on the banks of the River Reno. Any day now, as Doc Eddy had told me a few days ago when I had seen him with a bad cold and chest pains the final test would come as to whether it would be possible to sit out on guard all night with a collapsed lung. I was glad I had him in the medical unit at the front.

Daily shower-baths were a de rigeur that was coming to an end with the onset of the winter. They were used as a meeting place for discussion, news and portents. Meeting Jules Rider (the Major's ear) and Aga (the Major's damocles) together at the showers sent a cold shiver down my spine. Aga took one look at me with ferreting eyes while I was naked and some flesh restored to my bones, and the die was cast. I stuck my tongue out at Jules and he gave me a wink back.

MEESER

Meeser had always kept an ear open on many levels of regimental affairs and my abscondment from hospital, physical examination by Dr. Eddy on my return to the regiment and final relocation to his Squadron was not unnoticed. He briefly thanked me and had me earmarked eventually to run 'B' Squadron's wireless net which I took with a pinch of salt because the squadron was now back in infantry.

Aga, Meeser's ever faithful henchman was more impressed because he had had feedback from the convalescent camp down on the Volturno which hadn't known how to grade me and where I had become, with my history of mutilations something of a legend amongst new recruits and was not exactly flattered when I was addressed as 'Pop' by one of them and 'the walking scrap-heap' by another.*

Dr. Stan Eddy had high praise for officers like Ron Meeser who, when wounded, he had evacuated to the British hospital at Frosinone, just south of Rome. No sooner treated there Meeser persuaded the M.O. to release him and hitch-hiking, he was back again in two days with the regiment at the front where Eddy continued to tend him and replace his bandages. It was this kind of esprit de corps that kept the N.M.R. continually able to lead the 8th Army all the way in reconnaissance to Florence.

Friday, October 27th '44 – Appenines

Went for shower and saw Aga and Jules there together. After lunch our recall to the regiment came through and we left immediately after hastily packing. Went out to Bagnolo to join the squadron [which overnight had become an infantry company with its platoons and sections again.] Left some kit on the truck

---

*A reference to the many pieces of shrapnel I now carried around in me.

[duffle bag for storage.] Had letter from home. Got into vino in the local 'pig and whistle' [in Bagnolo] and had a very pleasant evening. Am in Bully's section.

Being back with my own kith and kin was a tonic that temporarily dissolved all doubts about physical disabilities. I was going into action again with guys like Bullimore, Richard Platt and Pooch Marais, who all had guts and that's what counted. Any hour the call could come but in the meantime we made hay while the sun shone.

Tuesday, 31st October '44 – near Ripoli

Went out to the range and did some Bren and rifle shooting [calibrating.] News of move up to the front and now I'm worried [about the infantry tasks.] Got all my [action] kit in readiness. Had some brandy with Richard and Joss. Joe very drunk.

Wednesday, 1st November '44 – Ripoli

Pulled out after early breakfast for Ripoli and made it by teatime. Passed over the Apennines [heights] in pouring rain and ice cold mists. Saw many pieces of pretty scenery. Arranged with Oscar for platoon's cooking to be done in an Ito casa by an old woman and then went with him for a walk up into the hills and bought mushrooms and cider to devour. Raining steadily. Slept well.

Thursday, 2nd November '44 – Ripoli

Weather cleared more and the platoon went out stalking fowls. I am now Bren gunner in Yank Collins' section with Joe as 2 I.C. Prepared for the front. Slept well. Snow on the nearby mountains.

Our own operation now became clearer. Our company of the N.M.R. was to relieve an infantry company of Guards who were holding three strong points on the River Reno. They and artillery observation posts were under sustained shellfire and attack from German fighting patrols. The three strong points were a small concrete footbridge cross the Reno, a village at the other end of it and a casa at the southern end. These three sisters looked on to a railway tunnel that opened out from its path under the Apennines. The river had a stony bed and the dry summer meant it could be forded almost anytime.

As usual we would be undermanned with a company trying to do a battalion's job. The problem was complicated by the fact we were on the extreme of the 8th Army's left wing which flapped around into the territory of the American 5th army. Crafty Aga had got me to organise the feeding of our platoon from a cottage in Ripoli. He had given me Oscar to help and we organised it so that hot food could come up at least once a day from Ripoli.

Friday, 3rd November '44 – Gardaletta

Helped with the preparing of food in the casa and flirted with 'Bella of Ripoli.' Packed kit after lunch and moved in trucks up to the front. A bridge was washed away and had a terrible battle carrying all my kit and ammo across the river. Moved into position vacated by the Guards and had a sleepless night doing guards [listening posts] and drawing rations. Have a very sticky job holding the bridge here. Had a couple of scares. Plenty of mortaring. As it was we had not enough men to hold all three positions and instead held both ends of the bridge and the shallow crossing below it. The tunnel opening had to be covered by fire from the position my section was holding, the cottage at the south end of the footbridge. Richard Platt's section held the village at and beyond the north end of the same bridge. His section's defence of the village strong point won for him the Military Medal. The citation for his bravery reads:

CORPORAL RICHARD EDWARD PLATT
6 S.A. ARMOURED DIVISION, N.M.R./S.A.A.F.

"Corporal Platt has commanded a section of infantry since August 1944, with outstanding success and has always proved a first class leader. On the night of 5/6 November 1944, this N.C.O. was defending the bridge at Gardaletta. It was imperative that this bridge be held at all costs, being the only Line of Communication available at that time. About midnight he observed an enemy patrol approaching, subsequently found to be 13 strong. Having engaged the enemy with hand grenades, he took up a position in a nearby house from which he could cover the bridge.

The enemy engaged the house with machine guns, spraying all windows and attacking with L.M.G.'s and grenades. Corporal Platt organised the defence and maintained complete control throughout, moving from man to man with words of encouragement and transferring his own L.M.G. from window to window with complete disregard for his personal safety. Several of the men in the section were in action for the first time that night and this N.C.O's coolness and courage was an inspiration to all. Having beaten off the attack, wounded four of the enemy and taken two prisoners, the section stood-to until dawn and only then was it known that Corporal Platt had been wounded with the first burst of enemy fire.

Saturday, 4th November '44 – Gardaletta.

Got some sleep in during the day. Heavy guards [and persistent vigilance] every night. Lovely weather. Under full view of the enemy who are less than a thousand yards away. Watched them bashing one of our [artillery] observation posts. Len and Pooch out on a deadly night patrol but came back through our position safely.

News about the attack on our bridge and Gardaletta soon got around and who should appear in the aftermath but the terrible two, Bernie and Ron. Bernie was standing in for the signalman allocated to our section and Ron said he knew I would want help with heaving and lugging. It was good to see them but I suspected an ulterior motive which turned out to be Bella of Ripoli who, quietly suggested she might vist our casa with the rations truck! They stayed till dark and went mooching off. 'cher chez les femme'.

We heard later that Gardaletta was important to hold because it was a salient feature in the Spring assault on Mount Sole which towered above it and against which Archie McLachlan led a platoon in the Grand assault.

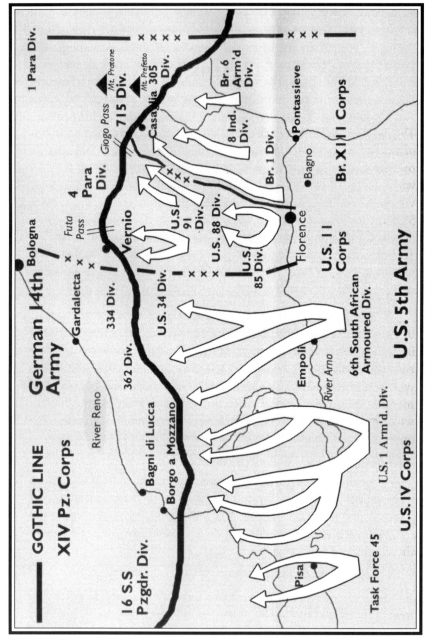

The Gothic Line, 5th November '44

CHAPTER XXX

The rush of water over the round stones and giant pebbles in the bed of the River Reno awoke me early. I had slept beneath the window overlooking the shallow crossing that connected the casa I was holding with a section on the near bank, to Richard's section holding the small village of Gardaletta on the far bank. It was Guy Fawkes Day, Nov. 5th, which celebrated the capture of the Catholic terrorist who had nearly managed to blow up the Houses of Parliament in England in 1605. Known as the 'Gunpowder plot,' since kids we had observed it with fireworks and stuffed incendiaries called 'guys' which we burnt with fireworks.

Today the sun was shining very brightly after many weeks of it being overcast. From my casa I could see across the river to Richard's house and his open bedroom window. To celebrate I took up a 303 rifle and put a shot across the 200-yard gap into the wall of his casa just outside his window. A very frosty Richard showed himself momentarily and I waved a white handkerchief at him from my window. A minute later the signallers phone went. It was Richard of course.

He asked, "What do you want?"

I said "It's Guy Fawkes."

"You're fucked up" he ejaculated.

"So are you; just getting your range." I went on "I have a feeling there'll be fireworks here tonight."

Richard grunted "Why so?"

"Several groups of Itos have crossed the bridge. They're all leaving town," I pointed out. "Perhaps they know something we don't."

Richard concluded. "Could be."

The bridge as it stands today, rebuilt, capable of taking motor traffic. Beneath it is the ford across the river Reno which was also under attack on 5th November.

He rang off and slammed the shutters of his window shut. I threw an empty beer bottle at the ford over the Reno below. It fell short. If I threw grenades at enemy crossing there, I would miss them. My scapula was still weak. I really shouldn't be in infantry at all.

There was some desultory shelling but I managed to rest most of the afternoon in the sunshine. Then I prepared the guards for the night's operation, which was to use the Bren gun on anything approaching the bridge. Just half-an-hour before midnight a German fighting patrol attacked Richard's section in Gardaletta village. For his personal courage and his leadership in repelling this attack he was awarded the M.M:

During the furore at Gardaletta on Guy Fawkes night with Richard and his section in top form, my eyes had been scanning the riverbanks for movement of any kind especially an attack from the ford. There was faint moonlight, and with the rushing waters it could be casting illusions of movement. Suddenly I heard a cry and then low toned voices coming from the ford, which was just visible. I had tracers in my magazines and plastered the shallow strip from one end to the other. Then all went quiet.

It was just getting light when I thought I saw or heard movement on the bridge. It seemed to be a small group of people. Then I saw helmets and shouted a challenge and cocked the Bren gun. A frightened voice called back "Don't shoot, don't shoot. We're friends." There was something funny about their language and their movement. "We're friends, we're Yanks. We've got a friend with us here, he's hurt." I opened the front door and two G.I.'s stumbled into the casa carrying a wounded comrade. They were absolutely exhausted and could hardly speak. "My friend Homer here has hurt his foot." I pulled up a chair and they flopped him down on to it. His right leg had been blown off at the knee. Homer was either partly blinded by the shoe mine that had wounded him, or in such a state he did not know the extent of his injury. Thunderstruck and out of courtesy more than anything I said: "How are you feeling Homer?" He answered piteously, "My foot hurts." His two exhausted friends were stretched out on the floor of the casa the log fire catching their tense features and open mouths gasping for breathing. Lost, they had carried Homer a long way. Then my horror mounted. Homer had no dressing on at all and the main artery just below the knee was pulsing blood out in jets. The G.I.s' main concern had been to hide from Homer the fact that his right lower leg was no longer there. I made one of the two Yanks press on Homer's femoral artery and grabbed kitchen towels and tore them into strings for ligatures. Then I got on to the phone to our medics and in twenty minutes they had an ambulance and stretcher to the casa. I don't think by then we had completely stopped the haemorrhage. Homer had passed out.

In a few moments after arrival of our ambulance the two were gone and I was left with a bloodied kitchen to clean up. I cursed the fact I had not got Homer's surname and I can't say to this day whether he survived. The G.I.'s had seemed a little embarrassed before they left. It took me some time to realise why. In the stress of carrying their wounded comrade to safety, they had to dump their weapons and other equipment. I knew this, because in carrying Terry Smedley out of battle at Gazala I had had to shed everything except my rifle. In the British army you were never allowed to discard your rifle.

<u>Sunday, 5th November '44 – Gardaletta</u>

Shall not forget this Guy Fawkes day in a hurry. Had a restful day in glorious sunshine and made the most of it. Slept when possible and did some cooking. Started the guards [in the casa] but were awakened just before midnight when a Jerry parole attacked out positions. Bully and Co. did well and gave them hell. Richard in action with grenades and did wonderful work but was wounded slightly in the shoulder. Captured two of the six and the rest fled. Hell and Tommy for the rest of the night. Only had one hours sleep.

<u>Monday, November 6th '44 – Gardaletta</u>

The stand-to and excitement lasted till dawn. A Yank patrol brought a comrade (Homer) into our casa with his leg off. I had the horror and nauseating job of bandaging the leg. Did all I could for them though I nearly vomited. Got Bill Janks with his stretcher and got Homer away to safety [Episode of Bill Janks and the salvo latile].* On the bridge with Joe (Rawlinson) when Richard passed on his way back (to hospital). I don't know how

Gardeletta today.

The house (centre) occupied by my section on the South bank near the footbridge. The extension to the right has been added since the war.

much longer I can stand it as I am far from fit. Pinpointed German machine gun on hill when he opened up as we pulled out at dawn. Slept fitfully during the day.

Tuesday, November 7th '44 – Gardaletta

Slept badly last night and am having nervous reaction as well as physical.

Put on a swine of a job in the evening guarding a tunnel exit in no-man's-land with not enough men. Sat for four hours staring into the blinding wind. Fortunately nothing happened and by dawn we were pretty shaken.

Wednesday, 8th November '44 – Gardaletta

Had a murderously cold day in the tunnel with a gale (blowing through) strong enough to test a Messerschmitt plane. Kept in my sleeping bag as much as possible. Roosevelt in again. Softly away and rations (fatigue).

Thursday, 9th November '44 – Gardaletta

Rather colder today. Hibernated during the day. Went on guard after sunset and we had a freezing shower (of rain). It got very cold after that and snow fell on the surrounding hills during the night. Started reading 'The Patrician'. Can't stand much more of this weather. Parcel of books from Valerie.

No wonder the guards hated this part of the Line and were glad to get relieved. Mid-winter on the top of the Appennines in tunnels, on bridges, in lice-ridden casas, stand-to fatigues, listening posts and guard with only one functioning lung was hardly Turkish delight, but I had stuck my neck out for it and this was the 'chop.'

Friday, November 10th '44 – Gardaletta

Some bombing while on guard tonight. Have been trying in vain to shoot a fowl or two which are stalking around here, but they are too bomb-happy, or we are!

---

* The scenario at this stage was so traumatic that when Bill Janks (M.M.) handed me the bottle of salvolatile to rescue me from nausea, I had to use it to rescue him from passing out completely.

<u>Friday, November 17th '44 – Bagnollo</u>

Slept well and rose early to shave and pack my kit. Said goodbye to closest friends but avoided publicity. Major Meeser wished me all the best and seems to think I've done something praiseworthy. I think I've been rather foolish. Went by ambulance through various C.C.S.'s and reached 108th Hospital in Florence in late afternoon and was made comfortable and had some good food.

Assisted generally in the ward, especially with a badly burnt chap wreathed in bandages. Cannot stand the stink of decaying flesh. To bed early.

<u>Saturday, 18th November '44 – Florence</u>

Was evacuated after breakfast and went to the airfield. Here we waited till the plane came in and left at 11a.m. for Naples. A very splendid trip and saw many splendid sights. Reached Naples by 1:30p.m. and have been sent to 103rd British Hospital, and am a bit worried (about absconding). Did the 30-mile ambulance journey and finally settled in by sundown. Am in a very cheery ward and there are not many serious cases here. Finished 'It's A Battlefield' and slept well.

ARCHIE MCLACHLAN

On the 17th/18th April '45, Archie McLachlan M.M., now a second lieutenant, lead No.2 Platoon of the R.D.L.I. in the Grand Assault on Mount Sole which had towered above us when Richard Platt M.M., and I had been attacked on Nov. 5th 1944.

On 25th April '45 in establishing a bridgehead near Picozzi across the River Po, 2nd Lieutenant McLachlan M.M., was again involved serving with the R.D.L.I. In a few weeks we were both back in Civvy street at John Dickinsons & Co. with business discussions over morning tea and anchovy toast at Greenacres.

Whereas the N.M.R. was involved ultimately in every conceivable condition and situation in W.W.II. for which it would have greatly profited by having dashing, young, intelligent colonels in command, it inherited a succession of misfits ranging from a schoolmaster, a grocer, and a policeman to farmers and sycophants. They were all nice guys but when someone is placed in precarious situations and whose command can materialise for you all kinds of infernal experiences, you tend to take a second look. Colonel No.1 had been a headmaster and still viewed all soldiers in his regiment as old boys whose welfare was paramount as long as they could come together when the sun went down and give a few Zulu war cries in concert. He was an old darling and went sick every time things hotted up. Years later I helped him in politics and consoled him when the battle between parties was lost. In Cape Town, attending parliament he often cried on my shoulder between drinks.

I had met No.2 when I was selling Croxley pads in civvy street for John Dickinson's. He owned a wholesale merchant business and as war approached was anxious to see his business well stocked as he was expecting call-up. Once or twice at army barracks and in the Officers' Mess at Ladysmith where I was on fatigue serving as waiter and at Gazala, he had met my gaze and may have remembered me.

When the long-awaited German attack came on May 26th '42 at Gazala, that colonel was away sick and another ferocious looking one replaced him. I think No.2 made a clever and calculated decision because during his absence we got the hiding of our lives fleeing through Tobruk to Alamein.

No.3 greatly resembled his nickname "Biltong", barked like a dog and was officer commanding the battalion during the fiasco on June 7th '42. He should never have ordered a composite company to attempt the job of a battalion and must be held responsible for our losses. I never saw him at the front or ever visiting the wounded in the hospitals where I lay. Even General Patton had the courtesy to do that.

We had a policeman by trade for No.4, and after the war he returned to his profession where he really belonged. This colonel was totally lacking in human psychology and a sense of humour. Instead of understanding that his men, some with four years of war service were worth more than squad drill and church parades, he brought out their resentment and bitterness. Wounded in Italy and again in hospital on the D.I. list for a long period, I never once saw him at the 92nd British General Hospital in Naples or in the South African hospital at Bari and never in the armoured line advancing up the Italian Peninsula.

Why the N.M.R. by-passed in promotion its most experienced soldiers, heroes by example to their men, will never be known. The much loved Bello Theunissen M.C., should have been colonel in the early stages of the North African campaigns. Captain Vic Paul and Pat Lyster both rose from the ranks through sheer valour in action. They were the victors of Miteirya Ridge at Alamein and should have been Commanding Officers of the N.M.R., long before any outsider was considered.

AUTHOR'S ARMY DETAILS

Enlisted: 1939 Age 16

Served in: South African 1st Infantry Division – 1940/43.

East Africa, Abyssinia, Egypt and Libia.

The Army of the Nile – 1940/41.

British 8th Army in Sept. 1941/44 in Egypt, Libya and Italy.

American 5th Army in Italy – 1944.

6th South African Armoured Division – 1943/45.

7th British Armoured Division – 1941/42.

Invalided out of S. African Army, April 1945 – multiple shrapnel wounds.

HOSPITAL IN BARI

Letter, 19th November 1944:

> "I'm sitting in a brightly lit ward… What a joy it is to sleep in the comfort of a warm bed & in peace whereas a week ago I was never warm and shells and machine gun fire screamed over our heads all night and we did on an average six hours of sentry guard between dusk and dawn every night. And my tummy is full & my chest is easier.
>
> I'm reading *Vanity Fair* at the moment. It's about time I started on Thackeray. My childhood was sadly lacking in good literature. I used to read the books mother read – mainly by Joseph Hocking and A.J. Cronin. There's a wireless giving it hell here, but I love it to death: the relaxation after the strain of the last few weeks is great."

My two extended convalescences in military hospitals gave me time to think about the sick, the lame and the lazy as well as the dead and the dying. Even then it took some years to come to strange conclusions related to that favourite of subjects which so often confronts those faced with violent death or mutilation......the matter of 'Fate.' Are our most excruciating experiences somehow pre-ordained? Are they nodes in the criss-crossing vicissitudes of our lives, synchronised to exact perhaps the utmost learning from life's challenges? It seemed to me, not just because I was one of them, those suddenly burdened with pain, especially in the war, were so often turned upon again and again to be afflicted by fate.

Fred Clarke in the N.M.R. had a leg shattered in W.W.II. which then necessitated amputation. We met again in 1958 attending Medical School in Cape Town. Successful and charming there, he was struck down a few years later with terminal cancer.

Jack Miller, an infantryman badly wounded with me at Alamein, happily employed in a large oil company was similarly struck down with cancer only a few years later.

Shorty Carneson, on the other side of me in the bayonet charge at Alamein, afflicted in childhood with poverty and later with alcoholism was wounded in the jaw by a piece of ricocheting shrapnel and after the war shared in the agonies of his younger brother at the hands of apartheid.

Bernard Notcutt, information officer suffering agonies from heat-stroke in the Western Desert became professor of psychology at my university only to be struck down mortally by a brain tumour eight years into the peace.

Eddy Sayer, taken prisoner in the Gazala fighting on June 7th, suffered frightful psychological disorders while in captivity. He joined me in peacetime celebrations only to die of cancer in his mid-forties.

For his action at Gardaletta, Richard Platt won the Military Medal and because later he also rendered distinguished service in Italy:

On the night 17/18th April 1945, his Company was laid on to take Covo and this N.C.O. was in command of the leading section. Having led them to the start line, through a mined area, which necessitated lifting and taping, he waited on the start line, under heavy enemy fire, for the orders to go in. Owing to a considerable delay there and eventual cancellation of orders, the men were subjected to prolonged shelling, but Corporal Platt, by his cheerfulness and calm behaviour, kept complete control of a difficult situation and brought his section out without loss. Again on 28th April 1945, when the Company was advancing along the road through Noventa, it was fired on from the rear by the enemy positioned in the houses on the East of the road. Corporal Platt was directed to clear the enemy from the area and immediately went in and mopped up the position so quickly that the advance was never even halted. Throughout operations, Corporal Platt has shown himself an outstanding N.C.O. displaying courage beyond the call of duty.

Dick and I were to remain firm friends both in the world of commerce and outside of it, where we often sought each other's opinions and advice. Richard's ageing father gave me an opening in the printing industry, which led to my lifetime in publishing.

DECEMBER IN BARI

December '44 was a dreary and disturbing month living in hospital and finding ways and means of getting back to South Africa where I would be finally invalided out of the army. As Christmas approached I watched matinee operas in Bari and took over some of the harder work from the nurses in the ward. My main task was to provide a Christmas theme for several wards and get patients involved in their ward decorations. In my own ward I created a giant mural bon-bon and each patient was to draw in the explosion part of the mural his own ideas about its content novelties. The nurses loved it. I thought it was awful and had to discreetly cull some of the horrors imaged on it by sick, distorted and resentful artistic potential. There was not much food around but if you were kind the nurses would do you Horlicks during the frosty nights. Regimental friends, aware of the vacuum I was in sent helpful advice. Pooch Marais had a brother in the S.A.A.F. who eventually managed to swing a flight back out of Italy for me.

Saturday, 23rd December '44 – Bari

Had a pretty heavy drink up of champagne with Olifants and two Carbineer boys. Saw the *Barber of Seville* – very few nurses. Had a lift down and back. Read 'Zulu Paraclete.'

Sunday, 24th December '44 – Bari

Went to performance of *Aida* in the afternoon. It was a (fine) all round performance with brilliant dancing, singing and scenery. Best opera so far. After dinner went to (carol) service and then to bed.

Monday, 25th December '44 – Bari

The day dawned fine. We soon got stuck into the liquor we had secreted into the building. Threw a cracker under a sister and incurred her wrath. Had a fine Christmas dinner and two bottles of beer. Slept in the afternoon and listened to carols in the evening and was called upstairs by Joss' cousin and the blonde sister in our ward. Had a very pleasant evening and two bottles of beer.

Wednesday, 27th December '44 – Bari

Left hospital at 9:30a.m. and was surprised at being taken to the S.A.A.F. transit camp. Expected R & I (?) therefore interviewed Pooch's brother asked him to do something for getting me home by air. A very good chap. Not very happy or comfortable at the camp. Read late into the night Frankau's '*Martin Make-Belief*'. Gave Joy Waller a jersey. The sisters are badly looked after up here.

The interview worked and in a couple of days I was scheduled on to a flight back to South Africa.

Friday, 29th December '44 – Bari

Left early for the drome. The cold was bitter and the plane didn't pitch up. Back again to camp for lunch. Over to hospital and found a stack of letters awaiting me. Went in and spent the afternoon at Blonde's bedside. She has a bad cold and found my jersey a help. Sister Johnstone tried to bounce me but failed. Had a long wait, but enjoyed it reading my mail meanwhile. On draft again but the weather is vile and the moon full! (always an anxious time for allied soldiers). Went to an amazing lecture and demonstration of hypnotism. Wrote to Len.

Saturday, 29th December '44 – Bari/Foggia

There was plenty of driving rain at the aerodrome and was surprised that we tried to travel by air at all. Had a mishap before starting when we brushed another plane and then nearly had to turn back when we were thrown about in a squall. Travelled fairly low down the heel of Italy across the Bay of Taranto. Saw Etna's snowy peaks and Sicily's narrow beaches. Had a very rough passage and I got quite windy. Crossing to Malta the weather improved. The island was bathed in sunshine. Was pleased to land and made comfortable at the camp with beer and gin on tap. Was half-put under hypnotism before bed.

My own concern about rough air passage resulted from a history of air disasters plaguing flights to S.A. back from Italy. Planes being used were veterans of the war, some say damaged and shot up. Captain Wynn of the N.M.R. had been killed a few months earlier on a disastrous flight back and, a year earlier, Dan Pienaar O.C. 1st South African Division had also suffered the same fate.

Sunday, 31st December '44 – Malta

Were awakened at 4:30a.m. This is my 22nd birthday. Took off in the dark. Ran into bad weather just after dawn and had another nasty spell. Had to go around the storm. On land for a second breakfast at Castel Benito. Our pilot commented "Only fools and birds fly!" Flew at very high altitude rest of the way. Felt a few effects of it (high altitude). Had lunch at El Adem. Passed Bardia and Mersa and I saw many old and memorable spots.

Sitting in the plane after leaving Malta I had a dream about Ellis and we were back in the ward at the 92nd, both in our beds. His throaty movements were just audible with intermittent screams, curses and grunts. I saw myself in his circumstances but out in the world for all to hear. My conscience was goading me to tell the truth. Ellis had no chance and the scanty supply of penicillin was denied him. I too had had no chance and but for Hoddy, I may have been like Ellis, denied the penicillin. Startled, I awoke.

The sun had tipped the cloud lining them with gold and we were flying south over Alamein where 250,000 men had, two years previously joined in momentous battle.

ARMY DISCHARGE

After undergoing various therapies for the effect of multiple shrapnel wounds I secured a discharge from the South African Army in April 1945.

APPENDICIES

APPENDIX I

Short Historical Review of…

THE NATAL MOUNTED RIFLES

1854

The original parent unit, the Royal Durban Rangers, was a mounted corps formed at Durban in 1854. The uniform comprised a black helmet with black horsehair plume and the scroll R.D.R., tunic and trousers (this was before the days of riding breeches) of blue serge with red facings.

The Colonial Government supplied muzzle-loading muskets and heavy cavalry swords. A contingent from the Royal Durban Rangers was in active service in December 1854 against an unruly native chief in the Umkomanzi area and assisted in subduing this unrest.

1856

In this year the Rangers participated in an expedition to the Natal border, during the disturbances created by the fighting between Cetshwayo and Mbulazi, and again in 1861 when Cetshwayo's "hunting parties" near the Tugela gave rise to anxiety.

1879 Zulu War

The Victoria Mounted Rifles (formed 1862), Alexandra Mounted Rifles (1856), Stanger Mounted Rifles (1875, Durban Mounted Rifles (1875), which later consolidated into the Natal Mounted Rifles, took part in the Battle of Inyezane in January 1879 (The Regiment's First Battle Honour), and detachments were engaged in the action at Gingindhlovu.

1888

In this year the Victoria Mounted Rifles, Alexandra Mounted Rifles, Durban Mounted Rifles and Umzimkulu Mounted Rifles amalgamated under the name of Natal Mounted Rifles, with headquarters in Durban.

1894

In this year the Regiment was split into two wings, the Natal Mounted Rifles forming the right wing and the Border Mounted Rifles the left, the former operating in the northern coastal sector and the B.M.R. in the south.

It was in 1898 that the famous South African war/cry "Qobolwayo-ji" originated in the Bellair Troop of the Natal Mounted Rifles and is said to have been the war/cry of a famous Zulu regiment at the time of Tshaka, and is a challenge or cry of defiance. Another Zulu cry still used in the Regiment is "Se si Fikile," meaning "now we have arrived, so all is well."

Both the N.M.R. and B.M.R. were called out in September 1899 for the South African War. They took part in eighteen engagements and suffered eighty-four casualties. Both Regiments formed part of the Garrison during the Siege of Ladysmith, and twenty men from the N.M.R. formed the personal bodyguard of General Sir George White, V.C., Commander of the Garrison.

1914-1918

During the South West African Campaign the Regiment formed part of the 8th Mounted Brigade and rode from Luderizbucht via Aus, Beersheba, Gibeon and Rehoboth to Windhoek, some five hundred miles through desert and sand. The main action of this campaign in which the Regiment participated was at Gibeon, where a decisive defeat was inflicted on the enemy.

During this period no less than twenty-five decorations and medals were bestowed upon members of the regiment and fourteen were mentioned in despatches.

1939-1945

The N.M.R. mobilised for full-time service in June 1940. The 1st. Battalion (V) was soon one thousand strong and joined the 2nd. South African Infantry Brigade at Ladysmith.

Appendix II

EARLY DAYS
AUTHOR'S MEMOIRS OF 1940

Private Baker D.M. No. 77581, age 17
Platoon No.1 Headquarters N.M.R.Somewhere in Africa!
The months of June to October 1940, transcribed verbatim from
1940 diary.

Training

Week beginning Sunday 9th June 1940.

There was a colossal crowd lining the route to the station to see
the 1st N.M.R. off for active service. I was in the first platoon.
The crowds were enthusiastic like I have never seen them before.
The first troops left just before eleven p.m. Derek & Jock and I
grabbed a coupe' and pinched blankets & sheets & slept like
Lords. The train raced through to Ladysmith without a stop. It
was damn cold. The women's auxiliary had grub to meet us
with. The three of us were posted to the same bungalow.

That night the only warmth that the army offered us was one
blanket each. It was freezing. The three of us slept together for
warmth. The temperature dropped below 40° F. We have had
intensive training & squad drill for three solid days. Italy has
declared war and it looks good for us leaving for North Africa.

Our training has begun. It is mostly lectures on every subject
possible. We have been issued with beds at last and of course
make full use of them. The news in Europe looks bad. The
French are finished from what I can see. The B.E.F. will be cut
off. France has capitulated. Words fail me.

How right was my prophecy of a year ago. The French are nothing but a decadent race who lack all ideals of patriotism, who disgrace the very anthem they sing. That they should dare to make peace behind England's back. They are finished as a nation. They have been annihilated as a race. The very fact that they should surrender when the enemy had barely occupied a tenth of their land leaves me with not an ounce of sympathy, but an uncontrollable feeling of loathing for the ....! The French hate England but they will be more than hating in a short while. The supposed friend and glorious ally that would fight to save Paris, that would fight to a finish against Hitlerism will soon be fighting for Hitlerism. The non-surrender and the death of the glorious French fleet is but another demonstration of the French hatred of us. The French have begged England now to rid them of their Empire, which is a damn sight more loyal than their mother country.

Have just been home for the weekend and had a marvellous time. Our training is still going on as usual, but we have been issued with gas masks, which are a curse, and we are now doing bayonet training, which is a bigger curse. We are gradually being issued with our proper kit. The movements of the Petain government put me in the hell of a temper every time I read of them. Everyone seems apprehensive that England will be invaded. This is stupid. I say now England will never be invaded. By that I mean the Germans will never actually land in a large scale, but might of course put out a few feelers and make a few practice invasions. But they would not dare to land. I have a ten shilling bet with Derek about it and I shall win it. Have again been home for the weekend and again I had a good time. Things are beginning to move now in Ladysmith and I think we will soon be off for another destination. And won't we be pleased. Our training is as boring as ever. Kit is still being issued. We now have our battle dress or Maternity Jackets, and to crown it all I now have 3 pairs of boots. We will soon be having too much kit to carry. We have definite news that we are moving, and the general line of thought is Piet Retief. Yes we are off to Piet Retief tomorrow. Everyone is packed up and ready.

The ride to Piet Retief though rather boring and back breaking proved interesting as it was the first occasion I had entered the Transvaal. The northern Natal towns were friendly and hospitable, though Vryheid was rather cool.

Piet Retief... Hell, what a hole! The camp consists of straw huts with mud walls, and is situated about two miles from the town. The camp welcomed us with a wealth of dust and fleas. Our first job on arrival was to fashion ourselves beds from government stocks of timber. We do very little training and get plenty of rest.

In town on Saturday night had a bit of a spree with Derek. Place is like a blackout in the Congo. Derek, a friend and I wanted to clean a nationalist up but the police intervened.

Sensational news!!! We are off to Maritzburg tomorrow and thence to Durban on 5 days embarkation leave. The trip to P.M.B. was uneventful but the Vryheid women turned up trumps and gave us a feed on the station while most chaps had little or no clothing on. In Maritzburg we have been cleaning up and doing fatigues all day. Nearly missed the last train to Durban. Margaret was at the station to meet me having received my wire.

She's a champ and has been a pal during leave.

5 days leave.

For five hectic days I have let loose all passions held up in me since mobilisation. One day at the races, the next visiting relations and friends, the next wining, dining and celebrating; then buying requisites for Kenya, then another day at the races. Every night it's either a dance, a party, a wild orgy of drink or the flicks.

At least it is all over!! Here we are in Maritzburg kicking our heels waiting for the embarkation order.

We are getting hell laid into us during the day with manoeuvres, section leading and bayonet training. But at night it is a different tale. Leave is hard to procure, but we just walk through the guards when we like and they don't attempt to stop us. Nearly every night I either go into PMB or tear down to Durban. Most of us are physical wrecks. Seldom do we see our beds before 2a.m. I have had a few affairs with some of my old flames and while under 'fluence have come into contact with two definitely below the belt women. Kath has been up to take me for a drive on Sunday and Margaret as well. We are being frantically issued with kit. Expect to leave anytime. Am sick of saying goodbye. Received news that we are off on Monday. Have told the firm and Mr. Woods has given me our representatives' address in Nairobi. Had a spree with Derek on Saturday night and only got back just in time for roll call yesterday afternoon. Reveille to be sounded at four tomorrow morning. Went to service tonight.

An active service.

Monday morning when we entered the train we found ourselves for the first time on active service. Arriving at the wharf in Durban we found crowds to greet us. Everyone expected our ship the "Llangibby" to leave that evening but fortunately it didn't and leave was granted. Met Jock on the wharf. He looked very fit.

Margaret was waiting to meet me with the car as I left the docks. We arranged to pick Jock up later and Derek, Margaret and I went home to wash and get ready for the Roadhouse. We had a fine time and got back on board ship an hour late. We have to sleep on deck because of lack of space.

On the morning of October 15, after much hustle & bustle, our ship being second in a convoy of four ships and a cruiser, weighed anchor at ten-thirty and slowly slipped away from the wharf. Waving crowds on the quay though penned up behind the barb-wire and railings began to wave even more frantically while on board some enthusiastic troops struck up popular tunes and gave the N.M.R. call. Further and further the distance stretched and the liner, as if unwilling to leave the relatives of its protégé bade a mournful farewell with three long blasts. And now the voices of the men began to fade until barely a score were singing "Wish me Luck." In time these faded. In the throats of these well-trained men an unmoveable lump replaced the deep notes of Auld Lang Syne.

Meanwhile all was not well with the crowd. I have been told that every woman and even the men, though still waving their handkerchiefs stood silent – awe-struck. Then the national anthem arose as if by instinct amongst the sorrowful community. Men bit their lips, old men, fathers and veterans of the first war to end war; youths, brothers and pals; and women stood unashamedly with tears in their eyes and on their cheeks.

Well out into the Maydon Channel forged the convoy. In a quiet and removed corner I sat watching unable to stop or attempt to stop my flow of tears that sprung involuntarily from my eyes. Along the wooden quayside ran a woman, a young girl trying bravely to keep up with her brother, father or lover. But those which affected me most were the farewell salutes of British and foreign ships. As we passed, each one gave vent to a series of blasts. By now we were passing H.M.S. Royal Sovereign. All the jack-tars were on deck and they bade us farewell with three rousing cheers. Out across the bar we pitched.

Durban's last adieu to her sons was a brilliant array of flashing mirrors stretching from Glenwood to Beachwood, transmitting a last message from civilian to soldier.

Soon, very soon, the bluff and all we had cherished slipped from sight behind a barrier of deepest blue. The next few days the ship was transformed from a luxury liner to a gambling hell. To kill boredom and melancholy men sought relief in cards, Crown & Anchor and drink.

Before the end of an uneventful trip we were drenched regularly every night on deck by tropical downpours. I did well at Poker, but most chaps lost heavily at Crown & Anchor. The day that Mombasa came into sight I was on air guard. A Hurricane and a Hartebeest flew over to welcome us and we docked safely in a climate that had Durban's summer humidity and the tropical heat in perfect combination. Almost immediately we were put into waiting trains and then began perhaps the most monotonous journey I will ever experience. Momby impressed me as being pretty from the harbour and a likeness to Cornwall was existent on some parts of the coast.

<u>KENYA</u>

The journey on occasions where the scenery varied was interesting especially after Voi when it became slightly cooler. However, that night, when 28 of us were crowded together in a 3rd Class Compartment, can only be described as a night of horror. Our hardships have been unparalleled in history since the Black Hole of Calcutta. The best parts of the interior to sleep on were the baggage racks followed closely by the floor under the seats out of the way of feet. The latter position I adopted owing to my height. Windows were smashed to obtain air, regardless of mosquitoes. During the night two birthdays were celebrated and a general singsong under the most harrowing circumstances was adopted. Needless to say I had little or no sleep.

At long last dawn broke and we found the train lined on either side by wandering Thomson Gazelle which grazed in amazing profusion. Occasionally, giraffe could be seen cantering across the veldt, which was covered by a rich yellow grass. By 8 o'clock we steamed into Nairobi station. We had a good breakfast and were soon on our way again. Nairobi, though not much bigger than Maritzburg was extremely pretty with a distinctly modern touch about its buildings. Our surroundings began to change and throughout the whole day we were winding our way down steep valleys, now puffing up long hills, now passing huge volcano craters and finally the great salt lake of Navasha. This lake was fascinating and left its impression of blue and silver in our minds long after. Our destination Gil Gil is comparable with the Indian villages round Sea Cow lake in Durban. It was comprised mainly of a cluster of Indian stores and garages around the station. From here the line continued to Nakuru, but we branched off and eventually stepped out on to our camping ground. The first night we slept in tents, but the next night found us rather uncomfortably spread-eagled across the floor of a large shanty. On the whole I enjoyed my stay at Gil Gil. Our training was continued, as were air guards. Our three posts are named Point, Glenwood and Berea. Although hot during the day and cool through the night, the climate was quite tolerable. Flies were the biggest curse and jigger-fleas and snakes ran them a close second and third. During our hours of rest I spent my leisure in cycling on army bikes to all places of beauty and interest. The most momentous of my rides was to Flamingo lake one brilliant Saturday afternoon. Here was a shallow salt lake of deepest blue bordered by a smooth shore of white sulphur deposit. Encircling this veritable domain of the Flamingo was a verdant undergrowth of fever trees and bush. Like a drop of Prussian blue in a saucer of green it lay with mountain peaks reaching to the sky across which scudded the notorious white rain clouds. From various folds in the hills escaped voluminous spirals of vapour from a wealth of geysers. And now the crowning splash of an artist's brush on a beautiful picture, in the centre of the lake on an island of white mud stood the Flamingos. Thousand upon thousand of these birds in plumage from the palest pink to the deepest crimson basked in the last rays of the dying sun. And just before King Sol dipped behind the hills of mauve, his great host of subjects rose like a curtain in the breeze and thrice encircled their lake abode before the threat of darkness bade them descend. I can still remember as we trudged wearily pushing our cycles up the hillside, the last glance at that scene "so touching in its majesty."

Apart from fishing (which I detest) reading and card-playing were our only outlets for pleasure. Apart from many platoon and section squabbles it was a free life that we spent. It was not long before our section separated and moved to a large EPIP. Here we spent many happy days, which ended only too soon. Just before we moved I had the good fortune to have a flip in a plane.

Being one of a party of ten I arrived at Nakuru aerodrome after a bumpy 30-mile journey. As the car pulled up, six fighter-bombers were preparing to leave and bomb the N.M.R. camp. One seat was open for a flip and we decided to draw. The idea was to write a number on a piece of paper and the first man to give the number in rotation got the ride. I started off, and by some undeniable luck gave No.4. I drew the right number 25 and dashed across to the waiting plane. Sans goggles, sans overalls, I jumped into the rear cockpit. A hasty consultation with the pilot about how to fix the parachute left me just as ignorant. But now a devil-may-care mood possessed me and I didn't give a damn. In a few moments we were off. Surely there can be no more delightful sensation than rising from the ground in a tiny plane. It is as if a mighty invisible hand is drawing you away from the earth, higher and higher. In a matter of seconds we were high above the drome; homes became match-boxes and men merely specks. Miles and miles of the rift valley lay spread out below us. The three lakes, Navasha, Flamingo, and a third, whose name fails my memory, lay like three big puddles of silver on a carpet with a patchwork of green and brown. Now we roared in an arrow formation of three planes down the valley towards the camp. The blast from the propellers was terrific and my uncovered hair whipped into my eyes. A feeling of exaltation possessed me with all the valley like an open book before me, and I began to sing at the top of my voice and received a shock to find my ears had failed me completely. The reason for this I can not explain, but it had the effect of sobering me slightly. After encircling the camp twice the planes altered formation and prepared to bomb. And now came the most thrilling moment of the flight. Our plane suddenly dipped and down we went in a power dive from 3,000 feet following closely on the tail of No.2; 3000, 2800,2000, 1500, down we shot like a bolt from the blue. My stomach by this time was up by my neck but still we fell, and that peculiar high-pitched note often heard in cinemas when a plane is diving, screamed in my ears. The temperature changed rapidly. Specks became men; fantastic camouflage changed to gun emplacements. Then at a hundred feet, when I was becoming slightly uneasy we rose. My entrails promptly descended to well below their former position.

The first dive was over and as I turned in the cockpit I noted our own tent and even gun positions and most of all the uplifted wondering faces of several soldiers. This performance we repeated eight times and then we circled and flew hell-for-leather back to the drome. No sooner had my Hawker Hart landed, then another pilot ran up and asked me if I would like another spin. I told him I would. Here now was a different type of pilot to the first, who though obviously well trained was level headed.

Tall and fair with blue eyes, he was the youngest pilot in the squadron. Though he was eighteen, he was considered the most skilful and daring, with several wrecked planes to his credit.

In a matter of seconds I was again in the air. This time however, we hardly rose above 500 feet. Making for the neighbouring lake he descended to about 100 feet and flew round the soda caked edge. So low were we that the stench of the sulphur deposits was nearly overpowering. Lower and lower he flew, 50 feet, 30 feet, 10 feet, and then for a split thrilling second he touched ground, bumped along twice, and took off again flying towards the eastern shore which was clothed with dense undergrowth. Never higher than 50 feet, he frightened and stampeded a herd of zebra, chased an ostrich almost decapitating it, and finally roused several hippos from their muddy lair. Soon, too soon was this crazy adventure over and as I walked back to our lorry I realised why the Empire was able to beat the superior German planes over Dunkirk. We have men of a calibre equalled only by the men of our navy and although outnumbered, our planes are the cream of our industrial attainments.

In vain did I try for Nairobi leave. And when it seemed certain that I should get leave our regiment was given orders to move. Before we left Gil Gil it became imperative for a certain number of the platoon to be transferred to a rifle company. Like a fool I remained in ack ack and lost some of my best friends. If I had gone to a rifle company I would, I am sure, never regretted my action.

It was towards the end of November, 1940, that we forsook our life of ease and comparative luxury and headed northwards to meet the advances of the Italians who had begun their invasion of Kenya. The S. African army met the enemy thrusts with three brigades of white troops and some black K.A.R's and Nigerian troops. There were two fronts on the north east frontier around Wajir, where the first brigade operated with native troops and on the north west frontier around Marsabit. This was our destination. To reach Marsabit a desert had to be crossed and for many, many days we wound our way through the comparatively flat scrub country passing intermittent koppies and hillocks whose queer stony formations often intrigued us – one resembled Gibraltar and others human likenesses. At night we more often than not camped near an oasis. At one of these "Liasamis" I saw the biggest scorpion of the whole campaign. It became a pastime matching scorpion against scorpion in a small densely packed arena of soldiers.

It took some days to cross this semi-desert and finally we crossed the last river we were to see for many months at Archers Post. Marsabit oasis is, I think, one of the most amazing and intriguing places on earth. The oasis is really a gigantic forest, which sprawls over a sudden clump of small hills in the otherwise flat waterless country. How this forest exists I cannot say. There are no rivers for hundreds of miles, and there are only water holes in the area. The forest is far thicker than any in the Union and is comprised of large trees as old it seemed as the hills themselves. A green moss or fungus draped each tree giving it the appearance of a weeping willow. Luxuriant grass, long and green, grew in the patches, which were not already covered by the veritable jungle. This then was to be our home for five weeks and was the army's forward base. In between two great nipples with their brassiere of green reaching up to the windswept sky, was our temporary home. Nestling under the trees were many grass huts known as "bandas." Two or three of us lived in each of these. They were exceptionally well made and were weatherproof warm and comfortable. Their furniture consisted of beds made of sticks and odd shelves for kit. We gave them names and made them quite homely with pictures and other knick-knacks. My particular banda which I shared with one other was called "Ye olde Brothel" it being an outsize in bandas and thus a congregating place for card games and binges. Those were happy days, and our only duty other than bayonet training was to mount an air sentry on the summit of the larger of the two hills. Each morning just before dawn, three of us had to take the path up the hill. Laden with rations we spent the day up the top reading, writing, cooking and spotting for aircraft. The path was rather a precarious one, for it had to be navigated before sunrise and after sunset. It wound through the forest and skirted a cliff, rising all the time. If a person strayed off the path he was lost in a few minutes. One party in another camp did this and were lost for days before a search party of local "patriots" found them. A tribe of baboons lived in the cliff and all day long we could watch them prancing in the trees and barking. To many of us – born and bred in the towns they were rather frightening, and many a time did I cock my rifle and walk past the cliff with my heart in my mouth.

There were still many buck and an odd buffalo, which we left very much alone. At night we were particularly wary and more so when a few roars were heard in the distance. The only curse that was upon us was that of insects, or rather vermin. By day we were entertained by flies – at night mosquitoes started their antics. Not content with these there were plenty of fleas. But by far the biggest inquisitor was the tick. These ticks were no bigger than a pin head and plagued us in their thousands. I met quite a few of these in my first never-to-be-forgotten encounter. In about five minutes I took ninety off my legs and burnt hundreds more off my clothes with a cigarette. Such a curse these became, that on air guard we were forced to sit in the centre of a ground sheet and watch them cross the edges, whence they were quickly eradicated. In the cool of the trees life was pleasant and birds of many colours, species and sizes chirped and chattered above us all day. A small red speckled butterfly swarmed over the countryside all day and added colour to the already picturesque scenery. It was in these surroundings that we spent our first Christmas in the army and a very pleasant one it was. A couple of gazelle had been shot and these were roasted on an open fire on Christmas Eve. The whole platoon sat round in "braavleis" fashion, and in turn each member gave a song recitation or skit. We had ample supplies of liquor and our spirits were high. The party ended up going "Zulu" and "Hey Makadema" was the last refrain that echoed over the silent hills before we returned to our bandas. A description of celebrations at New Year would hardly be proper in this account. But a few words must be spent on the "Dance of the veiled shifta."

Appendix III

GAZALA near TOBRUK

Saturday, June 13th, 1941 – the nineteenth continuous day of battle – broke warm and clear. With the first light the two armies were engaged. Almost at once the battlefield was covered over with rolling sand and the smoke of burning oil. Confused orders and messages were flying over the radio on both sides. The front-line British tanks called for assistance, and launched an attack from the north to cut through the base of Rommel's wedge. They ran at once on the 88-millimetre guns that had been concealed in the night. Simultaneously, the tip of the enemy wedge threatened the British armoured headquarters which were forced to decamp hurriedly eastwards. During this move the headquarters lost contact with a great part of the tanks joined in battle. And the battle was ferocious.

In an attempt to get within range the British charged headlong upon the German positions. In a few minutes it was a massacre for both sides. From dozens of concealed positions the 88s opened up a tremendous belt of fire. Those British tanks, which had somehow escaped the opening salvoes and got right up to the enemy, found themselves exposed and deserted by their comrades who had fallen by the way. Those who were only slightly hit at first and turned to get away were caught by the second and third barrages of gunfire. Those who came in as reinforcements found themselves in a confusion of blown sand, burning vehicles and deadly shellfire that raked the plain again and again. When at last the British sighted the German tanks and went forward at them they were led on to other guns and demolished. Then and not until then, the German tanks came out and ran upon the British forces that had been largely cut up by anti-tank guns.

To a great extent it was the repetition of the oldest tactic on earth. Little brother goes down the road and the footpad springs out at him. Little brother runs back to the spot where big brother is waiting with a cudgel behind a corner. Big brother springs out and knocks the footpad down.

Both sides had many times lured or tried to lure enemy tanks on to concealed anti-tank guns. The Germans succeeded here not because it was a new tactic, but because the British were bound to attack to stop the march on Tobruk, and to attack they had to run into the 88 barrage in order to get their own guns within range.

One after another the British squadrons reported that they were taking heavy losses and needed immediate support. It was the Germans who were charging now, charging past the burning hulks, and they forced the depleted defenders to give battle. In this tremendous follow-up the British became isolated from one another and were forced to fight in small groups. These groups in turn got separated from their own anti-tank guns and their supply vehicles. Many tanks ran out of petrol and had to be abandoned. All the confusion which had overtaken the Germans in their earlier retreat was redoubled here in the British lines, and at a time when we had no reserves, when only a few counters were left on the board, and so each counter was vital. This was the position that Rommel had reached in his big retreat from Sidi Rezegh in the winter except that it was we this time who had no more reserves. The great battle for the annihilation of the tanks – the only sort of battle that really counts in the desert – was nearing its end.

— From a *Year of Battle* by Alan Moorehead, 1943

Operation Lightfoot
– Plan for opening the battle of Alamein

The information contained in Lightfoot was to the effect that:

(1) 1 S. A. DIVISION was to attack and capture Sanyet el Miteyira Ridge before 1st light on 'D' plus 1, and to exploit southwards.

(2) 2 N. Z. DIVISION would be attacking on its right.

(3) 1 S. A. DIVISION would be attacking on 2 BRIGADE front: right – 2ND BRIGADE; left – 3RD BRIGADE and that 1ST S. A. BRIGADE would be protecting the Division's southern flank.

(4) The attack by 2 BRIGADE was to be carried out in two phases, the N. M. R. co–ordinating with C. T. H. and F. F. B. by first light 'D' plus 1.

There was to be an extensive programme of air support.

The main attack was carried out by the 9TH AUSTRALIAN (Right Coast), 51ST HIGHLAND (Right Centre), 2ND NEW ZEALAND (Left Centre) and 1ST SOUTH AFRICAN DIVISION (Left); the objective was to cut two corridors through the enemy's fortifications.

Every available man, including drivers and batmen, in the N. M. R. Battalion took part in the Battle. Support Company Men acted as riflemen, to add weight to the attack. The battle strength of the regiment was:

	Officers	Other Ranks
Regimental Headquarters Group	9	32
Headquarters Company	4	19
'A' Company & Supports	6	82
'B' Company & Supports	5	90
'C' Company & Supports	6	94

The N. M. R. Battalion's objective was the main enemy position on the Sanyet el Miteiriya Ridge, on a three company front, each company operating with three platoons forward, with full advantage being taken of the supporting artillery, V. M. G. and mortar barrage.

Under cover of the barrage, the advance continued up to 300 yards from the enemy main minefields, where intense artillery, mortar and M. G. fire retarded progress. Extensive and deep though the minefield was, the assault group advanced, despite the heavy casualties, especially through anti-personnel mines. Once through the minefield, a successful bayonet assault was made on the enemy posts, which fell one by one. Prisoners-of-War collected were evacuated by Cape Corps Guards, through the Report Centres on the Axis of Advance. At 2325 hours, a gap through the minefield had been established, and five minutes later all organized opposition had been overcome, the objective gained, and success signals received from the companies. Lieutenant-Colonel Harris was then able to report by line to Brigadier Poole the success code-word SHERRY, indicating that the N. M. R.

had achieved its object. The support group was thereupon ordered up immediately, and consolidation proceeded with, in face of enemy artillery fire, which was continuing. Several captured enemy anti-tank guns were utilised in the defence system which was rapidly achieved.

At 0200 hours on 24 October, instructions were received for one company to be sent to support ½ F. F. B. 'B' Company (Captain R. V. Paul) was detailed for this purpose, and left the Battalion's area at 0300 hours, its strength having been reduced to 5 Officers and 42 Other Ranks. On arrival in the ½ F. F. B. Section, it attacked the objective with mortars, using high explosive and smoke, and, after heavy fighting gained the objective at 0605 hours. Its casualties were:

3 Killed (Lieutenant Dennis Platt, Privates B.M. Lloyd,
     C.R. Joyner.)
1 Died of Wounds (Corporal W. J. M. van Niekirk)
22 Wounded (including the author)

An uncounted number of German paratroops of 433 REGIMENT were captured by the Company, during this engagement, and handed to the ½ F. F. B. Fifteen minutes later, after a desperate struggle, all resistance had been quelled and the gallant force began to consolidate their gains. Shortly afterwards they were relieved by the F. F. B.

Captain Paul's planning and leadership was superb and 'B' Company had every reason to be proud of their achievement for every officer and man acquitted himself with distinction. But the toll had been an extremely heavy one, for only one officer and twenty-eight men returned unscathed to the battalion; the rest had been either killed or wounded. Of the five officers who went into action, Lieutenant Dennis Plat was killed, while Captain Vic Paul, 2/Lieutenants Pat Lyster and Bunny Evans were wounded. When Captain Paul fell, severely wounded, 2nd Lieutenant P. J. Lyster immediately took command of the Company. For his courage and devotion to duty, he was awarded the Military Cross.

AL AMEIN BY FIELD MARSHAL LORD CARVER

1st Natal Mounted Rifles captured 'Red' line in 2nd Brigade's sector without difficulty. Cape Town Highlanders, due to pass through on the right, got involved in serious and confused fighting on their start line and suffered considerable casualties, including the two leading company commanders. This led to the artillery programme for the second phase being postponed several times, while attempts were made to deal with the opposition and sort out the confusion. Although it started again at five minutes past two, it was not until half past four that the infantry advance was resumed. It then met no serious opposition and the battalion was established on Miteiriya Ridge by first light. On the left first / second Field Battalion also ran into trouble, including an unexpected minefield. After some difficult and confused fighting the battalion established itself just east of the ridge, a mile short of their final objective, having had 42 men killed, 8 officers and 133 men wounded and having captured 36 Germans.

– El Alamein by Field Marshal, Lord Carver.
Publisher: B.T. Batsford Ltd.

It was the N.M.R., the author's own regiment that rescued the 1st Field Battalion from it's massacre in the minefield of Miteiriya Ridge (see map page 275).

– Author

BATTLEFIELD AT ALAMEIN

While we were busy consolidating our positions, a much-distracted N. C. O. of the F. F. B. came to me appealing for help as his company had come up against a particularly strong enemy post. His comrades had been severely mauled in fruitless efforts to take their objective. Under the circumstances I could not leave my own sector to go to their assistance but, while the fellow was still with me, I telephoned Col. Harris explaining the position.

At 2am the C.O. received instructions to send a company in support of the F. F. B. 'B' Company of the N.M.R. was detailed for this difficult task under the leadership of Capt. Vic Paul. An hour later the company left the regimental area in order to make the preparations for an attack on the original F. F. B. objective which was still in enemy hands. At 5.40am Capt. Paul and his men, supported by F. F. B. mortars, using smoke and high-explosive bombs, stormed the strongpoint in the face of heavy machine-gun fire. Fifteen minutes later, after a desperate struggle, all resistance had been quelled and the gallant force began to consolidate their gains. Shortly afterwards they were relieved by the F. F. B.

It is unfortunate that I have not been successful in obtaining an account of this fierce engagement but as a result of my enquiries. I do know that Capt Paul's planning and leadership was superb. "B" Company had every reason to be proud of their achievement for every officer and man acquitted himself with distinction but the toll had been extremely heavy. Only one officer and twenty-eight men returned unscathed to the regiment; the rest had been either killed or wounded. Of the five officers who went into action, Lieutenant Dennis Platt was killed, while Capt. Vic Paul, Lieutenant Pat Lyster and "Bunny" Evans were wounded. When Vic fell, severely wounded, Pat immediately took command of the company. For his courage and devotion to duty he was awarded the military cross, a copy of the citation reads as follows:

ACTION FOR WHICH RECOMMENDED

Attack on Sanyet Miteyriya Ridge, night 23/24 Oct. 42. In this action in spite of being slightly wounded, 2/Lieutenant Lyster displayed great personal courage and leadership in an advance which culminated in a successful bayonet charge on an enemy position. In another action a few hours later, when his Coy. Com. became a casualty, 2 / Lieutenant. Lyster took comd without hesitation and gallantly led the advance under heavy fire. He fell wounded a second time. His gallantry at the critical stage preserved the impetus of the charge and enabled the Coy to launch a final successive offensive on the objective.

(Sgd.) L. M. Harris, Lt-Col., N. M. R.

Recommended by:

(Sgd.) W. H. E. Poole, Brig.,

Comd. 2S.A. Inf. Bde.

APPENDIX IV

BOOKS READ 1943-44

Too much should not be read into this list of some of the literature read by the British 8th Army more than 60 years ago. The books circulated amongst the N.M.R. Regiment being then passed on from Army unit to Army unit until they fell to pieces. Ones with a bit of "stick" in them circulated much faster than those without. Some authors appeared much more frequently than others like Gilbert Frankau, Somerset Maugham and James Hilton.

Taking myself as an average reader I am surprised that Rex Warner's famous book *Aerodrome* only scored 3 points. Ten years later doing English at University it was regarded as a classic. On the other hand some of the genuine classics like *Vanity Fair*, *War and Peace* and *Northwest Passage* were greatly appreciated.

We live in an age in which reading is no longer encouraged with great persistence, probably due to displacement by the Internet.

We have to remember that in W.W.II. reading material that carried news, especially war news, was grabbed but so were crossword puzzles, which were at a premium. The main motivating factor was always some degree of boredom and the need for diversion.

Book titles noted in the author's war diaries:

Year	Rating	Title	Author
1943	8	The Pied Piper	Neville Shute
1943	10	Dynasty of Death	Taylor Caldwell
1943	8	Random Harvest	J.B. Hilton
1943	8	Born to Trouble	Pat Alexander
1943	7	Thee Are No South Africans	G. Calpiens
1943	3	Fortune's Fool	R. Sabatini

1943	5	Fragment from A Surgeon's Log Book	
1943	6	The Impatient Virgin	
1943	3	Clementine	A.E. Mason
1943	10	The Way of The Transgressor	Fanson
1943	2	If I Were Your Wodehouse	
1943	5	The Mother	Pearle S. Buck
1943	8	Spanish Maine	P.C. Wren
1943	9	"My Son, My Son"	Howard Spring
1943	1	The Road to Glenfairlie	
1943	8	Contango	James Hilton
1943	9	Cage Me a Peacock	Noel Langley
1943	5	The Powers of Darkness - Short Stories	
1943	7	The Sword of Fate	D. Wheatley
1943	6	The Loom of Youth	A. Maugh
1943	8	Thirsty Land	Jane Sutherland
1943	8	Rebecca	Daphne Du Maurier
1943	7	No Homeward Journey	Havigh Hurst
1943	7	Goodbye Mr. Chips	J. Hilton
1943	10	Dr. Bradley Remembers	F.B. Young
1943	10	The Keys of The Kingdom	A. J. Cronin
1943	7	Solomons Vineyards	
1943	8	Aphrodite	
1943	6	Shadow of Wings	S.
1943	4	Beatrice	R. Haggard
1943	6	World Without End	G. Frankau
1943	10	Leopard For Spots	Noami Jacobs
1943	6	Jim Redlake	Francis B. Young
1943	4	The Doomsday Men	J.B. Priestley
1943	3	All This And Heaven Too	Rachel Field
1943	9	Thursday's Child	J.B. Young
1943	9	Frenchman's Creek	Daphne Du Maurier
1943	7	Break the Bars	
1944	5	Winter Of Discontent	Gilbert Frankau
1944	9	All That Glitters	Francis P. Keyes
1944	5	Put Out More Flags	Evelyn Waugh
1944	5	Experiences of Irish R.M.	
1944	10	I'd Live the Same Life Over	Philip Lindsay
1944	7	Kindred of the Dust	Peter B. Kyne
1944	8	Young Ames	Desmond
1944	9	Northwest Passage	Kenneth Roberts
1944	-	Youth and Sex	

1944	9	Return via Dunkirk	Gun Buster
1944	6	Action Front	Boyd Cable
1944	9	A Man's Man	Ian Hay
1944	1	Brainy Eye	David Gardner
1944	8	Quo Vardis	
1944	7	The Faithfull Years	Robert Eton
1944	9	Trial of Mussolini	Cassius
1944	-	Brush Up Your Reading	
1944	6	Garden of Paradise	V.S. Morton
1944	7	Hocus Pocus	Noel Langley
1944	5	1066 and All That	
1944	8	Cakes and Ale	Somerset Maugham
1944	8	Nana	Emile Zola
1944	7	The King Liveth	
1944	3	Thirty-Nine Steps	John Buchan
1944	9	Enter Three Witches	
1944	5	Flamingo	
1944	3	The Aerodrome	Rex Warner
1944	10	Les Miserables	Victor Hugo
1944	8	My Sister Eileen	
1944	7	Mysterious Mr. Waye	P.C. Wren
1944	9	Victoria Regina	
1944	6	Ladies Paradise	Emile Zola
1944	8	Women at Abysinnian War	
1944	8	Queen Anne's Lace	Frances P. Keyes
1944	10	Vindication	S. McKenna
1944	9	Dodsworth	Sinclair Lewis
1944	6	Alone N.	Douglas
1944	6	It's a Battlefield	Graeme
1944	9	Martin Make-believe	Gilbert Frankau
1944	7	Ashenden	Somerset Maugham
1944	6	Zulu Paraclete	
1944	9	Cosmopolitans	Somerset Maugham
1944	6	Flaming Youth	Fabian
1944	10	Vanity Fair	Thackery
1944	9	Self Portrait	Gilbert Frankau
1944	10	Escape to Yesterday	Gilbert Frankau
1944	7	Time for Silence	Andre Maurois
1944	6	The Interpreter	Gibbs
1944	7	Christmas Holiday	Somerset Maugham
1944	9	Madame Curie	Evelyn Curie

Appendix V

POEM

When the author was fourteen years old a history class fired his imagination at Durban High School. Charlie Evans was teaching on the subject of the Treaty of Versailles and how its harsh nature was certain to provoke wars in the future involving Germany.

At the same time he had read how Charles Darwin's grandfather, Erasmus Darwin, had written a poem on evolution before even Charles had been born. The author was fired up by the implications of this familial association and by the fact that four of his own antecedents had died in recent wars and began to compose a poem on Versailles and the first world war reproduced below:

In Three Decades

Europe a shambles, of nations
Exhausted yet smitten with hate,
Guided by anger and passions,
Warped by folly and fate,
Blundered on to insanity
Till God cried, "Enough! This must cease!"
And for her sins and vanity
Entrusted her with peace.

From the quagmire our allies merged,
The battle had been won and lost,
For German tyranny was purged,
And all had paid the cost.
To cure the eagle of its lust

Came four great men from four great lands
To make a peace severe yet just
Where regal Versailles stands.

In spirit the Orlean Maid
Was there, draped in a tricolour
All drenched with the blood she had paid
For freedom and honour.
Stepped forth, to champion her claim
Clemenceau drunk with hate
Vengefully sealing without shame
That unhappy country's fate.

When she thought the allies must win,
Italy clambered from the fence
And though defeated, saved her skin
At minimum expense.
With greed of gain Orlando came,
Quoting her military feats
But history records the fame
Of Italy's retreats.

FIFTH SUPPLEMENT

to

The London Gazette

of Friday, the 20th of April, 1945

Published by Authority

Registered as a newspaper

TUESDAY, 24 APRIL, 1945

Air Ministry, 24th April, 1945

The KING has been graciously pleased to confer the VICTORIA CROSS on the under-mentioned officer in recognition of most conspicuous bravery:-

Captain Edwin Swales, D.F.C. (6191V) S.A.A.F., 582 Sqn. (deceased).

Captain Swales was "master bomber" of a force of aircraft which attacked Pfotzheim on the night of February 23rd, 1945. As, "master bomber," he had the task of locat- ing the target area with precision and of giving aiming instructions to the main force of bombers following in his wake. Soon after he had reached the target area he was engaged by an enemy fighter and one of his engines was put out of action. His rear guns failed. His crippled aircraft was an easy prey to further attacks. Unperturbed, he carried on with his allotted task; clearly and precisely he issued aiming instructions to the main force. Meanwhile the enemy fighter closed the range and fired again. A second engine of Captain Swales' aircraft was put out of action. Almost defenceless, he stayed over the target area issuing his aiming instruc- tions until he was satisfied that the attack had achieved its purpose.

It is now known that the attack was one of the most concentrated and successful of the war.

Captain Swales did not, however, regard his mission as completed. His aircraft was damaged. Its speed had been so much reduced that it could only with difficulty be kept in the air. The blind-flying instruments were no longer working. Determined at all costs to prevent his aircraft and crew from falling into enemy hands, he set course for home. After an hour he flew into thin-layered cloud. He kept his course by skilful flying between the layers, but later heavy cloud and turbulent air conditions were met. The aircraft, by now over friendly territory, became more and more difficult to control; it was losing height steadily. Realising that the situation was desperate Captain Swales ordered his crew to bale out. Time was very short and it required all his exertions to keep the aircraft steady while each of his crew moved in turn to the escape hatch and parachuted to safety. Hardly had the last crew member jumped when the aircraft plunged to earth. Captain Swales was found dead at the controls.

Intrepid in the attack, courageous in the face of danger, he did his duty to the last, giving his life that his comrades might live.

Eric Gregg is the longest surviving friend of the author. The two met at the YMCA in Durban in 1938. He has raised three children and served with the author in North Africa and Italy throughout the war years.

INDEX

A

A Company 218
Abassia 325, 326
Abyssinia
  campaign 73
Acroma 136, 142
Adam, General Ronald 256
Adama 64
Adams, Captain Dixie 233
Afrikaans 15
Aga Kahn
  318, 320, 323, 332, 356, 371
Alam el Halfa 226, 264
  battle at 226
  German tanks lost 228
Alamein 221, 222, 224, 239, 275
  approach to 214
  before the battle 264
  concrete bumkers 215
  contaminations in 224
  final victorious battle 264
  first night of 272
  policy of the Allied forces 231
  training for 237
Alamein Club 330
Alamein line 264, 272
Alanbrooke, Field Marshall Lord
  77, 255, 256, 371
  war diaries 222
  war diaries 235
alcohol rations 207
Alexander 82, 256
Alexander, Doug 357, 358, 438
Alexander, General 413
Alexander, Sloppy 438
Alexandria 111, 339, 359
Ali Baba 84
Altamura 354, 363
American Browning 132
American Honey tanks 116
Anderson, Joan 315
Anglo-Boer Wars 17
anti-aircraft defence 212
anti-tank gun
  six pounder 79

antibiotic
  sulphonamide 224
Anzio
  Allied landings 389
  landings 389
apes, exotic 332
Appenines 456
Armstrong, Aunty 6, 185
Arnold's Hill 1
artillery barrages 212
Askham, Bill 434, 442, 446, 447
Askham, Jules 442
astrology 298
Auchinleck, General Sir Claude
  82, 114, 116, 164,
  207, 234, 236
  Crusader operation 79
Aunt Rose 141
author
  21ST birthday 355
  22nd birthday 473
  army details 469
  army discharge 474
  arrest 91
  at Heliopolis 250
  begun to write novel 326
  books read 1943-44 496
  brings down a plane 150
  case dismissed 96
  concerts at Marine View 6
  dream about Ellis 473
  dream of Dennis Baker 10
  dream of Jack Gray 329
  dumb insolence 96
  hit by shrapnel 284
  hospital in Bari 469
  keeping a diary 222
  memoirs of 1940 479
  morse code classes 326
  on trail 94
  poetry and song 210
  sense of immortality 109
  strange dreams 98
  surgery again 430
  thigh abrasions 180

Abbreviations

A.W.O.L. .... Absent without leave

A.D.S. .... Advanced Dressing Station

A.C.R. .... African Corps Regiment

A.F.V. .... Armoured Fighting Vehicle

B.E.F. .... British Expeditionary Force

C.T.H. .... Cape Town Highlanders

C.C.S. .... Casualty Clearing Station

C.I.G.S. .... Chief Imperial General Staff

C.I.C. .... Commander-in-Chief

C.O. .... Commanding Officer

D.I.L. .... Dangerously ill list

D.F.C. .... Distinguished Flying Cross

D.H.S. .... Durban High School

E.N.S.A. .... Entertainments National Services Association

F.F.B. .... Field Force Batalion (S.A. Regiment)

F.D.L. .... Forward Defence Line

F.T.D.S. .... Forward Transit Depot ...??

G.S. .... General Service (3 ton truck)

H.M.S. .... Her Majesty's Ship or Service

H.E. .... High Explosive (grenades)

H.A.C. .... Honourable Artillery Corps

I.L.H. .... Imperial Light Horse

K.R.R.C. .... Kings's Royal Rifle Corps (Gen. Gott Co.)

L.M.G. .... Light Machine Gun

M.A.P. .... Medical Aid Post

M.O. .... Medical Officer

M.M. .... Military Medal

N.M.R. .... Natal Mounted Rifles

N.A.A.F.I. .... Navy, Army and Air Force Institutes

N.Z.C.C.S. .... New Zealand Casualty Clearing Station

N.C.O. .... non-commissioned officer

O.P. .... Observations Post

O.C. .... Officer Commanding

O.T.C. .... Officers Training Corps.

P.T. .... Physical training

P.M.B. .... Pietermaritzburg, South Africa

P.O.W. .... Prisoner of War

R.S.M. .... Regimental Sergeant-Major

R.A.M.C. .... Royal Army Medical Corps.

R.A.S.C. .... Royal Army Service Corps.

R.D.L.I. .... Royal Duban Light Infantry

R.D.R .... Royal Durban Rangers

R.H.A. .... Royal Horse Artillery

R.N.C. .... Royal Natal Carbineers

R.N.V.R. .... Royal Naval Voluntary Reserves

2 I.C. .... Second in Command

S.M. .... Sergeant-Major

S.I.L. .... Seriously ill list

S.A.A.F. .... South African Air Force

S. L. .... Springbok Legion

E.P.I.P. .... standard army tent

T.S. .... Transvaal Scottish

W.A.A.F. .... Womens Auxiliary Air Force

Y.M.C.A. (Y.M.). .... Young Mens Christian Association

Bibliography

Amery, Julian: .... Sons of the Eagle, A Study in guerrilla War

Bader, Douglas: .... Fight for the Sky, The Story of the Spitfire and
the Hurricane

Baldwin, Hanson: .... Battles Lost and Won, Great Campaigns of
World War II

Barnett, Corelli .... The Desert Generals [2nd edition]

Bingham, J.K.W. & Haupt, W.
.... North African Campaign 1940-1943

Blaxland, Gregory .... The plain cook and the great showman: the First
& Eighth Armies in North Africa

Blumenson, Martin: ...... Rommel's Last Victory, The Battle of Kasserine
Pass

Bullock, Alan: .... Hitler, A Study in Tyranny

Cartland, Barbara: .... Ronald Cartland

Carver, Michael .... El Alamein

Collier, Basil: .... The Defence of the United Kingdom

Connell, John: .... Wavell, Scholar and Soldier, to June 1941

Cooper, R.W.: .... The Nuremberg Trial

Cruickshank, Charles .... The German Occcupation of The Channel
Islands

Deakin, F.W. .... The Brutal Friendship, Mussolini, Hitler and the
Fall of Italian Fascism

Divine, A.D. .... Dunkirk

Douglas-Hamilton, James
.... Motive for a Mission, The Story Behind Hess's
Flight to Britain

Forty, George .... Afrikakorps at War

Frank, Anne: .... The Diary of Anne Frank

Gray, Brian: .... Basuto Soldiers in Hitler's War

Green, Colonel J.H. .... After the Battle, Number 52

Groves, Leslie R. .... Now It Can Be Told, The Story of the Manhattan
Project

Guedalla, Philip .... Middle East 1940-1942, A Study in Air Power

Gwyer, J.M.A., and Butler, J.R.M.
.... Grand Strategy, Volume III, July 1941 –
August1942

Hall, J.W.: (editor) .... Trial of William Joyce

Hamilton, Nigel .... Monty: master of the battlefield 1942-1944

Hamilton, Nigel .... Monty: the making of a general 1887-1942

Handel, Michael I. (editor)
.... Strategic and Operational Deception in the
Second World War

Heckmann, W. .... Rommel's War in Africa

Hyde, H. Montgomery .. Stalin, The History of a Dictator

Irving, Charles .... The trial of the fox: The life of Field-Marshal
Erwin Rommel

Irving, David .... Hitler's War

Jackson, W.G.F. .... The North African Campaign 1940-1943

Law, Richard D. & Luther, Craig W.H.
.... Rommel: a narrative and pictorial history

Lewin, Ronald .... The Life and Death of the Afrikakorps

Lewin, Ronald .... Montgomery as military commander

Lindsay, Captain Martin & Johnston, Captain M.E.
.... History of 7th Armoured Division, June 1943 –
July 1945

Lucas, James .... War in the Desert: the Eighth Army at El Alamein

Macksey, Kenneth .... Rommel: Battles and Campaigns

Majdalany, F. .... The Battle of El Alamein

Martin, Lieutenant-General H.J. & Orpen, Colonel Neil D.
.... Eagles Victorious, The Operations of the South
African Forces over the Mediterranean and
Europe, in Italy, The Balkans and the Aegean,
and from Gibraltar and West Africa

Messenger, Charles ...... The Tunisian Campaign

Mitcham, Samuel W. Jr. . Hitler's Field Marshals and their Battles

Montgomery of Alamein, Bernard, 1st Viscount
.... The Memoirs of Field-Marshal, The Viscount
Montgomery of Alamein, KG

Perrett, Bryan .... Wavell's Offensive (Armour in Battle)

Pitt, Barrie .... The Crucible of War: Western Desert 1941

Plant, Richard .... The Pink Triangle, The Nazi War Against
Homosexuals

Playfair, I.S.O. .... The Mediterranean and the Middle East (History
of the Second World War: United Kingdom
military series 4 vols

Pryce-Jones, David .... Paris in the third Reich, A History of the German
Occupation, 1940 – 1944

Robertson, John: .... Australia at War 1939 – 1945

Shircr, William L, ... The Rise and Fall of the Third Reich, Λ History
of Nazi Germany

Slim, Field Marshal Sir William
.... Defeat into Victory

Speer, Albert .... Inside the Third Reich

Stewart, I. McD. G. .... The Struggle for Crete 20 May – 1 June 1941

Strawson, John .... El Alamein: Desert Victory

Adalbert, T. .... Tobruk 1941, Der Kampf in Nordafrika

Toynbee, Arnold & Toynbee, Veronica M. (editors)
.... The Initial Triumph of the Axis

Trevor-Roper, H.R. .... The Last Days of Hitler

Trevor-Roper, H.R. (editor)
.... Hitler's War Directives 1939 – 1945

Tute, Warren .... The North African War

Warner, Philip .... Alamein

Warner, Philip .... Auchinleck: The Lonely Soldier

Wheeler, Harold .... The People's History of the Second World War
September 1939 – December 1940

Worm-Muller, Professor Jacob
.... Norway's Revolt Against Nazism